The Hyperorchestra

Sergi Casanelles

The Hyperorchestra

Screen Music and Virtual Musical Ensembles

Sergi Casanelles
New York, NY, USA

ISBN 978-3-031-75192-9   ISBN 978-3-031-75193-6 (eBook)
https://doi.org/10.1007/978-3-031-75193-6

© The Editor(s) (if applicable) and The Author(s), under exclusive license to Springer Nature Switzerland AG 2024

This work is subject to copyright. All rights are solely and exclusively licensed by the Publisher, whether the whole or part of the material is concerned, specifically the rights of translation, reprinting, reuse of illustrations, recitation, broadcasting, reproduction on microfilms or in any other physical way, and transmission or information storage and retrieval, electronic adaptation, computer software, or by similar or dissimilar methodology now known or hereafter developed.

The use of general descriptive names, registered names, trademarks, service marks, etc. in this publication does not imply, even in the absence of a specific statement, that such names are exempt from the relevant protective laws and regulations and therefore free for general use.

The publisher, the authors and the editors are safe to assume that the advice and information in this book are believed to be true and accurate at the date of publication. Neither the publisher nor the authors or the editors give a warranty, expressed or implied, with respect to the material contained herein or for any errors or omissions that may have been made. The publisher remains neutral with regard to jurisdictional claims in published maps and institutional affiliations.

This Palgrave Macmillan imprint is published by the registered company Springer Nature Switzerland AG.
The registered company address is: Gewerbestrasse 11, 6330 Cham, Switzerland

If disposing of this product, please recycle the paper.

Acknowledgments

The genesis of this book started during my Master's program before I began my research in the area during my PhD studies. As a classically trained composer who also studied and worked in computer science, I was immediately fascinated by the potential technology had in the development of screen music aesthetics. During my Master's, I found in Elias Constantopedos a like-minded friend with whom to create a series of practical workshops for our colleagues devoted to technology and virtual instruments. We were dissatisfied with the idea of calling the process of creating music with sample libraries virtual orchestration or mockup creation. It seemed an already too-reductionist terminology that could not encompass the potential virtual music creation had to offer to produce music that could not be created with acoustic means only. The hyperorchestra emerged throughout our discussions in finding the best way to frame a set of practices that had not been studied.

Elias and I were encouraged to create these sessions for our peers by our mentor, Ron Sadoff, whose contributions to the field are immense. Ron became my doctoral advisor and academic mentor; since then, we have worked as colleagues. Ron also helped and encouraged me to create my first class—*Contemporary Scoring*—which was directly related to this area, just after I started my doctoral studies. He both asked and helped me think beyond the purely technical aspects to develop a class that engaged in a deeper level of aesthetic inquiry. In addition to Ron and I, Tim Starnes was also instrumental in developing the *Contemporary Scoring* class. Tim's ideas and approach to conceiving music mixing as a discipline directly connected to music composition have influenced my definition of hyperorchestration.

After a couple of years, the class became widely popular beyond the screen scoring students (who were also growing in number). Due to the innovative way the class taught about technology and aesthetics, I asked some former students to join me in teaching the class. Ariel Marx joined me as an instructor. Ariel was part of the first student cohort to take the class. She was already working with me when the class was evolving in parallel with my finishing my doctoral dissertation. We were also joined by Lillie McDonough and, afterward, Alex Rodriguez, Kat Vokes, Hunter Hanson, and Colton Dodd. All of them have been instrumental in refining the ideas of the hyperorchestra, hyperinstruments, and hyperorchestration.

To that end, I am also immensely grateful for our students' effort and feedback and for their practical and theoretical engagement with the class concepts. I was positively surprised by how naturally they engaged with the ideas behind the hyperorchestra, the creation of hyperinstruments, and hyperorchestration. This has not only encouraged me to write this book but also given me plenty of data from which to further refine the ideas in a manner that supports a wide variety of creative endeavors. For instance, I recall how Jordi Nus, a fellow Catalan composer who now works in the industry in LA, created a score that had to incorporate hyperinstruments exclusively by bowing everything he could find in his apartment. He made a group of suggestive hyperinstruments from these sounds that generated a compelling and innovative score.

I am also grateful for the continuous support and feedback from the impressive and welcoming group of scholars who come together yearly at the *Music and the Moving Image Conference*. Their thoughts, ideas, and questions have also been an asset in writing this book. From all of them, I would like to show my special gratitude to the late Danijela Kulezic-Wilson, a prominent scholarly voice in the field and a supportive colleague who is greatly missed. Danijela was a supportive mentor when I wrote my first approach to describing mixing as hyperorchestration. In conjunction with Liz Greene, their feedback was invaluable. I would also like to thank Miguel Mera for their insightful comments on his manuscript review, which helped me improve its content and readability.

I would also like to enthusiastically thank Jim Buhler for agreeing to read the manuscript and for providing a significant number of insights and ideas to make it better. Jim is one of the few scholars who has published about some of the technological areas covered in this manuscript. In addition to many ideas, I took his suggestion to call the first approach to sample design analytical. Thanks, Jim, for all your input!

Finally, none of this would have been possible without a nurturing family that was always supportive of my varied interests and curiosity.

Contents

1	**Introduction**	1
	Screen Composers as Filmmakers	2
	The Computer and Audiovisual Storytelling	5
	Is This a Treaty on Hans Zimmer's Aesthetics?	6
	A Theory Informed by Practice Approach on Timbre, Organology, and Technology	9
	Structure of the Book	11
	Scope	12
	Terminology	13
	A User-Friendly Glossary of Concepts	14
	References	22

Part I	**Theoretical and Practical Foundations**	23
2	**From Hyperreality to Digital Cinema: A Theoretical Overview**	25
	A Philosophical Model for the Hyperreal	27
	Disneyland and the Hyperreal	28
	Baudrillard's Hyperreality	30
	McLuhan's Theory of the Media	35
	A Process of Virtualization	39
	Digital Cinema, Virtual Realities, and the Hyperreal	42
	Narratives and Virtual Reality: Worldbuilding	43

Digital Cinema and the Ontology of Cinema	46
Prince's Perceptual Realism	52
Cinema and Hyperreality	54
Conclusion	56
References	58

3 Conceptualizing the Hyperorchestra — 61

A Process of Increased Virtualization	62
Musical Notation	64
Recorded Music	68
Sound Objects: The Studio Recording, the Acousmatic Sound, and Film Music	72
Synthesizers and the Evolution of the Musical Instrument	81
Sampled-Based Virtual Instruments and the Digital Revolution	85
Defining the Hyperorchestra: Two Preliminary Approaches	92
A Technological Approach	92
A Philosophical and Aesthetic Approach	93
Conclusion	97
References	103

4 The Digital Tools for the Hyperorchestra: MIDI, Virtual Instruments, and Digital Music — 107

The End of Pen and Paper: The Toolkit for the Contemporary Screen Composer	107
The Interface Effect and the Musical Instruments Digital Interface	109
A Brief Overview of MIDI Messages	112
MIDI Mapping, Musical Mapping	114
The Effect of MIDI	115
The Effect of the Mockup: Replica and Simulacra of the Film Orchestra	120
Modeling the Real: Sampling Techniques for the Hyperreal Production	128
Multiple Performance Techniques	133
Looping and Time Stretching	133
Layering	134
Deep Sampling	137

Dynamics: Layering and Crossfading	137
Round Robin	139
Legato and Note Transitions	139
Recording Locations and Sound Perspectives	146
Capturing Performances and Performance Practices	148
Synthetic Techniques, Processing, and Modeling	150
Classifying Virtual Instruments: Taxonomies	151
Origin of the Sound Sources	152
Design Paradigms of Sample Libraries	153
Relationship with Reality	160
Creative Role	163
A Practice-Induced Typology of Virtual Instruments	166
Reproducing the Western Orchestra	167
Reproducing Sounds Outside the Western Orchestral Paradigm	171
Epic Percussion, Accent Libraries, and Loops	173
Analog Synthesizers, Digital Synthesizers, and Analog Emulations	176
Hybrid Synthesizers and Ethereal Timbres	177
Interactive Hybrid Virtual Instruments	178
Conclusion	180
References	184

Part II The Hyperorchestra and the Contemporary Aesthetics for Screen Music — 187

5 Hyperorchestral Aesthetic Frameworks for the Screen Music Composer

	189
Hyperorchestral Screen Music Analysis: A Sonic Approach	190
Sonic Analysis	192
Music Creation Frameworks	195
Example: Synthesizers and the ADSR Framework	196
Creating Music in the Digital Age: A Collaborative and Nonlinear Mode of Composition	198
The Traditional Linear Scoring Process	200
The Contemporary Framework for Audiovisual Music Creation	201

    Example: Inception (2010), *Challenging Reality and the Impossible Orchestra*   204
    Example: A Small Light (2023), *Nonlinear Process and the Artisan Score*   209
    Example: Bear McCreary, Sparks and Shadows, and the Composing Teams   210
  Hyperinstruments: A Timbral Revolution   212
    Example: Man of Steel *(2013), a Multicultural Drum Orchestra to Represent Humankind*   216
    Example: Chernobyl *(2019) and the Sound of Radiation*   219
    Example: World Building Through Hyperinstruments in Dune *(2021–2024)*   220
  The Hyperorchestra and the Generation of Meaning   225
    Example: Gravity *(2013): Scoring the Soundlessness of Outer Space*   230
    Example: Annihilation *(2018) and the Organic Corruption*   234
  References   241

6 Hyperorchestration: Sonic Strategies for the Creation of Meaning   245
  On Orchestration: A Birdseye Overview   246
    Spectral Orchestration   247
  Hyperorchestration   250
  Hyperinstrumentation and Virtual Organology   252
    Sound Source: Materialization and Musicalization of Sound Objects   254
    Sound Source: Musical Traditions and Globalized Culture   257
    Sound Source: Expanding Instruments   259
    The Design Process   260
  Mixing as a Mode of Hyperorchestration   261
    Acoustic Mixing in Mahler's First Symphony   261
    The Parameters of Sound (and Music)   263
    Synthetic Sound Design Principles   268
    Defining Mixing   270
    Combining Microphones: Sound Perspectives   271
    Spectral Shaping Through Equalization   275
    Frequency: Harmonic Density   277
    Volume and Dynamic Control   280

Virtual Space Design	281
Primarily Creative Processors	285
Sound Processing and Aural Fidelity	286
Spectral Transformations: Timbre, Harmony, and Dynamic Hyperorchestration	288
Expanding Western Orchestration Principles with the Hyperorchestra	291
Augmenting and Expanding the Orchestral Sections	291
Sonic Combination	293
References	295
7 Conclusion	299
References	301
References	303
Index	317

List of Figures

Fig. 2.1	This graphical model describes performance based on David Fincher's approach to performance and acting as described by Prince (2012, 102)	51
Fig. 2.2	This graphic summarizes the distinct roles that contribute to generating a performance in audiovisual media. The graphic is divided between physical and virtual processes	52
Fig. 3.1	The graphic shows three different *crescendo* representations	66
Fig. 3.2	Representation of a *crescendo* utilizing traditional musical notation	67
Fig. 3.3	Schematic for an octave of a musical keyboard	84
Fig. 3.4	A general classification for synthesized and sampled instruments based on their connection to the acoustic or the analog domain. Pure synthesizers are instruments that create sounds solely from oscillators (VCOs). Hybrid synthesizers are virtual instruments that employ one or more samples as the sound source to produce the synthesizer's sound. Sample libraries are designed by creating computer programs that utilize a generally extensive set of samples to generate virtual instruments. The last typology, the recording, refers to any other typology of music recording as presented before	87
Fig. 4.1	Conceptual representation of an interface	110
Fig. 4.2	Graphical schematic to represent MIDI communication	112
Fig. 4.3	MIDI communication and human interaction	118
Fig. 4.4	Generic representation of a piano roll in a DAW	119
Fig. 4.5	Conceptual graphical representation of the structure of a virtual instrument inside a sampler	130

Fig. 5.1	A graphical representation to show how music is a subset of sound, which is also a subset of mechanical waves	192
Fig. 5.2	Visual representation of the main principles of the Attack, Decay, Sustain, and Release (ADSR)	197
Fig. 5.3	Graphical representation of the sound wave of a timpani hit, with the ADSR labels superimposed	197
Fig. 5.4	Music in the hyperreal. This graphic shows how sound sources from the physical world are transported to the virtual area for processing. Once this happens, music becomes hyperrealistic	199
Fig. 5.5	Graphic visualization of the processes involved in a traditional movie scoring composition process	201
Fig. 5.6	Graphical visualization of a framework for contemporary music scoring. As it is a nonlinear process, there is no specific linear set of steps. Instead, the DAW becomes the core of the process	202
Fig. 5.7	A progressive crescendo written utilizing a traditional musical score notation	207
Fig. 5.8	Progressive crescendo representation based on a DAW piano roll. The top frame is used to write the note, whereas the bottom frame is used to write continuous data. In this figure, a 0 value in this lower area means the lowest possible dynamic and the highest value (127) means the highest possible value. The top numbers are the measure and beats	207
Fig. 5.9	Graphical representation of the hyperinstrument design framework	214
Fig. 5.10	Graphical representation of a conceptual framework for the hyperorchestra	227
Fig. 5.11	Graphic representation of direct and reversed sound waveforms	231
Fig. 5.12	Graphic representation of different amplitudes in sine waves	232
Fig. 6.1	Score reduction for Mahler's *First Symphony* (m. 17–25)	262
Fig. 6.2	Visual representation of the piano mixes in *The Social Network* (2010). The composers utilized three different microphone positions at varying distances from the source	273
Fig. 6.3	Mixing perspectives with different panning	274
Fig. 6.4	String EQ Processing in the Strings of Daredevil. Transcribed by the author	278
Fig. 6.5	Frequency representation of adding different levels of distortion to a sound	279
Fig. 6.6	Sketch of the effects of a compressor	280
Fig. 6.7	Representation of multidimensional spaces based on the example from *The Social Network*	282
Fig. 6.8	Two-dimensional possible mental representation of the previous figure	283

CHAPTER 1

Introduction

In just a few decades, computers have transformed our lives at a pace never seen before by humankind. From aiding humanity in sending the first men to the moon to having similarly powerful computers on our desktops just a few years later, computers have been increasingly integrating into our lives. To quote the title of Ray Kurzweil's (1990) foreshadowing book, the *age of intelligent machines* has also already arrived. In parallel, music technologies rapidly evolved from allowing sound to be recorded to creating music synthetically through electric devices. With the new millennium, computers became the centerpiece for music production and creation.

Filmmaking underwent a similar evolution, reaching an important milestone in introducing film editing using nonlinear software in the early 1990s. *The English Patient* (1996), the first movie edited digitally (using computer software) by the legendary Walter Murch, won the Oscar in the editing category. Murch (2001) detailed the film's editing process in his book *In the Blink of an Eye*. Murch explained how significant evolutions in the software made it a viable option by the time he edited *The English Patient*. The software used for editing (Avid Media Composer)—along with more powerful hardware—allowed for two people (the editor and the assistant editor) to work on the movie at the same time (97–101). This is an essential landmark because editing is the only art specific to cinema, and, at its core, editing as an art immensely benefits from being nonlinear. Nonlinear editing refers to the capacity not to edit a film sequentially so

© The Author(s), under exclusive license to Springer Nature Switzerland AG 2024
S. Casanelles, *The Hyperorchestra*,
https://doi.org/10.1007/978-3-031-75193-6_1

the editor can modify any sequence at any time (Kmet 2018, 211). Editing software is nonlinear and nondestructive, allowing the editor to make changes without altering the original material (Kmet 2018, 211). While there are many movie classics with extraordinary edits created by cutting and pasting pieces of film, the analog editing process was tedious and limiting. Therefore, the capacity for editing to develop further as an art was restricted without the technology to support it.

This book is about the aesthetics of screen music since the emergence of digital technologies at the start of the twenty-first century, which I conceptualize through a virtual ensemble that I call the hyperorchestra. Digital technology involves converting information or data into numbers to be stored and processed using computers. For image and sound, it involves converting the recordings and photographs into a set of numbers for the same purpose. As I will define throughout the book, the hyperorchestra is a term that I coined to describe a virtual musical ensemble that is the product of the interaction of musical devices and technology to create sounds that carry narrative meaning for the audiovisual material they are part of. The use of digital tools liberates music from using the limited sounds that a group of acoustic instruments playing together can produce, unlocking virtually unlimited possibilities. Akin to film editing, I believe that digital music is the best medium to unfold screen music's full capacities within an audiovisual narrative. In fact, digital music is the medium that propelled the emergence of *filmscoring* as a discipline openly distinct from music composition. Of all the arts that converge in crafting an audiovisual narrative, editing is arguably the closest to filmscoring. However, many editing techniques are more straightforward to describe than similar ones for the music. For instance, explaining what it means to increase the amount of blue in a scene and its emotional or narrative effects is reasonably straightforward. On the other hand, it is more challenging to describe what it means to reduce some of the content of the sound (a portion of its frequency content) and its possible narrative effects. This is why a significant part of this book is dedicated to unfolding and detailing statements like this one above.

Screen Composers as Filmmakers

In my opinion, the best way to describe a screen composer is as a filmmaker responsible for the music department, as a natural consequence of the shift in film scholarship introduced in the 1990s by authors such as

Michel Chion (1994). While we do not hesitate to consider screenwriters, editors, cinematographers, or directors as filmmakers, this denomination somehow eluded screen composers. Therefore, the musical score is not something that helps the narrative tell a story; it is part of the narrative and, thus, storytelling. To do so, music must have the power to be malleable and sonically innovative as the rest of the elements of the audiovisual narrative, which is much better achieved through digital means that go beyond the classical film standard for filmscoring: the Western nineteenth-century orchestra.

By defining the hyperorchestra, I put the generation of meaning through musical means at the center of screen scoring, in alignment with considering the score as storytelling and narrative content. Further, the hyperorchestra unlocks all the properties of sound to become a vessel for meaning generation through music. In addition, for the musical score to be wholly integrated into filmmaking, it requires the *screenscorer* to communicate their ideas efficiently with the rest of the team. Technology has enabled the possibility of reshaping the scoring process to become nonlinear, thus having continuous points of interaction and communication with the team; at the same time, it has provided the tools for a fruitful interchange of ideas. In this context, nonlinearity applied to music is much more extensive than the definition of nonlinearity in film editing. The scoring process—while generally regarded as part of the post-production part of filmmaking—has a conception (composing), production (recording), and postproduction (mixing) phases. In other words, while film editing already has all the materials from the production stage (unless there is a need for re-shoots), music material is conceived and produced as part of the scoring process. Technology has made it possible to merge all the stages, thus making the whole process nonlinear.

One of the earlier developments in this area was the music mockup. Before using electronic devices, one of the biggest challenges for film composers was conveying the musical result to the director and the rest of the filmmaking team (Karlin and Wright 2004, 101). One reason is the lack of objective reasons to assess whether or not a scene is working. Director Rod Lurie says, "You know a cue is working in a simple, visceral way, that it's either there or it's not" (Karlin and Wright 2004, 101). Before computers, a composer would play on the piano (accompanied by comments indicating which instruments would be playing and possibly some singing) for a director to demonstrate the music for a scene. This process not only involved a significant amount of trust but was also an obstacle for the music to become fully integrated within the storytelling.

The mockup is a computerized realization of the music for the audiovisual narrative with the purpose of serving as a temporary placeholder before it is entirely replaced by a (generally orchestral) recording. To achieve that, a mockup is created using virtual instruments—conceptually, a digital version of a musical instrument. Some of these instruments utilize recordings of acoustic instrument performances to generate a digital sound based on them. In its idealistic technical conception, the objective of some of these virtual instruments would be to emulate an acoustic instrument as closely as possible. For example, a violin virtual instrument aimed to sound as close as possible to an acoustic violin. With that in mind, a mockup would be created using the instruments and techniques the composer envisioned in the final product, thus creating a digital replica before the expensive recording process started. However, the emulations were frequently underwhelming, especially in its early stages. Quickly, mocking up evolved when the replication objective was replaced by an aim to create a convincing result to emulate the feeling and overall impact of the final recorded sound. For example, a composer could create a mockup for a string passage combining virtual instruments of string sounds playing regularly and with the mute on. The intention was not to record it in that way but to create an impression—a rendering—that was verisimilar in terms of its dramatic effectiveness to the recorded result (Karlin and Wright 2004, 103). While most of the discussions and interviews from industry professionals from the early 2000s would generally mention their intent to make their mockups sound realistic, I believe that verisimilitude is a better concept. Thus, a composer would aim for the mockup to sound as verisimilar as possible while being an effective tool to convince the filmmaking team to approve the cue and sound close enough to the final recording so the filmmaking team would accept the final recording as an improvement from the mockup and would not perceive it as a different piece of music in its function within the storytelling.

In that process, there was a detachment from reality as a principle that governed the mocking-up process, unfolding the potential that virtual music has in expanding its expressive power. Almost inevitably, the mockup lost its meaning—a temporary version of the final score that would eventually replaced it—when at least a subset of its sounds became part of the score. When this happened, composers still presented temporary versions of their work to the filmmakers. In that case, though, I prefer to call these versions demos, sketches, or drafts instead of mockups to differentiate the process. To create an analogy, aiming for the music mockup to remain as only a demo would be the equivalent of using computer graphic imagery (CGI) to mock up practical visual effects and expecting CGI not to be used in filmmaking to create visual effects in its own. In a significantly reduced set of instances, CGI could be just a mockup tool. However, once the power of CGI is unfolded, it expands beyond what practical effects could achieve as it is not attached to reality. This is one of the central ideas of this book.

Nevertheless, in the 1990s, the technology to create mockups could only render underwhelming prototypes of the final recorded result. One of the reasons for the emergence of Hans Zimmer as the most influential figure in contemporary filmscoring is his success in creating better tools to produce mockups that were increasingly more verisimilar and compelling. Zimmer asserts that his initial objective was twofold: to have an efficient communication tool and to be able to write music with sounds that were nicer for them to listen to (Zimmer 2021). It is important to emphasize that, at the core of Zimmer's idea for developing these tools, he felt that they were necessary to overcome the communication barriers composers had. Thus, the development of these technologies helped to facilitate the integration of the score into storytelling. Therefore, Hans Zimmer's model and the emergence of his company, Remote Control Productions, became central to the development of the hyperorchestra.

The Computer and Audiovisual Storytelling

Based on what I described above, one of my theses in this text is that the computer—and digital technologies attached to it—are the most appropriate medium to create music that is part of an audiovisual narrative. Further, digital music seems to be the best way to truly integrate music as storytelling and composers as filmmakers. I also mentioned that this is not dissimilar to the editing process (including the sound design of the film's sound), which also seems to reach its top potential using digital tools.

While this is mostly out of the scope of the book, I would like to provide my hypothesis as to why computers have become a central aspect of the postproduction process of audiovisual stories. Storytelling comes from, literally, telling stories that generally have mythical content embedded in them. Telling a story involves imagination, which is one of the reasons why our perception of realism in a movie is not directly connected to its capacity to become a very accurate depiction of reality but to provide the data for us to recreate a compelling reality for the story that is being told.

Films (and any mode of storytelling) skip real time (we would not watch a character sleep for 8 hours) or reshape the perception of sonic material to tell stories better. However, movies rely on moving images that closely depict reality, which is a powerful device for storytelling but that also constrains our imagination. For instance, in *The Lord of the Rings* (2001–2003) movies, Gandalf needs to be depicted as much taller than the hobbits as part of the storytelling. If the movie presented the actors to appear to be at their actual heights, audiences would not be able to imagine this aspect of the story. Thus, capturing reality is, sometimes, an obstacle to boundless storytelling.

The computer allows filmmakers to render captured elements of reality, which become the seeds for developing the audiovisual narrative. Once rendered, these pieces can be transformed, edited, and modified much more easily to meet the story's requirements. As rendered elements can be processed and transformed, it is much more natural to create an audiovisual simulation of the story and its elements, which is the goal of audiovisual narratives. In other words, the computer removes at least some of the limitations of audiovisual storytelling, as its sound and visuals anchor us to a depiction of the reality of the storyworld.

This does not mean that movies created before the digital era are inferior or that depicting Gandalf as taller than Frodo using a camera effect instead of digital editing is an inferior solution. On the contrary, this idea could only speak of the impressive results that filmmakers were able to achieve while dealing with the limitations of the physical world. Editing a film by manually cutting and pasting film frames is a tedious task that can generate the same effective results as if it were done digitally. Thus, their success speaks to their mastery of the art and their inventive solutions to overcome the multiple challenges they faced to tell the stories they wanted. Nevertheless, when done digitally, I believe film editing and screen scoring achieve their full potential as an art form inside audiovisual storytelling.

Is This a Treaty on Hans Zimmer's Aesthetics?

This book is an aesthetic exploration of contemporary scoring techniques, which originated with digital technologies, and I conceptualized them by defining the hyperorchestra. The examples provided aim to illustrate the aesthetic features I am describing, but they are not a comprehensive history of screen music at the start of the new millennium. Thus, the aim is to define the hyperorchestra as a theoretical model that can describe myriad contemporary aesthetic approaches.

Having said that, Hans Zimmer's influence on the model is significant due to his relevance in not only capturing but also creating a zeitgeist for screen scoring from many angles.[1] Many of his scores have become milestones that have influenced the aesthetics of his contemporaries and, thus, have become central elements in the description of the hyperorchestra.[2]

With the Oscar-winning score for *Lion King* (1994), Zimmer collaborated with Lebo M—along with South African musicians—to include non-Western orchestral content into the score. While he was not the first to do that—the Oscar-winning score for *The Last Emperor* (1987) is one example—it certainly propelled Hollywood composers to expand their instrumental palette. With *Gladiator* (2000), Zimmer reshaped the structure of the orchestra, switching the paradigm from music written for orchestra to music that sounded orchestral. For instance, by recording sections of the orchestra separately, Zimmer was able to create orchestral sounds that would not have been possible if the orchestra had been recorded together. In tandem and partly thanks to the reshaping of the orchestral sound, Zimmer successfully crafted what would become the sound of the epic drums for the beginning of the twenty-first century: a combination of electronic and acoustic sounds that were heavily processed using computer tools. Zimmer detached from its own signature sound a few years later to explore other means of narrative storytelling through music. *The Dark Knight*'s (2008) score (in collaboration with James Newton Howard) presented a heavily processed violin sound with constant panning to represent the Joker, breaking the idea that orchestral instruments mimicked the orchestral default. It also contributed to improving a software synthesizer, U-he *Zebra*. I will describe synthesizers in much more detail later on. For now, a software synthesizer is a virtual instrument that creates sounds using electronic means only. One problem they faced was a lack of emotional intensity and expressiveness compared to acoustic instruments or even hardware analog synthesizers—the same kind of instrument but in which the sound is generated electrically instead of electronically. U-He *Zebra* has been celebrated for its groundbreaking capacity to overcome these shortfalls, in part due to the contributions of Zimmer and his team. More importantly, the improvements were almost immediately released to the public, making *Zebra* a scoring standard tool. Again, Zimmer was able to contribute to the zeitgeist of scoring aesthetics.

Similarly, *Inception* (2010) popularized the braams—a loud and processed instrumental brass sound that sounds like a screaming thunder and has been associated with apocalyptic epicness since then—to the scoring vocabulary, which many composers immediately adopted. While the origin of the braams technique is disputed (Abramovitch 2015), Zimmer certainly created a version of the sound that was more orchestral, could combine with an extended Western orchestra, and had a clear emotional and storytelling function.

With *The Man of Steel* (2013), Zimmer showcased another angle of his conception of the orchestral sound as a substitute for music played by an orchestra. He combined the orchestral concept of an ensemble with a non-orchestral instrument that was always famously played by one performer: the drumkit. In the movie, Zimmer created a drum sound by combining 12 drummers playing simultaneously, subverting their roles and performance practices, and exploring the concept of an instrumental drum section. This concept became widely popular for developing new virtual instruments by creating recordings of sections that did not exist in the orchestral vocabulary (e.g., an ensemble of marimbas).

Christopher Nolan asked Zimmer to write music for *Interstellar* (2014) before the script was completed, inspired by what—according to Nolan—was a core idea for the movie. This process highlighted my previous point of film composers becoming filmmakers and all the potential it has for telling sophisticated stories. Finally, Zimmer's score for Dune (2021–2024) presents a highly organic but fully non-orchestral sound palette that distances itself from most of the previous approaches to score world-building of futuristic civilizations, which were either based on synthesizers or in a traditional orchestra. While writing this book, it is still early to analyze the full effect of this score, but I believe it will impact the sounds of audiovisual narratives that depict futuristic civilizations. Nevertheless, I will analyze the intricacies of its design later on.

Relatedly, directors such as Christopher Nolan or Denis Villeneuve have been significant in releasing massively popular films that embrace complex modes of storytelling, in which music is undoubtedly an intrinsic part of storytelling. Nolan has been continuously criticized for mixing the music louder than the dialog, which he defended as a creative choice (Sharf 2020). Similarly, when discussing *Dune*, Villeneuve stated that he was against a too-dialog-centric approach to cinema, which he attributed to television. He even stated, "I hate dialogue. Dialogue is for theater and television" (Tapp 2024). In both cases, they were using a score by Zimmer.

I started to conceive the hyperorchestra through my attempts to describe and analyze the music and the narrative for *Inception* (2010). The dreamworlds depicted in the movie shared common ground with the concept of hyperreality, which was also a significant part of the design of the music. As I will detail in the next chapter, I use Baudrillard's concept of hyperreality to define the hyperorchestra. Succinctly, for Baudrillard, hyperreality is a simulation that generates things that are modeled from reality but that do not have reality as its referent or origin (Baudrillard 1994, 1). Nowadays, an approach that uses the hyperorchestra is dominant as a scoring practice across many different composers and composing teams. Nevertheless, I frequently find that many of Zimmer's movies are the clearest to illustrate hyperorchestral aesthetics. This is the reason why I feature Zimmer in quite a few of the examples in this book, which does not suggest that the hyperorchestra is exclusive to his aesthetic world.

A Theory Informed by Practice Approach on Timbre, Organology, and Technology

This book's approach is to create a theory that is closely informed by practice. Thus, while it is a theoretical book in its essence, it avoids being too abstract to disregard practice. Consequently, while it is not a practical book, it is a valuable theoretical framework to teach practice in a manner that proposes a sophisticated discussion on aesthetics. Along with my colleagues, we have used hyperinstruments (the term I created to describe an instrument within the hyperorchestra that is sonically specific in its aim to create precise meaning), hyperorchestra, and hyperorchestration (another term I created to describe the techniques to write and create meaning with the hyperorchestra) as the core theoretical concepts to teach our introductory practical course—aimed at future screen composers—devoted to the use of digital technologies to create music. Students start building hyperinstruments within a few weeks to expand their aesthetic world and include timbre—the sonic qualities of a sound beyond its pitch—as an essential aspect for the generation of narrative meaning.

In a general sense, this book focuses on the spectral aspects of the musical phenomenon and their relationship to the generation of meaning for audiovisual narratives. The study of the sound spectrum (and timbre) is complex, requiring technology to perform objective sound analysis. In other words, analyzing sound spectrally requires technology. This is one of the reasons why a serious study of the spectral qualities of the musical phenomenon did not start until the late 1960s. It was created by a group of composers who would be known as part of a spectral school of musical thought and had access to the technologies developed in IRCAM (Paris, France). Spectral derives from the concept of sound spectrum, which is an objective way to talk about timbre.

More recently, musicology has embraced timbre as one of its most vivid research areas. Dolan and Rehding (2021) alert in the introduction of *The Oxford Handbook of Timbre* that timbre is an ambiguous term that needs to be redefined constantly. Frequently, the study of timbre is associated with exploring the discrete sound spectra of musical instruments. My approach is a bit different, as it emanates from the ideas of the spectral composers to approach timbre as a mode for analyzing sound musically. On that train of thought, I suggest in the last chapter that music mixing—the process of combining and processing different sounds together to create the final piece of music—is a mode of hyperorchestration that shares the same goals and overarching approaches as traditional Western orchestration—the art and craft of writing effectively for the Western orchestra or any combination of instruments that emanate from that paradigm (e.g., a string quartet).

I want to note that the terms spectral and timbre are frequently used interchangeably. However, the term timbre makes the most sense when referring to the spectral properties of a physical musical instrument or sounding entity. For example, when digitally modifying the spectrum of a violin recording using a tool for that purpose (e.g., an equalizer), we will generally acknowledge that it produces a change in the sound spectrum rather than a change in the timbre of the instrument. Thus, generally speaking, timbre is associated with traditional processes of orchestration, whereas spectral manipulation is associated with sound manipulation in the studio. With digital technologies, though, both these concepts have increasingly merged, especially from the perspective of recorded music. Thus, my definition of hyperinstruments aims to incorporate this fusion by providing a conceptual framework to define and analyze complex sound entities.

Therefore, in the process of crafting customized and meaning-packed scores, I describe how composers design what I define as hyperinstruments. These are specific and curated virtual sound entities designed to provide unique meanings to each score. They are the product of combining or modifying existing virtual instruments and custom-made recordings of acoustic-sounding bodies. In doing so, I engage in what could be defined as virtual organology—the study of instruments—with an emphasis on the tools and processes to design these hyperinstruments. This is because hyperinstruments are designed to be specific and tailored to unique situations or needs, whereas the principles to build them become more universal and prone to the equivalent of an organological analysis.

At the same time, virtual instruments—a key tool for creating hyperinstruments—have become so significant and complex that they require analysis to classify them based on key features. In doing this process, I also provide a historical snapshot of the technologies for screen music for the first 20 years of the twenty-first century. However, the book does not offer a detailed history of these technologies or even a detailed history of virtual instruments. I only suggest a selection of aesthetically and historically relevant ones that serve as just a blueprint for these technologies.

From these ideas, I present the hyperorchestra as a conceptual framework that defines an approach to screen scoring that encompasses a spectral approach to music, taking full advantage of digital technologies. Its prime feature, though, is that it embraces a spectral attitude to music-making based on the generation of meaning for storytelling purposes.

STRUCTURE OF THE BOOK

To achieve all of these, I divided the book into two parts. The first part, *Theoretical and Practical Foundations*, provides theoretical grounds for the hyperorchestra in three areas. Chapter 2 focuses on the philosophical background from which to describe the hyperorchestra. It is divided into two parts. First, there is an investigation of how postmodern philosophy defined the concept of hyperreality and how it was informed by McLuhan's highly influential theory of media. Second, I analyze the aesthetic and philosophical foundations that emanated from the introduction of digital visual tools to cinema, with an emphasis on Prince's theory of perceptual realism. Chapter 3 is devoted to investigating the process of increased virtualization of the musical phenomenon since the introduction of recording technologies, culminating in a preliminary definition of the hyperorchestra. This chapter expands the ideas from the second chapter into music.

The first two chapters provided the theoretical foundations. Chapter 4 is dedicated to describing the innovations in the screen scoring practice through the use of digital tools. Thus, it provides an account and a taxonomical analysis of the tools for the contemporary screen composer. A significant part of the chapter is devoted to virtual instruments, proposing a set of taxonomies to describe and analyze them and a practice-induced typology.

The book's second part, *The Hyperorchestra and the Contemporary Aesthetics for Screen Music*, is devoted to aesthetics. Chapter 5 provides three frameworks and eight examples to describe hyperorchestral practices. First, I describe how screen scoring became a nonlinear process with the aid of digital technologies. Then, I propose a model to describe and analyze hyperinstruments and the hyperorchestra. I use a selection of movies and TV shows to exemplify these models.

Chapter 6 is dedicated to hyperorchestration, encompassing a set of techniques used in writing music with the hyperorchestra. I draw from the examples and analyses from the previous chapter and supplement them with examples from other movies to demonstrate the application of the hyperorchestration techniques I am describing. The chapter includes a description of the process of creating hyperinstruments based on the framework proposed in the previous chapter, along with a detailed description of how mixing should be considered analogous to any other orchestration technique in the domain of the hyperorchestra.

Scope

The scope of this book encompasses music for contemporary audiovisual narratives that embrace technological innovations to craft the score. I mainly focused on screen music that utilized these technological tools in a manner that was especially relevant to crafting new aesthetic approaches. For example, John Powell's impressive score for *How to Train Your Dragon* (2010) extensively used orchestral mockups (as defined above, a temporary digital version of how the music will sound once recorded) as a part of the scoring process to create a primarily orchestral score. Thus, John Powell used scoring technology as a means to create a mockup that served as a communication tool for a score that became mainly orchestral in a traditional sense. While there would be plenty of areas in which to analyze this score from a hyperorchestral perspective, I prioritized audiovisual narratives that were aesthetically more groundbreaking for the sake of clarity. With that, I am not implying that Powell's music is less original or noteworthy. I just tried to select the examples that were the clearest to illustrate the points that I was making. Conversely, this should not preclude analyzing scores such as this one from a hyperorchestral perspective, nor should it imply that only aesthetically groundbreaking scores defying the traditional orchestral sound define a hyperorchestral aesthetic.

Similarly, the hyperorchestra depicts a musical practice in which the creation of meaning is essential. Therefore, it works best in audiovisual narratives that are created for audiences to enjoy. This does not restrict the scope to blockbusters or wide-audience film releases. However, it is a model that would not work as well in audiovisual products in which audience comprehension and engagement are less relevant.

Finally, to maintain cohesion, I purposely avoided discussing labor, authorship, and the general narrative function of the music unless it was relevant to the discussion. Therefore, while the use of technology has an enormous impact on screen music as an industry, I restricted the discussion to just a few relevant points to contextualize the hyperorchestra. Similarly, I have only described the narrative function of the scores I analyze when they exemplify the techniques I am defining.

Terminology

The term audiovisual narratives encompasses movies, episodic narratives (TV shows), video games, most documentaries, and so on. Therefore, this is the most accurate way to approach what screen scoring and this book is about. However, in terms of discourse and prose, the expression *audiovisual narrative* might become wordy and somewhat repetitive. At the same time, audiovisual narratives started with cinema, which was recorded in film. During the book, I took the stylistic license to sometimes use cinema or film as a synonym for audiovisual narrative for the purpose of making the prose flow better.

Similarly, we generally name a person who works in audiovisual narratives a filmmaker, which has become a generic term. Therefore, I frequently refer to the filmmaker(s) when talking about someone in the creative team of the audiovisual narrative (e.g., the director). For clarity purposes due to the musical focus of this text, I refer to the composer as a composer instead of a filmmaker.

Storytelling has also become a generic term encompassing much more than the traditional story. I generally incorporate diverse modalities and narrative levels when I refer to storytelling. For instance, a documentary (nonfiction) contains storytelling, even when it documents actual events. Similarly, the narrative layers that provide deeper meanings, such as philosophy or more complex ideas, are also conceptually included in storytelling.

A User-Friendly Glossary of Concepts

Many concepts I use in this book are rather new terms, especially from a scholarly perspective. For instance, industry professionals might define the term mockup differently from each other, and it has not been established as a concept in screen music scholarship. To avoid confusion, I am providing a glossary and definition of these terms, which I will use in this text. I tried my best to make these definitions as user-friendly as possible, avoiding unnecessarily technical complexities and simplifying as much as possible. Thus, in some cases, the definitions below are my definitions, which sometimes—such as in the case of the difference between a mockup and a demo—emanate from a theoretical need to differentiate and classify practices. I hope that this list is helpful for the reader who is discovering these terms for the first time, as well as for the reader who is familiar with this terminology to understand the way I am using these terms.

Acoustic Instrument: A musical instrument in which the sound is produced through the vibration of physical elements only or a sounding body used musically. A violin, a cymbal, or a glass hit by a mallet is an acoustic instrument. However, a synthesizer such as the Moog is not an acoustic instrument as it requires electricity to produce sound.

Amplified Instrument: This refers to an acoustic instrument that uses or requires electrical sound amplification. An electric guitar, which generates a very quiet sound without amplification, would be an example of an amplified instrument.

Amplitude (Volume, Gain): Amplitude is the technical term for defining the intensity of a sound. The higher the amplitude, the more intense the sound. We generally refer to amplitude as volume, and while not scientifically accurate, it works for our understanding. Similarly, an increase in Gain is an increase in the amplitude of a sound. Therefore, a sound with a higher amplitude is generically louder than a sound with a lower amplitude. However, our ears do not perceive changes in amplitude linearly, and they change by frequency (see **Loudness** and **Frequency**).

Audio Domains: Conceptual frameworks to define how we work with audio.

Acoustic Domain: This is the "natural" way sound is transmitted using particle vibrations.

Analog Domain: This domain uses electricity to generate, store, or transport music. A microphone is an analog device that converts sound from the acoustic domain into electricity, making it part of the analog domain. Similarly, a loudspeaker converts electrical signals from the analog domain to air particle vibrations in the acoustic domain.

Digital Domain: It is sound from the analog domain that has been converted into a discrete sequence of numeric data to be processed and stored in a computer or digital system. Electricity representing sound is measured several times per second (frequently 48000 times) and given a discrete number. The number range in CDs (compact discs) was between 0 and 65535 (2^{16}). In modern systems, the range of numbers is even higher (generally 2^{24}).

Audio Effect Processors (Audio FX): Tools in either the analog or the digital domain that serve to transform audio.

Compression: A processor that reduces the amplitude range of a sound (generally described as the dynamic range). This means that it reduces the loudest sounds, making them quieter.

Distortion: A processor that transforms the signal by adding harmonic content to the sound (most common) or inharmonic content.

Equalization: A processor that can alter the amplitude of a sound in frequency areas or at specific frequencies.

Panning: Placing a sound in the stereo field. Stereo sound is achieved by having two audio signals: left and right. Panning is the process of deciding how much sound signal is routed into the left and right channels.

Reverb: A processor that generates the equivalent of the ambiance produced by the reflections and bounces of a room or a hall.

Braams: Most likely a combination of the word brass and onomatopoeia of a scream, braams denote a very loud sound that resembles a distorted, loud brass sound. Abramovitch (2015) defined it as "a foghorn on steroids." Since around 2009, they have been a staple of trailer music, amongst other scoring usages.

Demo, Sketch, Draft (of a digital music piece): A version or iteration of a piece of music for screen music (a cue) while it is being used as a communication tool between different members of the filmmaking team. While a mockup (see below) is a similar tool designed for a much more linear process of scoring, the demo is an iterative process in which the music is constructed until it is finalized. Recordings are not merely substitutes, as in the case of the mockup, but additions to the piece of music, susceptible to being manipulated and transformed nonlinearly after the recording process.

Digital Audio Workstation (DAW): A software designed to edit and create music nonlinearly through the arrangement and combination of digital audio material and MIDI data. DAWs contain a timeline similar to nonlinear video editors and several lanes to place either audio elements or MIDI data that will become audio.

Digital Cinema: A movie in which digital means are used as part of the creative process. This means that the movie information is, at least at some point, converted into digital data, and it is processed in a computer.

Dynamic: While dynamic is sometimes used as a synonym of amplitude (see compressor), I will always use dynamic in its traditional musical sense. A violin player who applies less bow pressure to the violin is performing at a lower dynamic than when it applies more bow pressure. A piano player who hits a key with less energy than the following one is performing the first at a quieter dynamic. Generally, the results are that higher dynamics have a higher amplitude and, therefore, sound louder. However, this is not all. A change in dynamic generally carries a change in the acoustic instruments' timbre (the sound spectrum). Hence, I refer to a change in volume or amplitude when there is a change in the instrument in which the spectrum remains intact. At the same time, I use the term dynamic to emphasize the effect that playing louder has on the resulting timbre of acoustic instruments.

Frequency/Frequency Spectrum (sound): Frequency is the number of times a particle vibrates per second. The human ear can perceive vibration from about 20 times per second (Hz) to up to 20,000. Lower-frequency sounds are generally described as low, and high-frequency sounds are generally described as high. Most sounds contain a large number of different frequencies together at different amplitudes. The Frequency spectrum is a way to describe and analyze a sound based on which frequencies it contains and how loud they are.

Gain: See **Amplitude**.

Harmonic Content: Musical instruments have a frequency spectrum that contains frequencies mathematically organized as multiples of the lowest frequency. These frequencies are described as the harmonic content of the sound (also called **Overtones**). For example, if an instrument's lowest vibrating frequency is 100Hz, its harmonic content will contain frequencies such as 200Hz, 300Hz, 400Hz, 500Hz, and so on. Generally speaking, the amplitude of the harmonic frequencies decreases gradually. The first four harmonics generate a major chord, which is one of the reasons why they are called harmonic content.

Hyperinstrument: A term I created to describe an instrument within the hyperorchestra that is sonically specific in its aim to create precise meaning.

Hyperorchestra: A term that I created to describe a virtual musical ensemble that is the product of the interaction of musical devices and technology to create sounds that carry narrative meaning for the audiovisual material they are part of.

Hyperorchestration: Akin to orchestration, a term I created to describe the techniques to write and create meaning with the hyperorchestra.

Hyperreality: As defined by Baudrillard, "the generation of models of a real without origin in reality" (1994, 3). It is frequently used to describe virtual realities or simulations, although Baudrillard's concept was more sophisticated. The term is complex, and it is covered in detail in Chap. 2.

Inharmonic Content: All the frequencies in a sound that are not part of its harmonic content. For example, the sound of the bow friction with a string in a cello will generate frequencies that are not part of the harmonic content of the sound the string produces.

Loop: An audio fragment (a sample) designed to be repeated continuously. This means that the end of the sound needs to be able to concatenate with its beginning.

Loudness: The human perception of how loud a sound is. For example, lower-frequency sounds require more amplitude to be perceived at the same loudness level than higher-frequency sounds.

MIDI: Musical Instruments Digital Interface. It is a digital protocol that provides a set of instructions that are equivalent to a musical score in the digital realm, with the capacity to interact with virtual instruments that can understand these instructions and convert them into sound, much like a performer would do using a score. Therefore, MIDI is not sound but a set of instructions for generating sound. It has many elements similar to a musical score, especially the concept of a note that is fundamentally the same as you would find in the score. MIDI is organized over time like a score with an associated tempo.

Mixing (music): The art and craft of combining sounds to produce a final musical result. The process of mixing might involve selecting which sounds will appear in the final result (imagine recording several takes of a musical passage and selecting one), their amplitude level, their position in the space, and any sound transformation applied to an individual sound, a group of sounds, or the whole musical result.

Mockup: This term does not always have a unified meaning across the industry or among amateur composers. In this book, I refer to a mockup as a computerized temporary realization of a piece of music, mostly orchestral and mainly used for screen music with the objective of being replaced by a recording. The mockup—understood from this angle—is an especially relevant term to discuss the scoring practices of the late 1990s and the first decade of the twenty-first century. Created using virtual instruments, the objective of the mockup is to sound as close as possible to the orchestral recording that will eventually replace it. Thus, a mockup is a temporary tool that will be replaced entirely by live instruments that will be recorded at the final stages of the process. The objective of the mockup is to help the composer imagine the music they are writing and to facilitate the communication and approval process of the music, minimizing possible surprises after the recording.

If part of the mockup ends in the final score, it is no longer a mockup. This becomes a piece of music created with digital means (the industry term for this is also "in the box"). There was a period of time when some people used the term mockup to refer to any digital piece of music that carried a pejorative meaning (e.g., they could not afford an orchestra for this film, and they are using mockups instead). I will call a piece of digital music that is not finalized and is part of the review and discussion process a demo.

The term mockup has been fading away since the second decade of the twenty-first century as most scores incorporate digital elements into the final mix. This is also due to the proliferation of a nonlinear scoring process, which I will detail in Chap. 5. In this contemporary framework, composers frequently do not know which musical elements will need to be recorded and which will remain digital only, which makes the term mockup ineffective unless this is clear (e.g., the composer knows that there will be an orchestra session that will fully replace their digital rendition).

Music Production: Creating or processing music in the analog or digital domains. Music production is all the processes that are not related to composing music in the traditional sense (score, paper, pen) and acoustic performances. Therefore, recording, editing, mixing, or generating music using digital devices are part of music production.

Nonlinear Editing Software: A piece of software (Avid Media Composer, Adobe Premiere, Apple Final Cut) designed to edit movie material. Nonlinear editing refers to the capacity not to edit a film sequentially so the editor can modify any sequence at any time (Kmet 2018, 211).

Nonlinear Creative Process: A linear creative process in music involves sequentially conceiving the music, writing it, creating the musical scores, and performing or recording it. A nonlinear process of music-making involves creating music with all these steps simultaneously or not necessarily in linear order.

Organology: The study of instruments. In the context of this book, the study of musical instruments.

Overtone: See **Harmonic Content**.

Pitch: The fundamental frequency of a musical note that has a standard harmonic spectrum. In other words, a pitched note is a sound that has a spectrum dominated by a harmonic structure. Thus, saying that the A above middle C pitch is 440Hz, we are indicating that it is a sound that has a harmonic spectrum in which the fundamental frequency is 440Hz.

Round Robin: For the purposes of this book, Round Robin is a technique used to create sampled virtual instruments in which the same sample (e.g., a staccato A3 in *piano* dynamic on the flute) is recorded several times. Each time that the virtual instrument uses this sample, it will iterate from the collection of samples recorded. This is done to avoid the perception of artificiality produced by repeating the same sound over and over.

Sample (sound): Generally speaking, a recorded sound fragment. However, I will primarily refer to samples as sound fragments that are recorded and edited to become part of a virtual instrument, generally a sample library, a (hybrid) synthesizer, or a loop.

Sample Library: a virtual instrument that uses a significant amount of audio samples. The term originates from the process in the 1990s of manually assembling and organizing a set of sound samples to be used in a piece of hardware that could create sound, the original sampler. At that time, composers or the users of the hardware sampler collected sound recordings to feed to the sampler to create sound. Therefore, the composer would need to properly organize hundreds of audio files using the resources available in the 1990s, which could involve several disks. Currently, though, a sample library only refers to a virtual instrument that uses a significant amount of distinct samples to generate sound.

Sampler: Originally, a sampler was a piece of hardware that could create sounds at different pitches from one or more audio sources (the samples). Currently, it is a piece of software used to create virtual instruments that contain or use any amount of audio samples.

Scripting: Scripting is programming—or, more specifically, programming a computer program. In this book, scripting will refer to the process of programming a sampler to create a virtual instrument. Samplers act as tools that allow designers ample flexibility to create the equivalent of subprograms, each of which is a virtual instrument created within their paradigm.

Sequencing: A sequencer is a piece of software that works with MIDI information that will be used to produce music. In other words, sequencing is the equivalent of digital score writing using the MIDI protocol instead of the Western score.

Sound Design: In film studies, sound design refers to the creation of the film sound. In electronic music, sound design is the process of creating sounds and programming synthesizers or virtual instruments to generate specific sounds. In this book, I always use the latter definition.

Interestingly, both processes use similar tools and resources and share a common aesthetic in many contemporary films. For instance, musical elements of a score might be generated by creating musical instruments that use sounds from elements that appear in the audiovisual narrative, such as the nuclear plant in *Chernobyl* (2019) or the pipes of *How to Blow Out a Pipeline* (2022).

Spectrum, Spectral (sound): The combination of frequencies and their amplitude that constitute a sound.

Synthesizer: an electric, electronic, or virtual instrument that generates sounds without using acoustic means or acoustic recordings. A synthesizer always contains an artificial sound generator, such as an oscillator.

Hybrid Synthesizer: It is a synthesizer that uses sound samples to generate sound exclusively or in combination with artificial sound generators. The difference between a sampler and a hybrid synthesizer might be more aesthetic than purely technical. However, a hybrid synthesizer will generally use one or a few audio samples to generate sound instead of the dozens to thousands of samples a virtual instrument in a modern sampler would typically use. In addition, the samples will generally be transformed and processed in a hybrid synthesizer.

Timbre: The spectral properties of the sound of a musical note or a musical instrument that are not related to its pitch.

Time Stretching: A software process that alters a sound to make it slower or faster. The process will try to compensate for the loss of quality using algorithms that attempt to keep the stretched sound as close to the original as possible. The process also allows for to change the pitch of a sound by playing it faster or slower. In this case, the resulting fidelity is higher when the new pitch is closer to the original one.

Virtual Instrument: A digital version of a musical instrument. Virtual instruments might or might not be created to resemble an acoustic musical instrument. Some of these instruments utilize recordings of acoustic instrument performances to generate a digital sound based on them. Other ones generate sounds on their own without the need for recordings (a virtual synthesizer). Virtual instruments receive information similar to a musical score (using the MIDI protocol) and generate audio.

Virtual Space: A digital creation that simulates a space in terms of its acoustic properties. Virtual spaces might emulate or replicate existing acoustic spaces or might not. Virtual spaces can also generate acoustic results that would be impossible in the physical world.

Volume: See **Amplitude**.

Notes

1. In addition to the movies I am highlighting here, it is well-known how many composers were mentored and started their careers through Zimmer. To name a few: John Powell, Tom Holkenborg, Ramin Djawadi, and Harry Gregson Williams.
2. As I will detail in Chap. 4, Hans Zimmer and his team also created one of the first—albeit private and not publicly released—high-quality sample libraries that became legendary in the industry at the end of the twentieth century.

References

Abramovitch, Seth. 2015. "'Braaams' for Beginners: How a Horn Sound Ate Hollywood." The Hollywood Reporter. https://www.hollywoodreporter.com/movies/movie-news/braaams-beginners-how-a-horn-793220/.

Baudrillard, Jean. 1994. *Simulacra and Simulation*. Ann Arbor: University of Michigan Press.

Burton, Byron. 2019. "How 'Chernobyl' Composer Found Inspiration in a Real (and Radioactive) Power Plant." The Hollywood Reporter. https://www.hollywoodreporter.com/news/general-news/how-chernobyl-composer-found-inspiration-a-radioactive-power-plant-1228682/.

Chion, Michel. 1994. *Audio-vision: sound on screen*. New York: Columbia University Press.

Dolan, Emily, and Alexander Rehding. 2021. "Timbre: Alternative Histories and Possible Futures for the Study of Music." In *The Oxford Handbook of Timbre*, edited by Emily Dolan and Alexander Rehding. Oxford Handbooks Online: Oxford University Press.

Karlin, Fred, and Raybund Wright. 2004. *On the Track: A Guide to Contemporary Film Scoring*. Routledge.

Kurzweil, Ray 1990. *The Age of Intelligent Machines*. Kurzweil Foundation.

Kmet, Nicholas. 2018. "Orchestration Transformation: Examining Differences in the Instrumental & Thematic Color Palettes of the *Star Wars* Trilogies." In *John Williams: Music for Films, Television and the Concert Stage*, edited by Emilio Audissino. Brepols.

Murch, Walter. 2001. *In the blink of an eye: a perspective on film editing*. 2nd edition. Los Angeles, California: Silman-James Press.

Nolan, Christopher. 2010. *Inception*. [Shooting Script].

Sharf, Zack. 2020. "Christopher Nolan Says Fellow Directors Have Called to Complain About His 'Inaudible' Sound." IndieWire. https://www.indiewire.com/features/general/christopher-nolan-directors-complain-sound-mix-1234598386/.

Tapp, Tom. 2024. "Denis Villeneuve: "Frankly, I Hate Dialogue. Dialogue Is For Theatre And Television"." Deadline. https://deadline.com/2024/02/denis-villeneuve-movies-corrupted-by-tv-1235838780/.

Zimmer, Hans. 2021. "Hans Zimmer's use of computers and samples in orchestral music" In "Mix with the Masters." https://youtu.be/_LHyNYRtwR8?si=VUrPPKEv0N3HB0Ep.

PART I

Theoretical and Practical Foundations

CHAPTER 2

From Hyperreality to Digital Cinema: A Theoretical Overview

NEO
This—This isn't real?

MORPHEUS
What is real? How do you define real? If you're talking about what you feel, taste, smell, or see, then real is simply electrical signals interpreted by your brain.

[...]

MORPHEUS
"The desert of the real."
—*The Matrix* (1999)

The Matrix (1999) became a cultural icon for movies that engage with hyperreality. The film is set in a dystopian future on Earth, where humans exist while connected to a computer-simulated reality in which they are enslaved by an aristocracy of self-intelligent machines that exploit them as a source of bioenergy. At the movie's beginning, Jean Baudrillard's book *Simulacra and Simulation* (1994) appears on-screen, acting as a secret container in which Neo, the protagonist, hides disks containing illegal computer data and software. This scene is just one of the numerous allusions to Baudrillard's ideas that appear implicitly and explicitly in the movie. The most significant of these references is the existence of a simulacrum, or a computer-simulated reality, which humankind, unaware of their enslaved status, virtually inhabits.

Baudrillard believed that the movie did not accurately represent his ideas (Lancelin 2004), which broadly suggested an absence of the real in contemporary Western societies as they have become symbolic systems unable to differentiate between the real and its representation (Baudrillard 1994; Chan 2008). For Baudrillard, *The Matrix* failed to portray the lack of differentiation between the real and its simulation. Instead, the movie presented an opposition between a dystopian real (but real, nonetheless) and a hyperreal (the simulated virtual world called the Matrix). From this standpoint, Baudrillard believed that the dichotomy between the worlds portrayed in *The Matrix* was closer to Plato's allegory of the cave than his concept of the disappearance of the real (Lancelin 2004). This view would still hold even when considering that the real in *The Matrix* is the sunless ruins of a lost human civilization, which Morpheus qualifies by paraphrasing Baudrillard as *the desert of the real*. However, the desert of the real is portrayed literally in the world of *The Matrix* (by showing the deserted ruins of cities), whereas the concept is allegorical in Baudrillard's work. For Baudrillard, the desert of the real meant the absence of a real or the inability of Western civilization to distinguish reality. For all of that, Baudrillard thought that *The Matrix* "is surely the kind of film about the matrix that the matrix would have been able to produce" (Lancelin 2004).

However, we can interpret the real and the simulated in *The Matrix* as narrative devices. From this angle, the movie does not depict an imaginary world that inaccurately resembles Baudrillard's ideology but employs an audiovisual narrative (and its created world) to discuss many philosophical ideas. Thus, we could describe *The Matrix* as an audiovisual narrative that engages in philosophical thought and incorporates philosophical concepts developed by Baudrillard, among others. The idea that audiovisual narratives might be a form of philosophy is not a recent concept. However, philosophically packed movies have been much more frequent in the twenty-first century, roughly correlating with the advent of digital cinema.[1] For instance, Baudrillard cites *The Truman Show* (1998), *Minority Report* (2002), and *Mulholland Drive* (2001) as movies that engage with the concept of the hyperreal as in *The Matrix* (Lancelin 2004).

If audiovisual narratives engage in philosophical inquiry, we should assume they do it beyond the script level. This means that philosophical thought would also be present in the musical meaning of the score, amongst other elements. Further, the heightened interest in creating movies that engage with philosophical topics since the start of the twenty-first century suggests that the musical score has also evolved to incorporate additional devices to help in that endeavor. By defining the hyperorchestra, I aim to describe a significant part of these devices and suggest their effectiveness in portraying contemporary narratives in their totality. If philosophy evolves with society, it is understandable that visual narratives and their musical scores also evolve. In a society where technology evolves as fast as at the beginning of the twenty-first century, embracing a technocratic approach to these transformations is tempting. In the end, without analog and digital technologies, none of the axioms for the hyperorchestra would be possible. However, we can also analyze this process as the opposite: technological evolution is a response to changes that produce new societal challenges.[2]

This chapter is a brief, non-musical, philosophical overview of essential concepts and ideas that will support defining and describing the hyperorchestra. The first part covers philosophical approaches that assist in framing humanity's history as a process of increased virtualization by utilizing the definitions of the hyperreal by Baudrillard and Eco and the theory of media proposed by McLuhan. The second part takes these ideas into the realm of visual storytelling by analyzing the effects of digital cinema on the medium. Analyzing some of the transformations that audiovisual narratives have endured as a consequence of the introduction of digital technologies is relevant to the present discussion because these transformations are not dissimilar to the changes in the music for these narratives and, therefore, with the hyperorchestra. Importantly, this summary is not an attempt to provide a detailed philosophical overview of Jean Baudrillard or Marshal McLuhan. Instead, it provides select snapshots of their ideas that are useful for defining the hyperorchestra.

A Philosophical Model for the Hyperreal

Nowadays, hyperreality is both a relatively common and polysemic term. Hyperreality is often associated with virtual reality, video games, or even social networks. From the point of view of the person who coined the concept, Jean Baudrillard, these definitions would be as imprecise as how *The Matrix* approached the notion. On the other hand, many of these approaches to the idea of hyperreality do fit well with Marshal McLuhan's theory of media, a philosophy that strongly influenced Baudrillard's thought. In this section, I approach central ideas from both authors in this area of inquiry as the context to describe the processes behind the emergence of the hyperorchestra. I also briefly discuss Umberto Eco's more straightforward definition of hyperreality as an example of an alternate approach.

From a practical point of view, McLuhan's model is groundbreaking, clear, and easily applicable to describe almost any element of culture and innovation. Eco's definition of hyperreal is also relatively practical and concise. Baudrillard's thoughts, though, are generally convoluted, difficult to grasp, and never clearly explained, but at the same time, intellectually stimulating. Further, it is probably the reason why Baudrillard felt generally misunderstood by many, while, at the same time, Baudrillard's ideas inspired numerous artists and thinkers. With that in mind, I will introduce Baudrillard's ideas that relate to hyperreality while contextualizing them into more straightforward approaches. As a first step, I will describe how Disneyland has been used (and popularized) to approach the idea of hyperreality. Disneyland's model is powerful as it is very illustrative while being reasonably easy to understand.

Disneyland and the Hyperreal

Disneyland and the city of Las Vegas are frequently used in discussions that revolve around hyperreality. There is a common assumption that Disneyland is a prime example of what Baudrillard defined as hyperreality. However, this is not precisely the case. Baudrillard's assessment of Disneyland presents a much different picture and introduces some of his philosophy's central axioms, such as the orders of simulacra, which I will detail later. In a subchapter called "The hyperreal and the imaginary" from his *Simulacra and Simulation*, Baudrillard (1994) states:

> Disneyland is a perfect model of all the entangled orders of simulacra. It is first of all a play of illusions and phantasms: the Pirates, the Frontier, the Future World, etc. This imaginary world is supposed to ensure the success of the operation. But what attracts the crowds the most is without a doubt the social microcosm, the religious, miniaturized pleasure of real America, of its constraints and joys. [...]
>
> Thus, everywhere in Disneyland the objective profile of America, down to the morphology of individuals and of the crowd, is drawn. All its values are exalted by the miniature and the comic strip. Embalmed and pacified. Whence the possibility of an ideological analysis of Disneyland (L. Marin did

it very well in Utopiques, jeux d'espace [Utopias, play of space]): digest of the American way of life, panegyric of American values, idealized transposition of a contradictory reality. Certainly. But this masks something else and this "ideological" blanket functions as a cover for a simulation of the third order: Disneyland exists in order to hide that it is the "real" country, all of "real" America that is Disneyland. [...] Disneyland is presented as imaginary in order to make us believe that the rest is real, whereas all of Los Angeles and the America that surrounds it are no longer real, but belong to the hyperreal order and to the [third] order of simulation. (Baudrillard 1994, 12)

For Baudrillard (1994), even though Disneyland "is a perfect model of all the entangled orders of simulacra," the park acts as a mechanism that masks the loss of reality in the contemporary world. In other words, by admiring its aesthetic hyperreality, society can acknowledge it as a perfect fake and thus forget that the world they live in is the actual fake. Umberto Eco's (1990) description of Disneyland's hyperrealism differs from Baudrillard's approach and concentrates on more practical and palpable approaches:

Disneyland is more hyperrealistic than the wax museum, precisely because the latter still tries to make us believe that what we are seeing reproduces reality absolutely, whereas Disneyland makes it clear that within its magic enclosure it is fantasy that is absolutely reproduced. [...] Disneyland can permit itself to present its reconstructions as masterpieces of falsification. [...]

Once the "total fake" is admitted, in order to be enjoyed it must seem totally real. [...] When there is a fake – hippopotamus, dinosaur, sea serpent – it is not so much because it wouldn't be possible to have the real equivalent but because the public is meant to admire the perfection of the fake and its obedience to the program. [...] Disneyland tells us that technology can give us more reality than nature can. (43–44)

Eco's account of Disneyland's features highlights a distinctive point of view. For Eco, Disneyland is genuinely hyperrealistic, and society enjoys it because it can produce a flawless (yet artificial) nature. However, from Eco's viewpoint, this does not negate the existence of reality outside of Disneyland. For Eco, the imaginary part of Disneyland makes it hyperrealistic, highlighting how technology can produce more and better reality than nature. Eco's conception of Disneyland implies that its visitors accept what he calls the "total fake." Conversely, for Baudrillard, "the imaginary of Disneyland is neither true nor false, it is a deterrence machine set up in order to rejuvenate the fiction of the real" (13).

Baudrillard's Hyperreality

As noted earlier, Baudrillard's writings are purposely enigmatic and sometimes contradictory. In Jean Baudrillard's entry at the *Stanford Encyclopedia of Philosophy*, Douglas Kellner's (2020) concluding remarks suggest that:

> Baudrillard is perhaps more useful as a provocateur who challenges and puts in question the tradition of classical philosophy and social theory than as someone who provides concepts and methods that can be applied in philosophical, social or cultural analysis. He claims that the object of classical social theory—modernity—has been surpassed by a new postmodernity and that therefore alternative theoretical strategies, modes of writing, and forms of theory are necessary. While his work on simulation and the postmodern break from the mid-1970s into the 1980s provides a paradigmatic postmodern theory and analysis of postmodernity that has been highly influential, and that despite its exaggerations continues to be of use in interpreting present social trends, his later work is arguably of more literary interest.

Baudrillard (2000) concludes one of his latest books, *The Vital Illusion*, corroborating Kellner's (2020) conclusion quite explicitly while still considering his writing in the realm of philosophical inquiry:

> Here, however, lies the task of any philosophical thought: to go to the limit of hypotheses and processes, even if they are catastrophic. The only justification for thinking and writing is that it accelerates these terminal processes. Here, beyond the discourse of truth, resides the poetic and enigmatic value of thinking. For, facing a world that is unintelligible and problematic, our task is clear: we must make that world even more unintelligible, even more enigmatic. (Baudrillard 2000, 83)

I would suggest that even in Baudrillard's simulation theories, there is a significant degree of unclarity, as illustrated by the author's critique of misrepresentation from *The Matrix*, among other artworks. Nevertheless, as Kellner advocates, these ideas are stimulating and thought-provoking enough to serve a meaningful role in describing current societal trends. To contextualize Baudrillard's thoughts on simulation and hyperreality, it is worth revisiting the interview about *The Matrix*, conducted just three years before Baudrillard's death, in which Baudrillard tries to clarify his approach to simulation:

> The most embarrassing part of the film is that the new problem posed by simulation is confused with its classical, Platonic treatment. This is a serious flaw. The radical illusion of the world is a problem faced by all great cultures, which they have solved through art and symbolization. What we have invented, in order to support this suffering, is a simulated real, which henceforth supplants the real and is its final solution, a virtual universe from which everything dangerous and negative has been expelled. (Lancelin 2004)

Thus, Baudrillard criticizes *The Matrix* for portraying the simulated world as a version of Plato's allegory of the cave. From this point, Baudrillard acknowledges that most cultures have tried to solve the problem expressed by Plato: humans are only able to perceive reality from their senses, and, thus, we are only able to create an illusion of the real, what Baudrillard calls a radical illusion. Through abstraction (symbolization), societies attempted to, at least, think they could connect with reality. For Baudrillard, Western society after the Renaissance attempted something different: to create a simulation of the real that humans could perceive, and its role was to replace the real, which is impossible to grasp. This process has been achieved through stages (or orders) that I will detail below.

The idea of simulation is also an important distinction for the hyperorchestra, which is not just an attempt to sketch *real music* using technology but implies a much more profound aesthetic transformation. As I will define later, the hyperorchestra is less about utilizing virtual instruments to mimic and replace their physical versions and more about the aesthetic impact that results from abandoning the conception that music is linked to our physical reality, even if just symbolically.

Baudrillard (2005), in *The Intelligence of Evil or the Lucidity Pact*, slightly approached the impact of digitally processed music as part of a simulated reality:

> Integral reality is also to be found in integral music: the sort you find in quadraphonic spaces or can 'compose' on a computer. The music in which sounds have been clarified and expurgated and which, shorn of all noise and static, is, so to speak, restored to its technical perfection. The sounds of such music are no longer the play of a form, but the actualization of a programme. It is a music reduced to a pure wavelength, the final reception of which, the tangible effect on the listener, is exactly programmed too, as in a closed

circuit. It is, in a sense, a virtual music, flawless and without imagination, merging into its own model, and even the enjoyment of it is virtual enjoyment. Is this still music? The question must be open to doubt, since they have actually come up with the idea of reintroducing noise into it to make it more 'musical' (Baudrillard 2005, 27–28)

Contrary to Baudrillard, I will argue that this music mode is still music with an increased potential to work with audiovisual narratives and storytelling. To that end, I am presenting my interpretation of some of these concepts in a manner that helps define the hyperorchestra to encompass a distinct set of musical processes that emanate from digital music-making.

The Three Orders of Simulacra and the Hyperreal

To better grasp Baudrillard's thoughts on hyperreality and simulation, I will briefly examine the main points concerning the three orders of simulacra. Baudrillard describes three orders of simulacra that correlate with different stages of modern human evolution (1993, 50, 1994, 121). Etymologically speaking, a simulacrum is an image or a representation of an object. Baudrillard defines the first order of simulacra as the stage of human evolution when representations are based on imitation or counterfeit (1994, 121). In this order, images are naturalist, and they attempt to become a reproduction of the world. Still, images are not linked to the world but act as an arbitrary referential sign of it (Pawlett 2007, 74–75).

Baudrillard utilizes Saussure's ([1916] 1998) semiotic concepts, which include the definition of a sign. For Saussure, the sign comprises two elements: the signifier (the form the sign takes) and the signified (the concept the sign represents). For example, the word "bird" signifies the concept of a "bird," although it is not directly connected to any specific element taken from reality. Moreover, the word bird is advantageous as it points out an abstract idea that can be applied to both an instance of a bird and its abstract version. The equivalent of a sign in the physical world is called a referent. From this viewpoint, the link between the referent and the sign is arbitrary. For instance, calling both an ostrich and a nightingale bird is a convention and thus is arbitrary. Once defined as a planet, Pluto lost this status without any apparent physical change. This loss of status suggests that society constructs reality from imagining a model based on observations. Consequently, the association linking the concept of what a planet is to its referent is arbitrary, as it can change without the referent changing.

Subsequently, Baudrillard highlights a binary opposition between the notion of the 'world' (or reality) and the 'signs' (the symbolic) humans construct to interact with (Pawlett 2007, 75). Images are no different from other signs, even though they aim to reproduce reality naturalistically. Thus, Baudrillard (1994) defines the first order of simulacra as the "imaginary of the Utopia" (121). According to Baudrillard (1993), the first order appeared with the Renaissance (50), when the "bourgeois class dismantled the fixed ranks and restricted exchanges of the feudal order through the introduction of democratic parliamentary and legal institutions" (Pawlett 2007, 74). By breaking fixed ranks and norms, the signs that governed society were no longer sacredly connected to a referent. In other words, society learned that there was no divine order. Thus, the signified part of a sign became adaptable to changes in fashion or social values. In terms of art, Baudrillard emphasizes the development of stucco during the Renaissance, a material that facilitated the imitation of nature on walls. In addition, he mentions the importance of theatrical illusion. In both cases, their naturalistic approach aims to provide an imitation or counterfeit of nature (Baudrillard 1993, 50–52).

The beginning of the second order of simulacra corresponds with the Industrial Revolution, governed by the idea of mass production. In the first order, the difference between the real and the simulacrum is still presupposed (50), but this changes with the second order:

> The second-order simulacrum simplifies the problem by the absorption of appearances, or by the liquidation of the real, whichever you prefer. In any case it erects a reality without images, without echo, without mirrors, without appearances: such indeed is labour, such is the machine, such is the entire industrial system of production in that it is radically opposed to the principle of theatrical illusion. No more semblance or dissemblance, no more God or Man, only an immanent logic of the principle of operativity. (Baudrillard 1993, 54)

This change was made possible by the mass production associated with the industrial era. An object might be reproduced on an industrial scale, losing its attempt to be a counterfeit of its referent, as "serial production gives way to generation through models" (56).

The third order of simulacra corresponds to the current code-governed society, where simulation is the dominant schema (50). It might be associated with a postmodern society, even though Baudrillard disliked using this term. In this order, signs become modeled signifiers when signifiers detach from what they signify. Thus, the meaning of a signifier is not determined by what it signifies but by its relations with other signifiers.

In the third order of simulacra, the simulation becomes "the generation by models of real without origin or reality: a hyperreal" (Baudrillard 1994, 1). Meaning becomes unstable, as it is dependent on the relationships based on a symbolic system that now does not exist anymore: "Without the stable equivalence of sign–referent and signifier–signified, meaning becomes highly unstable, and binary distinctions implode, reverse or become radically uncertain in their meaning(s)" (Pawlett 2007, 77). Therefore, a simulation not only precedes any possible experience of the real but also highlights how meaning is volatile. Kellner (2020) summarizes Baudrillard's hyperreality as follows:

> In addition, his postmodern universe is one of *hyperreality* in which entertainment, information, and communication technologies provide experiences more intense and involving than the scenes of banal everyday life, as well as the codes and models that structure everyday life. The realm of the hyperreal (e.g., media simulations of reality, Disneyland and amusement parks, malls and consumer fantasylands, TV sports, virtual reality games, social networking sites, and other excursions into ideal worlds) is more real than real, whereby the models, images, and codes of the hyperreal come to control thought and behavior. Yet determination itself is aleatory in a non-linear world where it is impossible to chart causal mechanisms in a situation in which individuals are confronted with an overwhelming flux of images, codes, and models, any of which may shape an individual's thought or behavior. (Kellner 2020, "Symbolic Exchange and the Postmodern Break")

Kellner's Inclusion of Disneyland and similar experiences is surprising as it does not align with Baudrillard's thought. At the same time, it is also a good indicator of the difficulties faced in any attempts to summarize or even clarify this concept. For the purposes of the hyperorchestra, I also engage with these concepts in the limited scope of the aesthetics and the music's capacity to engage in new ways to generate meaning in audiovisual narratives. One of the most striking elements that pointed me to define the hyperorchestra is the observation of how transparent and well-accepted its devices were from the very beginning: the utilization of sounds that connected us with mainly orchestral models at first but at the same time were impossible to produce orchestrally was immediately bought and absorbed by audiences without hesitation. This situation is easier to understand if we encapsulate this behavior within hyperreality. Next, I continue to develop the ideas of simulation and implosion by exploring McLuhan's theories, which are closely related to Baudrillard's model of simulacra and hyperreality.

McLuhan's Theory of the Media

McLuhan's theory of the media, containing his famous statement "the medium is the message" ([1964]1994, 7), proves to be a practical resource in elucidating some of the effects of the hyperreal in society. Not surprisingly, Baudrillard drew significant inspiration from McLuhan when developing the concepts of simulacra and hyperreality. McLuhan developed a theory of the media in the well-known book *Understanding Media* ([1964]1994). The beginning of the first chapter, aptly titled "The Medium is the Message," explains the partially cryptic yet well-known statement:

> In a culture like ours, long accustomed to splitting and dividing all things as a means of control, it is sometimes a bit of a shock to be reminded that, in operational and practical fact, the medium is the message. This is merely to say that the personal and social consequences of any medium - that is, of any extension of ourselves - result from the new scale that is introduced into our affairs by each extension of ourselves, or by any new technology. (McLuhan [1964]1994, 7)

Thus, a medium, in McLuhan's terms, is any kind of extension of ourselves. For example, the hammer extends our arms, and the wheel may extend our legs (Federman 2004). In addition, the message of a medium is "the change of scale or pace or pattern that it introduces into human affairs" (McLuhan [1964]1994, 8). McLuhan provides several examples, which constitute the book's body, to demonstrate his proposition and provide a social explanation of humanity linked to its developments. One of his first examples, the railway, is remarkably eloquent to pinpoint his overarching philosophy:

> The railway did not introduce movement or transportation or wheel or road into human society, but it accelerated and enlarged the scale of previous human functions, creating totally new kinds of cities and new kinds of work and leisure. This happened whether the railway functioned in a tropical or a

northern environment and is quite independent of the freight or content of the railway medium. (McLuhan [1964]1994, 8)

Thus, the message of the railway lies in how it transformed society by generating, for example, new models of cities. McLuhan's thoughts on the medium and the message become ontologically relevant for understanding both terms as they acquire a broader meaning than what is usually assumed. No less striking than McLuhan's famous quotation is the introduction of the book (especially for a text written in 1964):

> After three thousand years of explosion, by means of fragmentary and mechanical technologies, the Western world is imploding. During the mechanical ages we had extended our bodies in space. Today, after more than a century of electric technology, we have extended our central nervous system itself in a global embrace, abolishing both space and time as far as our planet is concerned. Rapidly, we approach the final phase of the extensions of man - the technological simulation of consciousness, when the creative process of knowing will be collectively and corporately extended to the whole of human society, much as we have already extended our senses and our nerves by the various media. (McLuhan [1964]1994, 3)

If the medium is an extension of our bodies, the evolution of Western society may be described as a process of expansion (or explosion) by different mediums. McLuhan argues that the world has imploded since the electric era because of instantaneous communication: "As electrically contracted, the globe is no more than a village" (5).

Assessing why McLuhan describes this process as an implosion instead of a continuation of the expansion of our bodies is essential to our understanding of how this view relates to the concept of hyperreality. Electricity travels closer to lightspeed, the fastest speed possible. What comes after electricity will necessarily go beyond the physical because the limits of the physical have already been reached. In that sense, McLuhan labeled the process as an implosion, as it allowed for the merging of social and political functions. Similarly, it virtually eliminated the physical distance between people by bringing humanity together in a global village. However, McLuhan's implosion process may also be analyzed as a route of expansion that goes beyond the physical and the real, thus driving further into the hyperreal. McLuhan termed the process an implosion because he focused on humankind and the extension of their bodies. If railways extended the distance a human could travel, this distance was extended further by employing airplanes. With space travel, humanity became able to travel beyond Earth. However, the global village concept does not continue to expand with the same rationale. Instead, post-electrical development focuses on connecting the consciousnesses of human beings. As this is not strictly an extension of the body, and, for McLuhan, consciousness precedes any technology, he thus defined the process as implosion.

Therefore, the implosion process entails a disconnection from the real, as the power of transformation of the new media is not focused on the physical world. In this sense, McLuhan's concept of implosion intersects with the notion of the hyperreal. McLuhan's theory of the media is closely related to his views on the evolution of language in Western culture, which can also be linked to Baudrillard's orders of simulacra and the conceptualization of the hyperreal.

The Spoken and the Written Word

"Language does for intelligence what the wheel does for the feet and the body. It enables them to move from thing to thing with greater ease and speed and ever less involvement" (McLuhan, [1964]1994, 89). Furthermore, McLuhan emphasizes that Western society is rooted in the written word based on a phonetic alphabet (89). The utilization of such an alphabet is relevant because "the phonetically written word sacrifices worlds of meaning and perception" (91). Consequently, using a phonetic alphabet separates the visual and the auditory experiences, thus giving Western individuals "an eye for an ear" (84). As a result of this separation, phonetic language becomes central to civilized society. However, the power to civilize humanity comes at a cost. By separating "both signs and sound from their semantic and dramatic meanings," (87) there is a detachment "from the feelings or emotional involvement that a nonliterate man or society would experience" (79). Then, language becomes a technology that enables a process of abstraction from reality. In using a phonetic written language, the process of abstraction is even more significant than the spoken word. Using a phonetic written language, all the emotions and nuances natural in the oral language must become part of a rational, step-by-step description.

Because of the social and psychological effects of detachment produced by the phonetic alphabet, contemporary society has attempted to recover its contact with imagination and emotion to regain "wholeness" (89). In addition, McLuhan believed that "consciousness is not a verbal process"

(89). Thus, he thought that the process of expanding consciousness would bypass spoken and written language:

> The computer, in short, promises by technology a Pentecostal condition of universal understanding and unity. The next logical step would seem to be, not to translate, but to bypass languages in favor of a general cosmic consciousness, which might be very like the collective unconscious dreamt of by Bergson. (McLuhan [1964]1994, 89)

Before this transformation occurred, he observed that electric technology would threaten the ideology that emanated from the phonetic alphabet because by "extending our central nervous system, electric technology seems to favor the inclusive and participational spoken word over the specialist written word" (89).

McLuhan could not predict that, with hypertext, written language would evolve and maintain its status. In contrast, instant written communication (email or instant messages) would become indispensable for offline interactive communication. Still, both hypertext and instant written communication transformed the written language enough to corroborate, in a broad sense, his statement. His belief that consciousness, if taken literally, is separated from language is unclear at least. If language is one of the first technologies of humanity, it is because language is essential for humans to become *conscious* humans. Therefore, it seems more appropriate to understand consciousness in McLuhan's media theory less literally and closer to the idea of implosion.

Media and Simulacra
Examining McLuhan's theory on how language and humankind are connected helps to elucidate how his theory of media is related to Baudrillard's orders of simulacra. By underlining the phonetic language's detachment from perception and emotion, McLuhan presents a similar argument to Saussure's conjecture about the arbitrariness of the link between the sign and its referent. In a related manner, for McLuhan, the phonetic language is responsible for creating the Western *civilized* society by detaching *civilized* humans from reality. McLuhan (1969) defined art as "specialist artifacts for enhancing human perception" (32). The statement also applies to the perspective image (the drawing technique that allows a person to create a three-dimensional representation utilizing a two-dimensional surface). One key feature of the perspective image as a medium, compared to

other media such as the railway, is that it expands human senses virtually, thus detaching from its referent—only two dimensions can represent a three-dimensional space. From this viewpoint, the perspective image resembles the phonetic language. The similarity in how perspective image and language detach from the environment stresses another connection: if language is essential to define Western civilization and the perspective image is similar to language, producing simulacra is also crucial to define Western civilization.

A Process of Virtualization

Accepting the framework outlined above is equivalent to arguing that the history of Western society is effectively a process of virtualization, understood as any process that involves generating a simulation of reality. Thus, McLuhan's approach to media as an extension of the human body and mind outlines a process of virtualizing human existence. If Western civilization flourished with the creation of a phonetic language, this indicates that it was born when humans could detach from reality and construct their knowledge by virtualizing it. In his book *The Singularity Is Near*, Ray Kurzweil (2005) goes even further:

> The word "virtual" is somewhat unfortunate. It implies "not real," but the reality will be that a virtual body is just as real as a physical body in all the ways that matter. Consider that the telephone is auditory virtual reality. No one feels that his voice in this virtual-reality environment is not a "real" voice. With my physical body today, I don't directly experience someone's touch on my arm. My brain receives processed signals initiated by nerve endings in my arm, which wind their way through the spinal cord, through the brain stem, and up to the insula regions. If my brain – or an AI's brain – receives comparable signals of someone's virtual touch on a virtual arm, there's no discernible difference. (Kurzweil 2005, 203)

Similarly to Baudrillard's description of the radical illusion that I mentioned earlier, Kurzweil states that there is no direct connection between reality and human senses as physiology already mediates the process. Thus, in McLuhan's terms, the human body becomes the first medium for humankind. In these terms, the hyperreal is no longer a product of contemporary society. Instead, the ability to produce hyperreality may be considered a latent feature of the initial stages of humanity. Further, any virtualization process (which implies detachment from reality) tends to generate hyperreality. This is because if human beings who are intelligent and creative perceive reality through mediation, it is probable that their intelligence and creativity will attempt to modify the perceived reality.

Baudrillard and McLuhan identify the industrial and technological revolutions as two critical moments of transformation. The Industrial Revolution is essential for Baudrillard's definition of the second order of simulacra. For McLuhan ([1964] 1994), the printed book generated the modern world and the Industrial Revolution, as it "involves a principle of extension by homogenization that is the key to understanding Western power" (170–178). The homogenization produced by the printed word generated a further level of detachment: in a society with print, the human became more abstract.

The importance of the written language as a process of abstraction from reality becomes more evident if we utilize McLuhan's model to describe formal languages and hypertext. Computer languages are the most common form of formal languages. They are defined by a finite number of symbols and a finite and specific set of syntactic rules to combine them. Their main feature is that they do not require human intelligence to be processed. A closed set of grammatical rules generates content. Thus, they are the ultimate version of presenting knowledge through a set of instructions. Suppose the written language, as stated by McLuhan, requires the construction of a coherent sequence to express "what is quick and implicit in the spoken word" (79). Then, formal languages require a closed grammar to produce the language with total abstraction. However, if written language requires a large amount of text to describe a simple event of the spoken word, formal languages require a vast set of rules to process even the simplest form of written language. Computer languages became the next step in the homogenization (and simplification) of language to the degree that they no longer require human intellect to be executed.

From Text to Hypertext via McLuhan's Implosion
Hypertext and the widely used Hypertext Markup Language (HTML) are not formal languages, as they are only a set of markups that serve to format natural language texts.[3] They are just an extension of printed language. I will not discuss the implementation details of HTML here, as I will only focus on the essential changes that hypertext produces in society concerning the previous discussion. Broadly speaking, hypertext has provided a syntactical layer between texts.[4] If print allowed for the mass

distribution of existing texts, the hypertext allowed for the massive creation of relationships between them, which became a necessary step to continue producing knowledge efficiently. Before hypertext, modern libraries were created as a rudimentary syntactic system that paralleled the segmentation and isolation of knowledge in the contemporary world. Hypertext forces the abandonment of the linearity of this hierarchical classification. The written word requires defining a simple event based on oral communication linearly and causally. With hypertext, this process transforms. Any set of texts can be interconnected by complex networks of meaning, especially with the utilization of any tag system, a byproduct of hypertext.

McLuhan's concept of implosion is easier to understand in this context. He believed that implosion would revert humanity to a stage of development closer to the tribal era: pre-civilization but in a global village. From that angle, humans would regain what was lost during the process of abstraction of the modern world. By creating meaning for the connections between different texts, hypertext incorporates the nuances of the spoken word. The consequences that this approach has had in transforming the principles of Western civilization are enormous, as McLuhan stated.

One example is Wikipedia, which is generally rejected as a robust scholarly source because it is not peer-reviewed in the traditional sense and because its content may change at any time due to any user creating an update. In other words, Wikipedia has no identifiable authority and cannot be printed. Wikipedia's authority does not emanate from traditional Western authority systems, from the meaning produced by the connections of its contributors. The authority of the review does not come from the authority of the peers but from the power of the link. A change is accepted according to a combination of the number of users that support the change and the authoritative value of those users in terms of how their previous proposed changes have been accepted.

The previous definition of the hypertext also fits into Baudrillard's (1994) definition of hyperreality: "the generation by models of real without origin or reality" (1). For Baudrillard, the third stage of simulacra does not imply a partial return to a previous stage. The term implosion is used in Baudrillard to symbolize the destruction of not only the referents but also the signifiers. Therefore, accepting the premises of hyperreality implies that the basis of Western knowledge and science is not as robust as it once was believed to be. Baudrillard stated that the evident hyperrealism of Disneyland served to mask the absence of reality in the rest of society. For

McLuhan, media serves as a mechanism to augment the human body and senses at the cost of abstraction. The scrutiny of hyperreality within those lenses unfolds that the way to achieve the augmentation process involves exploring connections beyond the real, which is impossible to grasp, thus building the hyperreal.

After this broad overview centered on hyperreality in contemporary society, I will focus on theories and ontological approaches to digital cinema, a medium product of the abovementioned transformations. From the theories related to digital cinema, I feature Prince's concept of perceptual realism, which discusses the visuals of the medium with points in common with the hyperorchestra. Similarly, I discuss some of Auslander's theories on liveness, which serve as a foundation for some of the processes of the hyperorchestra.

Digital Cinema, Virtual Realities, and the Hyperreal

Digital cinema transformed the physicality of the seventh art so significantly that many scholars questioned whether it was still the same artistic medium. David Bordwell describes this process in *Pandora's Digital Box* (2012):

> The film is no longer a "film." A movie now usually comes to a theatre not on reels but on a matte-finish hard drive the size of a big paperback. The drive houses a digital version of the movie, along with alternative soundtracks in various languages and all manner of copy-guarding encryption. Instead of lacing a print through rollers and sprockets, the operator inserts the drive into a server that "ingests" the "content." (7–8)

Setting apart the purely technical aspects, the disappearance of a well-defined physical link between the image and its representation invigorated an ongoing discussion regarding film ontology. From my point of view, digital cinema should not be considered a different artistic medium from its celluloid counterpart, nor has it significantly altered cinema as a medium in terms of ontology.[5] Instead, digital cinema has definitively liquidated the assumed indexical property of the photograph. By analyzing the technological changes in digital cinema, I will discuss the most prominent elements related to cinema ontology to provide a philosophical ground for examining the interaction between cinema and hyperreality.

Narratives and Virtual Reality: Worldbuilding

Audiovisual narratives are a widespread mode of storytelling. However, not all audiovisual manifestations are the same, even if they employ the same set of technologies. For example, documentaries and movies use similar technologies. However, audiences need to perceive documentaries as faithful to what they are depicting to be effective, thus acting as an index that proves that a series of events occurred. This is not the case for a movie. Considering them in the same typology as movies or episodic narratives would complicate the approach. Therefore, this discussion will focus just on narrative cinema (and episodic narratives) that broadly follow the classical Hollywood form, regardless of their production location.

David Bordwell (1985) proposed a framework to define the classical Hollywood form in *Narration in the Fiction Film*. Bordwell references the Russian terms *fabula* and *syuzhet* to refer to what he later describes as story and plot, respectively. The story constitutes all the events of the narrative, including the ones that do not appear in the movie. By contrast, the plot contains all the film's information, including elements that would not be considered events in the story. The plot typically includes parts of the story only, which are not necessarily shown in chronological order (Bordwell and Thompson 2012, 80–82).

> Of all modes, the classical one conforms the most closely to the "canonic story" which story-comprehension researchers posit as normal for our culture. In fabula terms, the reliance upon character-centered causality and the definition of the action as the attempt to achieve a goal are both salient features of the canonic format. At the level of the syuzhet, the classical film respects the canonic pattern of establishing an initial state of affairs which gets violated and which must then be set right. (Bordwell 1985, 157)

Thus, narrative cinema is a character-centered "chain of events linked by cause and effect and occurring in time and space" (Bordwell and Thompson 2012, 79). Bordwell (2006) argues that postclassical era movies (produced after 1960) still follow, with some innovations, the classical form:

> American films have changed enormously. They have become sexier, more profane, and more violent; fart jokes and kung fu are everywhere. The industry has metamorphosed into a corporate behemoth, while new technologies have transformed production and exhibition. And, to come to my

central concern, over the same decades, some novel strategies of plot and style have risen to prominence. Behind these strategies, however, stand principles that are firmly rooted in the history of studio moviemaking. (Bordwell 2006, 1)

Bordwell's remarks regarding contemporary moviemaking practices define a common ground for cinema that would fit with the scope described above.[6] From this perspective, narrative movies produce two essential outcomes. First, they generate an imaginary world in which the story unfolds. Second, they generate an imaginary psychological world for each main character. These results constitute what is usually described as the movie diegesis, which has proved to be both a complex and controversial field of inquiry, predominantly when related to the musical score. Nevertheless, here, I will only focus on how these movie worlds interact with the concepts of virtualization and virtual reality examined before.

Storytelling relies on creating an imaginary world and a set of imaginary characters for a story to unfold. This statement is still valid when the story recalls a "real life" event. Even in this situation, the story must create a replica of this "real" world and its characters. In addition, the plot of the movie (using Bordwell's terminology) generally presents only a fraction of the story. Therefore, imagination becomes a fundamental element in understanding how we approach storytelling.

Imagination and Virtual Reality

In *Sweet Anticipation*, David Huron (2006) describes a cognitive process in which he terms the imagination response (8). It is the first step in Huron's well-known cognitive theory of human expectation based on five consecutive stages: imagination, tension, prediction, reaction, and appraisal. Huron calls it ITPRA theory, which is an acronym for these processes. He believes that the "*imagination response* is one of the principal mechanisms in behavioral motivation" as "*Imagining* an outcome allows us to feel some vicarious pleasure (or displeasure)—as though that outcome has already happened" (8). Hence, "we don't simply *think* about future possibilities; we *feel* future possibilities" (8). For example, thinking about a rose garden, "it is important to pause and smell the roses—to relish the pleasures of the moment. But it is also crucial to take the imaginative step of planting and nurturing those roses" (9). For Huron, imagination is essential for human survival and evolution. Thus, humans constantly imagine possible outcomes for different situations they believe they may encounter. Huron states that the process of imagination involves thinking and feeling simultaneously (9). Huron also argues that it is not possible for *healthy* humans to only think about what we imagine without actually feeling it. Therefore, by imagining a situation, humans experience the emotional outcome before the situation happens, which may aid them in shaping their actions (e.g., by planting roses).

In this framework, storytelling becomes a system that allows sharing possible outcomes of different events. That is why stories are customarily rich in mythical content, facilitating their application as a reference for a broad set of specific situations.[7] In accepting Huron's findings, perceiving a story involves a process of imagination and feeling the results of each situation as if they had happened to the audience. Stories are not only a form of entertainment but also a vessel to funnel the imagination's response and share ideas with each other. In doing so, we can process an imaginary situation created by someone else and feel it as if it were our own. Using McLuhan's theory of media, I believe that storytelling is a powerful tool for having a shared *consciousness*.

From this angle, the capacity to create psychological worlds for the characters of a story becomes fundamental. We engage with these types of stories by connecting with what happens to the characters in them. The psychological world and the values that justify the characters' actions are vital to establishing social patterns for the benefit of the receivers of the story, which is one reason why a character-centric mode of storytelling has become dominant in our society. In this mode of storytelling, the characters' psychology is central to unfolding the narrative's events.

Moreover, a story that utilizes the structure of a myth has the power of acting as a template. As a result, each viewer unpacks the content of these stories to imagine specific outcomes to their subjective experiences while modifying and complementing the content freely. Describing storytelling in terms of Huron's cognitive theory of imagination reveals that any process of imagination produces the equivalent of a virtual reality. Huron's findings suggest that the imagination process is so potent that it delivers the same emotional outcome as if experienced physically. By stating that imagination makes us feel as if the event actually happened, Huron implies that imagination generates alternate virtual realities. In each of these virtual realities, the emotional pay-off is equivalent to everyday physical experiences. Narrative cinema, as a form of storytelling, does not deviate from this framework. Compared to a written tale, cinema can operate within a complete set of audiovisual materials in addition to language, including music. Each of these materials contributes to shaping the imaginary world (or the virtual reality) that the narrative portrays.

Digital Cinema and the Ontology of Cinema

Digital cinema is not a different artistic medium compared to analog cinema, as it does not significantly modify cinema as a medium. Instead, digital cinema has assisted in elucidating ontological questions on the properties of film and photography, the most relevant being the concept of indexicality and the authorship of a performance.[8] These two areas of inquiry are relevant to discussing the ontology of digital cinema and providing a framework for a similar discussion regarding music and the hyperorchestra. For instance, using a virtual instrument that uses a set of sampled recordings to generate its sound in a musical score challenges the indexicality and authorship of the performance. Therefore, this discussion will also become helpful when approaching an ontology for the hyperorchestra.

Digital Cinema and Indexicality

One of the fundamental elements of Peirce's semiotics is the division of signs into three non-exclusive categories: icons, indexes, and symbols (Atkin 2013). A sign is an icon when it resembles its object; it is an index when there is a factual connection with the object; finally, it is a symbol when the relationship is arbitrary.[9] Following this rationale, both a painting and a photograph should be an icon of what they portray. However, it was once believed that the photograph was an index of the reality it captured. It was believed to be true since the painter did not necessarily need any reality to create a painting.

Conversely, this was impossible with a photograph, which requires a reality to capture. Following this line of thought, the camera would become a device capable of objectively capturing the reality in front of its lens, which acts as a record of its existence: the chemical process that converts the light emanating from the objects in front of the camera into a negative becomes the physical proof of its indexicality. An equivalent logic may be applied to film.

Using a digital camera would eliminate the indexical property because there is no physical film to capture the light from the objects. Instead, a set of digital light sensors mediate and generate a collection of binary code for the digital version of the picture. From this perspective, the digital image is simply a collection of single-colored dots (the pixels) that produce the impression of what photography once was. Due to the digital mediators and its pixelation (fragmentation of its surface into discrete single-colored dots), digital photography loses its indexical property.

Friedrich Kittler (1999) underlined the weaknesses of attributing an indexical property to the photographs or films produced by any camera. In discussing why film is not indexically linked to reality, Kittler states: "Instead of recording physical waves, generally speaking, it only stores their chemical effects on its negatives" (119). By emphasizing the chemical process, Kittler also reveals a further consequence: if the chemical print were accepted as indexical, digital photographs should likewise be accepted as an indexical medium. A photographic negative has a finite number of molecules, which implies a finite resolution. Thus, in terms of indexicality, it is similar to the limitations of pixelation. At most, the difference between analog and digital photography is a resolution problem (there may be more molecules in a negative than pixels in a digital photograph). Kittler's statement aligns with Baudrillard's concept of the radical illusion I outlined earlier: humanity suffers from the fact that we are incapable of perceiving reality as an abstract, as it is always mediated through our senses. Photography became the last hope to deal objectively with reality.

To further dismantle the possible indexical feature of the photograph, Stephen Prince (2012) challenges it by observing that the camera does not capture an amount of light comparable to the human eye. Prince challenges the camera's indexical capacity from the restricted point of view of the perception of the human eye. Prince intentionally modifies the definition of an index to apply only to the human-perceived reality instead of reality itself, which is impossible to grasp. For example, the intent of a regular camera is not to capture the infrared waves in reality, as the human eye does not perceive them. Nevertheless, Prince (2012) acknowledges that the camera fails to become an index, even when only considering a human-centered perception of reality. Therefore, the camera itself acts as a filter for anything it captures:

> Despite the important place that live-action-camera reality holds in the theory and aesthetic practice of realistic filmmaking, the camera is a poor instrument compared with the human eye. It is a lossy instrument that fails to capture the full range of luminosity in a scene or environment. The human eye can respond to a dynamic range of 100,000:1 luminance levels; a camera, depending on the speed of the lens, the latitude of the film, and the size

of its digital sensor, captures far fewer. Theories of cinema that take the camera as an indexical agent accurately capturing what is before it have neglected to consider the significance of this characteristic—a single analog or digital image created in camera is a low-level facsimile of the lighting environment from which it derives. (Prince 2012, 192–193)

Prince's statement implies that a photograph may be unable to capture, for example, the visual content of dark areas. Subsequently, the photograph would fail to index those areas. Even when considering an ideal situation in terms of lighting, Prince argues that a digital technology such as HDR (High Definition Range) is much better at capturing the full radiance of the environment than its analog counterpart.[10] In the previous section, I argued that any process of perception becomes mediated by the artifact employed for its capture. The human eye, the chemical components of the negative, and the optical transducer of a digital camera act as mediators between reality and what they capture. Consequently, the indexical property needs to be further diluted to acknowledge the interference of mediators in the link between reality and photography.

Digital cinema (and photography) has also allowed the incorporation of CGI and computer image processing into moving images. In terms of ontology, utilizing these techniques could become another possible dividing point regarding medium specificity. By adding objects generated by a computer or modifying the existing picture using computer software (eliminating the facial imperfections in a photograph, for example), digital cinema may differ significantly from analog film production. Following this rationale, analog and digital cinema would become ontologically diverse media due to the inability of analog cinema to incorporate objects that were not produced physically. In other words, even though the analog camera might not be able to become a strong index of reality due to the problems discussed above, at least it portrays what originates in the physical world. However, because of its inability to index the reality captured by the camera, a computer modification of the image should not be considered a medium-specific property. For example, makeup may carry out the same function as digital retouching, especially when assuming that part of the realistic effect of makeup is possible due to the camera's limitations. In other words, makeup that seems natural or verisimilar in a movie might look much more artificial when observed directly on set.

Further, in accepting CGI and visual effects as part of the moviemaking process, the indexical property of a product that utilizes those techniques weakens even more to become almost nonexistent. Instead, the association of meaning to an image combines its iconic value and symbolic attribution. Its iconic property (how the picture resembles the object it attempts to reproduce) is connected to its degree of fidelity, resolution, and clarity.[11] Hence, the iconic property alone is insufficient to ensure the truthfulness of a moving image. As the indexical property is not usable, the possibility of delivering verisimilar experiences (as moving images do) may only be attributed to a symbolic process. This capacity to deliver verisimilar experiences is only possible because the camera has become the symbol of a device capable of documenting the environment in Western society. Therefore, a movie is perceived as verisimilar due to the conjunction of its iconic power (how well it resembles the reality it is meant to represent) and the symbolic assumption that filmed events portray reality. However, these properties may not be enough to produce a verisimilar output. For this reason, the reliability of the author who captured the image may become the most substantial symbolic value in delivering verisimilitude.

Rethinking Authorship: CGI and the Gollum's Case
In *Liveness: Performance in a Mediatized Culture*, Philip Auslander (2008) discusses the implications of a CGI character like *Gollum* in *The Lord of the Rings* (2001–2003) trilogy in terms of the performance's authorship. In addition to its genesis through computer processing, Gollum's performance was also generated using an actor (Andy Serkis), who was recorded using motion and facial sensors. This virtual performance challenges the definition of what acting and performance really are, especially when considering its multiple ramifications:

> Once created, a digital clone can undertake an infinite variety of performances the actual performer never executed; such performances can also be extrapolated from other forms of information, such as motion capture data. Whether generated in a special-effects studio or a live, interactive dance performance, motion capture data can be stored and used to produce future performances that were, in some sense, executed by the performer but without that performer's direct participation. (Auslander 2008, 170)

Auslander focuses his discussion on the legal implications of the copyright of the performance. Nevertheless, his thoughts on the Gollum problem similarly challenge the ontology of performance and its authorship.

Hence, it becomes difficult to define what performance is precisely, and at the same time, assigning authorship to a given performance becomes equally challenging. Stephen Prince (2012) provides a compelling answer based on an idea coined by film director David Fincher, who advocates for differentiating the process of acting and performance:

> On stage, performance and acting often are interchangeable. In cinema, acting is a subset of performance. For our purposes, then, *acting* is the ostensive behavior that occurs on set to portray characters and story action. *Performance* is understood as the subsequent manipulation of that behavior by filmmakers or by actors and filmmakers. This distinction will enable us to recognize the ways that cinema employs technology to mediate the actor's contribution, via such things as editing, music scoring, lighting, makeup, and compositing. (Prince 2012, 102)

Thus, acting becomes just a part of the performance, contained in a finite set of actions, while performance involves many more processes. For example, when music is used to shape a character (the *Indiana Jones* theme, for example), this music becomes part of the character's performance. This definition also allows CGI to be included in the performance. In the graphical representation in Fig. 2.1, CGI contains more processes than virtual characters. Digital retouching may act as virtual makeup analogously to how color correction or artificial lighting relates to physical lighting or the selection of a lens filter. Moreover, the model reveals that performance in audiovisual media is a process that involves physical and virtual actions.

From a conceptual point of view, film editing and music scoring have always been part of the virtual process of film performance, as they are part of the postproduction stage. The editor is not cutting film for the sake of cutting it but for the sake of what it represents. Thus, cutting film stock is conceptually physical, but editing film shots has always involved a virtual framework. Defining the editing process as virtual does not preclude acknowledging the links between editing and the set of physical processes in production (e.g., the distribution and selection of takes or the instructions from the director and their team). Similarly, CGI usually incorporates data from the physical world into its digital processes. Equally, music

2 FROM HYPERREALITY TO DIGITAL CINEMA: A THEORETICAL OVERVIEW   51

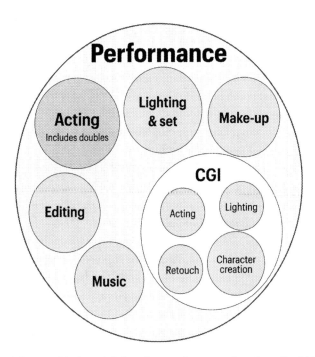

Fig. 2.1 This graphical model describes performance based on David Fincher's approach to performance and acting as described by Prince (2012, 102)

may incorporate recordings. Figure 2.2 attempts to represent this approach by modifying the previous model:

This division of the performance process underlines further connections regarding acting. For example, the instructions given to the actors by the director and their team will affect the acting result. Relatedly, music performance could be divided between the physical act of playing the instrument and all the aesthetic decisions that involve selecting a set of different playing actions. Influences from other performers, performances, or the instruments used become an integral part of the performance.

In lieu of this model, the concept of authorship dissolves. Regarding the ontology of the performance, this approach removes any possible distinction between a physical character, like Aragorn, and a digitally manipulated character, like Gollum in *The Lord of the Rings* (2001–2003). They are not ontologically different, as they only differ in the degree of performance attributable to the actor. The implications of this model are

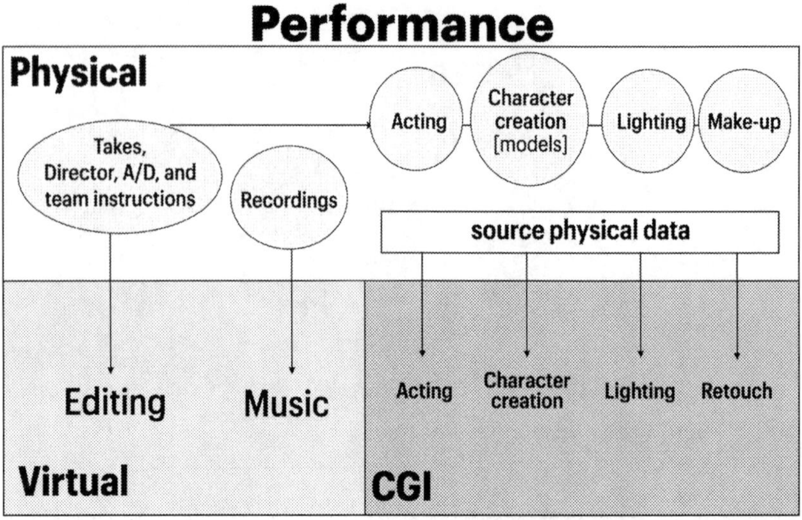

Fig. 2.2 This graphic summarizes the distinct roles that contribute to generating a performance in audiovisual media. The graphic is divided between physical and virtual processes

significant due to the disproportionate reliance on the concepts of authorship and authenticity in modern Western culture. The previous discussion reveals that both concepts are less stable than people in Western civilization might have assumed. Thus, authorship and authenticity hold a degree of arbitrariness, which ultimately means they are symbolic.

Prince's Perceptual Realism

Stephen Prince coined the term perceptual realism (Prince 1996, 2010, 2012) to describe better digital cinema, which helps investigate the connections between hyperreality and cinema. Perceptual realism will also help to elucidate a discussion between ontology and aesthetics. The term refers to objects in a movie that, even though referentially false, are perceived as realistic when depicted within the world of the movie (2012, 32). Prince argues that due to their perceptually realistic condition, "they are able to compel belief in the fictional world of the film in ways that traditional special effects could not accomplish" (33) and, therefore, "the more comprehensive a scene in evoking perceptual realism, the likelier it is to compel the spectator's belief" (33).

Prince utilizes the dinosaurs of *Jurassic Park* as an example of an object that is perceptually realistic, while CGI Gollum could be another example. The dinosaurs of *Jurassic Park* are exemplary as the movie's diegesis is set in 1993. The dinosaurs become an abnormal element of a depicted world that looks like it did in 1993. In addition, the movie combined physical models of dinosaurs with digitally generated ones. Hence, the dinosaurs will help exemplify a model for perceptual realism beyond CGI. Furthermore, the dinosaurs in the movie are a strong example of perceptual realism, as they do not currently coexist with humans, and no human has ever interacted with a dinosaur (2012, 32).

Prince (2012) also describes the scene in *Forrest Gump* (1994) in which Tom Hanks interacts with President Kennedy as perceptually realistic. In this case, President Kennedy's recording is real and may still exist in the memories of some audience members. Tom Hanks is similarly real and is a well-known actor. However, audiences likely know[12] that President Kennedy and Tom Hanks never interacted.

One of the main implications of Prince's definition relies on evidencing that perception has a quintessential role in generating a model of the real. Prince's concept signals how the limitations of the senses are relevant in perceiving a piece of art. In addition, Prince's conceptual approach associates the limitations of human perception in the movies with the limits of the senses in perceiving the world. The aesthetics of digital 3D exemplify this position. Prince (2012) argues that 2D (planar) cinema is "3D to the extent that it replicates the monocular depth cues that observers employ when viewing spatial layouts in the world at distances of six feet or more" (205). Thus, even though humans use both eyes to create a three-dimensional view of the world, this capability tends to be restricted only to the immediate space.

Consequently, planar movies or paintings that use perspective techniques still have spatial depth. Thus, it is not the painting or photograph that tricks the human eye into believing that a planar area has a third dimension. Instead, after a certain distance, the human perception "elects" not to perceive in three dimensions, thereby making a planar representation of a landscape and the landscape equivalent in terms of perception.

How human senses shape the perception of reality does not only apply to three-dimensional perception in cinema—human perception experiences movement by seeing 24 or more similar images per second. With less than 24 images per second, movement may also be perceived, but the illusion may become apparent. Similarly, with more than 24 images per second, a human may perceive a smoother sense of movement. The exact number of frames per second required for a person to perceive realistic movement depends on the limits of human senses and a certain degree of aesthetics, as humans are accustomed to adjusting their perceptual expectations to the environment. Similarly, a CGI object will be perceived as realistic depending on the degree of definition. A combination of perceptual capabilities and aesthetics will also determine the threshold.

In addition, Prince's (2012) definition of perceptual realism (32) provides the foundation for discussing the processes involved in perceiving something as realistic even though it is referentially false. The dinosaurs from *Jurassic Park* are a good example: they were generated by employing different models of the real, which were extracted from archeological findings and inferring animal behavior. Similarly, even though sound does not travel in outer space, it seems more realistic when it does, as is the case in many fantastic space movies. Space travel is yet to be a widespread human experience (although this is changing rapidly). Thus, the sound propagation quality is inferred from other physical media like air or water. I would speculate that even for audiences aware of this physical property of sound, a chase scene in space is perceived as more realistic with the sound effects of explosions, lasers, and collisions than without those.

Thus, perceptual realism is the product of aesthetics and the limitations of the human senses. Perceiving a dinosaur from *Jurassic Park* as realistic involves an aesthetic decision of acceptance because dinosaurs do not exist in contemporary reality. In addition, the previous discussion highlights the inability of human senses to distinguish between a CGI object and an image captured by a camera once CGI reaches a certain degree of resolution. Moreover, distinguishing something captured by a camera from something that has either been created digitally or manipulated becomes symbolic, as the indexical properties have been diluted. From this perspective, Prince's definition may be especially interconnected with the discussions concerning hyperreality.

Cinema and Hyperreality

Prince's definition of perceptual realism in the dinosaurs of *Jurassic Park* seems reasonably close to Baudrillard's definition of hyperreality: "models of a real without origin in reality" (1994, 3). However, Prince's scope is mainly aesthetic, as it describes an aesthetic process that surfaced alongside digital technologies. Nevertheless, the implications of perceptual realism may extend beyond aesthetics when considering the problems of indexicality and perception.

Regarding cinema's capacity to index reality, Prince contends that digital cinema might be even more indexical than its analog precedent. Prince asserts that HDR imaging (HDRi) is an example of a higher degree of indexicality when applying a digital process. However, by stating that indexicality may have different degrees, Prince transforms its meaning: it is no longer a binary property that would signal if the medium acts as an index of the reality it portrays. In fact, deciding the degree of indexicality of a given image requires an aesthetic evaluation. For example, the increase of lightness captured using HDRi should translate into a similar increase in the degree of indexicality. In addition, one must assess to which degree lightness contributes to the overall indexicality of the image. Based on this model, evaluating the indexicality of a given picture requires two elements:

- First, there needs to be an object against which it can be compared. If the object it will be compared against is the human eye, then a precise definition of what "human eye" means is necessary, as vision varies according to the individual.
- Second, a decision must be made to assign each pictorial feature's contribution (such as lightness or color) to the final degree of indexicality.

By following Prince's approach to evaluation, indexicality has become an aesthetic property, as its values are generated using a symbolic system. Hence, a process of assessment based on cultural codifications mediates the link between the moving image and reality. In addition, an object generated using computer software may become indistinguishable from an object captured by the camera. This statement especially holds true if one considers that CGI could incorporate captured elements to generate its digital objects, further complicating its relationship with reality and indexicality.[13] Hence, even with a culturally mediated approach to indexicality, problems arise due to the inability to distinguish between what was captured and what was artificially generated by using human senses alone.

The implications of redefining an index regarding the relationship between cinema and hyperreality are concentrated in three areas. First, McLuhan's position that Western civilization was given "an eye for an ear" ([1964]1994, 84), as it became visually biased with the phonetic language still holds. Thus, an analysis of the indexicality of the moving image tends to ignore the rest of the senses: reality is what is seen but not what is tasted, smelled, or heard. Second, the modified definition of indexicality reveals how it needs a comparison with other symbols to decide a moving image's indexical value. Consequently, the assumed direct connection between the real and the image is lost as the link is established by applying a set of rules based on cultural assumptions. Third, CGI generates objects with no apparent origin in reality, even though they may integrate some information captured from the world. Therefore, studying the relationship between cinema and reality becomes a perceptual inquiry. Digital cinema has been permitted to hide the illusion further, as it is able to work on a definition level that transcends the limits of human senses.

Conclusion

The overarching idea of this chapter devoted to presenting a philosophical overview of the hyperreal and the ontologies of digital cinema is the struggle humanity has had in knowing that we are incapable of perceiving unmediated reality. As a solution, we created a process of virtualization to generate a simulated world that can act as a replacement for the reality we cannot perceive, thus opening the door to the concept of hyperreality. Regardless of whether this statement seems to be an exaggeration, the philosophical ideas I presented outline the relevance of reality and truthfulness as core aspects of humanity's values. Therefore, subverting reality becomes significant, even if we know our perception of reality is always mediated.

The definition of the hyperorchestra starts from this idea: it is a virtual ensemble capable of generating meaning in any sonic way possible but that still feels the need to utilize models of the real to produce meaning that is engaging to human audiences. In the next chapter, I will use the frameworks and concepts described here to outline a *history* of the process of increased virtualization of music creation and production that will lead to a discussion on the ontology of the hyperorchestra and its definition.

Notes

1. Thomas Wartenberg (2003), in *Philosophy Screened: Experiencing The Matrix*, provides a general overview of the topic, while corroborating that "philosophers are turning with increasing frequency to film as a way of doing philosophy and that they see film as a resource for enriching

philosophic discussions of a range of ethical, social, and even metaphysical questions," (139) and concluding "that a film can actually make a contribution to philosophy is, no doubt, a surprising conclusion for many" (152).
2. James Buhler (2021b) in *Music, Digital Audio, Labor: Notes of Audio and Music Production for Contemporary Action Film* does provide a compelling discussion on these two approaches:

> "My point then is that the stylistic changes in the music reflect not just a response to the new kinds of narratives and basic shifts in audience taste—although they do that too—but also that the new kinds of narratives and apparent shifts in audience taste are themselves related to and determined in larger measure by the potential the new technological paradigm has to offer. This formulation may seem to commit me to a version of technological determinism—positing technology as driving the change in material production of the industry but also in style and aesthetics—but that would misconstrue the nature of this new technological paradigm, which was formulated in the first place by demands filmmakers and audiences placed on the technology to produce certain kinds of filmic experiences, and so encouraged technological innovation in those directions that facilitated the making of films that improved the delivery of such experiences, however we might define such improvement." (274)

3. The word hypertext was coined by Nelson (Xanadu), Engelbart.
4. It will also become semantic, as I will argue below.
5. In this context, medium refers to an artistic modality, regardless of its physical mode of delivery. Therefore, cinema is a medium regardless of whether the movie is projected in a cinema, watched on a TV screen or even on a cell phone. Similarly, literature is a unique medium regardless of whether the book is printed or if it is in an electronic version.
6. Similarly, this set of movies represents the majority of films that have been produced and released commercially.
7. Campbell's ([1949] 2008) *A Hero with a Thousand Faces* is widely known for depicting mythical structures in stories. Campbell's framework was adapted as a screenplay guide by Vogler (1992) in *The Writer's Journey: Mythic Structures for Storytellers and Screenwriters*.
8. In this discussion, the ontology of cinema will examine the properties of cinema as a medium. For example, defining photography as a different medium from a painting should be considered an ontological question. In order to properly demonstrate such a statement, a medium-specific quality (some property not applicable to photography) needs to be found to justify the separation of both media in terms of ontology.

9. The categories are not exclusive: a sign may be classified according to one, two, or all of the categories at the same time.
10. The same environment is recorded with different light sensibilities to register a broader light spectrum. After the recording process, the data from this set of light sensors is interpolated, creating a computer model. Prince's criticism evidences the problems that arise as a result of defining photography or cinema as an index of reality.
11. For example, a high-resolution image of a dark area will only serve as an icon for the darkness of the moment, but it will not serve as an icon for the objects that it could not capture.
12. At least the audiences that went to see the movie in 1994.
13. For example, a set of sensors can capture the precise amount of lighting in an environment using HDRi technology. Therefore, it is possible to get a precise 3D radiance map of a space. With this information, it is then possible to create computer-generated lighting that, as Prince argues, would become indexical of the radiance of the room (Prince 2012, 192–198). This lighting model, including an invented digital model, can illuminate any space digitally. This is similar to this discussion on motion capture sensors and using photographed textures to "paint" computer-generated objects.

References

Atkin, Albert. 2013. "Peirce's Theory of Signs." http://plato.stanford.edu/archives/sum2013/entries/peirce-semiotics/.

Auslander, Philip. 2008. *Liveness: Performance in a Mediatized Culture*, Second Edition. New York: Routledge.

Baudrillard, Jean. 1993. *Symbolic Exchange and Death*. Sage Publications.

Baudrillard, Jean. 1994. *Simulacra and Simulation*. Ann Arbor: University of Michigan Press.

Baudrillard, Jean. 2000. *The Vital Illusion*. New York: Columbia University Press.

Baudrillard, Jean. 2005. *The Intelligence of Evil or tile Lucidity Pact*. New York: Berg.

Bordwell, David. 1985. *Narration in the fiction film*. Madison, Wis.: University of Wisconsin Press.

Bordwell, David. 2006. *The way Hollywood tells it: story and style in modern movies*. Berkeley: University of California Press.

Bordwell, David. 2012. *Pandora's Digital Box: Films, Files, and the Future of Movies*. The Irvington Way Institute Press.

Bordwell, David, and Kristin Thompson. 2012. *Film art: an introduction*. New York: McGraw-Hill.

Campbell, Joseph. 2008. *The hero with a thousand faces*. Third ed. Novato, California: New World Library.

Chan, Melanie. 2008. "Virtually Real and Really Virtual: Baudrillard's Procession of Simulacrum and The Matrix." *International Journal of Baudrillard Studies* 5 (2).

Eco, Umberto. 1990. *Travels in Hyperreality (Harvest Book)*. Mariner Books.

Federman, Mark. 2004. "What is the Meaning of the Medium is the Message?". http://individual.utoronto.ca/markfederman/MeaningTheMediumisthe Message.pdf.

Huron, David. 2006. *Sweet anticipation: music and the psychology of expectation*. Cambridge MA: MIT Press.

Kellner, Douglas. 2020 "Jean Baudrillard." The Stanford Encyclopedia of Philosophy, Winter 2020 Edition.

Kittler, Friedrich 1999. *Gramophone, Film, Typewriter (Writing Science)*. Stanford University Press.

Kurzweil, Ray. 2005. *The singularity is near: when humans transcend biology*. New York: Viking New York.

Lancelin, Aude (interviewer), Gary Genosko, and Adam Bryx (translators). 2004. "The Matrix Decoded: Le Nouvel Observateur Interview with Jean Baudrillard." *International Journal of Baudrillard Studies* 1 (2).

McLuhan, Marshall. [1964] 1994. *Understanding Media: The Extensions of Man*. Cambridge, Mass.: MIT Press.

McLuhan, Marshall. 1969. *Counterblast*. London: UK: Rapp &Whiting Limited.

Pawlett, William. 2007. *Jean Baudrillard: Against Banality (Key Sociologists)*. Routledge.

Prince, Stephen. 1996. "True lies: perceptual realism, digital images, and film theory." *Film Quarterly* 49 (2): 27–37. https://doi.org/10.2307/1213468.

Prince, Stephen. 2010. "Through the Looking Glass: Philosophical Toys and Digital Visual Effects." *Projections* 4 (2): 19–40. https://doi.org/10.3167/proj.2010.040203.

Prince, Stephen. 2012. *Digital Visual Effects in Cinema: The Seduction of Reality*. Rutgers University Press.

Saussure, Ferdinand. 1998. *Nature of the Linguistic Sign*. Boston: Bedford/St. Martin's Press.

Vogler, Christopher. 1992. *The Writer's Journey: Mythic Structures for Storytellers and Screenwriters*. M. Wiese Productions.

Wartenberg, Thomas E. 2003. "Philosophy Screened: Experiencing The Matrix." *Midwest Studies In Philosophy* 27 (1): 139–152. https://doi.org/10.1111/1475-4975.00076. https://onlinelibrary.wiley.com/doi/abs/10.1111/1475-4975.00076.

CHAPTER 3

Conceptualizing the Hyperorchestra

Philip Auslander (2008) suggests in *Liveness: Performance in a Mediatized Culture* that there is no ontological difference between a live cultural event and its mechanical reproduction in the form of live broadcasts for the radio or television (52–63). Auslander argues that both events exist "only in the present moment" (50) and, thus, they are ephemeral. Based on that, Auslander suggests that a live recording should be ontologically similar to a live experience or a live broadcast, as they differ only in the characteristics of the mediation. The possibility of repeating a live recording, which could differentiate both events, is not inherent to the medium. Instead, repeating a live event is the result of a cultural practice. In other words, Auslander suggests that if a viewer records a live television show, remains in isolation from additional inputs, watches the show only once a few hours later, and then deletes the show, in terms of its *liveness*, it is the equivalent of having watched the show live. Hence, the ability to store a live-recorded event is not a necessary property to define live broadcasting. Applying this concept to music, we could infer that it is not in the recording technology but in the techniques employed to record it that a recording of a musical piece ontologically differs from its live rendition. In a musical record, different pieces of musical information are recorded, selected, and mixed together to create a product that becomes a *virtual* live experience.

In this chapter, I explore how music interacts with hyperreality, as I defined it in the previous chapter. I begin by describing three different modes of virtualization: recorded music, synthesized music, and sampled music. In doing so, I align with the authors who have challenged the status of the notated musical score in Western music as its primary source to describe and analyze it. Further, the virtualization modes I describe are essential to unfold an analysis of musical timbre that goes beyond musical instruments. At the end of the chapter, I provide two preliminary definitions of the hyperorchestra and its relationship to the different modes of virtualization.

A Process of Increased Virtualization

Western musical notation acts primarily as an interface to communicate performance instructions to the players of a musical piece. Further, most Western music theory and analysis methodologies are grounded on the score. One can even apply these analytical tools to a piece of music without hearing a performance of that piece. An outcome of this perspective is that a musical work is often associated with its score. A musical performance is ephemeral and variable. The score is the opposite. A musical score grounds a piece of music to clearly define reality and authorship, allowing for a systematic analysis and discretization process. For instance, we can compare harmonies between two artworks using similar chord progressions. The vast advantages that the Western musical score provides to align music with the conventions of Western thought are wide-ranging. They span from copyright and authorship to the capacity to replicate performances efficiently. However, identifying a piece of music by its musical score also generates serious problems. Musicologist Nicholas Cook (2013a, 2013b) proposes an analytical methodology that incorporates performance—a core element for musical expression—to become an essential axiom to approach the musical phenomenon, downgrading the status of the written musical score.

> Like others working in musical performance and multimedia, I have attacked traditional musicological approaches for treating a part of culture as if it were the whole. To analyze music as performance is to critique a musicology of writing that treats performance as essentially a supplement to a written text; to study performance as a form of multimedia is to see it as a phenomenon that involves the body and all its senses, not a depersonalized sound

source. By implication, we in this field contrast our work to a truncated, narrow-minded musicology that reflects the autonomy-based aesthetic ideologies of the past, rather than the performative reality of music as a vital and unprecedentedly popular cultural practice in today's multimedia-oriented world. (Cook 2013b, 53)

Traditional musicological approaches, following the nineteenth-century aesthetics of absolute instrumental music, force a distinction between the "musical" and the "extra-musical," where the "musical" is essentially defined in terms of notation: everything that Michelangeli does before he plays the first note, then, falls into the category of the "extra-musical," from which it is but a small step (and one that musicologists and traditional aestheticians readily make) to dismiss it as self-indulgence or showmanship. (Cook 2013a, 72–73)

In both passages, Cook defends the importance of incorporating the resulting sound and the audiovisual performance. Following Cook's views, I argue against considering the score alone as a valid source to describe the musical experience due to its representational limitations. In addition, I support Cook's position that advocates for analyzing sound-only recorded performances from an audiovisual perspective. Even when audiences listen to a sound-only recording, they may still generate a mental representation of the stage on which the music was supposedly performed. Thus, they might mentally generate models of reality that bring the experience into a heightened emotional status by forging a hyperreal out of the sonic material, its context, and the audience's knowledge. Similarly, in conceptualizing the hyperorchestra, the capacity to create a mental representation of the imagined physical space is a feature that adds to the perception of realism (or lack of) in a piece of music, which carries meaning.

In the following paragraphs, I explore how the music experience underwent an increased virtualization process that started with the capacity to record music. I conceptualize Western musical notation to describe the impact of recorded music. Then, I explore the concept of a sound object that emanated when the studio became the centerpiece of musical creation. After that, I explore additional virtualization processes by incorporating synthesizers and sampled-based virtual instruments.

Musical Notation

Let's analyze the musical score through the lens of McLuhan's ([1964] 1994) approach to media. The score shares plenty of similarities with McLuhan's description of phonetic writing—as described in the previous chapter. The score is an abstract notation system aiming to translate an aural phenomenon that occurs over time into a static, visual, and symbolic representation. Moreover, the symphonic orchestra (and other similar ensembles) acts as a standardized ensemble that facilitates and fundamentally allows for Western notation to be operational. Emily Dolan (2013) presents in *The Orchestral Revolution: Haydn and the Technologies of Timbre* a similar argument from the perspective of timbral evolution:

> The orchestra functioned as a recording technology: like the machines designed to imitate it, it enabled repeat performances of musical works. Of course, many forms of musical technology do this, from pianos to flutes to timpani. But what the orchestra recorded was more than sound. The status of The Creation as a great work reflects its continued ability to have an effect on its listeners. Put another way, that the listener responded physically could be assumed: the orchestration and musical effects were a means for inscribing the listener into the fabric of the piece. (Dolan 2013, 200)

In addition to its almost mechanical property, standardized ensembles such as the orchestra are helpful because the Western score has no system to efficiently represent the differences in the sound of an ensemble if the players sit significantly differently in the space. For instance, if the string section of an orchestra were placed at the back of the concert hall, the woodwinds in the middle of the parterre, and the brass onstage, the resulting sound would significantly differ from a performance using the standard placement of the orchestra. Traditional Western musical score notation does not include the tools to portray those differences effectively, nor is the music theory derived from the score as a notation system. For instance, the theory of harmony can efficiently describe different chord permutations and propose effective and ineffective note doublings for chords. Still, it cannot define the harmonic impact when some of the notes of a chord come from separate locations.[1] Dolan (2013) alludes to this fact in its relationship to the establishment of musicology as a science during the nineteenth century:

> Those things that could be notated precisely in the score – that is, pitch, harmony, and so on – constituted the essence of the composition, and could be contemplated, studied, and analyzed, activities that were supported by the burgeoning availability of scores and complete editions during the course of the nineteenth century. Orchestration and timbre became secondary parameters, separated from the mainstream of music history. Timbre no longer marked an awareness of sensation or signaled aesthetic attention; it was no longer a condition of possibility for modern aesthetics, but merely an ornament to those musical elements – form, harmony, pitch – that were understood to endure. (Dolan 2013, 257)

Dolan's description is analogous to McLuhan's description of how the phonetic language gave us "an eye for an ear" ([1964]1994, 84). Consequently, the score serves only as a partial visual representation of sound when several restrictions are applied, such as using standardized ensembles strictly positioned on the stage. Even in this strictly controlled environment, the score still demands a high degree of interpretation to become an effective form of representation of the sound depicted on its pages. Applying another set of constraints (establishing harmonic, melodic, and rhythmic principles) further facilitates the process of interpretation. By definition, the score can only depict a limited amount of pitches and rhythms based on a meter.[2] Harmonic principles assist in creating a theoretical understanding of the sounds and their progressions that, in turn, enable imagining them. Even when considering all these restrictions, the score fails to provide a visual differentiation of timbral aspects.[3] The timbre differences of the instruments written in a score can only be depicted by applying the acquired knowledge of the sound properties of all the instruments used in the score. Further, this also limits the design of instruments by restricting them into an idealized mode of sound production, as I will analyze in detail in the final chapter of this book. Nevertheless, Western classical music is inherently linked to a score-centric vision of music, thus carrying its limitations.

In exchange for its restrictions, the musical score offers substantial advantages as a medium for music transmission. First, the score allows for a rapid distribution of complex musical content. For instance, a group of trained musicians can quickly perform a piece of music just by using the score. In addition, the score allows the separation of writing and performing music, thereby facilitating a division of labor similar to other practices that emanated from the Industrial Revolution. Within the score paradigm, the nascent musical industry could separate the labor of the composer and that of the performer at the same time the musical *production* became standardized.[4] Therefore, any trained performer can play a musical piece written by any composer. At the same time, these performers are interchangeable, if needed, as they are detached from the creation of the musical piece. The process of standardization also involves discretizing different musical features. For example, dynamics—a continuous parameter—is divided into a few steps (*f, mf, mp, p*); dynamic variations are mainly represented as a proportional transitional process expressed by terms like *crescendo* or *decrescendo*. Figure 3.1 portrays three different possibilities for a

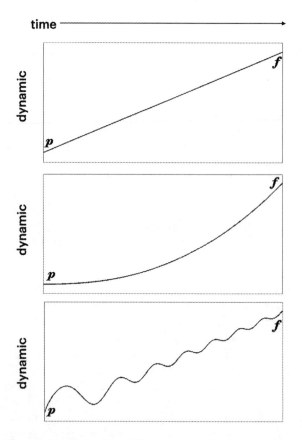

Fig. 3.1 The graphic shows three different *crescendo* representations

crescendo. The vertical axis represents the dynamic level, whereas the horizontal axis represents time. The first graphic refers to a linear and proportional process of *crescendo*; the other two are nonlinear. The first graphic symbolizes a performance that will increase the dynamic at a constant ratio during the *crescendo*. In the second, the dynamic increase will be slower at the beginning and more intense toward the end of the *crescendo*. The last example represents an increase in the dynamic that incorporates fluctuating dynamic variations.

However, the representation using the notation provided in a musical score to represent a *crescendo* of these three different processes of *crescendo* remains unchanged (Fig. 3.2).

Therefore, a performer will not be able to distinguish between these distinct types of *crescendo* by reading a musical score, creating a degree of ambiguity that must be resolved during the performance. The rest of the elements of the score undergo a similar process. The act of performing a musical piece written in a score involves the aesthetic process of interpreting the contents of the score.

The necessity of interpreting the score to produce a musical performance pinpoints an additional aspect of Western music practice: it still relies on a primarily oral tradition. Learning an instrument involves acquiring technical knowledge through instruction. In the training process, the student absorbs the performance practices necessary to properly decode the score based on a shared set of principles attached to Western classical music's styles. The nuances involved in interpreting a *crescendo* exemplify the impossibility of acquiring this knowledge from a manual due to the inexistence of proper notation procedures to describe it precisely.[5] Therefore, these practices are attained by aural communication, as they cannot be transmitted through written knowledge.[6] Applying McLuhan's framework, this is the type of interaction that would precede phonetic language. From this angle, the score becomes the only element capable of bringing part of the musical practice as close as possible to the other forms of intellectual knowledge that can be acquired by studying written information. Consequently, the score allows for isolating the necessity for oral transmission in music to a reduced set of situations.

Fig. 3.2 Representation of a *crescendo* utilizing traditional musical notation

The curated environment for music creation described above encompasses standardized models for the orchestral ensemble, a musical language, the concert hall, and music notation. However, in the evolution of Western music, the framework adapted to incorporate new sonic possibilities. The orchestra added new instruments and instrumental techniques, and the harmonic language developed beyond the structure of previously established harmonic transformations and tonality. Similarly, the rhythmic complexity expanded, stressing the limitations of what was possible to notate using the musical score. Each of these amplifications relaxed the restricted environment of a common practice Western music creation, which decreased the value of the score as a representation of music.[7] By losing its representational capabilities, the function of the score evolved to become just a blueprint for musical performance.[8]

When recording audio became a possibility, music experienced a shift in its perspective. Audio recording transcends the score and shifts the focus on the process and manipulation of sound. The possibility of editing a recording is a prime example of the conceptual revolution that the capacity of recording music triggered.

Recorded Music

Any process of capturing sound for either a recording or a broadcast involves the utilization of a medium to capture it: the microphone. More importantly, capturing sound involves (a) the decision of how many and which types of microphones to use, (b) the placement of those microphones, and (c) their contribution to the final sound mix.[9] Nevertheless, it is still possible to produce a live recording that, in principle, does not invalidate Auslander's statement on the ontology of live performances: a live recording might only utilize two microphones, one for each stereo channel, located in the middle of the hall.[10] In this situation, the microphones would not necessarily be mixed together or differently placed. Thus, the mediation process in a simple stereo recording only involves the transducing process of the microphone, converting mechanical sound waves into an electric (and then digital) signal. That means that using multiple microphones in diverse locations and mixing them together to generate a final mix is not necessary for the medium (audio recording). It is just an aesthetic possibility.

At the same time, each audience member of a live concert perceives a different *sound mix* depending on their location and the diverging capacity of their ears to transform a range of frequencies from sound waves they receive into brain signals. If a live experience can be so different between audience members, it is probably safe to conclude that the number and placement of the microphones do not affect the liveness of a live recording. What about the audience members who arrive late to a concert and have to listen to the first piece through the hall doors? In this case, we could probably conclude that the sense of liveness is, at least, compromised because their experience is significantly distinct from what the audience members inside the hall experience. Similarly, we can most likely define certain limits to the manipulation we allow in a live recording while preserving its liveness. That will, of course, differ from the aesthetic attributes of the music genre of the piece being performed.

The process of capturing sound implies an aesthetic intent along with a set of technical decisions that must be made to fulfill it. These technical decisions do not necessarily correlate with a trivial fidelity assessment to the original sound source, primarily because microphones and ears transduce sound differently. Knakkergaard (2015) summarizes this concept in *The Music That's Not There*:

> Placing microphones in a given location, for instance a concert hall or a recording studio, to pick up the sound signals that are emitted by sound sources will—unprocessed—hardly ever produce a sound image that matches what a human would experience when exposed to those signals in the same room. (Knakkergaard 2015, 395)

For instance, while recording an orchestral piece, a sound engineer might decide to recreate the sound from the conductor's position. To achieve this objective, the engineer might place two microphones near the conductor's position or recreate the position using multiple microphones.[11] The first possibility would not necessarily produce a result closer to what the conductor would be hearing. Microphones are not equivalent to human ears, which is why there are so many types of them.[12] Therefore, capturing the sound with microphones placed closer to the ears of the conductor would not result in a sound closer to their perception. Instead, combining a broader set of microphones deployed in multiple locations on the stage may produce a closer representation of what a conductor or an audience member would hear once they are properly mixed.

In terms of ontology, the properties of the microphone highlight their inability to become, just like the camera, an index of reality. That holds true even when acknowledging that microphones capture sound continuously, something that a camera cannot do with moving images. That applies to digital recordings as well. The nature of digital systems only allows for discrete data to be captured. For instance, a typical digital recording captures 48,000 samples per second (48KHz) in a grid of about 16 million different values (24-bit). However, this digital data is then used to generate a continuous signal when speakers reproduce it. Relatedly, that is not the case for moving images, which are reproduced as a succession of still frames. Thus, our ears receive a continuous sound signal and do not need to create an illusion of sound, contrary to what our eyes and brain need to do with moving images.[13] Nevertheless, the impossibility of making a microphone equivalent to an average human ear still challenges its indexical power analogously to the impossibility of capturing the same range of light as the eye challenges the indexical power of the camera.

The process of recording sound not only involves deciding which sound perspective to reproduce (e.g., the conductor's perspective, the perspective of an audience member located at the center of the floor, or the perspective of an audience member at the back of the hall) but also deciding how to achieve the desired sound by placing and combining microphones. Moreover, it is also possible to create a sound perspective that does not attempt to reproduce a specific location in the concert hall. Instead, the recording and mixing engineer may aim to replicate an ideal listening perspective that does not precisely correspond to any concrete spot in the hall. Furthermore, the recording may attempt to reproduce the composer's intentions for the sound of the piece better and more precisely than what could be heard live in the hall, separating the recording from the live sound result even more. Is the last hypothetical scenario a *lesser* live experience? This question can only be answered based on aesthetic and cultural conventions.

Therefore, a recording process is always associated with an aesthetic decision process that helps to define its final result. Further, the aesthetic decision process cannot be avoided because of the inexistence of an objective listening experience due to the different behavior of the human ear and any of the microphones available to us. More importantly, this mandatory aesthetic process alters the balance between music performance, the score, and the sound result, favoring the last. This statement will become more apparent by analyzing the aesthetics of the modern recordings of piano concertos.

The Piano Concerto Recording

The Western concerto involves a soloist and an entire orchestra performing together. The soloist has a prominent role in contributing to the final sound result of the piece while being clearly outnumbered by the orchestra. As an example, I use the piano concerto. Still, the ideas are directly applicable to any Western concerto for any instrument. Most orchestral recordings follow an aesthetic principle that aims to produce a sound that is similar to a live experience. In other words, the recording should sound verisimilar to be aesthetically recognized as a valid rendition of the piece. However, the solo piano is recorded with several dedicated microphones, which are regularly mixed louder than the orchestral microphones. In doing so, listeners of the recording can hear the solo piano in moments that would not have been audible within the environs of a live concert hall performance. For example, the piano is barely audible in most of the passages when the soloist is playing along with the whole orchestra in a *fortissimo* dynamic (very loud). In aesthetic terms, those passages are challenging. When looking at the score and examining the performance conventions for a piano concerto, it is implied that the composer's intention is for the soloist to be heard. At the same time, this becomes an acoustic chimera when the entire orchestra is playing loud.[14] Some conductors attempt to resolve this delusion at the performance level by making the orchestra play at a softer dynamic level. In doing so, the piano would then be heard again, but the timbral result of the orchestra would not be *fortissimo* anymore, which equally misrepresents what the composer wrote in the score. Thus, the aesthetic utopia of a soloist heard above a *fortissimo tutti* orchestra is not feasible with acoustic means only. In addition, those types of passages may visually confuse live audiences as they watch a soloist playing with courageous effort and strength without receiving a proportional sonic reward.

In a recording, it is possible to mix different sound sources to achieve the effect of distinctly hearing the soloist while the orchestra is playing in a *fortissimo* dynamic.[15] The result is a version of the piano concerto that could not be generated solely by live acoustic means yet still sounds convincing and verisimilar. In terms of aesthetics, a recording that mixes the solo piano louder than how it would sound in a live performance becomes an idealized version of the piece, implementing the utopia that a single instrument can overcome a hundred players when it is performed by an exceptional artist—a core part of the ideology behind the concept of the concerto itself.

Going back to developing a musical implementation of McLuhan's definition of media, a musical instrument is a medium that extends the human voice, as it can produce sounds that would not be possible otherwise. Similarly, the idea of the soloist in a piano concerto is to become a medium that can extend what a musical instrument can do by overpowering an entire orchestra. This romantic idea of a superhuman collides with the acoustic limitations of live sound. However, with the aid of the recording and mixing techniques, this artistic endeavor is realizable in a form that is still perceived as natural to the listener. In a live concert, the soloist could be amplified with microphones and speakers, thus generating a similar result. However, the process of amplification—which would not be visually and aurally neutral in a live performance—works against the epic metanarrative associated with the soloist acting as a superhuman artist. In a recording, the process of achieving the acoustic chimera is hidden, allowing for the verisimilitude of the musical experience to be preserved.[16]

Recording the piano concerto within these principles creates a process of virtualization.[17] In capturing the performance's sound from specific locations first and then mixing the captured sounds with a precise aesthetic intention later, creates a result that, although grounded in simultaneous captures of a real-life experience, transcends what the human senses would have perceived. From this perspective, the sonic result of a piano concerto recording becomes hyperrealistic.[18] The totality of the sound of the recording originates at the same time and space in the physical world. However, the resulting sound does not pertain to the same world, as it is transformed beyond the possibilities of the real. The transformation adheres to an aesthetic intention rooted in how the piece should ideally sound. In addition, the conflict between the possibilities of the physical world and the intentions of the musical creators stresses the necessity for human artistic expressions to transcend the physical limitations of the real.[19] Furthermore, the recording of piano concertos might reshape the audience's expectations of a live performance of the same type of piece. As the acoustic model of the recording is convincing and aesthetically coherent, audiences might expect the same balance in the sound of a live performance.

Sound Objects: The Studio Recording, the Acousmatic Sound, and Film Music

The aesthetic analysis of the piano concerto recording in its relationship with virtual reality uncovers how a recording in a concert hall that aimed to reproduce reality deviated from it. Further, studio recordings can detach even more from acoustic performances if they embrace the possibilities that a recording studio offers. First, the studio overrides the performers' need to share the same space simultaneously. In a studio recording, each instrument might be located in different isolation rooms, or they can be recorded at a separate time. In addition, the rooms are generally sonically treated to minimize the early reflections and the overall reverberation effect.[20] Hence, in the studio, the microphones broadly capture a malleable version of the sound produced by the instruments. This is due to the studio's capacity to produce sound isolation, to capture only a restricted amount of room sound, or for the capability to capture the instrument from diverse positions while using differnt types of microphones.

We can determine that the studio recording extends timbre by applying McLuhan's concept for media extensions to musical aesthetics. That is equivalent to stating that recording in a studio setting extends the sonic possibilities of music. However, recording in a studio does not expand on any musical features that a musical score could represent—such as harmony, melody, or counterpoint. Consequently, everything the studio recording adds to extend and advance musical aesthetics cannot be engraved in a traditional Western score. Furthermore, the aesthetic evolutions propelled by the capacity to record using a studio resonate with some of the aesthetic principles that defined *musique concrète*—broadly, creating music by combining and manipulating recorded sounds. In both cases, the new medium (the studio) allows the extension of the sound beyond the acoustic possibilities of the instruments[21] playing in a physical space. By transcending the necessity of a certain degree of fidelity (or resemblance) to an aural model from the physical world, the music created in the studio is sonically sculpted freely. At the very least, a studio recording requires the producer to generate a virtual stage and to determine the virtual positions of the sound sources on the recording. More importantly, a virtual stage implies that the sounds lack an identifiable visual source. This typology of sound was labeled acousmatic by Pierre Schaeffer, one of the founders of *musique concrète* and studio pioneer. Schaeffer ([1966] 2017) defined a sound as *acousmatic* when one hears it without seeing the causes that originated it (64). Strictly speaking, all recorded music should be considered acousmatic as it is reproduced without visually seeing the source.

Since the advent of the *musique concrète* and the development of electronic music, there have been attempts to expand our shared theoretical framework to encompass these new practices. Pierre Schaeffer's *Treatise of Musical Objects* ([1966] 2017) is arguably the first relevant endeavor in this area. Schaeffer realized that traditional Western music theory was constraining music creation into what he defined as *prose composition*, which means "to obtain from an instrument sounds that correspond to symbols" (391). Consequently, Schaeffer urged the expansion of notation to go beyond the concept of a note.

> But the need for musical signs that would communicate the real function of objects more directly is becoming urgent for composers. Given the growing importance of sounds that are more, less, or something other than notes, we now lack a link between musical thought and its realization. (Schaeffer [1966] 2017), 392)

Schaeffer proposed an approach that included two scores, one as a blueprint for performance and another to describe the piece of music accurately. As I mentioned above, Schaeffer also crafted the modern utilization of the word a*cousmatic*, which he derived from Pythagoras and his pupils, who "for five years, listened to his lessons hidden behind a curtain, without seeing him and observing the strictest silence" (2017, 64). For Schaeffer, an acousmatic setting breaks the symbolic connection between the sound and its visual source (65). Schaeffer precisely qualifies the connection as symbolic instead of indexical, as he believes that part of musical hearing involves visual information.[22] By proposing an acousmatic mode of hearing, Schaeffer argued in favor of focusing on the pure properties of the sound, regardless of its visual cues.

A listener of a recording might visually imagine its performers. This subtle process of imagination, divergent from the recording as an entity, would negate—if strictly following Schaeffer's approach—the acousmatic nature of the recording. However, I suggest that *acousmatic* should be considered an attitude, a conscious decision to disregard the visual cues in order to focus exclusively on the sound. The process of disconnecting from the visual source becomes much easier when the sound is not directly coupled with a physical object, unlike the experience of listening to an orchestral recording by an avid Western orchestra concertgoer. For example, a dynamically compressed and spectrally distorted sound from a guitar that is continuously panned from left to right does not represent a physical instrumental experience: the standard sound that one could imagine emanating from a guitar differs from the sound being reproduced in this scenario, at the same time that it is unfeasible to imagine a performer who can run around the spectators' aural range while playing the guitar. Hence, an acousmatic attitude of hearing concentrates on the sound of the music without a visual or cultural bias. In terms of the expanding aesthetics of music, I believe this is the most relevant innovation that recording, as a technology, has added.

From the previous example (a processed guitar sound), one could infer that making a sound acousmatic requires a detachment from any cultural referents or expectations (such as the sound of a symphonic orchestra in a traditional concert hall). This is not the case. An acousmatic attitude toward the sonic properties of music could still be compatible with its cultural connections. In fact, decoupling the sound from its source may even facilitate the creation of a level of signification that connects the sound with a more profound cultural background. For instance, Richard Wagner's design of Bayreuth's theater hid the orchestra to force the audience to focus on the sound of the music instead of being distracted by the visual cues of the performers. Aesthetically, Wagner attempted to push audiences to embrace an acousmatic attitude, as Schaeffer defined, for the orchestral sounds of his dramas. In this case, the cultural connections of Wagner's orchestra remain uncompromised. Audiences still recognize the orchestra, even when it is hidden. Michel Chion (1994) argues—contrary to Schaeffer's assumption—that an "acousmatic situation could encourage reduced listening, in that it provokes one to separate oneself from causes or effects" (32). Therefore, the listener will attempt to reveal the source of the sound first:

> Confronted with a sound from a loudspeaker that is presenting itself without a visual calling card, the listener is led all the more intently to ask, "What's that?" (i.e., "What is causing this sound?") and to be attuned to the minutest clues (often interpreted wrong anyway) that might help to identify the cause. (Chion 1994, 32)

Chion focuses on cinema sound, while Schaeffer's ideas were centered on *musique concrète*. Chion (2009) remarks that "if the source has been seen, the acousmatic sound carries along with it a mental visual representation" (465). Chion's observations are aligned with the concept of "source bonding," defined by Denis Smalley (1994), which is: "the natural tendency to relate sounds to supposed sources and causes and to relate sounds to each other because they appear to have shared or associated origins"

(37). For Smalley, source bonding is a deeply culturally embedded process because, prior to electroacoustic music, the sounds had always had an identifiable source (37). Chion (1994) asserts that, in most cases in cinema, the source of the sound is identifiable. Chion's approach to acousmatic sounds is practical and has been widely used. However, it deviates from Schaeffer's less practical and more philosophical discussion. For Schaeffer, an acousmatic sound broke the symbolic connection between the sound and its source. For Chion, this is just not the case in the majority of practical situations that he examined because the symbolic connection between the sound and the source is ingrained in the shared cultural background of the society that produced these sounds.

Chion's assumption accurately describes most of the off-screen diegetic sounds of a movie. However, it becomes a reductionist approach when analyzing the possibilities of music created in the studio. Examining, once more, the example of a processed guitar sound that is dynamically panned around the virtual soundstage, a listener could notice a symbolic connection with a physical source of the sound. They may identify that the sound physically originated in a guitar, but at the same time, they are cognizant that the panning effect is not a product of the movement of the source (the guitarist) during the performance. Consequently, the symbolic connection between the sound and its source becomes just a trace, a model of reality that collaborates with creating a more complex—acousmatic (and hyperrealistic)—sound model.

Hence, an acousmatic attitude—as defined by Schaeffer—toward sound becomes a further step into hyperreal sound and music. Moreover, when listeners identify the guitar as the sound source in the previous example, they also respond to an acousmatic attitude. In acknowledging that the guitar, the physical source of the sound, acts as an element that contributes to the shape of the final sound, the listener assumes a sonic attitude detached from exclusively physical forms of sound generation. Therefore, a listener who can incorporate the concept of detachment from the sound and the source demonstrates an acousmatic sensibility to sound.

Chion (1994, 2009) coined yet another concept, *materializing sound indices*, which will refine certain aspects of an acousmatic attitude toward sound. Chion defines them as the "sound details that cause us to 'feel' the material conditions of the sound source and refer to the concrete process of the sound's production" (1994, 114). Chion also notes that there are sounds that are prone to be more easily detached from their physical source:

> Among the most common noises surrounding us there are some that are poor in materializing indices, which, when heard apart from their source (acousmatized), become enigmas: a motor noise or creaking can acquire an abstract quality, deprived of referentiality. (Chion 1994, 114)

In this case, Chion develops Schaeffer's concept of acousmatic sound to describe how sound editing techniques can impact the perception of the characters and the story in a scene. Chion indirectly acknowledges the recording and performance practices of the musical soundtrack outlined above when discussing the effects of materialization in music:

> Take one image and compare the effect of a music cue played on a well tuned piano with the effect of a cue played on a slightly out of tune piano with a few bad keys. We tend to read the first cue more readily as "pit music," while with the second, even if the instrument isn't identified or shown in the image, we will sense its concrete presence in the setting. (Chion 1994, 116)

From the statement above, we can infer that a sound that deviates from the complete cleanliness of Western classical music recordings has the power to become a materializing sound index. For instance, Chion implies that a detuned piano would not be part of a recorded orchestral piece or film score. A similar conclusion could be extracted from a piano performance with noticeable audible mistakes.[23] Miguel Mera (2016) expands Chion's idea of materializing sound indices, which he acknowledges as reminiscent of Barthes' (1977) differentiation between voice and language, to encompass film music:

> Both writers [Barthes and Chion] identified how technical prowess and expressive force in much musical performance irons out the workings of the physicality of production. Indeed, this seems an entirely appropriate description of the vast majority of mainstream orchestral film music where instrumental recordings strive for effortless clarity and perfect evenness; microphones are carefully placed to avoid scratchy or breathy sounds, intonation is always precise. (Mera 2016, 157)

It is difficult not to think about Wagner's design of the Bayreuth Theater, which not only made the orchestra invisible but also attenuated any sounds that could highlight the "physicality of production" of the Wagnerian orchestra when discussing an aesthetic tailored to idealize the sound generated by symphonic orchestras. Therefore, the established orchestral recording aesthetic might be the consequence of an aesthetic trend in European classical music that started at the end of the eighteenth century, aiming to produce pristine-sounding instruments and acoustic environments. Mera's focus, though, is not on these "effortlessly clear" orchestral recordings but on the recent aesthetic trend that reincorporates noises (re-materializes) into music and "how musical noise in instrumental music is tied to material causality and announces its hapticity, creating an embodied connection with the audio-viewer" (158).[24]

In this context, musical noise is everything that deviates from the aesthetic framework of spotless orchestral recordings, even when these noisy sounds come from extended techniques that push the instruments beyond their stable classical state of sound production. For instance, when a string player is asked to play using *overpressure*, the sound result will deviate from the orchestral aesthetic discussed before, regardless of the recording technique. By making an instrument generate sound in a manner that is outside the general norm, we are also signaling the source of production and, therefore, its hapticity.[25]

Similarly, Baroque and early music performances using original instruments and performance practices have captivated contemporary audiences by materializing the music they played. These practices connect early music with the instruments used when the music was conceived, along with cultural axions from that era. For instance, listening to Andreas Staier's performance of Schubert's B♭ *Major piano Sonata D.960* (1997) in a fortepiano—an original piano from the nineteenth century or a modern reproduction of it—is shocking for an ear that is only accustomed to the pristine performances and recordings of Schubert's music. For instance, the rumble-sounding low trill, the unstable instrument tunning, the fragile harp-like sound of the *una corda* pedal, or the almost frustrating and weak *fortissimos* are all sound experiences that defy the expectations of how a classical piano piece should sound. In this case, the sound is not only materialized by making apparent that it is coming from a physical instrument but also by linking its sound to the sound world of another era and, perhaps, to the fragile health of Schubert, who died just after the composition of the piece.

Relatedly, audiences will be surprised by the sounds they hear, sometimes unable to identify the source precisely. They hear sounds detached from the shared expectations of what a piano should sound like. Listening to Staier's pianoforte rendition of this piece engages audiences in a much more acousmatic mode of listening than a performance using a modern piano. A great deal of the pleasure of listening to that performance is the exploration of the meaningfulness of each of the sounds produced while, at the same time, obfuscating a clear perception of harmony and musical balance.[26]

The increased popularity at the start of the millennium of early music performed with original instruments and performance practices indicates a change in the aesthetic taste in society. The soundworld that these performances and recordings produce defies the conventions on which Western classical music performances and recordings are based. At the very least, it shows an increased curiosity for new sounds and timbres that distance themselves from the ideal of perfection. In addition, it also shows an increased interest in sound materialization to reinforce or produce new meanings that go beyond what is expressed in harmony, melody, or discrete approaches to timbre.[27]

Comparing the sonic experience of listening to Schubert's sonata performed by (a) Staier in fortepiano, (b) a typical performance practice of the mid-twentieth century (e.g., Arthur Rubinstein), or (c) a more modern approach to performing this piece (e.g., Krystian Zimerman) results in discovering that they are different experiences that generate distinct significations and approaches to hapticity.

Based on Chion's definition of a materializing sound index, we could infer that a sound that excels in its capacity to materialize would lose its capacity to become acousmatic. That seems to be a workable assumption in the field of sound effects in an audiovisual narrative. However, Mera's (2016) adaptation of the concept into music for the screen shows a different picture. In the score for *There Will Be Blood* (2007), Mera describes how the music "consistently draws attention to its own physical materiality with textures—like the oil at the heart of the film's narrative—that seem to issue from the very ground itself, a space that I argue is embodied by and through the music" (158). By this process, strings are materialized by their connection to elements of the film diegesis, but not by being attached to the original source that produced the sound (a string section).

Moreover, Mera highlights how the score is an exploration of noise, which distances itself from our expectations when listening to a string ensemble. I believe that this process makes the music closer to Schaeffer's definition of an acousmatic sound. This is because the associations with actual elements of the diegesis further distance the sounds from the original source (the string ensemble), allowing for the generation of new meanings.

Further, Mera's (2016) discussion on Greenwood's *Popcorn Superhet Receiver* (2005) also highlights the inability of the Western score to be an accurate mode of representation for the sonic experience of that piece. In fact, Mera's reduction of bars 37–39 (163) presents a much more precise description of the sonic result of the piece than the original score. Schaeffer proposed a Generalization of Music Theory that started with his innovative idea at that time of the two-score approach: "We cannot escape the need to consider the possibility of two scores without risking falling into the most serious ambiguities: one score, essential, for musical description and the other, operational, for performance" (2017, 392). To that point, Mera's reduction could function as the second score of Schaeffer's two-score model. More importantly, Schaeffer believed that a notation system delimits which music can be produced using that mode of notation:

> If music theory as it is practiced in traditional music is indeed the means of notating musical ideas as much as translating these ideas into sounds, oral training reveals the basic direction of this discipline: to obtain from an instrument sounds that correspond to symbols. (391)

> If we compare classical and contemporary works, we observe that, for the former, theory enables an analytical representation of the work, which gives an account of it while leaving a certain degree of latitude for performance; for the latter the notations belonging to the same theory express less and less what is essential to music and tend to be valid exclusively on the operative level, which is itself more and more overloaded and persnickety. But as long as we keep to *"prose composition"* for the most modern musics and rely on traditional instruments, hardly anyone feels the need to change their habits: instruments being what they are, the notes on a staff faithfully transmit orders to the instrumentalist. (Schaeffer 2017, 391–2)

The inability of traditional Western theory and notation to accurately represent contemporary works was the reason Schaeffer proposed his two-score model. It also suggests that the Western notation system inevitably leads toward an aesthetic that privileges spotless, clear, and somewhat *dematerialized* recordings. This approach to recording and performance is the closest that one can get to accurately depicting the symbols on the Western Score. Therefore, we could infer that using a different notation system that can capture other elements of the sonic experience would better fit a more sonically grounded aesthetic approach to music, such as the one in *There Will Be Blood*. This is one of the reasons for the rapid assimilation, at the end of the twentieth century, of the Digital Audio Workstations (DAWs), a piece of software that implemented Schaeffer's two-score vision by providing an interface that allowed for a new mode of notation that is focused on the organization of many layers of sound objects over time.[28]

The description of sound objects, the acousmatic sound, and the studio highlights modes of virtualization based on the detachment between a sound and its physical source. The next step in the virtualization process involves removing the need for a material source to generate sounds by using a musical instrument that is the product of the electrical age: the synthesizer.

Synthesizers and the Evolution of the Musical Instrument

Applying McLuhan's media theory, the ability to synthesize music through the use of electricity is a new medium that expands on the new possibilities introduced by studio recording by adding the capacity to create sounds without the need to capture them. This is why synthesizers are a milestone in the evolution of music during the twentieth century. In this section, I will describe synthesizers for their role in virtualizing music and their crucial contribution to shaping the aesthetic framework in which the hyperorchestra is defined. In the next chapter, devoted to the tools of the hyperorchestra, I will expand on these ideas to describe how synthesizers are incorporated into the creation of music with the hyperorchestra while also inquiring further into their diverse functions and typologies.[29]

Conceptually speaking, synthesizers can generate sound without the need for a string (or another material) to vibrate. From a purely practical side, this is not sufficiently precise. Synthesizers generate an electric signal transduced to sound using a loudspeaker with a vibrating membrane. Thus, synthesized sounds are an intriguing form of an acousmatic experience in which the original source does not come from the acoustic domain before its sound is broadcasted through speakers.[30] Jonathan De Souza (2021) describes how synthesizers challenge the indexical relationship between timbre and instrument in *Timbral Thievery: Synthesizers and Sonic Materiality*. De Souza argues that "synthesizers are not simply machines for making sound. They also suggest ways of investigating and conceptualizing it. As such, they take on both musical and epistemic significance."

De Souza (2021) argues that synthesizers compose sound because they can "assemble new signals" and because "synthesizers generate sound through processes of mixing and filtering." This statement also clarifies what a synthesizer is for the purpose of this discussion: an instrument that creates sound without any connection to the acoustic domain at the moment of inception.[31] They generate sounds through what are called Volume Controlled Oscillators (VCO) using electricity. Thus, synthesizers can generate a new range of sounds that instruments cannot produce in the acoustic domain. For instance, they can create pure sine waves that repeat precisely through time. They sound significantly different from any physically generated sound because physical objects do not achieve this degree of mathematical purity in the sound waves. This fact highlights that the imperfections and unevenness of the timbre are essential for a sound to be associated with the physical world. In other words, natural sounds have a complex and variable timbre. Thus, the regularity of synthesized sounds becomes something beyond the physical world and denotes a definitive step toward virtualization.

The analysis of synthesizers as a new musical instrument of the twentieth century assists in clarifying that musical instruments are a medium in McLuhan's terms. Conversely, the definition of a musical instrument serves as a means to correctly identify the significance of the introduction of the synthesizers in Western culture. From the human perspective, the voice is the first complex natural instrument, as it is capable of producing a broad set of pitches and timbres at varied dynamic levels. In addition, hands and other body parts are the original source for percussive and rhythmic sounds. Applying McLuhan's framework, musical instruments are a medium that extends the musical capabilities of the human body by introducing new timbres, pitches, and the possibility of polyphony within a single instrument. They become a medium that extends the human voice analogously to how the hammer amplifies the arm by making it stronger.

In this framework, wind instruments (aerophones) are a natural extension of the voice, perhaps as an elaborate form of whistling.[32] Similarly, percussive instruments (idiophones and membranophones) are an extension of body percussion. String instruments (chordophones) are, however, a more sophisticated technology. They require a process of sound creation that is not found in a natural environment. It cannot be considered a direct extension of the human body in terms of organology. The sound of a plucked string is also significantly different from what can be achieved by the human voice. Bowing is even more complex, as it further distances the instrument from the mode of sound production of the human voice. On the other hand, from an acousmatic perspective, the sound of a bowed string, such as the violin, is probably the closest to the human voice singing.

Nevertheless, from an organological point of view, musical instruments are technological devices, and the mode of sound production of a bowed string is the furthest from the human voice. Thus, wind and percussive instruments naturally amplify the human body. With an increase in mediation, string instruments are still a technology that directly generates sound: a performer plucks a string, and the string produces sound. Thus, in all these cases, there is direct physical contact between the source of the sound production and the performer. This situation changes with the introduction of the keyboard. The musical keyboard virtualizes the process of performing music. By pressing a key, the performer does not directly interact with the source of the sound. Instead, the performer activates a mechanism that will produce the sound.

Jonathan De Souza (2017, 2018) provides a comprehensive approach to the critical aspects of organology and mediation in *Music at Hand: Instruments, Bodies, and Cognition*. De Souza explains Heyde's (1975) model of classification of instruments based on cybernetics, a science that "is concerned not with a system's material properties but with its abstract structure and behavior" (De Souza 2017, 32). De Souza describes that in Heyde's model, instruments are broken up into a set of elements that become black boxes that are connected with each other, creating a circuit diagram. All instruments have one component called an activator (the device that activates the sound, such as the muscle of a performer) and a transducer (the strings of a piano or a violin), which is the part of the instrument that converts the energy from the activator into sound. In this model, both the string bow and the piano keys are types of mediators, which are devices between the activator and the transducer (De Souza 2017, 33–35). Heyde's model is sophisticated and robust to describe musical instruments. At the same time, it fails to highlight the importance of the musical keyboard in a manner that is distinct from the violin bow. The keyboard adds an additional level of mediation, which also facilitates the standardization of music, as it is built using the 12-tone division of the octave. In addition, the 12 notes are divided between seven white keys and five black keys, which suggests a seven-note scale system. The musical keyboard is an interface that solidifies a scale-based 12-tone musical framework while detaching the process of playing (by depressing its keys) from the actual production of the sound (Fig. 3.3).

Emily Dolan (2012) stressed the importance of the musical keyboard in *Toward a Musicology of Interfaces*, concluding that "instead of thinking about music as a genus in which keyboard music exists as a species,

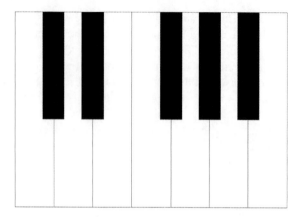

Fig. 3.3 Schematic for an octave of a musical keyboard

perhaps it could be productive to think of the keyboard—here standing in for all immaculately controllable instruments—as the genus, while this thing we have come to know as music as a species of keyboard" (12). For example, Dolan mentions the resistance to including a keyboard in synthesizers such as the Buchla. While the Buchla synthesizer was released without a keyboard, the Moog was released with one, making the latter more popular than the former (8).

Thus, most synthesizers, old and new, use the musical keyboard as the primary interface for music performance, in addition to additional controllers. In the case of the Moog, these were a set of controllable sound generators and processors that could be programmed using knobs and connected to each other using cables. These additional interfaces serve to shape the sound the instrument will produce. In terms of musical performance, playing a synthesizer is similar to playing another keyboard instrument. However, while synthesizers with keyboards seem to lack innovation in terms of evolving the musical interfaces, they offer the possibility of molding the sound they produce. Moreover, synthesizers can sculpt sound in forms that are not possible with purely physical instruments.

Hence, the incorporation of synthesizers as a new set of musical instruments highlights a new attitude in which timbre transformation and molding become increasingly relevant. Their utilization of electricity should be understood as a means to fulfill their goal of expanding the sound palette. Dolan (2012) argues that the keyboard "has represented a particular mode of instrumentality, namely one based on the idea of complete control" (10). Further, Dolan argues that to fulfill the idea of a modern music work that is repeatable and can be reproduced in a manner that is considered faithful requires "a composer in technological control" (11). With the synthesizer, the composer gains that additional capacity to control timbre in a way that was impossible with traditional instrumental/orchestral writing. However, synthesizers have not been able to reproduce all the sounds that an orchestra can create despite the early hopes of synth pioneers such as Wendy Carlos. In addition, a synthesizer alone is a limited and burdensome way to achieve total control. With the introduction of digital systems, this all changed. It allowed for the capacity to sample organic sounds, create virtual instruments, preserve the idea of a repeatable music work, and the capacity to store and process the musical material.

Sampled-Based Virtual Instruments and the Digital Revolution

Synthesizers can be either analog, digital, or virtual (software) devices. For instance, the Moog is an analog synthesizer, the Yamaha DX-7 a digital one, and any software synthesizer is a virtual one, including the emulations of the hardware ones produced by companies such as Arturia. On the other hand, sample-based instruments are always digital or virtual devices.[33]

Sample-based virtual instruments start with a sampler, a piece of technology (initially a hardware device but nowadays mostly software) that generates a broad range of musical notes and sounds from a short recording (or a group of recordings). This short recording is called the sample. Thus, they require the capacity to digitally store a sound sample that is then used to create the sound of the instrument. The sampler uses the sample or samples to generate a virtual instrument. Since the beginning of the twenty-first century, digital samplers have been able to handle thousands of samples per virtual instrument, making them generally very distinct from synthesizers in their function.

Nevertheless, sampled-based instruments were an evolution of a synthesizer. Technically speaking, sampled-based instruments utilize one or more sound samples to generate a new synthesized instrument.[34] Thus, this instrument does not purely originate from artificially generated sounds. Instead, a sampled instrument is the product of processing recorded sounds captured from the physical world and creating a computer program that generates a playable virtual instrument from these samples. This simple transformation has significant implications in terms of the ontology of musical instruments.

Samplers go a step further in the process of virtualization by going back to the physical world to borrow sounds from the acoustic domain that would have been unable to be produced, at least in 2024, by pure synthesis alone.[35] Even when a synthesizer embraces what Moog called "timbral thievery" (De Souza 2021) by trying to emulate the sound of physical instruments, the results are generally distanced from the acoustic model. For instance, Vangelis' score for *Blade Runner* (1982) incorporated many sounds from the Yamaha CS-80 that sounded close to a brass ensemble, but, at the same time, they were distanced enough from its acoustic model for the score to use these timbres to sound futuristic. On the other hand, the evolution of sampled-based instruments follows an aim to replace reality by creating virtual instruments that can replace live performances (at diverse levels of fidelity). Therefore, I argue that by capturing and processing sounds from the physical world, these instruments add a new layer of virtualization that did not exist with the synthesizers, as I defined before.

Sample-based virtual instruments are quintessential to defining the hyperorchestra as a virtual ensemble that is able to generate music that contains models of reality. For now, though, I am describing them superficially and only for the purpose of illustrating the process of increased virtualization of music. This process of virtualization will culminate with the hyperorchestra, as I will detail at the end of the chapter. As key tools for the hyperorchestra, these virtual instruments will occupy a central space in the next chapter dedicated to the tools of the hyperorchestra. Before doing so, I propose below a preliminary and unnuanced classification that will be further developed in the following chapter with a more detailed typology (Fig. 3.4).

Sampled-based instruments reside in a space between the world of synthesis and the world of recording and studio processing. Sound recording and the studio expanded the process of music virtualization by the processing and transformation of sounds that came from the acoustic domain. Conversely, synthesizers did a similar process by generating sounds in the analog domain that could not be produced by acoustic means. Samplers occupy a space in the middle and, as a consequence, contribute to the increase of virtualization from both perspectives. Sampled-based instruments create a sound that seems to replicate a physical performance by using short snippets of sound recordings that are programmed together. Nevertheless, they still present the same challenge that De Souza (2021)

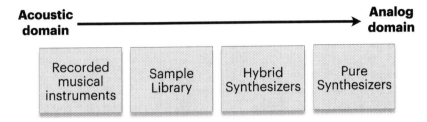

Fig. 3.4 A general classification for synthesized and sampled instruments based on their connection to the acoustic or the analog domain. Pure synthesizers are instruments that create sounds solely from oscillators (VCOs). Hybrid synthesizers are virtual instruments that employ one or more samples as the sound source to produce the synthesizer's sound. Sample libraries are designed by creating computer programs that utilize a generally extensive set of samples to generate virtual instruments. The last typology, the recording, refers to any other typology of music recording as presented before

described for the synthesizers: they equally, or I would say even more, "complicate phenomenological links between sound and source."

From the perspective of the connection of the sound they produce with physical reality, sampled instruments might be divided into two main approaches. First, some instruments use a sample as a source that is modified using synthesis techniques to produce the resulting sound (hybrid synthesizers). In most cases, the aesthetic intent in doing this process, at least since early 2000s, is not to replicate or emulate a physical instrument by virtualizing it but, instead, to create a new one by transforming a physically generated sound sample. The second group contains instruments that attempt to virtually replicate a physical instrument (or ensemble) by using multiple samples of the instrument to emulate it.

In many cases, the sample (or set of samples) that produces the sound for hybrid synthesizers carries a certain degree of signification to the newly created instrument. For example, a virtual instrument that uses the sound of a hammer hitting a metallic trashcan will probably have some sort of connection with the source of the sample in terms of its signified meaning. Thus, when the instrument appears in a piece of music, it will probably bring some references to the cultural connotations from the source. By incorporating meaning borrowed from the physical world, the new instrument becomes hyperreal, as it integrates models from the real without the sound having purely originated in the physical world. In the trashcan sound example, the resulting sound may have been transformed and then pitch-shifted to provide different musical notes. Hence, even though it might still preserve the connotations of a sound produced by industrial or urban objects, the sound produced by the instrument could not be generated just by physical means.

The third group of instruments constitutes the core of what is commonly defined by screen composers as sample libraries.[36] However, technically speaking, they are virtual instruments that utilize an extensive set of sampled sounds to produce a verisimilar rendition of the instrument or ensemble they aim to replicate. Even though hybrid synthesizers are crucial for contemporary aesthetics in screen music and are found in almost any score, sample libraries are the most relevant piece of technology for this stage of the discussion that revolves around the virtualization of the musical experience.[37] From that angle, sample libraries challenge the definition of a musical instrument when they become a virtual version of a physical instrument in a manner that goes beyond the concept of timbral thievery discussed above. From this viewpoint, to scrutinize their ontology, we should begin by asking the following questions: are sampled instruments an attempt to imitate a real instrument, making them a counterfeit, or are they a new instrument culturally connected to their physical counterpart? To answer this question, it is worth analyzing first how this dichotomy relates to a similar one between actors and their computer-generated counterparts.

CGI Actors and Sample Libraries

In Chap. 2, I discussed what Auslander (2008) described as the Gollum problem. The introduction of computer-generated characters, along with motion capture devices to record the movements of those characters, challenges our approach to the authorship of the act of performance. In these terms, the virtual instruments in sample libraries are closely related to CGI characters. Both CGI characters and sampled virtual instruments use samples from the physical world that are processed by computer models. In addition, they both require a certain amount of programming that is best achieved by experts who interact with specific interfaces. In the case of CGI actors, the experts are actors whose performances are incorporated into the computer model by the utilization of motion capture devices, generating a visual moving image. In theory, one could program the computer model without the help of a motion-capturing actor. Practically, the expertise of an actor becomes strategic in providing life and verisimilitude to the CGI character, mainly when the character is featured on screen.[38] Further, providing data for CGI characters is a skill that is somewhat different from traditional screen acting, which is the reason why an actor may become a specialist in motion capture performance.[39] That was the case of Andy Serkis, who came to fame through their CGI performance of Gollum in *The Lord of the Rings* (2001–2003) franchise, but also a few other well-known CGI characters, including Caesar in the prequel movies for *The Planet of the Apes* (2011–2017).

Music creation using sample libraries follows a similar process with a significant difference. Sample libraries are created to allow performance programming using the MIDI protocol. I will describe MIDI in more detail in the next chapter. For now, MIDI is a communication protocol that acts very similarly to a musical score in the digital realm, with the capacity to tell synthesizers, samplers, and other electronic instruments how to produce sound (which notes, how loud, which parameters to modify, etc.). However, performance programming is not achieved by hiring musicians with the equivalent of motion capture devices but by using a musical keyboard with a set of faders or knobs. Further, it is not the performer but a member of the screen composer creative team (including themselves) who programs these virtual instruments, regardless of which instrument they were replicating, with probably the only exception of drums, which, at times, have dedicated programming specialists. In other words, the same person would be programming a flute line or a pizzicato cello section, which means that no specialized musical performer is involved in the process, as an actor is involved in creating the CGI character.

The previous statement makes sense in music for several reasons. First, the composer, as a musician, has performance skills. Second, the input devices (keyboard and faders) do not capture musical performance as naturally as motion capture sensors do for acting. For example, a violin performance might be captured by simultaneously using a keyboard and some faders to control dynamics, *vibrato*, or a bow change. However, a keyboard and a set of faders cannot capture everything involved in a violin performance, while motion capture does capture the movements that constitute the actor's performance. Instead, the keyboard and faders capture a subset of musical elements, such as the amount of vibrato or the dynamics. Third, each instrument requires specific performance techniques, which complicates the task of designing capture mechanisms and the logistics of capturing the performance. Adding a musical performance capture player would not suffice because each instrument would require a specialist. Thus, even though MIDI wind controllers do exist, they are rarely used. That is because they require a wind performer to be fully effective. With all that in mind, it seems clear why, in music, the performance programming specialist for sampled virtual instruments comes from the composer's side of the creative process.

Considering all this, a sample library's user interface is generally designed according to the assumption that a member of the composer's team will act as the performer. That inevitably implies a much-simplified interface compared to the number of data inputs a performer provides when playing an instrument. Although a MIDI programming specialist is a profession (sometimes known as *synhtestrator*)—or at least a part of the skill set of many composing team members—their specialty is programming the library instead of an actual instrumental performance. Thus, when comparing music performance capture in sampled virtual instruments with CGI acting and capture, MIDI programmers are in a position that would be in the middle of a CGI programming specialist—due to their skills in the actual programming intricacies of the device—and the CGI actors—due to their abilities in musical performance.[40]

Sample libraries adapt to this situation by designing interfaces with composers and MIDI programmers in mind and by incorporating predesigned performance decisions that are reproduced automatically. For example, instruments in sample libraries routinely incorporate predesigned amounts of vibrato, instrument noises, or breathing sounds. The incorporation of predesigned performance decisions has an added effect: they reproduce the practices that follow a performance aesthetic, most of which derive from what is commonly known in the movie industry as the Hollywood sound. Consequently, the need for a simplified interface and a reduced set of performance decisions implies that these libraries incorporate a set of fixed cultural conventions, which are then partially introduced to the music created using these tools.[41]

The relationship between the physical instrument and its sampled counterpart becomes somewhat more explicit by analyzing the similarities between CGI characters and sample libraries. Motion capture actors provide an actual performance for virtually designed characters, which results in an actual human performance. Similarly, music created with sample libraries is also performed, even though the performance-capturing capabilities are not as extensive as motion capture for acting. This lack of precision in the performance capture process is partially supplemented by inserting predesigned performance practices. From this viewpoint, the actual performance (not the sound result) is neither synthetic nor computer-generated: it has been produced by humans. In the case of musical instruments, they act as a medium to transmit the musical ideas of the performer, comparable to how a virtual instrument from a sample library operates.

In addition, there is a supplementary consideration regarding audiovisual narratives: the importance of how music and acting support the narrative. For example, the character of Yoda in the *Star Wars* franchise was portrayed using a puppet for the first four movies (Episodes I, IV, V, and VI) and as a CGI character for episodes II–III. As a character, Yoda is the most powerful Jedi master who appears onscreen, implying he is also the best light-saber fighter. Yoda's supremacy as a light-saber warrior would be brutal to portray through a puppet or by employing physical means alone. Nevertheless, this is not a significant problem when Yoda is represented using a CGI character. Thus, from a narrative standpoint, Yoda is better portrayed by a CGI character than by a physical puppet or actor. Comparably, screen music adheres to the needs of the visual narrative as its primary function. Analogously, this need might be better achieved sometimes by using sample libraries.

Expanding What an Instrument Is
Sampled-based virtual instruments also expand the definition of a musical instrument even further by treating particular instances of an instrument and instrumental ensembles as types of virtual instruments. In the past, composers would typically be unable to specify a type or model of flute they require for the performance of their pieces, but they are now able to do so by selecting a different library. On the other hand, virtual instruments can encompass a group of instruments beyond the traditional string sections typical in orchestral writing. A virtual instrument might present a predefined orchestration of up to a full orchestra. As a consequence, the selection and design of the ensemble implies a degree of cultural signification. For example, a virtual instrument from a sample library that represents an orchestral sound would accomplish that goal by following a set of orchestration principles to fulfill the library's goal, which is generally attached to a process of signification. That highlights an important aspect that I have not discussed yet. The team that makes a library generally incorporates creatives with skillsets in the area of the composer's team, which would include orchestration.

Sample Libraries and Hyperreality

In Chap. 2, I discussed Prince's (1996, 2010, 2012) definition of perceptual realism and its connection with the hyperreal. CGI characters are ordinarily an optimal example of perceptual realism. Similarly, music produced using sample libraries interacts with the hyperreal. Sample libraries can create music that, even though it sounds verisimilar, cannot be produced by acoustic means alone. By using recordings from physical reality and transforming them into interactive virtual instruments, sample libraries engage with various models of reality that have been transformed into a virtual sphere. This approach differs from what synthesizers add to music, which is related to timbral expansion. Instead, with sample libraries, composers can interact with models of reality and transform them beyond what would be achievable in the physical world while still retaining their cultural value as physical artifacts.

These products are also prime examples of the immense effects of the digital revolution in music production, impacting each stage of screen music creation and production. Buhler (2019, 257–288, 2021) provides a comprehensive overview of this transformation for the entire soundtrack creation process. That will also be a central point for the second part of this book, concerning how it applies to the hyperorchestra and the compositional, orchestrational, and production practices that derive from it. Therefore, sample libraries have a fundamental role in the emergence of the hyperorchestra.

Defining the Hyperorchestra: Two Preliminary Approaches

In Chaps. 5 and 6, I will provide a detailed investigation and description of the hyperorchestra and the techniques associated with its utilization. Below are two initial definitions of the hyperorchestra as they relate to the technologies described in this chapter and the philosophical approaches to hyperreality that I described in the previous chapter.

A Technological Approach

In this chapter, I have described the essential elements that constitute the technological devices that facilitate and expand the music creation process. Exploring these different technological inventions shows their capability of expanding the available soundscape by expanding timbre. This process of sound expansion crosses the boundaries of the physical world through the introduction of musical synthesizers, and it opened itself up to the hyperreal by incorporating sample libraries and virtual instruments. From a purely technological viewpoint, I define the hyperorchestra as a virtual ensemble capable of incorporating all of these new means of music creation. The hyperorchestra inhabits hyperreality, as it goes beyond the physical world while maintaining its connection with the real whenever necessary. Thus, the hyperorchestra encapsulates all the music-creation processes that transcend the physical world's limitations.[42]

A Philosophical and Aesthetic Approach

As I described at the beginning of the chapter, recording music implies virtualizing the musical experience. As such, someone listening to recorded music will inevitably acknowledge this fact, as the only other possible explanation—that the musicians are somehow hidden in the room—is clearly not feasible. The only common exception to this principle occurs when recorded music is hiddenly played while a group of musicians makes the audience believe they are the performers. However, the degree of sophistication required to make a fake performance believable becomes more of a confirmation of the previous statement than a refutation.

To clarify how the progressive virtualization of the musical experience opened up for the advent of the hyperorchestra, it is valuable to create an analogy between the musical recording and Umberto Eco's observations on the wax museum and Disneyland to describe his approach to hyperreality. For Eco (1990), the wax museum "tries to make us believe that what we are seeing reproduces reality absolutely" (43), which makes it not hyperreal. Traditional Western classical music recordings seem—at least initially—the sonic analogous to the wax museum, as their aesthetic goal appears to be the exact reproduction of reality. As I argued in this chapter, this is not exactly possible with sound recording and, in some cases (the piano concerto), not even desirable. Nevertheless, while these recordings are a step into virtualizing the music experience that eventually produced the advent of the hyperorchestra, they are not strictly a representation of hyperreal or hyperorchestral music.

Similarly, a piece of music rendered using sample-based virtual instruments that aim to become a reproduction of reality would fall into the same category. This piece of music would be generated by one or more virtual performers who, using MIDI, a DAW, and a set of sample libraries, would create a performance of a piece of music with the intent to emulate a verisimilar recording of that piece. While this type of rendition of a piece might also become a technological attraction, it is still broadly a recorded performance of a piece in a traditional sense. It shows a higher degree of virtualization—in a similar manner to a heavily edited recording using many takes, which is more virtualized than a single-take recording—but it is not yet a clear leap into the hyperreal.

Eco details that Disneyland differs from the wax museum because "Disneyland makes it clear that within its magic enclosure it is fantasy that is absolutely reproduced" (43). Thus, Disneyland becomes hyperrealistic because it accepts its unrealistic status and attempts to reproduce magic in a manner that "must seem totally real" (44). As Eco points out, "a real crocodile can be found in the zoo, and as a rule it is dozing or hiding, but Disneyland tells us that faked nature corresponds much more to our daydream demands" (44). In other words, the fake crocodile in Disneyland will appear when it is supposed to appear, fulfilling its narrative role and the audience's expectations much more efficiently as if it were real, thus generating a hyperreal experience. Analogously, a piece of music that originates in the physical or virtual studio (DAW), becomes hyperrealistic when it is not attempting just to reproduce an acoustic musical performance. Music, though, renders subtler results in terms of perception compared to a fake rendition of a crocodile in Disneyland. At the same time, a musical recording is already a highly virtualized experience compared to the physical fake natural elements in Disneyland. Thus, the musical intent of transforming sound in order to fulfill a narrative function is fairly equivalent to using a fake crocodile that always appears to fulfill its narrative role.

Therefore, the hyperorchestra allows for the creation of instruments that become more pertinent to the narrative than a physical instrument, akin to Disneyland's fake crocodile. For instance, a hyperinstrument within the hyperorchestra might have its spectrum adjusted to become a better storytelling device. This will be the focus of Chap. 5 and especially Chap. 6. For now, let's imagine that the composer alters the spectrum of a violin in order to generate a violin sound that is able to provide more specific storytelling meaning to the audiovisual narrative the composer is scoring. In this case, the result becomes hyperorchestral, as I define it.

To recapitulate, the hyperorchestra does not rely only on the sound produced by physical sound objects, which would limit its scope to combining predesigned spectral shapes. Instead, the hyperorchestra operates directly on the sound spectrum. Similarly to Disneyland, though, the utilization of the hyperorchestra implies a storytelling purpose: music produced by the hyperorchestra is part of the audiovisual storytelling fabric and aims to be a better tool than the acoustic musical tools to fulfill this role. As I will detail in Chap. 6, writing for the hyperorchestra denotes a spectral attitude toward sound as defined by the French spectral school that started in the late 1960s by composers Gérard Grisey and Tristan Murrail. However, its main difference with the spectral movement is that the hyperorchesta's spectral attitude is guided by storytelling. Screen music is part of an audiovisual narrative and, in tandem with all the other narrative devices that constitute filmmaking, its primary function is to provide narrative meaning to the story that is being told.

The hyperorchestra unfolds music's uninhibited potential as a filmmaking tool. Cinema—as a fairly new art form that incorporates all the previous arts—has had a distinctive evolution in achieving increased levels of medium specificity for each of the arts that integrate it. For instance, acting for the movies is nowadays fairly distinct from acting for theater, whereas in the early stages of film at the beginning of the twentieth century, both acting approaches were much closer. Similarly, CGI has become an evolution of painting scenery for the mise-en-scène, and cinematographers are not just photographers but professionals of the moving image. From an editing standpoint, the capacity to edit nonlinearly and without physical limitations allows the art to develop and evolve in a manner that seems much more natural than cutting and gluing celluloid. For the music, the capacity to create music by working with sound directly using nonlinear editing systems similar to the editing software (the DAWs) and unlocking the power of sound manipulation and transformation beyond what acoustic instruments can do also becomes a much more natural way of partaking in audiovisual storytelling, making the *screenscoring* more and more a distinct discipline from music composition.

Baudrillard and the Hyperorchestra

Western orchestral music is a product—in its early stages—of the seventeenth century, while its full development did not arrive until the establishment of the classical orchestra around the second half of the eighteenth century. Therefore, one could argue that what we frequently vaguely regard as *classical music* is a product of what Baudrillard called the first order of simulacra. Orchestral music operates without clear referents compared to vocal music, for instance. However, the early orchestras and ensembles had significant connections to reality due to earlier versions of instruments that preserved the connection to activities such as hunting (the natural trumpets) or the materiality of the instruments (the gut strings in the string instruments). Through the implementation of standardized notation (as detailed earlier in this chapter), orchestral ensembles, tunning, performance practices, and a process of de-materialization of the orchestral instruments to make them sound as pure as possible, the orchestra underwent its transformation into the second order of simulacra. Finally, the use of recording technology and the capacity to manipulate and transform sound in the studio facilitated the migration of music into the third order of simulacra and, thus, into Baudrillard's hyperreality.

In the previous chapter, I mentioned how Baudrillard (2005) considered computer-generated music (in a generic sense) as music "which sounds have been clarified and expurgated and which, shorn of all noise and static, is, so to speak, restored to its technical perfection" (27). Thus, "it is a music reduced to a pure wavelength, the final reception of which, the tangible effect on the listener, is exactly programmed too, as in a closed circuit. It is, in a sense, a virtual music" (28). I believe that the process of *sound clarification* and *noise expurgation* began much before, as I just described, with the advent of the Western orchestra.

This is probably why music created without the audience understanding its sound source has generally been quickly embraced and incorporated into our culture without the need for an aesthetic revolution. Thus, sound manipulations in the studio or the utilization of synthesizers have been much more evolutionary than revolutionary from a broader aesthetic standpoint. In addition, the statements above connect with Schaeffer's *acousmatic listening* mode, highlighting that acousmatic listening is, indeed, hyperreal.

Listening to a movie score created by recording an orchestra potentially carries an association with the orchestra as an acoustic ensemble, diminishing its acousmatic effect by linking the sound to a sound source (even if it is virtual and not physically present). Thinking about film music, this association is not necessarily a negative thing as it can contribute to the sense of spectacle and epic of the audiovisual narrative. In a certain way, it would be analogous to the theater-like type of acting of earlier films. However, creating these associations makes film music more obtrusive from a storytelling purpose than if music were a purely acousmatic experience. This kind of obtrusiveness is a great aesthetic tool to have when telling stories, but having alternatives to this approach can only enrich the medium.

On the other hand, the hyperorchestra is capable of negotiating the degree of acousmaticism of its sounds to fulfill their function within the audiovisual narrative. Therefore, the sounds of the hyperorchestra can become heavily materialized to connect with clear physical entities to the point of implementing a sense of hapticity—as Miguel Mera (2016) suggested—and thus remove any sense of acousmaticity. Or, they can become a pure acousmatic experience that blends into the rest of the audiovisual narrative. While orchestral music can also negotiate with diverging degrees of acousmaticity—a slow, quiet, sustained string passage is more acousmatic than a passage that incorporates loud brass—the hyperorchestra allows for a much more expansive and fluid process. From this viewpoint, the hyperorchestra also becomes a more efficient approach to integrating music into audiovisual narratives.

Conclusion

In this chapter, I have outlined the evolution of music primarily during the twentieth century in its virtualization process, which is connected to the need for music to expand on its timbral possibilities while maintaining the capacity to be notated and reproduced precisely. In doing so, it has become clear that digital tools play a crucial role at almost any of the levels of music production: from providing new modes of music notation (DAWs and MIDI) to allowing for advanced techniques in editing and processing recordings, to the generation of virtual instruments. Then, I provided a definition for the hyperorchestra that engaged the topics I outlined in this chapter as well as in the previous one.

The next chapter pauses the aesthetic discussion of the hyperorchestra to investigate and describe the digital tools that constitute the hyperorchestra and their potential aesthetic contribution. This will allow us to have a much more specific and richer analysis of hyperorchestral aesthetics. The chapter is not designed to become a comprehensive and practical catalog of all the tools used by screen composers in the present day but to describe them from the point of view of aesthetics. That necessarily includes a description of MIDI and its role in providing a new mode to notate music. MIDI's full potential was only fully implemented with the introduction of Digital Audio Workstations. Then, I create a typology for virtual instruments that develops from the model presented in this chapter.

Notes

1. Would a second inversion triad sound as a second inversion in a string ensemble where the bases were located at the back of the hall and the celli were playing the fundamental note of the chord in the stage? When we do make the effort to imagine the result, we generally do it with frameworks that are immediately outside the traditional approaches to music theory.
2. Mainly based on a 12-tone scale. Although it is possible to notate quartertones or even smaller musical distances in the score, these new pitches are still subordinate to a 12-tone scale framework.
3. For instance, to acknowledge that a trombone sounds different from a bassoon.
4. In this context, production refers to the act of creating musical performances.
5. Even though performance treaties exist, they face the same limitations as the musical score: they are unable to properly reproduce sound or firmly represent practices that cannot be represented in a score. Thus, their value is limited, which is why learning an instrument still requires several hours of individualized instruction. Thus, learning how to perform a *crescendo* implies assessing a diverse set of musical parameters to decide what would be the best shape to execute the change in dynamics. It does not necessarily require awareness of the exact dynamic evolution of the sound by the performer. Instead, aural communication serves as a tool to sonically assess when a particular performance of a *crescendo* fits the needs of a passage.
6. For this example, I replaced the term oral with aural to acknowledge a communication system that involves the sound of the instrument being learned. Further, the fact that, even in the twenty-first century, the vastly predominant mode to teach how to play an instrument is through individualized lessons, which are expensive and inefficient from a productivity point of view, reinforces this point. Individualized instruction have been significantly reduced over the centuries, yet, it is still irreplacable for teaching musical performance.
7. For example, scores that use approximate notation such as Penderecki's well-known *Threnody for the victims of Hiroshima* (1960) are much less useful as a representation of the resulting sound than a piece by Haydn or Mozart.
8. Aleatoric notation is another good example to support this idea. Terry Riley's score for *In C* (1964) is only a blueprint for performers and would fail to faithfully serve as a representation of the sound produced by a performance.
9. The amount of signal from each microphone that will be sent to the final mix.

10. It could even just utilize a single microphone, which will produce a monophonic result.
11. Which might also include a set of microphones from the conductor's perspective.
12. There are several types of microphones that capture sound differently in terms of their sensitivity to specific frequency ranges, the capturing area (cardioid, directional), or the physical process of how the microphone converts sound to electricity (condenser, ribbon). For a further description of microphone typologies, see Owsinski (2013, 3–51).
13. In other words, the eyes will receive a discrete number of still images per second that the brain will interpret as movement. In the case of sound, the ears already receive a sound wave that has the same properties as any other sound.
14. Jonathan De Souza (2021) argues that the "rock organ–orchestra hybrid is a kind of chimera, situated between the individual expression of the rock soloist and the transcendence of the orchestral collective." De Souza describes how the concept of an auditory chimera has been used in timbre studies such as in Bregman (1990). Bregman describes an instance of an auditory chimera when "a heard sentence that was created by accidental composition of the two voices of two persons who just happened to be speaking at the same time. Natural hearing tries to avoid chimeric percepts, but music often tries to create them" (459–460). For instance, "a composer may want the listener to group the sounds from different instruments and hear this grouping as a sound with its own emergent properties" (460). As a consequence, this result grouping becomes a virtual source, which, nevertheless, "plays the same perceptual role as our perception of a real source does in natural environments" (460). In the example of the piano concerto, I use the same idea to propose that, in many instances, the intended sounding result is an impossible negotiation between the aesthetic desire for the solo performer to be featured and the acoustic result of the performer being engulfed by the sound of the orchestra.
15. This is a clear case in which mixing involves the production of a specific timbral result that is analogous to orchestration. I will discuss how I consider the process of mixing as hyperorchestration in the second part of this book. It is also important to emphasize that dynamic is different from loudness or volume. When an instrument or an ensemble plays a *fortissimo*, their timbre changes significantly than if they would be playing the same passage *piano*. The result is also that the first scenario is louder than the second, but, with recordings, you could make a *fortissimo* passage sound quieter and still preserve its timbral properties, which is one of the ways in which the piano in that context could be heard.

16. Western classical music—and operatic music in particular—are full of controversies when a microphone is spotted on stage, or when amplification is perceived. In both cases, the consensus is negative. To give an example, Anthony Tommasini wrote in the *New York Times* an article titled "Wearing a Wire at the Opera, Secretly, of Course" (2013) when the cameras captured a performer secretly wearing a microphone at the Metropolitan Opera in New York City. The executives from the Met rushed to explain that this was not to amplify the performance, but to allow for the singer to be heard in the live recording when they were singing at certain areas of the stage where the microphones were not properly capturing them. In a much more critical manner, Sebastien Turgeon (2019) wrote for the Opera Wire a critique of the use of amplification at the Royal Swedish Opera. Turgeon writes, "The production of sound in opera has always been acoustic in nature. [...] Natural sounds produced by voices and instruments are untouched and vocal technique accounts for the ability to project in a concert hall. [...] However, for some time now, there have been suspicions that some opera companies are utilizing discreet amplification systems to support singers with weaker voices."

    Then, the author criticized a performance of *Król Roger* for its use of amplification: "Dramatically, if amplification attempted to reinforce the sense of obsession or schizophrenia, it was at the price of the operatic nature of the performance. The continuous use of amplified sounds constantly created musical imbalances, contrasting unnatural and acoustic sounds, voices synthetically boosted and stripped of their natural quality. The result was a musical mess, disorienting and difficult to follow."
17. See Knakkergaard (2015) for a mostly phenomenological discussion on this topic.
18. In Baudrillard's (1994) terms described in the previous chapter.
19. The musical creators may include the composer, the performers, and the recording team. This is important as some creative decisions (the size of the ensemble, for example) are generally not specified in the score and might affect the relationship in terms of the comparative loudness of the soloist and the orchestra.
20. Early reflections are the first bounces of the sound to the walls of the stage or the studio, which are key to define its timbre. This is because we cannot hear a sound in regular conditions without early reflections. However, studios control early reflections to different degrees, thus practically changing the timbre of the sound, and, at the same time, allowing for the recorded sounds to be more malleable.
21. In this case, an instrument is any physical object that is able to produce sound.

22. For instance, Schaeffer writes: "For the traditional musician and the acoustician one important aspect of sound recognition is the identification of sound sources. When this takes place without the help of sight, musical conditioning is thrown into disarray. Often taken by surprise, sometimes uncertain, we discover that much of what we thought we could hear was in reality merely seen, and explained, by the context. This is why it is just about possible to confuse some sounds produced by instruments as different as strings and woodwind" (2017, 66).
23. Amy Blier-Carruthers (2020) compellingly discusses the differences and conflicts generated by classical recordings in relation to live performances from the performer's point of view. Blier-Carruthers offers data to support that most of the time, performers stop takes due to either tempo issues or mistakes in the performance (203). The author also details how expectations of perfection (200) are now a given even in live performances.
24. In Chap. 6, I will revisit these concepts in the description of the process to create hyperinstruments.
25. In contemporary Western music, it is, somewhat confusingly, described as "extended techniques." For instance, asking a string player to play closer to the bridge (*sul ponticello*) would have been considered an extended technique at the beginning of the nineteenth century, but not now, whereas using overpressure on the same instrument is still considered an extended technique.
26. In a following chapter, I will explore how the expansion of piano sounds is a feature of twenty-first-century aesthetics for Screen Music. Composers currently have a wide variety of virtual piano libraries that reproduce myriad piano timbres, including some esoteric sounds, such as a piano with only one string per note or the recording of a piano that was set on fire.
27. By "discrete approach to timbre," I mean the idea of musical instruments as abstract and general entities. Writing for a violin—or a flute—implies writing for a discrete number of timbres associated with musical instruments, which are also generic enough to be interchangeable. A violin part is meant to be performed by any violin (or violin section of any orchestra).
28. DAWs also implement the Musical Instruments Digital Interface (MIDI) mode of notation, further expanding their capacity to notate music.
29. A first glance at the diverse ways we can classify synthesizers is presented in the next section of this chapter to connect them with sample library-based virtual instruments.
30. In contemporary audio production, we identify three domains of audio: acoustic, analog, and digital. In the analog domain, music is transmitted using electricity, which is why any recording or process in a studio setting would at least start in the analog domain. Contemporary studios would

generally convert analog signals into digital signals for further processing. A more detailed explanation can be found in Mayfield's (2012, 2016).
31. In some instances, synthesis and sampling might be treated as a single instance. In *Music Technology*, Julio d'Escriván (2012) introduces synthesizers by mentioning four synthesis methods: Processed recording, spectral models, physical models, and abstract algorithms (72). However, the first two methods involve sampling, which, at least for the purpose of this text, is a significantly different paradigm. Pejrolo and Metcalfe, in *Creating Sounds from Scratch* (2017), define two types of sound sources for music synthesis: "the oscillator (which forms the foundation of subtractive, frequency modulation and additive synthesis) and digital playback (the basis of sampling, physical modeling, wavetable, and granular)" (53). Thus, this section is devoted to synthesizers that generate sound through oscillators (what I will call pure synthesizers). In the next section, I will be discussing the introduction of sampling. Historically, the capacity to create sound from digital playback came after the invention of the first synthesizers.
32. The following discussion does not aim to be a faithful history of organology but to apply McLuhan's framework to organology. Aerophone instruments are a part of a widely known classification of musical instruments was developed by Hornbostel and Sachs (1961), and it is acknowledged in key orchestration books such as Adler (2016, 473) or in De Souza (2017, 32).
33. There is one notable exception, though, the mellotron. The mellotron is an analog hardware sample that uses tape to reproduce samples mechanically (Pejrolo and Metcalfe 2017, 14–15).
34. Sample-based synthesis is generally considered one of the latest evolutions in sound. For an introduction to this type of synthesis, see Pejrolo and Metcalfe (2017, 203–62). It is also worth pointing out that even though Sample-Based synthesis is a digital process, this does not mean that it has to be accomplished with computer software. Sample-based synthesizers originated as hardware synthesizers before software synths were even created.
35. The application of the Fourier theorem makes it possible to create a synthesizer that could theoretically reproduce the sound of any sound produced in the physical world using an appropriate combination and mix of sine waves. Synthesizers that aim to accomplish that use a technique called physical modeling (Pejrolo and Metcalfe 2017, 263–90). There are currently few products that generate virtual versions of acoustic instruments (Pianoteq has a piano, and Sample Modeling offers some strings and wind instruments) that are competitive. However, this technique has been revolutionary to create software versions of analog synthesizers (Arturia is one of the leading companies in this matter) or analog sound processors

(Universal Audio's software renditions are virtually impossible to distinguish from its analog counterparts). This is an area in which it is possible that it will quickly evolve with the utilization of artificial intelligence.
36. In practice, the first group is regularly considered just to be synthesizers. However, the distinction was required to precisely define these instruments.
37. Especially when they fulfill the function of portraying what Dolan and Patteson call "ethereal timbres" (2021).
38. This is coherent with McLuhan's thesis on the limitations of the written language. Programming language, as an even more formal type of written communication, requires massive data to represent body movements.
39. Marci Linoff's (2022) article in the popular website Backstage titled *How to Become a Motion Picture Actor* is an example that highlights the existence of a distinct set of skills for this area of acting.
40. It could be argued that MIDI programmers are closer to CGI actors than it might seem because, many times, these actors enact performances of a wide variety of non-human creatures. In this situation, acting might be considered a comparable challenge to performing an instrument for which the musical performer is not trained to perform.
41. This will be explored in detail in the following chapter.
42. As mentioned in Chap. 1, the term hyperorchestra was created by joining the words "hyperreal" and "orchestra." From this term, I generated related words such as hyperinstrument and hyperorchestration.

References

Adler, Samuel. 2016. *Study of Orchestration*. Fourth ed.: W. W. Norton & Company.
Auslander, Philip. 2008. *Liveness: Performance in a Mediatized Culture*, Second Edition. New York: Routledge.
Barthes, Roland. 1977. *Image-Music-Text*. Hill and Wang.
Baudrillard, Jean. 1994. *Simulacra and Simulation*. Ann Arbor: University of Michigan Press.
Baudrillard, Jean. 2005. *The Intelligence of Evil or tile Lucidity Pact*. New York: Berg.
Blier-Carruthers, Amy. 2020. "The Problem of Perfection in Classical Recording: The Performer's Perspective." *The Musical Quarterly* 103 (1–2): 184–236.
Bregman, Albert S. 1990. *Auditory Scene Analysis: The Perceptual Organization of Sound*. Cambridge, MA: MIT Press.
Buhler, James. 2019. *Theories of the Soundtrack*. New York: Oxford University Press.
Buhler, James. 2021. *Music, Digital Audio, Labor: Notes on Audio and Music Production for Contemporary Action Film. Music in Action Film: Sounds like Action!* New York: Routledge.

Chion, Michel. 1994. *Audio-vision: sound on screen*. New York: Columbia University Press.
Chion, Michel. 2009. *Film, a Sound Art*. New York, NY: Columbia University Press.
Cook, Nicholas. 2013a. "Bridging the Unbridgeable? Empirical Musicology and Interdisciplinary Performance Studies." In *Taking It to the Bridge: Music as Performance*, edited by Cook Nicholas and Pettengill Richard, 70–85. University of Michigan Press.
Cook, Nicholas. 2013b. "Beyond Music: Mashup, Multimedia Mentality, and Intellectual Property." In *The Oxford Handbook of New Audiovisual Aesthetics*, edited by Richardson John, Gorbman Claudia and Vernallis Carol, 53–76. Oxford University Press, USA.
d'Escriván, Julio. 2012. *Music Technology*. Cambridge, UK: Cambridge University Press.
De Souza, Jonathan. 2017. *Music at Hand: Instruments, Bodies, and Cognition*. New York, NY: Oxford University Press.
De Souza, Jonathan. 2018. "Orchestra Machines, Old and New." *Organised Sound* 23 (2): 156–166.
De Souza, Jonathan. 2021. "Timbral Thievery: Synthesizers and Sonic Materiality." In *The Oxford Handbook of Timbre*, edited by I. Dolan Emily and Rehding Alexander, 346–379. New York: Oxford University Press.
Dolan, Emily. 2012. "Toward a Musicology of Interfaces." *Keyboard Perspectives* 5: 1–13.
Dolan, Emily. 2013. *The Orchestral Revolution: Haydn and the Technologies of Timbre*. Cambridge, UK: Cambridge University Press.
Dolan, Emily, and Thomas Patteson. 2021. "Ethereal Timbres." In *The Oxford Handbook of Timbre*, edited by Emily Dolan and Alexander Rehding. Oxford University Press.
Eco, Umberto. 1990. *Travels in Hyperreality (Harvest Book)*. Mariner Books.
Heyde, Herbert. 1975. *Grundlagen des natürlichen Systems der Musikinstrumente*. Leipzig: VEB Deutscher Verlag für Musik.
Hornbostel, Erich M. von, and Curt Sachs. 1961. "Classification of Musical Instruments." *The Galpin Society Journal* 14: 3–29. https://doi.org/10.2307/842168.
Knakkergaard, Martin. 2015. "The Music That's Not There." In *The Oxford Handbook of Virtuality*. New York, NY: Oxford University Press Inc
Linoff, Marci. 2022. "How to Become a Motion Capture Actor." https://www.backstage.com/magazine/article/how-to-become-a-motion-capture-actor-73824/.
Mayfield, Matt. 2012. "AF002 Audio Domains and Waves." https://www.youtube.com/watch?v=I__cjo82SQY.

Mayfield, Matt. 2016. "The Acoustic, Analog, and Digital Domains - Digital Audio Foundations Video Tutorial: Linkedin Learning, Formerly Lynda.com." https://www.linkedin.com/learning/digital-audio-foundations/the-acoustic-analog.

McLuhan, Marshall. [1964] 1994. *Understanding Media: The Extensions of Man.* Cambridge, Mass.: MIT Press.

Mera, Miguel. 2016. "Materializing Film Music." In *The Cambridge Companion to Film Music*, edited by Cooke Mervyn and Ford Fiona, 157–172. Cambridge: Cambridge University Press.

Owsinski, Bobby. 2013. *The Mixing Engineer's Handbook*, 3rd Edition. Cengage Learning PTR.

Pejrolo, Andrea, and Scott B. Metcalfe. 2017. *Creating Sounds from Scratch: A Practical Guide to Music Synthesis for Producers and Composers.* New York, NY: Oxford University Press.

Prince, Stephen. 1996. "True lies: perceptual realism, digital images, and film theory." *Film Quarterly* 49 (2): 27–37. https://doi.org/10.2307/1213468.

Prince, Stephen. 2010. "Through the Looking Glass: Philosophical Toys and Digital Visual Effects." *Projections* 4 (2): 19–40. https://doi.org/10.3167/proj.2010.040203.

Prince, Stephen. 2012. *Digital Visual Effects in Cinema: The Seduction of Reality.* Rutgers University Press.

Schaeffer, Pierre. 2017. *Treatise on Musical Objects: Essays across Disciplines.* Translated by Christine North and John Dack. Oakland, CA: University of California Press.

Smalley, Denis. 1994. "Defining timbre - Refining timbre." *Contemporary Music Review* 10 (2): 35–48. https://doi.org/10.1080/07494469400640281.

Staier, Andreas. 1997. Schubert, F. – The Late Piano Sonatas D 958 - 960. Teldec - Das Alte Werk.

Tommasini, Anthony. 2013. "Wearing a Wire at the Opera, Secretly, of Course." https://www.nytimes.com/2013/06/30/arts/music/wearing-a-wire-at-the-opera-secretly-of-course.html.

Turgeon, Sebastien. 2019. "The Problematic Case of Sound Amplification at the Royal Swedish Opera." Opera Wire. https://operawire.com/the-problematic-case-of-sound-amplification-at-the-royal-swedish-opera/.

CHAPTER 4

The Digital Tools for the Hyperorchestra: MIDI, Virtual Instruments, and Digital Music

THE END OF PEN AND PAPER: THE TOOLKIT FOR THE CONTEMPORARY SCREEN COMPOSER

With the digital revolution, the iconic image of a composer writing at the piano using a pen and staff paper has been replaced, at least for screen composers, by a spaceship-looking computer desk with multiple screens. Pen and staff paper, while not wholly extinct, have been relegated to a minimal role in the music creation process. These computer workstations revolve around two pieces of software: the DAW and a set of virtual instruments hosted in a computer system. Generally, the computer in the DAW connects to one or more hardware devices capable of sending MIDI messages (such as a musical keyboard). At the very least, the workstation also includes an audio interface hardware device to output high-quality sound to either speakers or headphones. In addition, the workstation might include optional audio hardware devices such as effects processors or hardware synthesizers connected directly to the audio interface. This chapter focuses on these tools with a predominant emphasis on virtual instruments.

Virtual instruments are a centerpiece of the system, as composers generally have extensive collections of those that keep updating. An essential subset of virtual instruments employs audio samples—sample-based virtual instruments—but are usually referred to in the industry as sample libraries. These virtual instruments contain numerous short audio recordings (samples) of an instrument aiming to create an interactive digital

© The Author(s), under exclusive license to Springer Nature Switzerland AG 2024
S. Casanelles, *The Hyperorchestra*,
https://doi.org/10.1007/978-3-031-75193-6_4

replica. While this is a reason why the name "sample library" is appropriate, the origin of the term comes before the introduction of software samplers. Hardware samplers were a type of digital synthesizer that allowed the user to record short sounds (the sample) from which to generate a virtual instrument. Software samplers, along with exponential increase in computing power, allowed for a single sampled instrument to contain massive amounts of samples from which to be generated. Hardware samplers allowed for one or just a few. One of the tasks of the composer/user of the hardware samples was to collect and organize an expanding set of sounds to be used to program the sampler: the sample library. Dave Stewart published in 1994 a historically illuminating article called *Organising Your Sample Library*. In the article, Steward suggests techniques on how to record the best samples and how to store them, but mostly how to organize and name them so they become a usable library. Steward acknowledges himself as an early adopter of the technology by purchasing the first sampler in the market, released in 1981: the E-mu systems Emulator. Software samplers added a layer between the samplers and the samples: the virtual instrument. However, the term sample library was repurposed to refer to these virtual instruments as well.

Their capacity to create virtual versions of the instruments commonly found in all classical musical scores for the screen (primarily using the Western orchestra) made them a vital asset. Nowadays, they are an indispensable tool for screen music. Therefore, a sample library commonly refers to a set of virtual instruments that utilize an extensive collection of samples to produce sound. For example, a sample library that intends to replicate a violin ensemble playing a short staccato will contain several samples for each pitch the violin section can play. Sample libraries do not generally make their sample files easily accessible to their users. Instead, they are an integral part of virtual instrument programming.

Virtual instruments utilize the MIDI communication protocol. The introduction of MIDI in 1983 (labeled later as MIDI 1.0) facilitated the utilization of computer-aided technology for creating music. MIDI provided the grounds for establishing a new paradigm for music creation, which was different from the two main modes of music making: writing in staff paper music to be performed or using improvisation along with performance practices (and human memory) to generate music on the spot. Virtual instruments utilize MIDI to interact with the composer, constrained by MIDI's definition. In other words, MIDI provides a framework that delimits the musical instructions a composer can provide to operate a virtual instrument (or a physical instrument that uses MIDI). At the same time, it also constrains the design and conception of these virtual instruments, as the MIDI protocol determines which data input they might receive. Therefore, I will begin this chapter by describing and analyzing MIDI as a technological interface and exploring how MIDI's implementation relates to the models of Western musical practice. It will serve as a foundation to define the importance and influence of such an interface in contemporary music production. For clarity, I will provide a short historical overview of the evolution of sampled-based virtual instruments. It will lead to a description of their main technical aspects. The second part of the chapter is devoted to providing a typology for virtual instruments based on their function and design.

The Interface Effect and the Musical Instruments Digital Interface

Of the four words in the MIDI acronym, Interface is the only one that requires some discussion. Even though we generally use interface to refer to computer-related inputting tools, the idea of an interface can be generalized beyond computer input devices. Alexander Galloway (2012) succinctly describes interfaces as "those mysterious zones of interaction that mediate between different realities," which implies that "interfaces are not things, but rather processes that effect a result of whatever kind." Therefore, "Interfaces themselves are effects, in that they bring about transformations in material states. But at the same time, interfaces are themselves the effects of other things, and thus tell the story of the larger forces that engender them." Therefore, in a similar manner as to how McLuhan (1964) stated that "the media is the message," Galloway suggests we look into the effects of using specific interfaces, not only by what they produce but also by why they were chosen or created.

For instance, a person might be capable of using musical interfaces such as a violin, a piano, or a digital keyboard with a computer system to generate music. On the other hand, if the person uses a typewriter, the expected result from using this device would be to produce text (of course, everything evolves, and, nowadays, the typewriter has musical qualities that have been frequently utilized since the first decade of the twenty-first century). Therefore, the interface is central to producing the desired result. In this case, we need to use a music-generating interface to generate music.

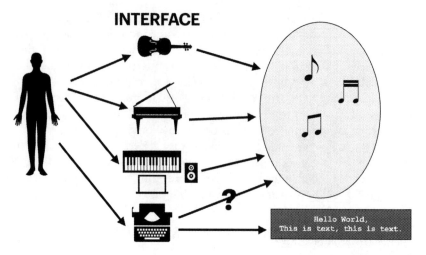

Fig. 4.1 Conceptual representation of an interface

What is relevant about Galloway's approach to interfaces is that it emphasizes the importance of examining the particular effects that an interface has on the result (Fig. 4.1).

Therefore, if we use a violin to produce music, we will generate violin music. Likewise, based on Galloway's approach, the interface becomes the effect of the culture it inhabits and, in this particular situation, the associations we give to the sound of a violin and how it is used to encode meaning. Interfaces can also evolve and expand. For instance, a text-only-based communication interface such as the one produced by the typewriter has evolved since the advent of instant communication devices to incorporate an ever-growing set of meaningful icons (first, emotional icons or emoticons, and later generalized as emojis). Following the previous approach, the effect of this expansion of an interface does not only imply that there is an added set of outputs (the emojis) available in the interface but that the effect of this addition reshapes our culture and the way we communicate. For instance, these emojis also highlight a change in society, and at the same time, they serve as tools that trigger further social and cultural transformations.

In Chap. 3, I described how the musical keyboard added an extra level of mediation for music production, acting as an interface between humans, a specific music theory, and sound production. The extra mediation layer was achieved mainly by establishing the 12-tone system as the standard system for Western music. One of the keys to the success of MIDI as a musical technology, which has lasted several decades without any significant change in its definition, is that its design affords a great degree of flexibility while at the same time allowing a natural and practical implementation of the Western canonic musical system.[1] Thus, MIDI is a remarkably flexible interface (or, at least, it has been made into) that is also practical in codifying Western musical practice.

Formally speaking, MIDI is a communication protocol, which implies that it is an interface that allows for interaction between other interfaces. From this viewpoint, MIDI is similar to the Western musical score, which acts as a communication protocol between two humans who either use an instrument to produce music or provide instructions in the score for how to perform it. Similarly, some attributes of the musical keyboard, which acts as an interface between the performer and the actual generation of the sound, relate conceptually with the inherent principles of MIDI. In other words, a keyboard facilitates the communication between a performer and a range of instruments that utilize the keyboard (piano, harpsichord, organ) in a comparable manner that a myriad of electronic musical devices are designed to employ MIDI to facilitate its use.

However, the differences between MIDI, the musical keyboard, and the score are numerous. For instance, the keyboard is reasonably objective as an interface: two identical events will regularly generate two identical sounds. However, the keyboard is sturdily charged with cultural connotations. Its 12-tone structure, divided into seven white keys and five black keys, suggests a seven-tone organization, which might condition the music produced with it. Technically speaking, on a keyboard instrument, it is generally easier to perform music that follows Western tonal principles than music that does not. Similarly, the keyboard prevents a flexible approach to the sound it produces, as it only allows the performer to depress and release the keys (a violin allows the performer to utilize many more techniques, for example). If the performer wishes to expand the sounds produced by the piano, they need to bypass the keyboard and directly interact with the strings.

The musical score is ambiguous and subjective, generating differing interpretations for most terms (e.g., dynamics or articulations). Utilizing the score as an interface requires a system for interpreting its symbols based not only on a direct musical translation but especially on discrete cultural practices. Even though the design of the musical score is culturally

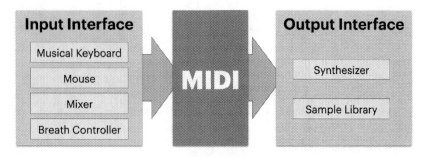

Fig. 4.2 Graphical schematic to represent MIDI communication

biased toward a Western classical musical model, it allows for a greater degree of flexibility compared to the keyboard. For instance, it is possible to notate extended techniques without significantly altering the most traditional notation.

MIDI allows for a great degree of flexibility while maintaining the objectivity associated with a communication protocol that needs to be programmed. For instance, programming a *crescendo* in MIDI will render a precise interpretation of the musical expression: it is both composition and performance. As a formal (computerized) communication system, MIDI comprises distinct types of messages designed for varying functions. One important aspect is that MIDI implements Western musical standards almost naturally while opening the door for other organizational systems. In other words, the flexibility and ease of implementation of Western music are achieved by a design that preserves enough elements from a Western musical framework without significantly compromising the possibilities of the interface. To that end, MIDI has been used to control and trigger live events that are not exclusively musical, which proves its flexibility.

Analogously to the musical score, MIDI is a communication protocol that acts as an interface between other interfaces. Figure 4.2 describes a preliminary (and simple) visual representation of this communication:

A Brief Overview of MIDI Messages

In this section, I provide a conceptual, limited, and very brief overview of MIDI messages as they relate to the current discussion.[2] This is not, by any means, a technical overview or a comprehensive conceptual description of MIDI. Instead, I provide an outline of the MIDI implementation most commonly used in virtual instruments. MIDI comprises a few distinct types of messages philosophically conceived to model the musical experience. In equivalence with Western practices, MIDI includes two main types of messages: the notes and the continuous controllers (CCs). All messages are time-stamped—they happen over time—regulated by the equivalent of a metronome. The note is central to the protocol, thus making it note-centric. However, the flexibility in implementing both types of messages is remarkable. By definition, two types of MIDI messages generate the musical note: a "Note On" and a "Note Off." In other words, a MIDI note is like a switch that can be turned on or off. It is a definition that facilitates the implementation of Western musical notes, which, by definition, are precisely timed pitches. In the Western musical framework, the Note On marks when a note or musical sound should start, and the Note Off marks when this particular event should end.

Each MIDI instrument is allowed enough different notes to map the modern piano, which has 88 keys.[3] However, strictly by its definition, each note is just a different number within a defined range. Therefore, this means that each MIDI instrument has a distinct number of on/off switches if we use the previous analogy. Further, MIDI notes do not have direct Western musical connotations, such as octave, scale, or pitch, as they are merely numbers. Although MIDI notes have no direct connection to pitch, it is easy to associate the piano notes with MIDI notes, as aforementioned. In addition, each MIDI note has another associated value called velocity. Thus, each Note On message has only one velocity value. The velocity name comes because this value is usually created by measuring the depressing speed of the keys in a MIDI keyboard. A higher speed encodes a higher velocity.

Continuous Controllers, the other core message type, are disassociated from the notes. Their values affect the whole instrument.[4] Similarly to MIDI notes, there is a finite number of possible Continuous Controllers (CC), which also have a value inside a numeric range. Therefore, they do not have a start or an endpoint. Instead, the Continuous Controller message changes the value of the controller at a given time, with the assumption that it will remain the same until there is a subsequent change.

In sum, MIDI was firstly designed with a Western music perspective in mind while focusing on the nascent market of synthesizers and other electronic musical instruments (mostly keyboard-based) that were developed at that time and required a standard to communicate and interact. Thus, the protocol was designed to be note-centric, as with keyboard instruments. At the same time, it allowed for additional parameters to be encoded and transmitted using Continuous Controllers (for instance, the overall volume of the instrument) that were generally associated with knobs or faders. While very flexible, this model is undoubtedly limited. For example, let us explore two aspects of a violin performance not immediately encoded in this model: a *glissando* and the capacity to play the same note using different strings. A *glissando* defies the concept of a note on and off model, while the overall notion of a note struggles when the same musical note can be achieved by playing in different strings, carrying a different timbre. Therefore, within this framework and with the subsequent development in virtual instrument design, a primal aspect to consider is how to associate different musical properties with distinct types of MIDI messages and values. This process is usually defined as mapping.

MIDI Mapping, Musical Mapping

Mapping is the process of associating one item from a set (e.g., the keys of a musical keyboard) with items from a second set (a note value in MIDI). In the context of this discussion, I distinguish two different types of mapping. First, there is a mapping between the devices we use to input MIDI and the MIDI protocol. Therefore, the model described in the previous figure implies that, by utilizing input interfaces, it is possible to map their events into MIDI messages.[5] Thus, a MIDI keyboard is a physical interface that converts a set of inputs produced by a musical keyboard into a set of MIDI messages. The mappings that convert physical gestures into MIDI values are arbitrary and do not necessarily follow any specific pattern. However, all MIDI keyboards are expected to map their events similarly into a conventional set of MIDI messages.

Moreover, different inputting devices are generally better suited for specific MIDI events. For instance, faders or knobs easily map Continuous Controllers, while keys are better fit for MIDI notes. The output interfaces (virtual instruments, synthesizers) will convert the MIDI messages they receive into sound depending on an arbitrary mapping that associates a sound with a particular set of MIDI information in the manner that best fits the needs of the instrument's design.

For instance, a MIDI keyboard will generally implement MIDI by associating each of its keys with a MIDI command that generates Note On events when they are depressed and Note Off events when they are released. In addition, it generates a velocity value based on how fast the note was pressed. The MIDI keyboard might not provide data for any of the Continuous Controllers, which will be assumed to have a default constant value unless the keyboard has faders or knobs that are associated with a Continuous Controller number. Similarly, a device such as a drum pad will also assign a distinct MIDI note number to each of its buttons. Thus, this implementation does not assume any particular pitch to be associated with any specific key or sound property of the sound to either a CC or the velocity value.[6]

The concept of mapping is also helpful in analyzing how designers use MIDI to create virtual instruments. If the virtual instrument attempts to replicate an existing physical instrument, the mapping process involves understanding the fundamental aspects that define this instrument. A piano virtual instrument is possibly the most simple mapping process. A virtual piano will have each of the keys become a MIDI note number (that will coincide with the MIDI note number of physical MIDI keyboards), and the note's velocity will determine the dynamic level. Additionally, CCs can be used to indicate if any of the piano pedals are being used. However, only some of the physical properties of the piano are easy to map in MIDI. For instance, it is unclear how to map the double escapement action in all grand pianos suitably using MIDI in a user-friendly manner. Non-key instruments are generally much more complex to map into MIDI accurately, leading us to the importance of the interface effect.[7]

The Effect of MIDI

In this section, I examine the effect that MIDI (1.0) had on music creation while examining how composers have thus far utilized this effect. Earlier, I stated that MIDI was a flexible protocol. I also suggested that MIDI encodes Western practices with ease. Encoding other musical systems is more convoluted, though generally possible. While a superficial inquiry might suggest the MIDI effect is minimal, I believe it cannot be overlooked. Further, it is essential to examine the effect of MIDI in terms of usability (the UX experience) for its target user: musicians. I divided the effect of MIDI into four areas.

The first area relates to the limited human capabilities in multidimensional thinking. Thus, a MIDI implementation of a virtual instrument unnatural to human thought will be impractical, rendering it useless. For instance, imagine a MIDI design that attempts to codify a violin performance using as many parameters as possible. Theoretically, MIDI would allow us to use different continuous controllers to determine, independently, the amount of bow pressure, the direction of the bow, the speed of the bow, the pressure of the finger in the left hand, the speed of the vibrato movement on the left finger, the string used to perform the MIDI note, the position of the bow, or the part of the bow used at each time. While a violin performer can keep track of all these parameters at once when performing, a MIDI programmer would struggle if they had to control each feature independently to render a virtual violin performance.

Further, it most likely would require more practice than learning to play the violin, making the solution impractical. The target users of virtual instruments are generally composers interacting with hundreds of virtual instruments simultaneously. Thus, the solution above becomes unsuitable for their needs. Conversely, a reasonable UX design should force interfaces, such as virtual instruments, to add an intermediary layer to negotiate some sound parameters automatically.

The second area of the MIDI effect revolves around the centrality of the MIDI note with a single attribute in the protocol. This means a MIDI note only has a note value and a velocity value. Following the example of the violin, a note can be played in multiple ways or articulations. However, due to the centrality of the MIDI note, virtual instruments tend to become articulation-specific.[8] A violin *tremolo* will become a virtual instrument different from a *pizzicato* violin, although they might represent the same physical instrument. Consequently, a musical passage that includes a violin playing a *tremolo* articulation simultaneously while playing left-hand *pizzicato* will need to be rendered with two virtual instruments. Moreover, Continuous Controllers affect the whole instrument as they are not note-specific.[9] Thus, polyphonic dynamic variation (having several notes with different dynamic shapes) would require two or more MIDI 1.0 instruments to modify the CCs that affect each line separately.[10] This all means that the music creator who wishes to use virtual instruments must detach from the physical act of performance (such as a violinist performing several string techniques). Thus, an effect of MIDI is that it forces users to think virtually and be much more sonically oriented. For example, it is easier to go beyond what is physically plausible in a violin performance once the composer uses one virtual instrument for the *pizzicato* and another playing the *tremolo* sound.

The third area of effect refers to a fundamental design decision: MIDI does not transport sound, just messages. Sound processors, such as reverberation effects, utilize an audio input to generate an audio output. Thus, the MIDI protocol is not a valid interface for such musical devices. Sound processors (e.g., equalizers) require another interface design to be appropriately integrated into the workflow of digital music creation.[11] This interface is integrated into the software that commonly serves as the platform to negotiate with digital sound creation: the DAW. As software, DAWs have evolved to integrate the programming of MIDI to generate sounds through virtual instruments (originally referred to as sequencing) with the capacity to record, edit, and manipulate sound. Common DAWs that are used to create screen music (e.g., Logic Pro or Cubase) started as software sequencers (they were only able to handle MIDI information). On the other hand, the leading software in audio recording (ProTools) started as an audio manipulation tool only. Strictly speaking, ProTools was a DAW, as it provided a virtual platform to record and edit audio that was analogous to the recording studio. With the development of computer technology and the increase in computing power, these two approaches merged in the modern DAW that is able to handle both. Thus, we now refer to a DAW as a software that is capable of recording, editing, mixing, and processing audio at the same time that is capable of sequencing MIDI and host virtual instruments that generate audio that is fed into the audio part of the DAW.

In the modern DAW, the user can modify and interact with the sound result of virtual instruments without leaving the DAW interface. The capacity of DAWs to integrate MIDI and sound simultaneously facilitates the integration of recorded sounds without the need to implement a MIDI layer to interact with them. Figure 4.3 expands on the previous graphical model based on what I just discussed. For clarity, I have only incorporated sample libraries as sound objects (which I called output interface to keep the centrality of MIDI in the chart). The graphic shows the different layers of mediation between the inputs from the composer and the people who recorded and created the library. In addition, it shows the dual input process that the composers are afforded to modify and program the sound results.

The fourth and final area of the MIDI effect concerns MIDI's graphical representations to become a feasible interface for music making. All DAWs visualize MIDI with a variation of what is referred to as a piano roll view.[12] It has a solid link to the Western musical score by using measures to show

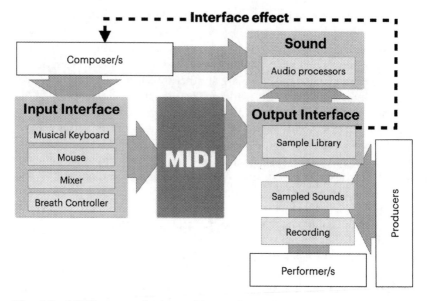

Fig. 4.3 MIDI communication and human interaction

musical events over time. However, the piano roll is a musical notation system that allows the composer to be more specific regarding the desired resulting sound than in a traditional musical score, as it is meant to represent a performance. Yet, it comes at the cost of decreased readability and the inability to write ambiguously (such as writing *crescendo*), assuming that a performer would later interpret the instructions. Figure 4.4—which will be confusing for anyone who is not used to this interface—represents how the piano roll looks like in most DAWs.

Let's unroll the piano roll view based on an equivalency with the musical score. Similarly to the score, it is read left to right based on measure numbers. In the MIDI note area (the top region), we find the notes in a manner similar to the score. The beginning of each rectangle marks the start of a note, and the end of the rectangle determines when the note ends. Thus, the length of each rectangle is the equivalent to the duration of a note. The MIDI keyboard at the left indicates the pitch of each lane. Instead of a 5-line staff paper, the piano roll has a lane per pitch using the Western 12-tone system. For instance, the first note in the representation above indicates that an E3 starts at measure 1 and ends after the first beat

4 THE DIGITAL TOOLS FOR THE HYPERORCHESTRA: MIDI, VIRTUAL... 119

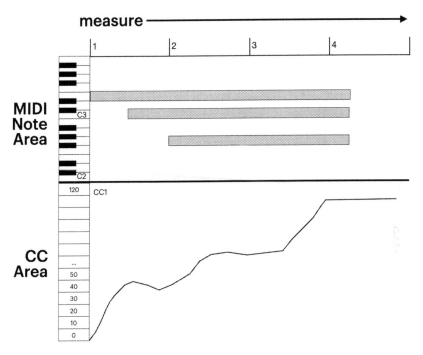

Fig. 4.4 Generic representation of a piano roll in a DAW

of measure 4. Thus, the graphic represents the following notes: E3, C3, and G2, which start every two beats and are all held until the end of the first beat in measure 4. In addition, the color intensity of each rectangle generally indicates the velocity of each note.

The other area is reserved to represent the Continuous Controllers (CCs). It is multidimensional because there are several different CCs (DAWS approach this area differently, some of them showing only one at a time and others representing several CCs). In the representation above, the area shows the values of CC1 (Continuous Controller number 1). This does not have a direct connection to the Western score. However, if CC1 was used to program the dynamics of the instrument, the graphic would represent the dynamic shape of the passage. In this case, the passage represents an overall nonlinear *crescendo*, which tends to be an accurate representation of how performers approach a *crescendo* marking (increasing the dynamic in an expressive manner instead of mathematically linearly).

The piano roll view highlights MIDI's note-centric design while allowing the user multiple types of control. The note area is fundamentally equivalent to how notes are represented in the score. However, as this was not designed for human sight reading, it is less compact and visually guiding compared to the 5-stave score model. It makes certain musical elements easier to represent (clusters), but it is more challenging to sight read (yet not impossible).

Looking into the interface effect of MIDI helps to explain why virtual instruments are designed the way they are, their constraints, and the creative ways that instrument designers have envisioned to overcome them. At the same time, it becomes a first step in examining the implications that using these technologies has had in the realm of music aesthetics and how creatives collaborate and distribute work. Before inquiring into how these virtual instruments operate, it is time to examine yet another interface effect: the effect of the MIDI mockup. The MIDI mockup, realized with sampled-based virtual instruments, transformed how creatives in the screen industry communicated and how they performed their teamwork.

The Effect of the Mockup: Replica and Simulacra of the Film Orchestra

The term mockup became ubiquitous in the screen music industry at the turn of the millennium. Succinctly, a mockup is a computer simulation of a piece of music, mostly applied to screen music. The book *On the Track* (Karlin and Wright 2004)—which captured the practice at the time—defined the term as the "electronic or acoustic audio replications of the music (sometimes a blend of both) varying in quality from rough demos to finely polished performances" (762). Similarly, composer Hans Zimmer explained how he started to incorporate the mockup as a tool to communicate between the creative teams of a movie soon after he arrived in Hollywood in the late 1980s:

> "When I first came to Hollywood, most people were still writing [music] on pieces of paper," he says. "The first time a director would actually get to hear something would be when the orchestra was wheeled in, which I didn't think was very efficient. I mean, there's a huge emotional distance playing somebody something on a piano and shouting at them, 'This is where the

French horns come in!' as opposed to at least [playing] an imitation of the French horns coming in." (Vary 2013)

Karlin and Wright's definition includes the possibility of recording several acoustic instruments that would be included in the mockup. These acoustic/electric instruments would generally be recorded in the composer's studio and integrated into the electronic track. Nevertheless, at the heart of the popularization of the mockup process are the sampled-based virtual instruments (known as sample libraries) that aim to reproduce orchestral instruments.

The exponential evolution of technology, especially in the first decade of the twenty-first century, made the mockup ubiquitous in screen scoring. Later, it rendered the concept outdated when virtually generated musical parts became routinely part of the final mixes. Hence, one of the effects of the mockup is that it stopped being just a mockup. This is the reason why the term mockup started to fade away at the beginning of the second decade of the twenty-first century, but not before a greater degree of ambiguity was added to the idea.

So, from this perspective, what is a mockup? The truth is that the combination of the exponential development of the technologies associated with the production of mockups and its almost exclusive use inside the industry precludes us from providing an established definition of the concept. To make things more challenging, the concept started to fade away in the industry in the second decade of the twenty-first century, diminishing even more the need for an established definition. Nevertheless, I believe that a definition of a mockup is important for historical purposes, to understand better the development of the technologies associated with the process, and to distinguish a subset of contemporary production practices. Below, I outline three possible definitions of a mockup, from which I propose to use the first one.

1. A computer simulation of an orchestra before an orchestral recording replaces it. This definition would allow some non-orchestral instruments to be part of the mockup, but generally in a restricted fashion.
2. Computer-generated elements that use sampled-based virtual instruments of a screen score. In other words, everything in a screen score that was not recorded in a traditional sense or was not clearly

coming from synthesizers. I call these elements an intrinsic part of hyperorchestral writing.
3. Drafts, sketches, or demos of a screen score before it is finalized (regardless of whether the elements will be replaced or not) are often referred to simply as demos or sketches, especially when knowing that recordings will replace none or only a small part of the musical elements.

While I restricted the scope of this text to philosophy and aesthetics, I feel that it is necessary to add the economic side of recording a Western orchestra in order to contextualize the emergence of mockups. In other words, if an orchestra was comprised of two or three performers instead of 80 or even more, I believe that the mockup, as I outlined in the first definition, would not have truly developed. To record an orchestra involves thousands of pages of scores that are created, printed, and taped by a team of orchestrators and music preparation services. It involves dozens of highly skilled musicians who are recorded in a dedicated space that contains expensive and state-of-the-art technology that is produced and managed by a team of engineers, mixers, and support staff. In other words, an orchestral recording is not only expensive but also a logistic endeavor.

Western composers, especially since instrumental timbre became more important in the compositional process, devoted many hours to mastering an imperfect capacity to imagine how an orchestra would sound in their minds. The fact that post-performance revisions of their compositions were frequent indicates the limitations of this imagination process and the tediousness of writing an orchestral piece without any accidental notation imprecisions. Film and screen music had the added challenge of needing to be discussed with the rest of the film creative team.

Therefore, the capacity to create a simulation of an orchestral performance had a clear utility. First, it allowed the composer to hear a simulation of their music that could contribute to both enhancing their capacity to imagine the final result and quickly catching notation mistakes that are fairly easy to miss. As I will exemplify later, the development of the mockup technology also improved the working conditions of the composers by allowing them to hear sounds that were more amenable to our ears. Further, the mockups allowed for better communication with the director and the creative team with the objective of getting the music recorded in the most efficient way possible to avoid the need for changes during the recording (e.g., the director or producer asking for an instrument to be removed because they do not like how it sounds) or even for the need to re-do and re-record parts of the score. From this perspective, the mockup should sound like both a close but inferior version in every aspect of the final orchestral recording.

Based on this definition, the mockup concept starts to collapse the first time a director tells a composer that they prefer the mockup—or certain aspects of it—over the orchestral recording. When that happened, naïve recommendations between screen composers could include something like, "You should create a mockup good enough for the director to get an impression of how the music will sound but not too good that they feel that there is no need to record or, worse, that after the recording, they prefer the mockup." However, the virtualization process acts like an intense gravitational pull that, once it crosses a threshold, attracts everything into a simulation. It is a process not dissimilar to the Disneyland allegory I discussed in the previous chapters: virtually created music might appear more realistic than what the real could produce in its capacity to obey and satisfy the needs of a program better than its acoustic and naturalistic counterparts. Thus, in their pursuit of a great replica, mockup artisans developed techniques that went beyond the replication ideal—which also triggered the development of virtual instruments—in order to achieve a higher degree of *realism*, which should be understood as an aim for the perfect verisimilitude.

To better understand this inevitable transformation, let's go back to the initial process of mocking up an orchestral piece. Similar to how music notation programs still operate, a mockup would have one virtual instrument for each acoustic instrument of the orchestra, with the exception of the string section which would get one instrument per section. In other words, one virtual instrument per staff line in an uncompressed orchestral score. The need for a more accurate rendition of the music triggered some basic expansions. For instance, instead of just having one virtual instrument with one type of violin section sound, the mockup would have several virtual instruments that contained collections of samples that encompassed different performance modes of the instrument (short notes, long notes, tremolo notes, and so on). Now, instead of one single Violin I virtual instrument aimed to replicate the Violin I acoustic section, there were several ones that could be easily joined together at the orchestration stage because two articulations for the same instrument or section would not be programmed at the same time ... until they were. At some point, someone noticed that the sound of strings playing *tremolo* (quietly) under a sustained string moment created the impression of a more emotional and *realistic* rendering of that passage. Thus, the objective was not to suggest to the orchestrator that the first violins should be divided between *tremolo* and sustained techniques but to render, using the available technology, a more emotional and verisimilar sustained passage. Conceptually, though, the limitlessness of the virtual became a part of the process, and it became available, and there was no way back. It is understandable that with the evolution in the quality of these virtual instruments, a director would feel that a sound that combined *tremolo* and sustained strings was different than a very expressive sustained acoustic recording of the same passage. It is also likely that they would prefer the former version for storytelling purposes.

Concomitantly, composers would start to embrace the power of the virtual that was able to be modeled by acoustic realities without the need to be restricted to the limitations of the physical world. I defined this aesthetic attitude as hyperorchestral, which is clearly distinct from the process of creating a temporary mockup that an equivalent acoustic recording will eventually replace. Therefore, while the emergence of the mockup is key for the development of the hyperorchestra, hyperorchestral aesthetics fully develop after its demise.

Let's revisit the definition of sample libraries from the perspective of the mockup as I delineated it. A sample library is a sample-based virtual instrument constructed using a vast collection of typically short recordings from an instrument or a musical ensemble. The recordings are assembled to allow the recreation of a performance of the sampled instrument or ensemble virtually by interpreting MIDI information.[13] Thus, sample libraries aim to become a virtual replica of a physical instrument or ensemble (e.g., the violin I section in an orchestra) to aid the mockup process and to simplify the process of orchestration from the mockup. In the next section, I will provide an overview of the techniques associated with the creation of a sample library. For instance, each note might be recorded multiple times, in various dynamics, with several levels of vibrato, multiple articulations, and using numerous techniques. With this information aggregate, a software called a sampler is built and scripted to generate the output sound result.

Sometimes, sample-based virtual instruments are made with few recordings or do not aim to replicate an instrument and are still called sample libraries due to their similar aesthetic intent and function. For specificity and clarity, I will restrict the definition of a sample library to the original concept while providing a detailed taxonomy of virtual instruments in the second part of this chapter. This allows us to distinguish the original historical function of virtual instruments that were designed as purely mockup tools. In contrast, other virtual instruments, such as synthesizers and sample-based synthesizers, were already used as part of the final product at the time when mockups were emerging.

Historically speaking, Hans Zimmer was a pioneer in establishing the mockup as an indispensable communication tool between the composer team and the rest of the creative team. Further, he was the first to release some of his mockups officially. Frequently called sketchbooks—to utilize a much more familiar term for the audiences—they are fascinating for two reasons beyond their musical value. First, they serve to document the creative process. Second, they become a historical artifact that acts as a blueprint for the state of the art of virtual instruments at a given time. This is because Zimmer was always at the forefront of both the technology and the programming techniques of virtual instruments.

One of Zimmer's most significant innovations in the process of scoring a movie is the creation of a musical suite at the very beginning of the process (frequently at the preproduction stage), inspired by the themes of the movie. Once written, the suite becomes the starting point to discuss the score with the movie's creative team (Hurwitz 2011). Putting aside the aesthetic implications of this process, which broadly imply that the music is less focused on visual synchronization and much more connected with the story's deeper meanings, Zimmer's suites are generally created with virtual instruments. This means they are a valuable tool to capture state-of-the-art snapshots of sampling technology at a given time, as stated above.[14] For instance, in his album *More Music from the Motion Picture "Gladiator,"* Hans Zimmer released a track called *The Gladiator Waltz* (2001), which was a selection from the original suite.

Similarly, in the deluxe edition of the soundtrack album for *The Man of Steel* (2013), the composer released a track called *Man of Steel Hans' Original Sketchbook* (Zimmer 2013). For *Dune*, a 74-minute album called *The Dune Sketchbook* (Zimmer 2021a) was released before the movie's premiere. Comparing the production of these pieces written by Hans Zimmer, arguably the leading composer in creating highly realistic mockups, the evolution that sample libraries have experienced is apparent, especially in the first decade of the twenty-first century.

In a video interview with *Mix with the Masters*, Zimmer (2021b) explains that he and his team have used sample libraries since sampling was invented, corroborating my previous explanation of the advantages of the mockup. The initial objective was to manage to "get directors to feel the intention of the music behind the mockup and let them know what the piece of music is about. What the emotional intent is." Zimmer elaborates even further to explain that, in addition to the communication with the directors, better sample libraries allowed him to both "spend all day [while composing] listening to better sounds" and to "listen to my favorite players" after having sampled them in his custom-made sample libraries.

The mockup track from *Gladiator* (2000) is a testimony of the original function of the mockup: to make the composing experience more pleasant and become a helpful tool to communicate with the director and the rest of the creative team. However, the sketchbook from *Man of Steel* (2013) shows a significantly different picture, in which the sketchbook is no longer a mockup but already incorporates musical elements of the finished product. It also marks the time in which the concept of mockup started to become an inappropriate term to describe these pieces of music and, therefore, an increasingly outdated term.

The mockup can also be analyzed as an interface for communication between creatives. From this viewpoint, it is worth examining the effect of the mockup on the creative process and how its effect implied its evolution beyond being just a mockup. When Zimmer states that sample libraries allowed him to listen to better sounds while working, it highlights their importance in reshaping the creative process. While the following two chapters will focus on developing this radical transformation, for now, I would like to reiterate the transformative importance of utilizing the mockup to open the door to creating hyperorchestral music that effectively invalidates the term. While the initial purpose of the mockup was to serve as an imperfect replica of what would later be recorded in reality, the power of the tools used to produce it quickly surpassed the scope of the mockup to become a means to use models of reality to generate music that could never be replicated in a live performance with only physical means, while completely subverting the process and aesthetics of composing for the screen.

In 2012, Zimmer stated in a reply on the vi-control forum, where the topic was precisely the "Hans Zimmer Sound," that he does not "understand why people don't sample their own stuff." Similarly, in the 2021 interview referred to above, Zimmer explains that generally, each of his projects starts with sampling: "Once I have an idea of what I want to do, then becomes this safari of sampling, you know, it's like we're hunting down sounds, we're making sounds. Each movie has a load of custom sounds in it" (2021a). While the sampling process was not as accessible in 2012 as it became a few years after, and most composers' introduction to producing music for the screen was coming exclusively from commercially available sample libraries, the statement serves to highlight the importance of sampling in the music creation process.

Therefore, an added effect of the mockup is that it puts the process of sampling at the core of the creative process in a manner that makes it unbefitting to describe the vast majority of screen music from the twenty-first century without considering them. Hence, the mockup has evolved from being ubiquitous during the screen music composition process to being diluted when its tools permeated into the final product. In the process, mockup techniques facilitated the generation of a new sonic model for music that has become fundamental in the creation of the hyperorchestra.

The evolution of the mockup to become much more does not imply its total extinction. Traditional orchestral music still plays a role in screen music, which would generally require a mockup process prior to its recording (John Powell's scores of the second decade of the twenty-first century are frequently a good example on that end). However, for clarity purposes, I will still differentiate between what I defined as a mockup and what could be defined as a demo, draft, version, or sketch. The demo is any piece of music that is not final and approved. It might include musical elements that will not be recorded at any stage of development (more or less polished), mockup elements that are meant to be recorded, and broad textures that might or might not end up being recorded. The role of the demos is to become an iterative tool for creative conversation with the rest of the filmmaking team for the music to be approved. Sometimes, this involves incorporating some or all the recording parts before the demo gets the full approval to become the finished cue.

Next, I will describe some of the most prominent sampling techniques. After, I will delve into a process to classify and explain the different types of sample-based virtual instruments.

Modeling the Real: Sampling Techniques for the Hyperreal Production

As I just described, the mockup's original goal was to create a musical piece that was close to how the subsequent Western orchestral recording would sound. Further, the mockup would also ideally facilitate the orchestration process later on and smooth the transition of staff-paper composers into the virtual. In other words, a composer who wrote orchestral scores in a traditionl sense would feel the nascent mockup process to be more user-friendly if it replicated their composition process. While the utilization of digital technologies unfolded composition approaches that were completely detached from staff-based composition, it is understandable that the earlier stages of development incorporated and took into consideration centuries of Western musical composition practice.

A subset of orchestral sample libraries is the primary tool for creating mockups. To fulfill the staff-writing equivalency goal I outlined, sample libraries were designed to generate virtual instruments that acted as good-enough replicas of their acoustic counterparts that would eventually be used to replace them in the final result. Hence, multiple sample-library design techniques were invented with this goal in mind.

Creating a virtual instrument that models an acoustic instrument means designing a virtual reality system that can produce similar sonic outputs based on human-friendly inputs. In this context, the composer was the person tasked with inputting the information to render the sonic output, which means that the input mimicked the Western orchestral score writing based on pitches. At the same time, generating verisimilar sonic outputs that mimic an acoustic instrument is a rather complex task. The sound of an instrument is the combination of multiple physical bodies vibrating, reinforcing frequencies, bouncing, and so on. For instance, one single long note in a cello might accumulate more overtone content over time as the instrument starts to vibrate, which will also influence the sound of the following note performed by the instrument. Frequencies of the sound might be reinforced or attenuated by the body of the performer, other instruments playing—they also might be reinforcing the sound produced by the cello in their bodies—and so on.

With these two factors in mind and with the objective of creating a good enough temporary rendering meant to be replaced by a recording, the design process of these virtual instruments was established. The design principles that I will outline started by discarding the most complicated acoustic challenges that I just briefly described to focus on an approach that assumed that it was possible to model reality through the deconstruction of it into the smallest but also still meaningful units. This analytical approach has several advantages. First, it allows for an equivalency between music notation concepts (e.g., *sustained* vs *staccato* sounds) and the units that serve as the building blocks for the technology. Second, it discards the acoustic complexities by both acknowledging the temporary function of these virtual instruments and by embracing a sort of Frankenstein-like belief in the capacity to recreate reality out of its own fragments. Third, it is an approach that is similar to how object-oriented programming is defined for modern computer systems. Finally, the design approach is also directly connected to the central axioms used to create synthesizers. This is because a subset of synthesizer design became the first attempt to generate virtual replicas of acoustic instruments. These techniques reside in the sampler, the software responsible for interpreting MIDI information, selecting and processing the sampled sounds of the library, and generating the sound result. Thus, this section describes some of the most salient features that samplers incorporate to model the real.

Let's start with an imaginary example to illustrate these principles: a hypothetical library that aims to reproduce a bowed orchestral string instrument (or string section) when playing legato. Figure 4.5 is an abstract graphical representation of this hypothetical virtual instrument and its MIDI implementation. For the virtual instrument to be able to recreate the instrument, it requires a set of samples. The first critical step is deciding what to sample to replicate the instrument's sound as accurately as possible. For this imaginary virtual instrument, the designers are aiming to replicate the first violin section of an orchestra playing *legato*. A violin section can play a sustained note at a variety of dynamic levels, at varied levels of *legato*, in different strings, with varying bow attacks at the beginning, either up or down bow, and with the bow at various locations in the strings, to name just the most important performance procedures. Moreover, string players would customarily be able to change most of these attributes during the performance of even a single note (for instance, they can start the note without vibrato and increase the vibrato at any given time).

The number of possibilities is already gigantic with only the abovementioned variables. Therefore, deciding what to sample is a process of determining what matters most to capture the sound essence of a given

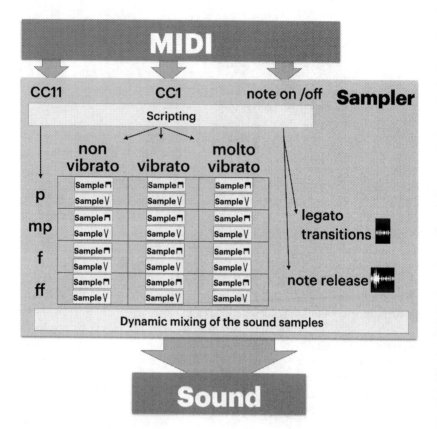

Fig. 4.5 Conceptual graphical representation of the structure of a virtual instrument inside a sampler

instrument to fulfill the role stated before in a manner that the musicians who are being sampled can play. For instance, a musician may have trouble providing samples of a note at 20 different levels of dynamics in the continuum that encompasses the softest sound they can produce to the loudest. Conversely, they will feel comfortable providing four or five dynamic levels that more or less align with the dynamic markings in a score. In the case of this hypothetic (but not unrealistic example), the sample library makers have decided to sample each note (chromatically using the Western scale) in all the possible combinations of

- up bow and down bow,
- four different dynamics (p, mf, f, ff), and
- three different types of vibrato (non-vibrato, regular vibrato, and exaggerated vibrato).

Consequently, for each note, there will be 24 sample recordings that encompass all the possible combinations above (2 bowings × 4 dynamics × 3 possible vibrato states = 24). In addition, the producers will also ask the performers to play each of the notes legato with each of the possible notes that are an octave or less apart in order to capture the sound produced by transitioning from one note into another. If the designers were to capture the sound of the transition at different dynamic levels and various speeds of transition, the number of additional recordings would grow exponentially.

The second important part revolves around combining all the recorded samples to create the best replica of the instrument possible with the given material and, simultaneously, provide an interface for the composer or programmer to interact in a manner that is as natural as possible. MIDI notes will be used for the composer/user to tell the sampler which pitches they intend to program. Because the designers want to offer the possibility to change the dynamic or the amount of vibrato of a note while it is sounding, they will use Continuous Controllers for the user to tell the sampler the dynamic and vibrato level they expect the instrument to be playing. The reason for using CCs is that the MIDI note is only a message that tells for a note to start and another one that tells when to end, but it is not designed to affect a note that is already sounding.

In this example, the information from CC1 (Continuous Controller number 1) will be used to signify the amount of vibrato in the sound. Similarly, CC11 controls the dynamic level. While CC1 and CC11 are common CC numbers used for virtual instrument programming, the decision of which CC number does what is completely arbitrary.[15] MIDI notes will be used to indicate which pitch should be played. Simplifying a bit, the sampler mixes a set of these sounds (selected by using the pair of numbers received from CC1 and CC11) in different volume levels to generate the final sound. When a note changes, a legato transition is triggered to perform the sound of a note transitioning into another. Similarly, the end of a line triggers a note-release sound extracted from the end of the recorded sample.

To summarize, this hypothetical analytic design process identifies Western pitch, bow direction, amount of vibrato, dynamic, and the sound produced when one note slides into another one as the fundamental building blocks to define the sound of a violin playing legato. In addition, it aims to reproduce many dynamic and vibrato levels just by combining a subset of dynamics and vibratos. For example, if the sampling process only recorded a *piano* and a *forte* dynamic, it would aim to create a *mezzoforte* by combining the *piano* and the *forte* recordings together.

This example encapsulates the most common sampling techniques developed to replicate reality virtually from the point of view of the original mockup process—good enough sound before it gets replaced. The success in terms of perceived fidelity of this model was impressive enough that filmmakers quickly started to suggest that the result was good enough as a score for their projects, removing the need for (expensive) recording sessions. At the same time, the aim to make these realizations closer and closer to real acoustic performance started to negate the replicative approach that I outlined so far. Instead, the objective switched to rendering a sound output that was a verisimilar representation of the musical idea instead of the best possible sounding exact replica. When that happens, though, it is less and less likely that an acoustic recording would be able to replace the digital rendition that preceded it. And, if it does, it will be by providing an equivalent emotional shape for the story instead of a better version of the same music.

The original mockup process aimed to create the best possible sense of musicality by generating a sound that was as realistic as possible via replication. The second approach (which I prefer not to call a mockup), though, reverses the approach to acknowledge, as James Buhler suggests, that it is "musicality [that] creates the impression of realism." In doing so, it brings the process closer to how realism is approached in contemporary visual storytelling.[16] While the change might seem trivial or just an expected evolution of the mockup process, it is significant in terms of aesthetics. While the mockup is a computer-generated simulation, it is not hyperorchestral or, at least, it does not highlight a hyperorchestral attitude to music creation. It is closer to Baudrillard's first stage of the simulacra, in which the artists aim to reproduce reality as closely as possible without ever attempting to replace it or surpass it. At the same time, the many economic and practical advantages of the mockup allowed for the quick development of technologies that are at the core of the hyperorchestra while unlocking the aesthetic constraints derived from an acoustic approach to music creation.

Therefore, following the hypothetical virtual sampled instrument above, I will describe these sampling techniques in more detail as they are exemplars of the process and challenges involved in creating a virtual reality of the musical phenomenon. These techniques will inform the following discussion about the typology of sample libraries while highlighting the tensions that emanated from their impossibility of replicating reality fully.

Multiple Performance Techniques

The first step for the analytical project of virtually replicating an instrument is dividing it by distinct performance techniques. Even though a performer can continuously switch from playing *legato* to sustaining sounds to *staccato*, these are different ways to produce sound with the same instrument. Therefore, they will be sampled and treated independently.

For example, a violin sample library will regularly incorporate separate virtual instruments that depict *legato*, sustain, *staccato*, *pizzicato*, harmonics, *tremolo*, *sul ponticello*, and other performance techniques. However, the performance techniques might extend beyond what should be considered regular string techniques. For instance, different types of staccatos might respond to different aesthetic intentions.

Looping and Time Stretching

The looping technique is at the core of even the most basic sustained virtual instrument based on a sample. A sample is a recording of a limited duration, often just about 2 seconds long. The sampler loops the middle of the sample (generally cutting the start and the end as they sound distinctly different) indefinitely until the note is released to recreate the illusion of a longer sustained sound.

As a technique, looping is as indispensable as problematic. The human ear detects a looped sound fairly quickly, breaking the illusion of the real. In addition, for a short sample to be adequate at looping, it must be reasonably stable and neutral, which is one of the reasons why the sounding results of sample libraries are frequently described as dead. Most of the following techniques were developed to diminish the effect of the loop and increase the perception of realistic replication in the sample library. At the same time, the problem of looping remains the main challenge of an approach of virtual instrument creation based on the aim to become a virtual replica of a physical instrument.

Similarly, but way less problematic, is the utilization of time-stretching processes to make samples play at different pitches. Time stretching allows recording as little as just one sample for a whole instrumental range at the expense of sound quality. By using sound processing algorithms, the sampler can adjust the sample's pitch, which increasingly decreases in fidelity when the distance between the original and the new pitch increases. However, time stretching is very effective at smaller intervals, at the expense of aggravating the problem of using loops. If all the contingent notes of the instrument are created with the same sample, it will become more apparent that there are loops even when there is a melody with different pitches. Nevertheless, if recreation is not an objective, time stretching becomes a very powerful tool for sound design.

Layering

Layering is an early sampling technique that has found multiple uses, which is also central to understanding the analytical design model that deals with the limitations of computing power (at the early stages especially), economic resources, recording limitations, and the complexity of the performance experience. The early stages of sample library development involved moving from hardware-based sample machines to software-based samples at a moment in which computers were way behind of what composers needed and what it was able to produce using sampling technology. Hans Zimmer explained how in the mid-1990s, when they were creating their first custom-made orchestral sample library, their original idea was to fit it all in eight Roland S760s hardware samplers (Wherry 2002). It soon became obvious that this was not possible due to the limitations of the hardware, and the library ended up residing in a set of network-connected computers, which were designed especially for the purpose of sampling and were way beyond the capacity of a regular personal computer at the time. Zimmer acknowledged that in 2002, he was using 10 of these computers simultaneously, but his colleague Klaus Badelt, a key person in the development of the library, was using 40. Therefore, at this time, additional computing power involved tens of thousands of dollars and a complicated setup in which computers had to be interconnected with each other. Thus, techniques that served to alleviate the need for additional resources were key even for the top composers at the time.

Layering means combining two or more samples to create the illusion of a different performance technique. For instance, to emulate a sustained note that started with an accented attack, it is possible to combine a sample of a short accented note that will play at the beginning of each note with the sustained sound that will not only play at the start of the note but as long as the note is sustained.

The technique allows for the virtual generation of performances that were not recorded with the hopes that the virtual rendering is convincing enough to seem realistic. Following the example above, instead of recording all possible attacks of a sustained note at all possible levels of dynamic and so on, the attack is layered on top of the existing one with the aim of replacing it (a sustained note would have been recorded with a soft attack).

Another common early use of layering was to increase the verisimilitude of a sustained note. The length of the sample in a sustained virtual instrument is between two and three seconds, which makes the loop recognizable after a few instances. In addition, sampling techniques tend to require a modification of the spectrum in order to make all the samples similar enough so the transitions between them seem to come from the same instrument. One of the first approaches to layering involved using a synthesizer that played a smooth and slightly undulating sinusoidal sound (a sound produced by a sine wave and, therefore, having only one or a very limited number of frequencies on its spectrum) with a sustained sampled instrument. The result increased the perception of verisimilitude of the virtual instrument because it reinforced its fundamental frequencies akin to the resonance chamber of an instrument and because it added some sonic variability that diminished the impression of a loop. Once sampled instruments reached a certain quality and quantity in terms of available products, layering extended to combine two or more libraries that represented the same instrument. For instance, a composer would mix together a sustained cello library from two or three different developers (or different libraries from the same developer). In doing so, the composer was hoping to diffuse the loop because each virtual instrument would have slightly different loop lengths (e.g., if one library loops every 2 seconds and the other one every 2.5 seconds, the combined loop would be its least common multiple, 10 seconds). In addition, each library would have recorded also slightly different areas of the spectrum, which hopefully would represent a more accurate depiction of the sound of the instrument when combined. If each of the virtual instruments is also programmed slightly differently, the variation can be increased significantly more. Another option—which I briefly mentioned above—is to use a layering technique that involves using quietly a tremolo sample to make a sustained sample more alive. It is a very similar technique to using an undulating synth (which uses a software version of a tremolo using what is called amplitude modulation).

Layering can also be achieved at the programming or composing stage after the virtual instruments have been developed. As I will discuss in the following chapters, this has an immense impact on the generation of the hyperorchestra since the concept can be expanded to create new articulations that would not be possible in a real-life performance (e.g., a string ensemble playing *staccato*, *pizzicato*, and *col legno* at the same time).

The layering technique also has problems that demonstrate the impossibility of recreating the sound of a performance from pieces. The main problem revolves around what is known as phasing issues, a rather complex area of music and sound production. Without entering into too much detail, any musical sound is constituted by a repeating pattern that iterates between positive and negative air pressure. If you have the same exact sound twice but you reverse the positive by the negative (and vice versa), you have created a phase-inverted version of the same sound. If you play both of them at the same time, they will cancel each other, and no sound will be produced. The reality is much more complex, though. A string section sounds smooth partially because some frequencies get canceled with each other due to multiple instruments at different distances playing the same type of sound. With these two ideas without much technical specificity, we can deduct that phasing is both a good and a bad thing. When you combine samples from two different libraries to play a duplicated musical line, it is possible that "good" phasing happens, which generates a sound that feels more rounded. At the same time, it is also possible that "bad" phasing happens and eliminates areas of the sound that you were aiming to reinforce. Or worse, it generates a sound that seems like two distinct entities playing at the same time. This last case is a common outcome when trying to apply the layering technique to solo instruments (e.g., individual elements of the woodwind section or solo string moments). This is a known problem with acoustic instruments as well. A well-known orchestration rule states that you need at least three instruments to create a sound that could resemble a section. This is another way of saying that you should generally never double a line with two instruments (you either use one instrument or three or more).

The fact that sound is the result of positive and negative alterations in air pressure, which we translate into positive and negative changes in electricity, poses great challenges for the development of technologies based on significantly processing recordings. Generally, hundreds of hours are spent in what is called phase-locking, ensuring that all the samples within a library start exactly with the same phase. One common problem comes from *vibrato*, which is the slight and undulating alteration of the fundamental frequency of the sound, and it is present in most performance practices at different degrees. Combining two samples that have varying vibrato tends to be a challenge due to phasing, which has been one of the most unsolvable challenges in the analytic approach to sample design.

Deep Sampling

Once computers were powerful enough to handle vast collections of samples, the first approach to attenuate the looping problem was to use as many samples as possible. By capturing as many recordings as possible, the aim is not only to provide a timbre as close as possible to how it would sound in reality but also to distract the human ear with multiple sounds from recognizing loops. It is achieved in two main ways: by capturing multiple dynamics and by sampling the same event multiple times.

One of the barriers that deep sampling faces is the human condition. As I will develop more in the next technique, you cannot ask a performer to provide a reliable set of 20 different dynamic levels on a single note that is stable enough to be usable for integrating into a virtual instrument that can move from sample to sample seamlessly.

Dynamics: Layering and Crossfading

When a performer makes their instrument louder or quieter, the instrument changes the volume of the sound and its timbre. A French horn playing softly or loudly sounds like two vastly different instruments. Therefore, any aim of replicating an instrument virtually requires considering the timbral differences produced by the change in dynamics. Intuitively, a solution is to record the instrument at multiple dynamic levels. MIDI 1.0 would easily allow up to 128 different dynamic levels, but this would be an impossible ask for a human performer. Therefore, a much smaller number of dynamic levels (about 3-5) are generally captured. The sampler's task is to utilize these limited recordings to try to reproduce a dynamic continuum that covers the value range offered by the MIDI protocol.

One approach is to use crossfading, which, in the design of sample libraries, employs a discrete set of sounds and maps them onto an array of numbers to generate a more realistic approach to the sound produced at different musical dynamics. This first approach would combine the recordings with changes in their volume to simulate the dynamic continuum divided by a number of dynamic regions based on the number of dynamic recordings. The instrument would start as quietly as possible using the softest dynamic at a low volume. Then, the volume would increase until it arrived in the new region, beginning with the following dynamic at a lower volume that matches the endpoint of the previous dynamic, and so on.

An evolution of the crossfading technique, which might be defined as musical dynamic layering, dynamically mixes different amounts of the sounds recorded at different musical dynamic levels to provide a much more varied timbre. Instead of playing one sample at a time, it combines a few dynamics at various volume levels in an attempt to merge the sound to simulate more timbral variations than the ones that were initially recorded. It assumes that the timbre between two dynamic levels is closer to a mix of both of their spectrums, which is not always the case. This technique is most effective with instruments with timbres that are reasonably cohesive (e.g., the orchestral strings), and it is the least effective when the opposite happens (e.g., orchestral brass). This approach has also been utilized, albeit more modestly, for other properties of the sound of an instrument, such as the amount of vibrato. The challenges I presented above when describing the layering technique for the first time are still present in this instance: phasing is an issue that sometimes has a limiting effect on the effectiveness of the technique.

Regardless of the specific details of the implementation of the technique, the use of multiple recordings at different dynamic levels is vital in getting the virtual instrument to match the timbre of the physical counterpart. While it is impossible to reproduce an instrument's continuum timbral change thoroughly, it provides enough resolution to give a solid approximation. Thus, the technique cannot capture the entirety of the timbral changes as the product of the shift from one dynamic to another during a *crescendo* or a *diminuendo*. Instead, it creates an approximation by combining changes in volume within a set of pre-established dynamic levels. Layering dynamics becomes a technologically feasible solution that aims to trick the human ear. Still, it does not entirely remove the lifeless sensation that samples produce compared to an acoustic performance in passages with very expressive *crescendos* or *diminuendos*.

Round Robin

Round robin is a common computational technique that allows the distribution of CPU time evenly among processes. This computational technique is adapted in samplers to employ a pool of similar sounds for the same note (Rogers et al. 2009, p. 24). The technique is intended to overturn an acoustic effect produced when repeating the exact sound multiple times in a short period. The brain recognizes that the same sound is triggered repeatedly. This effect is commonly known as the *machine gun effect*, as it is sonically unpleasant. Multiple samples of the same note at the same dynamic are recorded to avoid repetition of the same sample. Instead, the repetition occurs after several iterations. Round robin is primarily used in short or percussive sounds, as they are the ones that are more susceptible to being repeated at a similar dynamic range. Nevertheless, the same technique is used to alternate up and down bow samples in a sustained string library.

The effectiveness of the technique also unveils certain limitations in sampling. The technique is a welcome addition to a sampled instrument because a performer will play slightly differently every time they perform the same type of sound. Thus, it affords sampled instruments a tool to provide a viable approximation to these performance variations. Concomitantly, the technique also uncovers that many variables are at play in producing sound with instruments. Consequently, it foregrounds the limitations of capturing a predesigned subset of these variables that unavoidably are removed from a musical or expressive context.

Legato *and Note Transitions*

A fundamental aspect of (at least) Western performance musical practice is how to perform an expressive musical line, especially in how to approach the connection between its notes so they evolve from a collection of successive pitches into becoming a melody. One of the key elements of this process lies in a technique called *legato*. Following the analytical approach of the early sample library design I have been describing, *legato* is the sound produced when the performer changes from one note to another. Or, more technically, the recorded sound is produced at the transition between two notes.

Legato, as a sampling technique, aims to model a crucial Western musical practice that involves the performer connecting the sound of two consecutive notes. Buhler (2024) discussed the implementation of this technique in sample libraries in a discussion that centered on what he called the "fetish character of Legato" (153). Drawing from Roland Barthes' thoughts on the subject by analyzing the performance practice of the singer Fischer-Dieskau, Buhler suggests that "legato is fetishized because the arc as breath is a figure that allows belief that soul and spirit infuse the line, and that a representation of soul and spirit, rather than the articulation or musical expression, is the aim" (155). This is a deep and essential idea that helps to grasp the relevance of this process in music, especially when the music is created to mean something.

The idea of *legato* comes from the voice and is directly related to what we understand as lyricism. At a physical level, we do not possess a set of several vocal cords (similar to strings on a violin), which means that any change from one pitch to another will be accompanied by a necessary transitional moment in our only set of vocal cords. Singing a melody legato emphasizes the line and the musical gesture and tries to hide the note as a foundational element of music. It almost acts like a refutation of the Western musical system, which is grounded on an analytical approach to music that divides the phenomenon into equally tempered pitches and time distributions. At the very least, it is the remaining and arguably essential aspect of a tribal, in McLuhan's sense, musical expression without which Western orchestral music (which we could call "phonetic music" to continue with McLuhan's analogy) would struggle as a medium of sonic expression. It also highlights the importance of the human experience, represented by the performer, as a key element for musical expression—the soul and spirit, as Buhler puts it. All the small changes that happen between note transitions connect the audience to the performer's ideas, personality, or even worldview. To put an example, listening to how the solo violinist plays the first two notes (A and F#) of the main theme in Tchaikovsky's violin concerto is almost an open door to the performer's inner feelings.

Playing a melody *legato* has additional advantages in screen music beyond its added capacity to mean and portray feelings. As I mentioned, it converts a line constituted by notes into a sonic gesture that is not only more malleable but also would mix better under dialog. It allows us to keep the focus and the attention on the dialog—a character telling the other, "I love you!"—while also being able to engage fully with the lyrical melody. The dialog is a distinguishable *staccato* set of sounds—especially in dramatic moments in which we tend to emphasize the sound of the consonants—over a melody in which the pitches are partially hidden by a technique designed to smooth attacks out.

As I said, Western modern notation cannot encode the details of what happens in the transitory moment from one note to another. This is expected of a system that cannot—as I described before—represent in detail a process much more straightforward, such as a nonlinear increase in the dynamics. At the same time, these are the details that are at the core of lyricism and melodic expressivity in this musical system. From the point of view of an analytical approach to designing sampled virtual instruments—capturing fragments of what constitutes a performance to recreate any possible performance by using these models of reality—this phenomenon is a major challenge. Except for the round robin technique, all the other sampling techniques I described had a direct link with musical notation. With the problem of the machine gun effect, round robin became a solution that was detached from any connection to how music was notated. It solves a problem not that different from the note transition one as it deals with the importance of the slight differences between the same musical entity (a note) to create something that sounds musical. Round robin becomes a sort of brute-force solution to the problem by using the field of psychoacoustics, which deals with how humans perceive acoustic phenomenons instead of focusing on the acoustic phenomenon on its own. Round robin exploits the theoretical limitation of seven items in humans' short-term memory to convince them that a set of repeated notes is actually real. During the recording process of the sample, the designers just ask the performers to play the same note a few times with small variations and select the subset of the performances that will best fulfill the goal of the round-robin. However, as a brute force option—think of a kind of DDoS attack on our short-term memory—it does not ask why, how, and when performers vary the attack of a note. Further, performers would most likely not be able to reply to these questions, as these performance decisions tend to be intuitive and motivated by the idea of the musicality of a passage.

Recreating the transitions within a musical line becomes an even more daunting challenge from the perspective of analytical sample library design. At the same time, it is also an imperative area of development if the aim is to generate a tool that can produce the impression of liveness of a performance. Going back to Eco's discussion on Disneyland and the hyperreal (1990, 43–45), recreating the transitions would be the equivalent of recreating a sort of movement of a fake dinosaur in Disneyland in order to fulfill its role. For instance, a fake T-rex designed to scare the audience would probably need to move a little bit to fulfill its role in the storytelling. And the smoother and more verisimilar its movement will generally translate into a more scary experience. I believe the design of the legato technique in sample libraries is equivalent: it needs to produce an impression of performance that is necessary to fulfill the emotional role of a musical line. At the same time, it is also just a shadow of what happens in a performance. In the end, it is complicated to sample a model of a real you don't know about.

Based on all of that, the design of a technique to represent the transition sounds was developed with a set of axioms that followed the analytical approach, which simplified the process significantly. From this angle, the design assumes that *legato* notes sound different: before the start of the following note, there is a short moment in which we hear the sound mutating from one note to the other while the attack of the new note is masked. In our acoustic instruments, this is only achievable between notes in specific ranges in bowed and wind instruments. On the other hand, the nature of a percussive instrument, such as the piano, does not offer the possibility of *legato* from that point of view.

The first approach to producing legato was not a new sampling technique but a MIDI programming technique that replicated piano performance. Piano players imitate the lyrical effect of legato in their instruments by slightly overlapping the notes of the melody, placing the transitions strategically within the accompaniment, and playing with the dynamic intensity of the notes to mask as much as possible the attack of each note of the melody. MIDI programmers applied this concept to any virtual instrument (e.g., a violin section). With this technique, there is a moment when both notes are being reproduced simultaneously, blurring the attack of the second note. The technique is most successful when creating an accompaniment to a melodic line (sustained strings when there is a solo instrument playing a melody). Still, it is generally quite unsuccessful when attempting to reproduce the lyricism of a melody, which is a significant aspect of screen music expression.

A second approach to producing legato did not involve additional recording, but it was achieved at the programming stage of the virtual instrument. At this point, the focus of the designers was already on producing a transition sound. Commonly known as scripted legato, the design reproduces the transition by creating a fast pitch change between the notes using artificial pitch stretching algorithms. The result is that the sampler plays the sound of the original note at the moment of transition, progressively pitching it up or down for just a few milliseconds to create the impression of legato.

Once computing power and budget allowed it, sample libraries added a new sound object to their collection of samples: the transition. As I suggested, codifying the note transition becomes the next step in the analytical attempt to deconstruct an instrumental performance into workable and interconnected structured patterns. It is a particularly flawed technique, but the aim is that it can provide good enough results to enhance the musical expression of a melody. This is because the complexity required to properly replicate what happens during the transition from one note to another is exponentially more sophisticated than the techniques described above. The sound of the transition depends on, to name the most important, the dynamics of the note, the amount of vibrato, the speed at which the transition takes place (think about a very emotional slow violin performance), or the amount and the quality of attack that each note in the legato passage will have. In addition, each possible note pair will have a distinct transitory sound. Further, this does not only apply to the *legato* technique but also to similar techniques that live in the transition from one note to another, such as *portamento* or *glissando*. Thus, codifying the technique required a major simplification of the process to be represented with a single transitional sound. Still, the complexity of implementing the technique is major, as it required to record a transition sound for almost every possible note transition an instrument can play. Generally speaking, legato transitions were recorded for every possible interaction within an octave, which means that they had to record up to 23 different transitions for every note an instrument could play.

The *legato* transition was first introduced as early as 2003 in the Vienna Symphonic Library, based on a more than a decade-long conception and development process by his founder, former Vienna Philharmonic cello performer Herb Tucmandl. In their review of the library, Stewart and Wherry (2003) describe the *legato* technique as a technological wonder:

> VSL's solution is both brave and slightly mad; in their own words, they've "sampled every interval from a minor second to an octave, upwards and downwards from each note in the instrument's range" and trimmed the front of each sample so that only a few milliseconds of the starting note remain. By retaining a trace of the previous note, these "real legato" samples (played by all instruments except the harp) preserve the smooth transitions between one pitch and the next.

Buhler (2024) states that, for strings, "the favored legato for media composers is not, as one might expect, a relatively transparent connection between notes that is in fact the most common legato or orchestral strings, but rather a legato that transitions frictionlessly into a gentle swell on the note or arrival along with progressive vibrato to emphasize the swell" (155). This is, understandably, the model that most sample libraries recreated when recording their transitions. This makes more sense if one considers that the technique is an addition to the two approaches I just mentioned. This means that to recreate a transparent legato on a sustained string accompaniment, using the overlapping technique might be the best solution.

Regarding the MIDI implementation, sample libraries used the existing practice of overlapping notes to program legato transitions into playable instruments. When a composer or MIDI programmer overlaps two notes using a *legato* instrument, the sampler, instead of playing both notes simultaneously, crossfades the sound of the first note with the appropriate transition corresponding to the notes simultaneously depressed. Once the transition sample is over, it is crossfaded into the second note's sample. A consequence is that the sound of the second note (and thereafter) will be delayed by at least the duration of the transition, generating additional but solvable complexities in MIDI programming.

8Dio, a virtual instrument company, aimed for a slightly different approach to *legato* that hoped to improve on the limitations of the model I just outlined. First, they recorded a set of *legato* styles based on stylistic approaches connected to the themes of some major screen music. For instance, their *Adagio Violins* (2011) library included different *legato* instruments named Extra Terrestrial Legato, Schindler's Legato, Instinct Legato, or Village Legato, to name a few. The idea is that they asked the performers to play legato as if they were playing the themes from the movies that are suggested in the title. In addition, their approach had only two pieces. The first piece was the original note. The second piece was the transition and the second note together, acknowledging that the transition process on a *legato* line also impacted significantly the beginning of the note that followed. While this approach was abandoned by 8dio, it has had some impact. It is not uncommon that libraries now provide a version of the legato called *lyrical* and another version that is generally called *legato*. They might also include a couple more options which might be integrated into a single virtual instrument that tries to react to the playing technique to provide the most adequate transition for the performance. While this sounds like a leap forward, the results are only marginally better. In the end, there are too many variables in the process that relate to how to implement myriad ways of musical expression for this to be accurately codified in a discrete set of outcomes.

Nevertheless, the introduction of the transition sounds was a leap forward toward the ideal of creating virtual replicas of existing instruments as much as a realization of the impossibility of replicating the real with those analytical approaches only. Even with its limitation, the *legato* technique allows for an approximation to the creation of a musical line over a series of pitches placed one after another. It highlighted that the complexity and the high number of variables involved in the process of transitioning from one note to another during a human performance was an essential aspect of expressive music. The aim for codifying transitions is both an attempt to get as close as possible to the physical performance and a hope that this is good enough to fool a human ear in the context of a piece of music involving multiple instruments. With all its limitations, the *legato* technique remains a technological marvel at the end of the first decade of the twenty-first century. This is probably the reason why, as Buhler (2024) indicates, it became such a strong element for the marketing purposes of these libraries.

Finally, the importance of the nuances in the transitions for musical expression anticipates a feature common in hyperorchestral music, which I will describe in the next two chapters. Composers increasingly collaborate throughout the creation process with individual performers who can provide musical lines that are uniquely customized to fulfill the expressive means of the music they are creating. This is facilitated by a nonlinear scoring process but also highlights the importance in screen music of crafting a musical line that can express and transmit highly nuanced meanings.

Recording Locations and Sound Perspectives

The theoretical importance of this technique goes beyond the sound improvement it produced. It underscores the first design crisis based on a performance-based analytical model extremely tied to the musical score. In fact, it is a technique that states the defeat of a model that aims to replicate reality by combining a subset of parameters deemed to define it. Thus, the development of the technique revolved around a debate that questioned whether it was possible for the hall's acoustics, what we routinely refer to as the reverberation (reverb), to become a separate parameter. In other words, the question would lie in deciding if it was possible to separate the ambiance of a hall from the sound of the instrument.

A naïve analytical perspective would deem this as possible and desirable in terms of design. One of the first reviews of the first extensive commercial sample library released to the market, the *Vienna Symphonic Library* (2003), already captured the debate:

> There are two schools of thought when recording samples: you either place the players on the stage of a big hall and record the instruments from the perspective of the conductor or audience, taking advantage of the hall's natural acoustics; or else, you record the instruments as accurately as possible in a controlled acoustic space, and allow users to add their own ambience. (Stewart and Wherry 2003)

In the case of the *Vienna* library, their design approach suggested that it was indeed possible to separate the sound of the instrument from the hall in which it was performed. Therefore, the company created a unique studio, the Silent Studio, designed to record samples at the lowest amount of noise possible in a room that sounded as neutral as possible.

> To ensure acoustic consistency for hundreds of thousands of samples—including the vast spectrum of technical nuances, articulations and volume levels—each instrument must be recorded at an accurate and constant distance from the microphone. This fixed distance combined with an ultra-amplified signal—used especially for pianissimo sounds—can lead to unwanted environmental noise. No existing professional studios could offer the noise absorption we needed for this caliber of recording.
> Naturally, we had unique space requirements for larger ensembles, acoustic prerequisites and needed 24/7 availability. That's why in 2001, our custom recording facility, dubbed the "Silent Stage," was built in Ebreichsdorf,

25 kilometers south of Vienna. With an ambience of 0.8 seconds, it's neither a "dry," nor a "wet" environment, and it provides well-balanced reflections that the instruments' sound can evolve and the musicians can hear themselves well. (Vienna Symphonic Library)

The sound from the Silent Studio is generally considered dry for orchestral standards as it does not attempt to capture the reverberation of a hall that would be suited for orchestral performances.[17] In other words, it would be incredibly challenging to rehearse and record music (not samples) in this studio. The ambiance was supposed to be added later using sound processors that fulfilled that purpose. A year after the release of the Vienna Symphonic Library, another expansive orchestral library was released: the EastWest Quantum Leap Symphonic Orchestra. This library took the opposite route: it recorded its sounds in a concert hall and provided samples captured by the different microphones that would habitually capture an orchestra. They were microphones close to the instruments, from the conductor's perspective, and aimed to capture the hall's resonance. The overwhelming success of this second approach (Vienna eventually switched to the same model a few years later using a state-of-the-art recording studio) became the first blow to the most orthodox analytical approach to sample library virtual instrument design. The consequences were multiple. Commercially, this implied that users of these products would be willing to purchase libraries recorded at different locations because each studio would be able to provide a distinct sound.

Further, it helped to unlock music creative practices (which are spectral in nature) that detached the composer from a pitch/score-centric approach to composition. Hans Zimmer emphasized that composers should write specifically with the hall they are recording in mind. Discussing the differences between two popular London recording venues, Zimmer (2022) stated: "I would argue that the room—and a profound knowledge of the room—is as important as the notes performed in it. [...] You must write differently for Abbey Road than AIR." This quite phenomenological statement on music (which is not dissimilar to the ideology of conductors such as Celibidache, who embraced phenomenological ideas to shape their views on performance) embraces the importance of its spectral side and how each hall might significantly modify the spectral shape of a piece of music.

Another relevant consequence is the incorporation of the concept of sound perspectives in virtual instruments. The concept of sound perspectives refers to the utilization of different microphone positions to represent how a particular instrument might be heard from different locations. Technically speaking, it falls into a subset of layering with the advantage that controlling the phase is much more simple as it captures the same acoustic phenomenon. It is an important concept because the effect of microphone placement significantly alters the recorded sound. Sample libraries contain a set of perspectives for the user to mix. They add an extra layer of sound variation based on the instrument's hypothetical and hyper-realistic sonic placement.[18] The utilization of sound perspectives reveals the dynamism of sound and how it significantly changes with slight variations in the listener's location or the microphone, creating distinct sound objects. The physical interactions between the space and the sound produced by instruments are impossible or exceptionally complex to recreate virtually.

Capturing Performances and Performance Practices

Incorporating the sound of the recording location and microphone perspectives in the recorded samples is a sign that the ideal of building a virtual instrument from isolated pieces is considerably challenging, if not impossible. These sampling techniques are an even more radical reaction to the archetype of building a virtual and objective replica of a physical instrument that could behave analogously to its physical counterpart. Further, these techniques highlight the highly skilled role of performers in producing sounds with their instruments by using a level of complexity that is onerous to model objectively. The concept behind capturing a performance or a performance practice is to create a virtual instrument that does not necessarily attempt to be a flexible replica of its physical counterpart but to record pre-designed performances in the most flexible possible manner to be used by the composer.

Due to a combination of the Western music bias of MIDI 1.0, its standard implementations (most composers would program MIDI using a MIDI keyboard that resembles pianos), and a shared lack of knowledge and experience with non-orchestral Western music by most of the composers who used sample library products, the first libraries that substantially employed these techniques were the ones who sampled those instruments. Less fortunately, as a product made primarily by Western companies, sample libraries created virtual instruments of many non-Western instruments by referencing common codifications of its sounds in

Western cultural tradition. Ron Sadoff (2013) provides an early overview of these practices:

> Virtual instrument libraries constitute a broad, yet selective sonic ethnography spanning popular, traditional, and world cultures. They provide an expansive pool of sounds that all commercial media composers draw from. Their file names reflect the practical, prejudiced, and esoteric: "viola solo legato mp," "tundra travel," "Singapore squeak," and "Jihad" (an evolving soundscape combining dark "Middle Eastern" timbres, a driving rhythmic loop, and a male chorus chanting "Arabic" phonemes). [...] In the case of non-Western instruments, they are often assembled as an aggregate of culturally related sounds, such as "Silk" and "Desert Winds," which contain ethnic "eastern" instruments that may encompass the music of entire continents. (Sadoff 2013)

Thus, instead of attempting to replicate an instrument, these virtual instruments offered the composer either minute-long prerecorded performances or performance fragments that, from a Western music perspective, would be similar to note ornamentations or melismas. The virtual instrument is much less flexible as it only allows the composer to choose from a predesigned set of performance options, but it is at the same time more expressive as the sound it produces is actual performances. Due to the limitations of predesigned performance elements and phrases, using easily recognizable tropes, as I mentioned above, seemed inevitable. Hence, the importance of the connoted meanings and their influence on the composition process should not be overlooked. Sample libraries are not ideologically neutral, as they provide an aesthetic that emanates from a particular cultural viewpoint.

This design technique is not exclusive to non-orchestral Western instruments as it has also been widely incorporated into virtual instruments or ensembles that are comprised of Western orchestral instruments. For instance, as I described above, many orchestral sample libraries provide a legato instrument named "Lyrical," which tries to capture the type of legato technique and performance practice that string players use in highly melodic passages. More importantly, some sample libraries are created with long-sample recordings that generally evolve in terms of instrumental technique or dynamics. These virtual instruments, commonly called evolutions or a similar term, are much less flexible than virtual replicas but have an increased potential for expressiveness.

Synthetic Techniques, Processing, and Modeling

All virtual instruments require a certain degree of techniques that come from sound synthesis. A sampler is not more than an evolution of a synthesizer in which the sound source is not an oscillator but a collection of recordings. From this point of view, the looping technique I described above is borrowed from synthesizer design as well as the sound envelopes found in almost all sample libraries (such as ADSR). Further, all sample libraries provide ways to automate the volume of the samples to offer even greater dynamic simulation or to combine different samples as if they were different sound sources in a synthesizer. In other words, all sample libraries require the utilization of a set of synthesizer-like techniques to be completed to some extent.

With that in mind, it should come as no surprise that other techniques that could be considered less transparent have been utilized in the process of creating realistic sample libraries. While deep sampling is rooted in the necessity of achieving realism by capturing as much reality as possible, these techniques focus on the model to create the best simulation possible that is perceived as realistic to the target customers and passed on to the audiences. At the same time, they cover the shortfalls of the sampling process whenever other techniques have not been able to overcome problems. If the previous techniques describe a set of processes designed to achieve realism by capturing more of reality, these techniques are focused on recreating reality artificially with the hopes of creating a better replica. One example was the controversial decision of the team behind *EastWest Hollywood Strings* at the time of release to not record samples of the string section with mutes (*con sordino*) and use a simple equalizer to cut some frequencies and replicate the effect synthetically (Stewart 2010). The result was somewhat surprisingly accurate and verisimilar, involving a straightforward equalization process. Another process used commonly for similar resource-saving reasons is to use one sample for a set of nearby pitches by using pitch-shifting processes. This process also allows sample libraries to adjust to the tunning of other recordings (e.g., 440Hz vs 442Hz) or even non-Western scale systems.

In addition, these techniques can be used to solve problems such as the challenge of reproducing a continuous process of increased vibrato by only recording a few samples. While combining dynamics is reasonably effective, combining different degrees of *vibrato* recording for the same note frequently produces problems related to phase cancellation. A typical solution is to use another synthesis tool, frequency modulation, to assist in this purpose, generally in combination with recordings of different levels of vibrato.

The final group in this area relates to the utilization of these techniques to model the real by generating sounds that do not come from recordings. These techniques are commonly called sample modeling, although they do not use samples at all in the end product. Instead, these products are sophisticated synthesizers that create a genuinely virtual instrument governed by algorithms generated from the analysis of the sound samples of an instrument. Similarly, it is also possible to generate audio layers that simulate additional dynamics based on recording a small set of dynamics. In other words, it is possible to infer 100+ different levels of dynamics by generating audio based on the model of four or five different recordings of an instrument playing the same note at different dynamic layers.[19] This technique becomes an alternative to dynamic crossfading that aims to achieve a higher degree of verisimilitude by further detaching the generated sound from the samples of reality.

Classifying Virtual Instruments: Taxonomies

While there is a shared industrial and commercial vocabulary that aims to distinguish and classify virtual instruments, their importance in the production process and the vast number of available products make it advisable to attempt to provide theoretical ways to classify them. While I will provide a typology of virtual instruments that is more or less consistent with how these products are divided in practice, I believe that any analysis of a virtual instrument should engage in different taxonomies based on various approaches.

The scope of this book and, consequently, this classification lies mainly in the aesthetics of the contemporary screen music industry. Thus, I will not inquire about the commercial and marketing processes used by virtual instrument developers. Similarly, my focus is on how these tools are used by professionals in the industry, which excludes the hobbyists who are increasingly constituting the majority of the customers for these products. At the beginning of the second decade of the twenty-first century, the average computer was powerful enough to produce music at a higher level than a network of more than a dozen expensive computers just a few years before. Virtual instruments were also becoming more and more affordable because their consumer base was also increasing exponentially. As a consequence, virtual instruments have even started to be developed with this new population in mind: the hobbyists. Buhler (2021) presents a compelling description of this landscape in *Blank Music: Marketing Virtual Instruments*. Buhler's focus is on how these companies advertise these products, which also generates a classification of these libraries based on typologies that will not be dissimilar from some items of my typology at the end of this chapter. While it is not entirely possible to describe these products with a total detachment from the commercial practices, my focus will be much more on the aesthetic and the professional practice than the commercialization and marketing strategies of these companies.

The analytical approaches I present below combine technical aspects (how these instruments are made), design paradigms, relationship with reality, and aesthetic function. More than an exclusive classification, I believe they become useful tools to describe virtual instruments based on key elements of their design and function.

Origin of the Sound Sources

I first mentioned this classification in the previous chapter. It is possibly the simplest as it relates to the origin of the sound sources used to create the virtual instrument. Based on this paradigm, there are three broad approaches to instrument design: sample-based, synthesis-based, and hybrid.

Sample-based virtual instruments are created mainly from a generally sizeable collection of sampled recordings. While some synthesis techniques might be applied, these are primarily restrained to the reproduction and mixing of the samples. Therefore, the sound produced by these instruments comes from either a single recording or a combination of recordings mixed together. These virtual instruments tend to follow a logarithmic curve in relationship to the number of samples and the perceived increase in quality and verisimilitude. While, in the beginning, adding samples produces exponential returns (e.g., having a few samples for the whole instrument to have a few dozen), there is a point in which a slight increase in quality requires an exponential in the number of sample data.

Synthesis-based virtual instruments are generated exclusively via the artificial generation of sounds using a synthesizer. If the objective is to achieve a degree of realism (sample modeling), the starting point is overly complex algorithmically and in processing power (aka CPU). However, if the aim of the instrument is not to create a verisimilar virtual counterpart of a physical instrument, they require very modest resources.

Finally, *hybrid* virtual instruments use samples as sound sources in combination with synthesized sources and sound processing to generate their sound. While they require more processing power than simple synthesizers, they have the potential to provide highly suggestive sounds that are connected to physical instruments. Due to the advantages of utilizing synthesized techniques, these virtual instruments achieved a level of organicity at the beginning of the twenty-first century that was difficult to accomplish with sample-based instruments, at the expense of being more limited in their capacity to become a replica of reality.

While accurately outlining the differences in their design based on the sound source, this classification considers a sample-modeled virtual instrument of a violin that attempts to become a replica and a sampled-based one with the same purpose conceptually separated. Further, the stage of the development of these instruments is also not acknowledged. Thus, the following categories will focus on both the stages of development of virtual instruments and how they interact with reality.

Design Paradigms of Sample Libraries

The sampling techniques and conceptual approaches to the design of sampled virtual instruments have followed an incremental process. I have identified four main iterations that constitute paradigms of the design process. It is important to mention that each paradigm of virtual instruments does not invalidate the previous one but, instead, adds a new design approach and viewpoint for the composer. Thus, these paradigms are non-exclusive. Each paradigm has continued to evolve, improve, and generate new products.

The "first paradigm" aims to establish guidelines for creating virtual replicas of physical instruments as abstract sound objects. Its goal is straightforward and fundamentally aligns with the primary axioms of replication of the real. Arguably, the best product that represents this paradigm is the Vienna Symphonic Library (VSL), initially released in 2002. The samples were designed with the utmost analytical design principle and recorded in the driest room possible.

As I mentioned earlier, the founder of the company, Herb Tucmandl, was a professional cello player who left their job to go to film production, which included film scoring in the 1990s. During that time and out of frustration with the existing tools, he conceived the main design paradigms for the library:

> His approach was fascinatingly innovative, as Herb not only wanted to record single notes but also note transitions, which would allow for a living and believable performance for the very first time. The recordings would include a wide variety of articulations such as legato, repetitions, trills, fast runs, arpeggios, harmonics, flutter tongues, clusters, and so much more. While the largest conventional sample libraries at that time offered a mere 6,000 samples to replicate an entire orchestra, Herb developed a structure of more than one million single notes and short phrases! (Vienna Symphonic Library)

The VSL established the foundation for the analytical approach to sample design. The only popular technique they did not conceive was the round robin. Instead, the VSL solution incorporated a set of samples playing up to eight repeated notes that also served to alleviate the machine gun effect in its most egregious circumstance. As a reference, the Spitfire Audio BBC orchestra sample library, released in 2019, also contained just over one million samples, which indicates that the overall design approach of that model has remained fairly constant since then. This paradigm, in addition to aiming to create a realistic performance by deconstructing the musical phenomenon in malleable building blocks, is designed with an idealistic perfect performance free of "mistakes" or noises. It is, again, a version of Eco's description of Disneyland in that it "tells us that technology can give us more reality than nature can" (1990, 44). Thus, all the notes are perfectly tuned, all the attacks are smooth out to become similar, and there are no imperfect room reflections that could alter the pristine nature of the recording.

Technologically speaking, it contributed to the commercial leap from sample libraries that could be contained in a CD (a few hundred Megabytes) to sizes in Gigabytes, which required a computer instead of a hardware sampler. The now-defunct sampler *Gigasampler* (2000)—which evolved into Tascam's Gigastudio—is a clear indication of the significance of entering the Gigabyte realm, to the point of becoming part of the product's name.

The "second paradigm" approaches sampling in a more naturalistic way by incorporating the sound of rooms and halls, acknowledging at least some performance practices, and even allowing for some imperfections to permeate. The result is more naturally sounding out of the box at the expense of making the virtual instruments more specific and less flexible. If the objective of the first paradigm was, for instance, to achieve the perfect replica of a violin ensemble playing *pizzicato*, the second paradigm aimed for a successful representation of several types of *pizzicati* played in spaces that are commonly used to record screen music. Thus, this paradigm distances from what I called the replication pursuit of the first: the creation of an absolute virtual representation of an acoustic instrument that is also equivalent to its representation in Western notation practice. In the case of the example above, the first paradigm would aim to create a virtual instrument that represents all the acoustic violin ensembles when playing *pizzicato* to represent a composer writing *pizzicato* in the score.

While most of the libraries created in this paradigm in mind share design axioms of the first paradigm—and arguably many borrowed from VSL ideas—there is a significant conceptual change. The approach to realism in the first paradigm is grounded on the Western score, which means a sonic representation of the music that aims to be neutral, pristine sounding, and that complements the imagination process that a score-based composer already has when writing the piece of music. It is a design that comes from established Western music theory—which is why the analytical model is so apt—instead of the sound itself. Considering that a violin ensemble playing the *pizzicato* technique produces different music (as sonic results) depending on the hall or how they are recorded fundamentally defies the axioms of classical music in which authorship is anchored to the score and not to the sonic realization. The second paradigm approaches realism from its sonic realization. More specifically, its reality is not the live performance but the recorded result.

While the first paradigm mediates the real through theory and the musical score, the second paradigm mediates it through its practical output in screen music: the recording. Both cases are based on a simulation that allows us to properly analyze and discern mediated reality due to our incapacity to deal with reality directly and objectively. Live music has the problem that any assessment will always be mediated by both the location of our ears and our capacity to perceive sound through them. A recording provides an objective result that can both be assessed by different people to overcome the biological bias of our ears and objectively analyzed using sound processors. Similarly, a score-based model does have the objectivity that emanates from an analytical framework.

The greatest advantage of the first paradigm is that it smoothly integrates into a traditional and linear approach to film scoring, making acoustic orchestration almost trivial. Its biggest problem is that it fails (or it makes the task much more difficult) to become a great sonic equivalent to the final recorded result.

The second paradigm is based on the sound recording, which is essentially connected to the sample. It is a more natural evolution from early sampled products that were widely used by composers who did not approach music creation from the written score in a traditional Western sense. For those reasons, it was also a more user-friendly tool for other groups of creatives who were also not traditional composers: movie directors and producers.

The first product in this realm was not released commercially but is a sample library that had a great impact on the history of screen scoring. It is the private library that Hans Zimmer developed for his own use (and his peers). In an article/interview by Mark Wherry (2002), the author states that "Hans' custom-recorded orchestral library has become something of a legend for those who create orchestral mock-ups with technology." Zimmer explained how they recorded and created this library around 1996–1997:

> I always work with pretty much the same orchestra in London, so I did a deal with them, which was basically 'Let me go and sample you guys at AIR Lyndhurst sitting in the chairs you sit in whenever we do an orchestra recording, so the perspective is right.' And the other part of the deal I made with them was that I wouldn't use the samples without using any real musicians—it wasn't to replace real musicians. In fact, I think 90 percent of the movies I've done ever since I've recorded in London and kept those musicians busy. (Wherry 2002)

Zimmer acknowledges that his lack of formal training requires a sonic approach to music creation: "My musical education is two weeks of piano lessons and anything else I picked up on the way, so for me to orchestrate things—and I like doing all the stuff myself—I needed to be able to hear it" (Wherry 2002). And by hearing it, Zimmer refers to a version of the final mixed result, not a reproduction of an orchestral recording session. While Zimmer clearly states that the objective for his library was still to create a mockup that would be replaced by real musicians, there is a significant aesthetic transformation. These recordings don't assume the traditional film orchestra and its traditional recording process (players could be recorded isolatedly or in sections). Instead, they aim for a sonic result that frequently would not be able to be produced anymore in a single orchestral performance. As a consequence, there is no direct equivalency between the mockup, the realization of the mockup into a score (orchestration in a traditional sense), and the recordings of these scores. It is all about the final mixed result. Thus, the musicians playing the score, the hall, or the engineers might be as important for the sonic result as the notes written in the score. As Zimmer describes when explaining the success of his library over other products:

> It's partly the players. I managed to get hold of who I consider the best players in the world, in one of the best halls in the world, with one of the best engineers in the world; and I've worked with these guys forever, so I'm not going to let them get away with anything. It's very hard to give meaning and intent to a single note in isolation, and a sample needs to have some sort of sense of a performance. (Wherry 2002)

Thus, this paradigm approaches realism differently and much more phenomenologically. First, the real in a film score is only the recorded result, not the acoustic performance. Second, the people, spaces, instruments, and technology involved in the process of creating the music are relevant, and their contributions are musical. Thus, noise or imperfections might be desirable over the total clarity of the musical message, which would seem the ideal of a performance that aims to be a representation of a traditional Western musical score written in staves. And similarly, the location from which we perceive each musical element does not necessarily need to reproduce the perfect spot in a concert hall.

The first widely acclaimed commercial library—albeit much more modest in size and complexity—that followed this paradigm was the *Miroslav Vitous Symphonic Orchestra* (2000). Released as a CD sampler for a set of hardware samplers, it was recorded in the Dvorak Concert Hall in Prague. In an interview in 2004, Vitous stated: "Basically, everyone in the Hollywood community of composers has the library. People all over the world use it too" (Prasad 2004). Similarly to Tucmandl from VSL, Vitous, a jazz bassist, created the library out of a personal need—much like Zimmer—to have a more suitable tool to compose: "I needed to make some sounds. […] I'm the kind of composer who composes with sound, not with pencil" (Prasad 2004).

EastWest released their *Symphonic Orchestra* in 2003, which was recorded in a concert hall and had a sample size more comparable to the VSL. However, the moment this paradigm became groundbreaking was when commercial libraries emulated Hans Zimmer's approach to sampling and created libraries recorded from the studios used to record film scores. To name a few, EastWest released *Hollywood Strings* in 2009, recording in EastWest studios; Spitfire Audio started around the same time, creating libraries in Air Studios; and Cinesamples recorded their libraries in the Sony scoring stage. One of the results is that the number of libraries could grow exponentially. A composer might want a collection of libraries recorded in different rooms that fit a wide variety of scenarios.

The "third design paradigm" acknowledged that specific expressive musical shapes could not be adequately translated using previous techniques, generating a sound result that seemed lifeless. It builds on ideas and definitions of realism from the second paradigm, but it does not attempt to provide a solution that can fully produce a piece of music. Thus, the products that followed this approach were generally presented as a complement to the existing libraries when they were released. This design paradigm proposes to record these expressive shapes into longer samples at the expense of flexibility and the necessity to multiply the number of virtual instruments. They no longer attempt to replicate an instrument in a defined room and musical tradition, but instead, they aim to produce a specific expressive shape (a slow *crescendo* or a transformation between two different string playing techniques).

This design paradigm also acknowledges that a flute and clarinet playing in unison together sound different than if we mix two solo recordings of these instruments. Or, more importantly, a section of four horns playing the same note will sound much different from four individual horns recorded separately and mixed after the recording. Similarly, a chord played by an ensemble together might sound more organic compared to producing it by individual recordings.

A prime example of this approach was the widely popular *ProjectSAM Symphobia* (2008), which was released and advertised as a complement to your existing orchestral libraries instead of an alternative. It became a revolutionary concept and opened the door to libraries whose intent was not purely the replication of an acoustic instrument but still based on recorded samples of instrumental performances. If the second paradigm multiplied the libraries significantly, this paradigm exponentially grew the possibilities and products.

While these libraries mostly aim for authenticity and a verisimilar result, their approach to realism in the acoustic or recording sense is greatly diminished. A widely used library such as Spitfire *Olafur Arnalds Evolutions* (2015) or its sister library *OA Chamber Evolutions* (2018) provides the composer with evolving string textures that use a group of extended techniques that are generally outside from the Classical Hollywood film music orchestral sound. Orchestrators are generally challenged if they have to create an acoustic orchestral score out of a demo that uses these sounds, and several orchestral studio musicians would require some rehearsal and careful explanation to be able to produce many of the effects that appear in these libraries. Many composers might find these sounds outside of their sonic familiarity, and, most likely, they might be unable to determine if they can be generated with acoustic instruments only. This generation bridges the gap between hybrid approaches to synth design (synths that utilize sound samples as sound sources) and orchestral sample libraries. They also served to expand the orchestral vocabulary in screen music, which was mainly anchored in late nineteenth-century techniques. These tools allowed composers to demonstrate that the extended techniques for the instruments developed during the twentieth century were not only capable of producing non-abstract music but also were, in many cases, a powerful tool to produce highly expressive and meaningful sounds.

Finally, the "fourth paradigm" aims to use samples to create algorithms that wholly replace the need to use reality (aka samples) altogether. It is achieved at the expense of capturing a musician's performance, which puts the whole responsibility of creating a realistic performance on the composer or programmer. While this could render this paradigm practically unusable, it is worth acknowledging that it is also possible to develop algorithms that are modeled after performance practices and act as virtual performers for the composer. This paradigm's products are still in nascent stages and not fully developed when writing this book. An early example of this paradigm is created by a company called Sample Modeling, which is the actual name of the process. Their instruments are generated by algorithms created from analyzing samples and recorded performances. Their website describes their technological approach, which is the state of the art of this still not fully formed paradigm.

> The identification of the "fingerprints" of high-quality instruments was carried out by state-of-the art recordings of chromatically sampled notes, typical articulations, and expressive phrases, played by first class professionals in

an anechoic environment; an "adaptive model", based on the physical properties of the instrument, and exploiting the knowledge of the features of a real performance was then constructed. The purpose of the model was to minimize the differences between the real phrases and those played by the virtual instrument; sophisticated technologies, including G.Tommasini's patented "harmonic alignment", and convolution with modal resonances, innovative techniques for sample modulation, along with advanced AI midi processing, are used for real time construction of all articulations and morphing across dynamics, vibrato, legato and portamento. (Samplemodeling)

Relationship with Reality

As I discussed, sample libraries were created to provide mockups—in the original sense—of future orchestral recordings mainly for film music, which means that, at their core, the original objective was to create a one-on-one equivalency with its acoustic counterparts. Through the generations I described in the previous taxonomy, the concept of realism and how these libraries interacted with it differed. For the reasons I already described in the previous paradigm, I believe that exploring whether and how a sample library engages with realism is relevant.

The first group of sample libraries in this classification is the one that attempts to "replicate reality," either from an acoustic or from a recorded result viewpoint. These libraries' main goal is to afford the composer a virtual tool that would serve as a sketching tool for a future recording or to replace the recording process altogether with a digital rendition created with these products. One feature is that there should be a relationship between each virtual instrument and its acoustic counterpart, or at least, with it recorded sound object. The association eases the process of converting digital music into a musical score written on a staff paper that can be performed. For instance, a virtual instrument that replicates a violin I section playing sustained notes using the *sul tasto* bow placement can be immediately translated into a performance-ready score. This model allows trained Western classical composers to apply their skills to write music digitally directly.

On the other hand, this approach generally becomes a barrier for the non-classically trained composer, who would need help understanding the name of the virtual instrument or why the register is limited to specific pitches. If, instead, the virtual instrument was called "airy" or "silky strings" and was the combination of all the string instruments playing *sul tasto* with some additional processing, this instrument would probably be more fitting for this second group of composers. This other approach would complicate the orchestrator's work and add a layer of complexity for the classically trained composer. The instruments in the first paradigm clearly fall into this category. While many libraries of the second paradigm could also be accommodated into this model, their approach to realism significantly changed, and it is not uncommon that they produce sounds that would go beyond strict acoustic realism.

A middle-ground between the aim to replicate reality and the alternative I propose is libraries that aim to become "functional toolkits." Their goal is still to replicate reality but shift the focus from replicating the instrument in a one-to-one relationship to focusing on the musical or dramatic function of the sound. A characteristic example of this group is a library of percussive hits or accents. The sounds produced by such a virtual instrument generally combine several instruments playing together to create a dramatic effect that is common in screen music syntax. While this approach increases the steps for the orchestrator, it is still a reasonably straightforward job.

Moreover, achieving a percussive hit effect with myriad instrumental combinations is possible, which would facilitate the orchestration process. For instance, if some of the instruments used in the recording of this library were not available on the ensemble that would record the score, the orchestrator could easily create a satisfying alternative. Orchestral *crescendo* effects or specific coded aleatoric effects (random string *pizzicati*) are other clear examples of this group. Early examples of this group were groundbreaking: EastWest *StormDrum* (2004) and Heavyocity *Evolve* (2006), both highly focused on modern and post-orchestral percussive textures.

The third group of sampled virtual instruments aims to "augment reality." Broadly speaking, this group of instruments shares in common the utilization of recorded samples that are connected with reality to achieve Mera (2016a) calls musical materialization. However, the captured sample is generally the starting point for unfolding a resulting sound detached from a plausible physical musical performance or instrument. Eric Persing (2009), sound designer and the founder of Spectrasonics, coined the concept called Psychoacoustic Sampling as one of the main attractions of Omnisphere, a virtual instrument released by the company in 2008. Psychoacoustic sampling–defined by Persing (2009) as a form of organic synthesis—aimed to discover hidden frequencies in the material recorded in a way that would alter the perception of the recording. Persing and his team first demonstrated this idea by presenting a series of virtual instruments generated by carefully recording and processing the sound produced by hitting a light bulb.

The instruments of this group are frequently called organic because their sound feels connected with reality even though the listener cannot create an association with a physical sound object entirely. The sources for these instruments can come from the following non-mutually exclusive categories:

1. **(Not ordinary) Extended techniques.** While some extended techniques are easily identifiable as performance techniques on an instrument, others are unusual and generate sounds that seem outside of an instrument's capabilities. For example, using a superball or a bow on a piano string would generate a very suggestive sound that is also not associated with the instrument.
2. **Implausible instrumental sounds.** These are sounds produced by an instrument but impractical or implausible to be heard in a physical performance. One example, coined by the sample library company Spitfire Audio, is the idea of a *super sul tasto*. This sound is a much more radical version of the strings playing on the fingerboard, requiring a close microphone to be captured accurately. Virtual instruments in Spectrasonics *Omnisphere* that originate from sampling the sound of a light bulb would be another example. At the same time, listening to all the string sections of an orchestra as if we were very close to the instrument is also implausible, and, as such, virtual instruments that generate this kind of sound could be analyzed from that angle.
3. **Musicalizing found objects.** These are sounds produced by an instrument that is not standard. Generally, there is an intention to carry meaning through the object that is making sound. In addition to the numerous examples in virtual instruments (*Omnisphere* being a primer example), this aesthetic process is commonly found in many contemporary scores, in which the process of sampling sounds to create bespoke virtual instruments for each project is frequently the first step of the creation process. Hildur Guðnadóttir's work in sampling the sounds of a nuclear power plant for the music of *Chernobyl* (2019) is a good example of this process (Emmerentze Jervell 2019; King 2021).

4. **Sound manipulation and transformation.** In addition to capturing a broader set of possible sounds to create groundbreaking virtual instruments, it is also habitual to transform more standard musical sources through sound processing to unfold new sonorities that augment reality. Through transformations on the pitch, frequency manipulation, and other sophisticated ways to transform the sound and its spectrum, ordinary sounds like a voice singing or a note played in any instrument can become almost unrecognizable new sound objects that can retain the connection to reality through the organicity of the sound source while opening the door to both new sonic worlds and significations of the material.

The final group of virtual instruments in this categorization aims to artificially mimic the natural dynamism of sounds in our reality. I name this method "Simulated Dynamic Realism." While the previous three groups approach the capture of reality as primarily a static sound object—leaving it to the composer to combine multiple sounds to produce music that is dynamic—this category attempts to capture the subtle but unique ways in which a sound might evolve. The main objective is to try to solve the perception of artificiality due to the static nature of a collection of short samples. These virtual instruments, which are aligned with the third paradigm of sample libraries, act less as instruments and more as virtual performer collaborators. As such, the composer loses flexibility but gains the capacity to interact with a virtual instance that feels more *alive* by capturing the element of time. Libraries in this group might be simple prerecorded phrases, such as non-Western instruments phrases in EastWest *Ra* (2005). A different approach is much more interactive and, arguably groundbreaking, focused on recording evolving textures. It was initiated by Spitfire Audio's release of *Scary Strings* (2013), which was a private library created by Christian Henson for his own project a few years before the public release.

Creative Role

A final approach to describe virtual instruments lies in their role in the creative process. Thus, I am examining virtual instruments from the viewpoint of how they interact with the creative process. Sample-based instruments started as a means to create a mockup, which means that they were just tools for collaboration and prototyping during the creative process.

On the other hand, the creation of bespoke virtual instruments for a project aims to incorporate the resulting sound into the final product. In determining the role that a virtual instrument has in the creative process, we also uncover radical changes to the creative process itself, which will be the main topic for the following chapter. Thus, this classification will also serve to pose questions and provide initial insights that will be developed and hopefully resolved in the next chapter.

The first role a virtual instrument can play is "instrumental." In this role, the virtual instrument becomes a virtual version of an instrument, acting as an evolution of what basic general MIDI sounds were able to produce. This group of virtual instruments is the most amenable to old compositional and scoring practices, being able to act as almost a transparent tool for the composer. They become a noteworthy tool for creating mockups (with the understanding that an orchestral recording will produce the final result) and for creating more than acceptable versions of the finalized product when there is no possibility of recording. These virtual instruments require the composer to have a robust knowledge of the orchestra and orchestration. It does not necessarily mean that the composers are traditionally trained, as it is possible to acquire this knowledge through working with these virtual instruments. However, for the untrained composer, these libraries might be somewhat daunting. In addition, there is an inevitable side effect of utilizing these libraries as an interface for composition, even when their role might just be to act as prototypes. The composer might be inclined to write music that sounds best with these tools, regardless of what a real orchestra would eventually accomplish if recorded later on. This is their interface effect. One example of this effect is the extended utilization of sustained string harmonics in screen music due to how realistic this technique was using samples since the very first sample libraries were released.

The second role relates to "performance." The instrumental role is attached to a traditional, Western-centric, and somewhat idealistic creative process. In this traditional Western process, composers abstractly conceive a piece of music, then write it down on a score, and pass it to the performers, who are expected to produce the result without further indications. The truth, though, is that most musical practices do not follow that process, and even in the ones that do, performers have had significant roles in shaping the final result of a musical piece.[20] Thus, the first tools to be produced in the performance category were pre-recorded drum performances (commonly referred to as drum loops) and phrases played by non-Western orchestral instruments and traditions.[21] While the virtualization process of the instruments in the instrumental group aimed to be transparent to the creative process, these ones significantly altered it. The virtualization process of the instruments in the second group generates an asynchronous one-directional collaboration process instead of the synchronous reciprocity of a live recording collaboration. Even in the case of bespoke libraries in which the composer conceives the idea and works with the performer to create the recordings that are sampled, bi-directional collaboration ends with sampling. This means that while the process of creating the library is synchronous and collaborative, once the library is created, the performances are fixed. Thus, this creative paradigm engages with certain aspects of the mash-up culture. Miguel Mera (2013) briefly states: "In its most basic form, a mashup (sometimes also called 'bastard pop') is where two or more samples from different songs are blended together to create a new track," while underlining that "mashup is considered transformative and playful, delighting in synchronic simultaneity and difference and actively demonstrating that meaning is not fixed" (Mera 2013, "Mashup: Beyond Counterpoint?").

The third role aims to encompass virtual instruments that represent a "style or a musical aesthetic." They are usually tasked to capture the musical zeitgeist of the moment when they were conceived. When this happens, it gives them a snapshot of their time period and is a significant resource for the historical study of musical style in screen music (as well as other musical genres). Other options in this role are to encompass a relevant stylistic tradition (e.g., Rock and Roll, Jazz, and different types of EDM). These virtual instruments allow music creators to engage directly in a combination of musical styles without the need to master them fully. They also serve to maintain and somewhat disseminate innovative aesthetic practices to then become a shared aesthetic trend across many musical creators. A well-known example of this process is the orchestral brass sound that Zimmer crafted for *Inception*'s (2010) score. Commonly regarded as "braaams," they were replicated and incorporated in multiple virtual instruments, becoming a staple for the music for trailers for the 2010 decade. Similarly, Heavyocity, a virtual instrument company, has dedicated most of its flagship products to continuously capture the zeitgeist of complex percussive textures with products that started with *Evolve* (2008) to the different versions of their *Damage* Library.

The final group of virtual instruments interacts with the creative process at the "narrative and signification levels." These libraries put at the

Table 4.1 A summary of virtual instrument taxonomies

Virtual instrument taxonomies			
Source of the sound	Design paradigms	Relationship with reality	Creative role
Sample-based	First paradigm	Replicating reality	Instrumental
Synthesized-based	Second paradigm	Functional Toolkit	Performance
Hybrid	Third paradigm	Augmenting Reality	Stylistic
	Fourth paradigm	Simulated Dynamic Realism	Narrative Function and Signification

forefront the fact that a screen composer is a filmmaker. The objective is to encapsulate musical signification in the sound design of a virtual instrument to provide a tool to embed instant meanings into a score. It is also a key reason why composers might decide to create bespoke libraries specifically for a single project, in their aim to encode a distinct sound that aims to provide narrative or philosophical signification to the visual narrative. They are also proof of the power of timbre to efficiently contribute to the generation of meaning through music in these narratives. While many composers embraced this approach, an emphasis on music-making from this perspective has undeniably been a staple of Hans Zimmer's corpus of work since the beginning of the twenty-first century. There are numerous commercial and publicly available tools as well. For instance, most Spitfire *Albion* volumes are dedicated to providing a restricted range of significations, while many of the virtual instruments packaged in Spectrasonics *Omnisphere* also aim for the same.

As a summary, the table above compiles all the taxonomies described above (Table 4.1).

A Practice-Induced Typology of Virtual Instruments

The four taxonomies proposed above are advantageous for describing virtual instruments and determining how they relate to each other from contrasting viewpoints. The taxonomies attempt to provide a robust theoretical background that can facilitate the task of discussing and classifying virtual instruments. To that end, there is a needed abstraction from the products themselves to focus on the inherent properties they exhibit.

The typology proposed below comes directly from praxis and divides virtual instruments into common categories that share a set of properties. While the following typology might be theoretically less robust, its value lies in representing the praxis of the field, at least in the first quarter of the twenty-first century. Moreover, this typology highlights the Western orchestra. Western orchestral music has been the default mode of musical expression for screen music, and this classification shows how the other instruments are conceived as musical extensions for the orchestra, from reaching a wide variety of musical traditions to incorporating synthesis and sound processing. Thus, I divide these tools into six groups:

1. Reproducing the Western Orchestra
   (a) Replicating instruments abstractly or in an acoustic environment
   (b) Orchestral ensembles and performance practices
   (c) Predesigned orchestrations, orchestral textures, and orchestral gestures
2. Reproducing sounds outside of the Western Orchestral Paradigm
3. Epic Percussion, Drums, Percussive loops, and musical accent libraries
4. Analog Synthesizers, Digital Synthesizers, and Analog Synth Emulations
5. Hybrid Synthesizers and Ethereal Timbres
6. Interactive Hybrid Virtual Instruments

The division between the orchestra and everything else is clear: the first group versus all the others. In addition, this typology can also be divided into instruments that aim to replicate physical counterparts (groups 1 to most of 3), synthetic instruments (some of 3 and 4), and hybrid approaches (groups 5 and 6). The following descriptions will refer to the previous classifications when needed to avoid redundancy.

Reproducing the Western Orchestra

I have already thoroughly described that one of the focal design affordances of sample libraries has been to be able to reproduce the symphonic orchestra by individually generating virtual versions of all its instruments and sections. This is why the majority of the libraries from the first and second generations of my design paradigms are devoted to this purpose, and they have a significant presence in the other two paradigms as well.

While the majority of these virtual instruments are sampled-based, the utilization of synthesis, frequently modestly, is not uncommon. The main goal is to replicate reality, but there is also a fair number of virtual instruments of this type that are functional toolkits. Similarly, their creative role can be either instrumental or performance-related. Due to the vast number of products and diversity of design approaches, I divided this first category into three subsections.

The "first" subsection, replication, is partially utopian, as it negotiates with an idealistic model of the orchestra as a musical ensemble for Western culture. It is not possible to establish a unique orchestral sound, and it is even less possible to define a unique recorded orchestral sound. The size of the ensemble,[22] the hall, and the recording techniques employed are variables that have a meaningful effect on the final sound. In addition, the orchestra is constituted of a diverse group of instruments that combine differently. For instance, a solo horn performing a note sounds different from four horns playing the same note. Moreover, if four solo horns were recorded individually and then mixed, they would sound different from recording the four horns together. The difference between an orchestral sound for either Mozart or John Williams is not only a matter of ensemble dimensions, but it is also aesthetic. Eras, styles, or even composers have an associated set of performance practices that affect the performing and recording techniques employed, ultimately affecting the resulting orchestral sound. As a result, attempting to generate sample libraries that reproduce an idealistic model of the Western orchestra becomes a chimeric enterprise.

Hence, the production of a sample library in this subgroup generally begins by selecting a particular overall aesthetic for the orchestral sound, narrowing the scope of its replication efforts. For practical reasons, most libraries aim to replicate a variation of the *Hollywood Studio Orchestra*, although this is not the only possible approach. For example, the *Vienna Symphonic Library* (VSL, released in 2004) aimed for a romantic concert orchestral sound. In the necessity to choose an encompassing aesthetic framework, the designers of sample libraries negotiate between the desire to generate an objective and versatile orchestral sound and the need to adhere to a codified set of principles. Moreover, the concept of the *Hollywood Orchestra* is neither static nor universal for the music written for audiovisual media. As Sadoff (2013) asserts, a library such as EastWest's *Hollywood Strings* "no longer reflects the live sound aesthetics of the concert hall or the Hollywood sound of earlier generations."

Furthermore, the target sound for these libraries is broadly shaped after iconic scores for the screen. For instance, many libraries are modeled after the orchestral sound of new Hollywood films, headlined by most of John Williams' classic scores, generally connected to vast and epic-sounding orchestras. Similarly, after George Martin opened the Lyndhurst Hall of Air Studios in 1992 (Air Studios), it attracted the attention of new generations of screen composers such as Hans Zimmer (Zimmer 2012). As I mentioned earlier, Lyndhurst Hall was used to record Hans Zimmer's sample library already in the mid-1990s, serving him and all his team of composers (and each of their music team members) as the foundation for their orchestral sound. Two decades later, once the sound became a staple of a new Hollywood sound, Spitfire Audio created a string library in that hall that aimed for a much more detailed sound by using a small (16-player) string section while taking advantage of the acoustics of the hall, still delivering a sense of epic. Spitfire's *Sable Strings* (2012), later renamed *Chamber Strings*, was only the first of multiple libraries and scores recorded in that hall.

The libraries in the "second" subgroup—orchestral ensembles and performance practices—are an attempt to overcome the limitations and problems outlined above by engaging in a less rigid relationship between their physical instrument counterparts. Frequently, they fill the gaps that the previous libraries left, attempting to provide a mix between a naturalistic composing solution for specific settings and a naturalistic sound by diminishing the amount of customization. One example is Spitfire Audio's *Albion* (2011), which was also recorded in Lyndhurst Hall and includes a set of instrumental sections. For example, an instrument called "Woodwinds High" is created by recording the flute, clarinet, and oboe playing together (within their registers). This instrument attempts to simplify woodwind writing while aiming to achieve a more natural sound in the woodwind section by recording the instruments together.

In practice, if the previous model intended to create a virtual instrument by sampling it in all its possible performing techniques, this approach attempts to grasp an expansive set of performance possibilities. Instead of attempting to create a model of a virtual instrument that could be programmed to reproduce any possible performance technique, these libraries present a varied set of techniques that serve specific purposes by employing a specific set of performance practices. The advantage of this approach is that the result should theoretically be more natural, as it has been created from a single recording instead of through the union and merging of several samples.

These two different approaches to sample library design highlight the tension between a framework based on highly analytical premises and another that relies on a much more phenomenological approach. The first method assumes that it is possible to describe a physical process by employing a discrete set of parameters that can be mapped onto a set of functions to generate an output. The progress and evolution of the tools based on this model lie in the exponential growth rate of technology. However, this method of modeling presents an inherent risk, which is eloquently exemplified by Borges (1999) in his surrealist story *On Exactitude in Science*:

> In that Empire, the Art of Cartography attained such Perfection that the map of a single Province occupied the entirety of a City, and the map of the Empire, the entirety of a Province. In time, those Unconscionable Maps no longer satisfied, and the Cartographers Guilds struck a Map of the Empire whose size was that of the Empire, and which coincided point for point with it. (p. 325)

This parable highlights that the risk of constructing a model that replicates reality is that you might end up with no model at all. In the case of sample libraries, increasing the complexity of the model could imply requiring the composer or programmer to spend the same time learning how to properly program it that it would require to become a virtuoso of the physical instrument. While this would make the libraries impractical, it can open the door to the utilization of artificial intelligence as a middle layer between the virtual instrument and the composer/performer.

The "third" subgroup—predesigned orchestrations, orchestral textures, and orchestral gestures—evolves from the approach of encapsulating creative aspects into virtual instruments, making these instruments almost an asynchronous collaborator of the composer's team. Therefore, the process of creating the library involves one or more creatives who provide orchestration or compositional expertise by creating textures that are malleable enough not to become pre-recorded phrases but also specific enough to be worthwhile. The main focus of some of these products is on the sonic result. For instance, *Project SAM*'s *Symphobia* (2008) series provides a wide variety of orchestral gestures and textures that aim to become a resourceful toolkit.

Reproducing Sounds Outside the Western Orchestral Paradigm

While the Western orchestra has been at the core of music for film and other audiovisual media, the pursuit of timbral specificity for the generation of meaning has welcomed the addition of every possible instrument on the planet. In addition to not being a default instrument in the Western orchestra, the instruments of this category share a different approach to music-making that is not based on the strictly notated Western score. While other notation systems are not uncommon (the lead sheet being a clear example), these systems are frequently designed to be less specific in terms of matching the final sound result.

This category includes Western band instruments (the guitar or the drum kit), Western traditional instruments (the Irish whistle), instruments that are outside the Western culture (the duduk or the shakuhachi, but also the native American flute), new instruments that have been created recently in any culture (the waterphone), and new sound objects (hitting a water pipe). I have avoided qualifying non-Western instruments as traditional because of an inherent connotation of the term within Western cultural structures, but calling them traditional is not uncommon. Nevertheless, the terminology used to describe a subset of these instruments has been historically questionable, to say the least. From being described as ethnic or world instruments to being considered popular as a contraposition to orchestral instruments, most of these terminologies had a derogatory demeanor. While the audience for virtual instruments has become global, most library makers are in Europe or North America, tailoring their offerings with Western consumers in mind.[23] This was especially true when the first libraries of this group were released during the first decade of the twenty-first century, while subsequent libraries aligned with a more culturally diverse and aware audience.

Independent from the target audience, these libraries share two significant properties that distinguish them from Western orchestral ones. First, for the majority of these instruments, their performance practices are detached from Western notation, which is closely related to the MIDI protocol. Second, most customers will most likely not be well-versed in the instruments and musical traditions these libraries represent. If this was already a challenge in the design of orchestral libraries, it becomes an even more onerous one when you multiply the number of cultures and traditions. It seems implausible to expect that a composer will become proficient in a sizable number of cultural traditions that generally take years or decades of practice and expertise to master.

The design objectives are similar to the ones described for Western orchestral libraries, although they necessarily incorporate specific solutions to the challenges outlined above. Most of the time, the essence of these instruments is closely tied to a particular performance practice.

One initial challenge is that the set of intonations that define how an instrument—e.g., the shakuhachi—is performed cannot be mapped onto a 12-tone pitch structure (or any pitch structure that could be mapped into MIDI). One of the solutions is to record a diverse set of topical phrases, which generate an instrument that, instead of delivering notes, delivers entire musical phrases. The scope for these predesigned musical phrases is necessarily restricted to limited musical situations that permit their integration within the overall musical discourse. Another solution is to record common gestures and note ornamentations. Therefore, the designers of the non-orchestral sample libraries are faced with the problem of creating a workable and flexible instrument that still expresses its original performance practices, which means they are regularly sampled with different performance techniques. Technically speaking, the sampling approach does not differ from how orchestral instruments are sampled. However, while creating a mockup of an orchestral instrument performance with just one articulation is possible, this does not seem to be the case with this group. While the description above is especially pertinent for Western traditional and non-Western instruments and practices, the complexity and approach are similar to how an electric guitar is sampled.

The design and implementation of these virtual instruments unveil several consequences that affect music aesthetics.

1. The utilization of prerecorded phrases engages with certain aspects of the culture of the mash-up.
2. They generate cross-cultural musical entities, allowing the combination of varied instruments to blend two or more cultural traditions into one musical entity.
3. They provide any music creator with easy access to at least some basic features of any musical tradition in the world, triggering a musical version of McLuhan's idea of a Global Village.
4. While the effectiveness of these libraries in becoming final products might not be great, they become the first step for the creator to engage with performers outside of their area of expertise. If we add

the capacity to collaborate and record remotely, they facilitate global music-making practices.
5. They highlight the capacity that timbre and musical gestures have in the generation of fast and efficient musical meaning.
6. They provide a vast canvas from which to innovate and create music and sounds that go beyond any traditions. Therefore, the possibilities in terms of aesthetics and the generation of new codified meanings are vast, which explains the popularity of those instruments in contemporary practices.

Epic Percussion, Accent Libraries, and Loops

In technical terms, the third group of virtual instruments does not significantly differ from the previous two groups. Most of the instrument samples in the third category are percussion instruments that can generally be found in either the orchestra or, especially, non-orchestral settings. Thus, they are usually included in libraries from the two previous categories. What makes the libraries in this third group different is that they share in common an utmost utilitarian goal while becoming pristine snapshots of the stylistic traits prevalent at the moment of their release. Further, their importance in screen music unveils fundamental aesthetic changes introduced with what I defined as hyperorchestral music.[24]

An epic percussion library refers to a set of percussion instruments that propel generally loud action sequences. These libraries become an expanded drum kit for hyperorchestral music. As a virtual instrument, epic percussion samples originated from libraries that provided electronic drum loops and beats. Quantum Leap's *StormDrum* (2004) was one of the first libraries of this kind. The following review by Peter Kirn at the time of its release elucidates the rationale behind the creation of a new concept of virtual instrument:

> If you've watched any of the more epic-styled Hollywood films lately, no doubt you've noticed a musical trend that is taking hold of the industry. Films such as the Lord of the Rings trilogy and Gladiator feature original scores from notable screen composers, and all films rely heavily on the use of what I affectionately call "boomy" percussion. This trend of large, hard-hitting and, at times, almost tribal percussion usage has crossed over into television, music, and of course videogames. [...]

> Orchestral libraries will typically provide bass drums, timpani, and possibly even toms of some kind or another. However, none of these quite capture the sound of those epic soundtracks from Hollywood composers. (Kirn 2005)

The text highlights the influence of *Gladiator* (2000) and *The Lord of the Rings* (2001–2003) in shaping a new paradigm for screen music scoring that included this type of non-orchestral percussion. For example, the taiko drum was employed to create the percussive texture of Isengard in *The Lord of the Rings* (Adams 2010, 388), and since then, they have become standard in the scoring of battle-related scenes.

StormDrum exemplifies the main attributes of the libraries in this category. In the case of *StormDrum*, it aimed to capture the stylistic zeitgeist at the moment of its release. Kirn (2005) further elaborates that for "the contemporary composer and studio musician, it can be a bit of a challenge to create these sounds with existing software, and it is even more of a challenge to find and record the instruments themselves." Thus, the library allowed every composer to embrace the stylistic trend derived from those films. The library also becomes a snapshot of the cinematic style of the time period that preceded its release. They have the effect of popularizing and firmly establishing the stylistic innovations that those films contributed while also contributing to the overuse of these devices that would quickly make them dated. This is the case in libraries such as *StormDrum* that use a sort of reactive design: they are modeled upon existing music. On the other hand, some libraries proactively contribute to advancing and developing the aesthetics of screen scoring. These libraries aim to provide the composer with tools that hopefully would shape the latest aesthetic trend.

StormDrum also exemplifies the utilitarian bias for these libraries. For instance, while one might expect to find a timpani in an orchestral library, the physical instruments sampled on *StormDrum* are less relevant than the function they provide. Sampling Taiko drums was not a decision related to the drums on their own but to their function in the epic action cues from which they are modeled. Consequently, its aim is to replicate a function instead of an instrument. Thus, the virtual instrument that contains Taiko drum sounds is not a faithful rendition of the drum. Instead, it renders the drum (in Chion's sense) as it would sound when fulfilling its epic action function (Chion 1994, 109–15).

Therefore, the library designers process and transform the sound recordings to produce a virtual instrument that fulfills a precise aesthetic purpose and intended function. They fall into the functional toolkit category. In doing so, the libraries are partially hybrid: a combination of an aesthetic idea of reality replication with sound processing to create a hyperreality that better fits their function.

A spin-off of epic percussion libraries are virtual instruments usually referred to as either risers or hits. While epic percussion libraries still try to balance function with a connection with the physical source of the sounds (e.g., the Taiko drum), hits and risers are all about function. The sounds are generally a combination of one or more physical instruments, synthesizers, and generous sound processing. One example of such a library is Native Instruments *Rise & Hit* (2014). It includes folders of virtual instruments named Orchestral, Hybrid Orchestra, Hybrid Sounds, or Hybrid Instruments. The virtual instruments under the orchestral folder seem to refer to orchestral instruments as their recognizable sources. The names of the individual virtual instruments, though, already tell another story: "Bowed to Burst," "Scary Winds," or "Pizz Up." While it is possible to identify that orchestral instruments were part of the source material to create these instruments, there is no attempt to make them clearly recognizable. Hence, these libraries tend to augment reality, as described before, with the purpose of functionality. This is because each instrument of the library provides both a riser (a functional crescendo that lasts for several seconds aimed to raise the tension to arrive at a climatic point) and a hit effect (any combination of a sound impact that would serve to accent a pivotal moment in an audiovisual narrative).

Risers, hits, and similar virtual instruments share another feature: they provide the composer with pre-composed snippets to integrate into their scores. Similarly, many of the libraries in this category provide pre-designed percussion patterns that can be repeated over and over (loops). Percussive loops emulate an established practice that relies on drummers to render the percussive groove of a piece of music without being provided with detailed notation. Thus, a drummer is not only a performer who is able to play a drum kit but also a performer who is able to create a percussion texture based on a few parameters that adapt to the needs of the music at a given time. All these cases constitute a form of nonlinear or distributed creative process that I will describe in more detail in the next chapter.

Analog Synthesizers, Digital Synthesizers, and Analog Emulations

This category of instruments does not use samples as their sound source (or at least not samples as captured sound recordings). They are all either digital synthesizers or hardware models that have been virtualized to be integrated into the composing process within a DAW. Thus, this category encompasses analog hardware synthesizers that are able to use MIDI to synchronize and work with a DAW as an integrated hardware extension, digital virtual synthesizers, and, similarly, digital emulations of hardware models.

Almost all hardware synthesizers created nowadays (including renewed versions of classic synthesizers) have the capacity to input MIDI to be programmed. Therefore, a composer can write down the MIDI information in their DAW, which will be sent to the hardware synthesizer. The synthesizer will then generate sound that will be routed back to the DAW as if it were a virtual instrument. Some of these synthesizers even have specific software to make the communication process even more user-friendly.

Digital synthesizers generate sound using algorithms only. However, many digital synthesizers are based on hardware synthesizers that either model or emulate. Digital emulations of hardware synthesizers are virtual replicas that aim to sound faithful to their hardware counterpart. Replicating a hardware synthesizer is a much less onerous task than doing the same process for the acoustic performance of an instrument. Synths have a finite number of parameters (the knobs and faders) to consider, which are designed using known sound processing techniques. Instead of sampling the sound of the synthesizer, the process of replicating it by creating a virtual emulation involves the analysis of how each of these parameters changes the sound result. Then, the emulation is built with algorithms that mimic the process. One example is Arturia's True Digital Emulation, which the company claims "accurately reproduces the tone, waveshape, tuning and other detailed characteristics of an analog synthesizer" (Arturia, tae). The result of these emulations is generally regarded as very successful, generating virtual instruments that are close to being indistinguishable from their hardware counterparts. Companies such as Arturia have created emulations for most classic hardware synthesizers. For instance, a composer now has the capability to virtually use several instances of the Yamaha CS-80, the synthesizer Vangelis used to create the scores for *Blade Runner* (1982) or *Chariots of Fire* (1981).

The second option for digital synthesizers to be inspired by their hardware counterparts is to be modeled after them. Instead of attempting to replicate one single hardware synth, the designers might try to model different parts of a few analog synths and combine them together in a single virtual instrument that is based on models of hardware but with no referent in reality. A referent in this area is the company U-he, which made popular virtual synthesizers such as *Zebra* (2003), *Zebra2* (2006), and *Diva* (2011). A slightly expanded version of *Zebra2* was extensively used by Hans Zimmer and his team for the score for Christopher Nolan's *The Dark Knight* (2008), which was later released with the name *ZebraHZ* or *Dark Zebra* (2012).

While orchestral instruments have remained unchanged since decades before the first movie scores were written, synthesizers came in after a few decades of movie music, constantly evolving. Some of them are fundamental elements to describe the sonic zeitgeist of the 1980s and the 1990s. Their virtualization allows composers to create historical sonic references from those two decades while also expanding the expressive capacity of sound to represent an era.

Hybrid Synthesizers and Ethereal Timbres

Hybrid synthesizers are virtual instruments that are at the midpoint between a synthesizer and a sample library.[25] Thus, these instruments are hybrid in the sense that they are the product of the combination of recorded sounds, sound synthesis, and sound processing. Their objective differs from all the previous paradigms, with the exception of some instruments in the epic percussion category, as they do not attempt to model a live instrument. Instead, these hybrid libraries utilize sound recordings to generate new sounds via processing or synthesis. The instruments resulting from this hybridization process generally retain some of the associated coded meaning that might be attached to the source of the sound (e.g., a metallic stick hitting a pipe evokes an industrial context). This meaning mutates depending on the amount of transformation applied to the sample. As a result, the instruments in these libraries fluctuate between new sound horizons and connoted meaning from everyday elements of our lives.

Dolan and Patterson (2018) describe a set of acoustic instruments, such as the Aeolic harp, by calling them ethereal timbres. Their definition, though, also applies to the instruments in this category. Dolan and

Patteson suggest that ethereal timbres break the link with the physicality of the sound source while simultaneously becoming an invitation to instrumentalize nature. They also suggest that these sounds invite the audience to "listen more closely to one's environment" by being "attuned to the landscape" (2018, under "Always Already Sound Art"). The design approach of most hybrid synthesizers aligns with the aesthetics outlined by Dolan and Patteson. They make these virtual instruments particularly effective for embedding musical meaning while being highly unobtrusive. They connect the musical result with the meanings attached to its physical sources without the need to become a virtual replica of those sounds. Instead, their design allows the generation of fluent soundscapes that evolve over time, creating a dynamic texture that results frequently from a single MIDI note.

Early examples come from hardware sample instruments that were capable of loading a CD-ROM of sounds to use as the sound source. Spectrasonics became one of the most prominent companies in that area by releasing CD products such as *Distorted Reality* (1995), which were a massive success. A few years later, Spectrasonics released a game-changing product: their first hybrid digital synthesizer called *Atmosphere* (2003). A few years later, Spectrasonics released *Atmosphere*'s successor, *Omnisphere* (2008). It still included all the sounds from *Atmosphere* while further expanding the number of sound recordings and processing possibilities. *Omnisphere* is still, in 2024, a leading product and is continuously used in many scores for audiovisual media. Since the end of the twenty-first century's first decade, many more companies have focused on this type of virtual instrument. For instance, Heavyocity has released dozens of products that would fall into this category.

Interactive Hybrid Virtual Instruments

The last category of virtual instruments is also the last one chronologically speaking. In a certain way, it is a category that builds upon the success of hybrid synths while wishing to return to the connection with an instrumental source. The virtual instruments in this category offer malleable prerecorded gestures or long notes that are performed by an ensemble. They mostly align with the simulated dynamic realism I outlined above.

This new category originated out of necessity. Christian Henson, the co-creator of Spitfire Audio, was working on a TV show that required orchestral music without the budget for the recording. In a forum post on the popular music technology KVR forum, user JessicaAS summarizes the event:

> Award winning composer Christian Henson was commissioned to write 13 hours of music for a sprawling epic TV series, yet there was no budget for orchestra and there was only 3 months to do it in. […] The result was a quick string sampling session where over a range of perfect fourths he recorded a series of greatly differing long strings evolutions, senza vib/ sul taste [sic] into sul pont trem and back again etc etc. When putting the sample instrument together Christian and those who work with him were staggered by the results. The sheer beauty was compelling, and the chaotic nature of different evolutions placed over different intervals made for exciting and unexpected results. (JessicaAS February 13, 2015)

The sample libraries from the project were later released as a free product called *Scary Strings* (2014). The product's success triggered Henson and Spitfire Audio's team to release a commercial and more sophisticated version of the concept called *Evo Grid 001 Strings* (2015). In the introductory video for the product, Henson recalls the reasons why he designed *Scary Strings*:

> The Scary Strings I designed basically as a means of being able to play long notes for a long time without the audience getting bored. I was working on a project that was full of mystery and horror, so I wanted something that started beautiful and turned horrible. So I could both write beautiful, lovely lyrical stuff, but if I just held the stuff down, things would kind of evolve, and change, and morph. (Henson 2015)

Scary Strings contained rather long samples, which were just over a minute long and had the capacity to loop. Spitfire's press release to announce *Evo Grid 001 Strings* acknowledged the product's success. They called *Scary Strings* a prototype and stated that, after its success, they decided to create a "range of recordings according to this prototype" (Spitfire Audio 2015). Spitfire hired Ben Foskett, a concert, dance, and theater composer, to create the orchestrations for these recordings. The length of the recorded samples in EVO Grid was reduced to about 25 seconds, generating loops of about 20 seconds. A sample length of 20 to 30 seconds has become the standard in Spitfire libraries of this kind.

An essential aesthetic consequence for these libraries is the need for a composer to shape and orchestrate the recordings. From this viewpoint, they go beyond the replicative intent of orchestral samples and the sound design or utilitarian focus of previous categories. It is probably why some of Spitfire's most successful products in this area have been created in collaboration with renowned artists. The partnership with Olafur Arnalds, who co-created a series of virtual instruments inspired by this concept, arguably had the most impact. Similarly, several companies started to produce similar types of virtual instruments based on the combination of evolving pre-conceived textures within a given aesthetic. Sometimes, the results might fall between instruments in this category and hybrid synthesizers, such as with the company Slate + Ash.

It is also necessary to distinguish this approach from a much older strategy based on pre-recorded phrases or motives. The content in these libraries is, by design, much more malleable, less specific, and textural in its approach. It makes the sounds easier to combine, helping to generate even more sonic outcomes without the rigidity of a predesigned phrase that needs to fit in the musical grid. It also foregrounds the emotional content of a performance with its constant timbral changes, which cannot be replicated with approaches based on short and isolated sample recordings.

Conclusion

In this chapter, I have explored the toolkit of the contemporary screen composer with an emphasis on the effects that technology has on the creative process. In addition, I provided a detailed approach to classify and discuss virtual instruments. The description of the design of virtual instruments indicates their importance in shaping the aesthetic of contemporary musical practices, which will be described in subsequent chapters. In addition, the utilization of these instruments opens up the possibility of creating music impossible to produce by physical means only, unfolding the true potential of the hyperorchestra.

One of the challenges of describing virtual instruments is that they are now widely accessible and commercially available technology to a wide range of audiences. As I mentioned, my focus is on the aesthetics as they relate to the production of contemporary music for commercially available audiovisual narratives. Sample libraries nowadays are, in a reduced scope, similar to sporting equipment such as sneakers. All professional athletes use them, and the companies design these products with these high-performing professionals in mind, but their true market is everybody else. Buhler (2021) provides a compelling overview of the landscape of commercial sample libraries from the point of view of their advertisement and what they are aiming to sell to their wide range of customers.

In the professional composer landscape (including seriously aspiring composers), most marketing is word of mouth, as there is nowadays a general distrust in sample library marketing. This market also has much more direct access to companies and their developers and is often offered some of the products for free. I would even suggest that the perceived role and utility of certain libraries significantly differ between the professionals and the hobbyists. This means that a library might be advertised as something aimed at hobbyists and be used by professionals in a different way or purpose.

With all of that in mind, while it is not possible to completely detach the analysis of virtual instruments from its commerce and marketing, my approach on this chapter has been to focus on the aesthetic and in the established practices within the screen scoring industry.

Notes

1. MIDI 2.0, while increasing exponentially the flexibility and the capability of the protocol, is backward compatible. This means that it does not significantly alter the capacity to flawlessly implement the 12-tone Western musical system.
2. For more information, see Pejrolo and DeRosa (2007, 1–19). The discussion that follows concentrates on the conceptual implications of the MIDI 1.0 protocol. Thus, for the sake of clarity, the specific descriptions of the technical implementation of the protocol are omitted unless they are necessary. Concomitantly, this present discussion analyzes MIDI in its practical objective definition, which does not imply that its original design was created as a mapping of the Western musical framework. However, the practical result of the protocol is much more flexible, and it is generally not attached to a Western tradition. For this viewpoint, it is important to remark that although most of the names associated with diverse aspects of the protocol generally have connoted meanings within the Western musical framework, the implementation of the protocol only registers numbers. For instance, naming Continuous Controller Number 1 as "Modulation" does not practically affect how this controller functions within the protocol. As I will describe later on, this controller is regularly used nowadays to control either the dynamics or the vibrato of the instruments.
3. For MIDI 1.0, all the ranges are generally from 0-127, allowing for 128 different notes, states, or values. The only exception is the *pitchbend*

message that is allowed 16,383 different values. MIDI 2.0 increases the range significantly in some of these aspects, providing even more flexibility. At the same time, it does not alter the overall conceptual framework.
4. The MIDI protocol offers the possibility to use 16 channels that could help to designate which continuous controllers affect which instruments.
5. The four input interfaces do not represent the totality of possible input devices, although they are a relevant sample. In the case of the mouse, it is regularly used in conjunction with a graphical interface in a computer DAW (Digital Audio Workstation).
6. Although the physical structure of the keyboard implies a 12-tone based musical model, this is the system that will work most organically when employing a musical keyboard.
7. Relatedly, the MIDI protocol makes it very complex to create a successful mapping of microtonal music. While the use of the pitch bend (with its 16,384 possible values) with all the MIDI notes could theoretically generate over 2 million possible values for microtonal music, the implementation to achieve this is fairly impractical. MIDI 2.0 is designed to facilitate a wide range of different tunings due to its increased capacity to encode data.
8. There are techniques that partially solve the instrumental techniques problem, by employing unused MIDI notes (key switches) or CC in order to trigger different types of articulation sounds (pizzicato, tremolo, legato, etc.). However, at a conceptual level, they are still different instruments that are triggered together in the same MIDI instance by using a sort of switch.
9. Continuous Controllers do have a MIDI channel though. However, a virtual instrument only uses one MIDI channel, which means that in the realm of this instrument, it affects the whole instrument. A variation of the protocol called MPE (MIDI Polyphonic Expression) developed by Roli exists while not part of the standard MIDI definition.
10. As I will describe later on, CCs are generally used to represent dynamic variation in instruments that produce sustained sounds such as a bowed violin note.
11. While it is possible to use MIDI to control the parameters inside an equalizer, MIDI as a communication protocol is unable to transport sound and therefore interface in the signal flow process.
12. More information for similar systems can be found in Pejrolo (2005, 76–83).
13. In this instance, instrument refers to the specific sound entity defined before (e.g., violin pizzicato), not to a specific physical instrument.
14. Sampling is the process of recording sound fragments in order to create a virtual instrument based on these recorded sounds.

15. While this is not strictly relevant for the discussion, which is more generic, it is common that there are consensus in the design of the user interfaces for virtual instruments across developers, with the aim to simplify the task of the music producer who uses products from multiple companies. To that end, CC1 and CC11 are frequently used to control either the dynamic or the volume of the sound and, by far, are the two most common CCs used for virtual instrument design, with the exclusion of CC7 that is exclusively used to control the overall volume of the instrument always in addition to any volume control that CC1 or CC11 might implement.
16. James Buhler, email message to author, June 26, 2024.
17. A dry sound is recorded in a studio that intends to cancel any possible reverberation effect as much as possible, by employing special sound treatment and microphone positions.
18. I called the sonic placement hyperrealistic because it is possible to render a virtual placement that results in a sound that could not be generated in the physical world due to the total freedom of mixing different perspectives.
19. The technique of inferring additional dynamic layers from a subset of recordings was first envisioned in the sampler *Soundpaint*, developed by the parent company 8dio.
20. To start, many Western classical composers were performers themselves. To give just one example, Franz Liszt's music for piano is intricately connected to Liszt being a virtuoso performer of the instrument and to his performance practices.
21. A simpler variation of a sample library is an actual collection of samples that are already designed to be looped. While these collections lack a sampler to trigger the sounds, they are equivalent for the purposes of this discussion.
22. An orchestra for a Mozart symphony is vastly different to an orchestra needed to perform a Mahler symphony.
23. For an examination of the extensive use of virtual instruments and sample libraries by Nigerian composers, see (Obumneke S. Anyanwu 2022).
24. While these libraries, especially the drum loops, are also indispensable for most of electronic dance music genres and other musical styles, I maintain the focus of this analysis in screen music.
25. For a more extensive discussion about this particular type of virtual instrument, see my chapter titled *Atmospheres, Synths, and Spectral Transformations in Scores for TV* (Casanelles 2024). While in the second decade of the twenty-first century, these types of virtual instruments were present in the majority of screen music, they were mostly used in TV scoring when Spectrasonics *Atmosphere* (2003) was released.

References

Adams, Douglas. 2010. *The Music of The Lord of the Rings Films: A Comprehensive Account of Howard Shore's Scores* (Book and Rarities CD).
Borges, J. L. 1999. Collected Fictions. Penguin Books.
Buhler, James. 2021. "Blank Music: Marketing Virtual Instruments." In The Oxford Handbook of Music and Advertising, edited by James Deaville, Siu-Lan Tan and Ron Rodman, 93–118. Oxford University Press.
Buhler, James. 2024. "Composing for the Films in the Age of Digital Media." In The Mediations of Music: Critical Approaches after Adorno, edited by Gianmarco Borio, 144–162. London: Routledge.
Burton, Byron. 2019. "How 'Chernobyl' Composer Found Inspiration in a Real (and Radioactive) Power Plant." The Hollywood Reporter. https://www.hollywoodreporter.com/news/general-news/how-chernobyl-composer-found-inspiration-a-radioactive-power-plant-1228682/.
Casanelles, Sergi. Forthcoming 2024. "Atmospheres, Synths, and Spectral Transformations in Scores for TV." In *The Oxford Handbook of Music in Television*, edited by James Deaville, Jessica Getman, Ronald Rodman and Brooke McClorke. Oxford: Oxford University Press.
Chion, Michel. 1994. *Audio-vision: sound on screen*. New York: Columbia University Press.
Eco, Umberto. 1990. *Travels in Hyperreality (Harvest Book)*. Mariner Books.
Emmerentze Jervell, Ellen. 2019. "Icelandic Artist Drew Sounds from Power Plant to Compose 'Chernobyl' Soundtrack." Billboard magazine. https://www.billboard.com/music/music-news/hildur-guonadottir-icelandic-artist-chernobyl-soundtrack-interview-8527454/.
Henson, Christian. 2015. "Spitfire Walkthrough - Evo Grid #1: Strings" Spitfire Audio. https://www.youtube.com/watch?v=xwxM14oSZnY.
Hurwitz, M. 2011. "Sound for Picture: Hans Zimmer's Scoring Collective - Composer Collaboration at Remote Control Productions." In The Routledge Film Music Sourcebook, edited by James Wierzbicki, Platte Nathan and Colin Roust, 254–257. Routledge.
Karlin, Fred, and Raybund Wright. 2004. *On the Track: A Guide to Contemporary Film Scoring*. Routledge.
King, Darryn 2021. "How Hans Zimmer Conjured the Otherworldly Sounds of 'Dune'." New York Times. https://www.nytimes.com/2021/10/22/movies/hans-zimmer-dune.html.
Kirn, Peter. 2005. "East West Stormdrum Sample Library: In-Depth Review." https://cdm.link/2005/07/east-west-stormdrum-sample-library-in-depth-review/.
McLuhan, Marshall. [1964] 1994. *Understanding Media: The Extensions of Man*. Cambridge, Mass.: MIT Press.

Mera, Miguel. 2013. "Inglo(u)rious Basterdization? Tarantino and the War Movie Mashup." In *The Oxford Handbook of Sound and Image in Digital Media*, edited by Carol Vernallis, Amy Herzog and John Richardson. Oxford University Press.
Mera, Miguel. 2016a. "Materializing Film Music." In *The Cambridge Companion to Film Music*, edited by Cooke Mervyn and Ford Fiona, 157–172. Cambridge: Cambridge University Press.
Nolan, Christopher. 2010. *Inception*. [Shooting Script].
Obumneke, S. Anyanwu, Emaeyak P. Sylvanus. 2022. "Music Production Technology in New Nollywood Soundtracks: Context, Application, and the Effect of Globalization." *Music and the Moving Image* 15 (1): 22–37.
Pejrolo, A. 2005. *Creative Sequencing Techniques for Music Production: A Practical Guide to Pro Tools, Logic, Digital Performer and Cubase*. Routledge.
Pejrolo, A., and R. DeRosa. 2007. *Acoustic and MIDI Orchestration for the Contemporary Composer: A Practical Guide to Writing and Sequencing for the Studio Orchestra*. Kidlington, GBR: Focal Press.
Persing, Eric. 2009. "Psychoacoustic Sampling" Spectrasonics. https://vimeo.com/5748896.
Prasad, Anil. 2004. "Miroslav Vitous: Freeing the Muse." Innerviews: music without borders. https://www.innerviews.org/inner/vitous-1.
Rogers, D., Phoenix N., Bergersen T., and Murphy, S. 2009. *EastWest/Quantum Leap Hollywood Strings Virtual Instrument User's Manual*.
Sadoff, Ron. 2013. "Scoring for Film and Video Games: Collaborative Practices and Digital Post-Production." In The Oxford Handbook of Sound and Image in Digital Media, edited by Carol Vernallis, Amy Herzog, and John Richardson. New York: Oxford University Press.
Spitfire Audio, 2015, "EVO GRID 1 - If you liked our 'SCARY STRINGS' you'll love this!!."
Stewart, Dave. 2010. "EWQL Hollywood Strings." Sound on Sound. https://www.soundonsound.com/reviews/ewql-hollywood-strings.
Stewart, Dave, and Mark Wherry. 2003. "Vienna Symphonic Library: Orchestral Cube & Performance Set First Editions." Sound on Sound. https://www.soundonsound.com/reviews/vsl-orchestral-cube-performance-set.
Vary, A. 2013. "Inside The Mind (And Studio) Of Hollywood's Music Maestro." http://www.buzzfeed.com/adambvary/hans-zimmer-film-composer-inside-his-studio.
Wherry, Mark. 2002. "Media Adventures: Hans Zimmer and Jay Rifkin." Sound on Sound. https://www.soundonsound.com/people/media-adventures.
Zimmer, Hans. 2001. The Gladiator Waltz. Universal Classics Group.
Zimmer, Hans (Rctec). 2012. "Hans Zimmer Sound?" VI Control. https://vi-control.net/community/threads/hans-zimmer-sound.24544/page-2#post-3614029.

Zimmer, Hans. 2013. "Oil Rig. Man of Steel (Original Motion Picture Soundtrack) Deluxe Edition." WaterTower Music.

Zimmer, Hans. 2021a. The Dune Sketchbook (Music From the Soundtrack). WaterTower.

Zimmer, Hans. 2021b. "Hans Zimmer's use of computers and samples in orchestral music" In "Mix with the Masters." https://youtu.be/_LHyNYRtwR8?si=VUrPPKEv0N3HB0Ep.

Zimmer, Hans (Rctec). 2022. "Abbey Road vs Air Studios." https://vi-control.net/community/threads/abbey-road-vs-air-studios.100100/post-5176469.

Zimmer, Hans, and Christopher Nolan. 2011. "Hans Zimmer - Making Of Inception Score" Hans Zimmer - Making Of Inception Score. https://www.youtube.com/watch?v=gL5en8Y10OU.

PART II

The Hyperorchestra and the Contemporary Aesthetics for Screen Music

CHAPTER 5

Hyperorchestral Aesthetic Frameworks for the Screen Music Composer

The changes in the screen scoring process that resulted from the introduction of digital technologies are vast. They changed how music was made, how the process integrated within the creation of the audiovisual narrative, and promoted the development of new aesthetic grounds. A sonic approach to music analysis allows to uncover the musical score's full potential that is generally hidden when using only a score-based reductionist analysis. At the same time, it allows music to be more relatable to other elements of the audiovisual experience, such as light and color. From this viewpoint, this chapter explores how screen scoring has become a nonlinear process, increasing the capacity to collaborate, communicate, and integrate within the whole filmmaking process. Further, it explores how the unfolding of the full potential of music through sonic transformation and digital technologies allows for more precise and extensive ways to produce meaning through the conceptualization of hyperinstruments and the hyperorchestra.

In the upcoming two chapters, I will examine the music creation process for audiovisual media using hyperorchestral resources from an aesthetic perspective. In Chap. 3, I described music in the hyperreal and the concept of the hyperorchestra from the point of view of technological development. The following chapters will explore the aesthetics of the hyperorchestra and its capacity to surpass what can be musically achieved with acoustic or electric means only.

© The Author(s), under exclusive license to Springer Nature Switzerland AG 2024
S. Casanelles, *The Hyperorchestra*,
https://doi.org/10.1007/978-3-031-75193-6_5

This chapter describes theoretical models of praxis, which I refer to as frameworks. The first framework discusses the evolving nature of what we consider music and our evolving process of aesthetic evaluation. While highlighting a timbral shift in musical analysis, I provide foundational concepts for analyzing screen music through sonic analysis in tandem with inspecting the score's generation of narrative meaning. Only through a mode of musical analysis that emphasizes its sonic properties can one fully discern the value and intricacies of hyperorchestral music. After that, I will describe three composition-related frameworks for the contemporary composer: a nonlinear model of music creation, the conception and creation of hyperinstruments, and the utilization of the hyperorchestra. For clarity and specificity, I will provide examples from twenty-first-century audiovisual narratives and screen music creatives that are particularly clarifying.

Hyperorchestral Screen Music Analysis: A Sonic Approach

As an artistic form, music holds an aesthetic status within a given culture at a given time. It is a status based on the consensus among the people of that society. In other words, defining what music is music in a society is arbitrarily determined by its people. This definition emphasizes that the appreciation of art depends not only on its intrinsic qualities but also on how it aligns with the values of the culture that experiences it. Thus, the aesthetic value of a piece of music is the result of the sensory stimuli it creates in conjunction with a set of cultural values.

Relatedly, a movie is a multimodal cultural object independently of its audiovisual mode of delivery. The narrative content is attached to the society that produced it and the tools and techniques that render the final product. Music is part of the audiovisual content of the movie, contributing to its meaning and aesthetics. Ron Sadoff (2013) stresses the importance of a multifaceted analysis of screen music in *An Eclectic Methodology for Analyzing Film Music* by including a referential level of analysis. The musical content of a movie might be described as the sum of (1) the music in the movie, (2) its referential meaning, (3) the assumed musical background to comprehend the referential meaning, and (4) the assumed meaning inside the narrative. For example, Kubrick assumed in *A Clockwork Orange* (1971) that the audience would possess some knowledge of Beethoven's music beyond what is stated in the movie's narrative.

In this context, analyzing contemporary screen music must account for how it operates within the audiovisual framework and its aesthetic value based on contemporary assessments. It is essential to separate musical functions and roles from the musical devices that have been traditionally attached to them. For example, tonal harmony has customarily provided structure to the musical discourse, generating moments of tension and release. However, it is possible to structure a musical discourse by other means. Further, that flexibility allows musical devices, such as harmony, to be employed to fulfill other functions. Hence, the increased sonic possibilities produced by the digital manipulation of sound provide new ways to shape musical function. Thus, two new interconnected areas appear with the expanded sonic landscape produced by digital music and defined within the framework of the hyperorchestra. First, new possibilities for associating meaning emanate from the musicalization of a wider variety of sounds. Second, there is a necessity for a sonically grounded analysis of music.

Concerning meaning associations, screen music commonly relies on understanding the cultural qualities of a piece of music, which is generally significant when it comes to discerning how the piece interacts with the rest of the elements of the audiovisual narrative. The meaning associations of a piece of music are a cultural construct within a culture. Denotative meanings (explicit or direct associations) of musical elements acquire an especially significant role in the expanded sonic world of the hyperorchestra. By expanding the sound sources beyond musical instruments, composers utilize a more extensive array of sounds chosen because they carry an attached denotational level of signification. For example, a hybrid synthesizer built using the sound of the wind will serve as a denotation of air or wind. Functionally speaking, they might replace the sound of a flute that, while airy, its link to air is much closer to connoted meaning (implied or second-hand). Therefore, the hyperorchestra highly increases the access to musicalized sounds that might become denotative, creating clear and direct associations. In doing so, it leaves additional room for connoted meaning to portray either deeper levels of signification or to add nuance to a denotative association. These processes will become much clearer after describing the primary axioms that would constitute a sonic analysis.

Sonic Analysis

The second area of hyperorchestral analysis of music involves the need to incorporate a sonic perspective, an analytical process involving technical ear training that involves critical listening skills.[1] By sonic analysis, I refer to the analysis of musical elements from the viewpoint of sound. However, in the expanded world of the sounds of the hyperorchestra, what constitutes a musical element? In the most objective terms, music is a subset of sound, which is, at the same time, a subset of acoustic waves (Fig. 5.1).

Acoustic waves, a type of mechanical waves, are objectively defined by Physics. To define sound involves examining the process of reception of these acoustic waves. Thus, it is expected to define sound as the range of acoustic waves the human ear can hear. In specific circumstances, sound could be defined as the sounds an animal can hear, which would differ from the range humans can perceive. Sound technologies (from microphones to digital music) are primarily anthropocentric. Thus, unless there is a need for specific uses, the way we store and reproduce sounds is designed to capture the range of sounds we can hear.

Further, each person perceives a different frequency range inside the human hearing range. Additionally, all people lose their capacity to hear the highest frequencies with age, at different degrees and rates. Thus, the essential information transmitted with sound is usually delivered in a much narrower range of frequencies than the ones the best and youngest human ear could perceive. For instance, a sound in a moderate amplitude at the higher range of the human hearing spectrum (e.g., 18KHz) will only be distinctly perceived by a minority of human beings. At the same time, it can be easily stored using our standard digital storage protocols. However,

Fig. 5.1 A graphical representation to show how music is a subset of sound, which is also a subset of mechanical waves

is it really sound, which is defined in terms of reception, if most of the receivers cannot perceive it?

With this highly concise introduction, I wanted to suggest that defining sound is more subjective and complex than one might expect. It impacts how music is made to ensure that all the information arrives at the broadest possible set of audiences and how we might analyze and understand its spectral properties.

In addition, as a subset of sound, music is defined arbitrarily according to a cultural framework. Thus, the borders that separate music from sound are variable and frequently blurred. They evolve over time and vary depending on the cultural background of each listener. The borders might even mutate depending on the musical style. Including new sounds in music has been common practice in Western music for centuries, with increased intensity since the second half of the twentieth century. In screen music, the score is part of the soundtrack, which includes dialogue, a non-diegetic narrator, and sound effects. They all share, along with the visual track, the common goal of contributing to the movie's narrative.

In *Sound Design Is the New Score* (2020), Danijela Kulezic-Wilson advocates for an integrated approach to the soundtrack. This involves not only applying sound design approaches to the musical score but also the musicalization of the soundtrack as a whole. Kulezic-Wilson states, "Instead of the conventional orchestral sound that existed on a different level of perception and functionality than sound effects and dialogue, we now have scores where the language is in many ways much closer to noise or ambient sound" (6). In parallel, Buhler (2020) argued in *The End(s) of Vococentrism* that contemporary films are less reliant on having dialogue as the centerpiece of the soundtrack. Buhler argues that in classical cinema, "vococentrism signified that everything in sound film passed through the voice, even when the voice was absent" (2020). However, in contemporary commercial cinema, "narrative still dominates the conception, to be sure, but that narrative is more complexly rendered and it no longer requires the voice to integrate the soundtrack" (2020).[2] Both Kulezic-Wilson and Buhler emphasize how the aesthetics that derived from digital cinema have blurred the distinction between sound effects and music:

> In any event, a world rendered with music and digital effects is, as Chion long ago pointed out, not a world of reality but a representation that attempts to get us to feel the impact of the world. Music focalizes feeling and renders emotion-as-we-hear-it. This is how most contemporary cinema

has approached the confusion. However, it is also possible to confuse the distinction in the other direction and create an equally stylized effect by lifting a sound out of the diegesis and into the music and thereby transform it into a motif. (Buhler 2020)

A sonic approach to screen music analysis is vital to analyzing music from a hyperorchestral perspective that connects with digital cinema aesthetics outlined above by Kulezic-Wilson and Buhler. Further, as I mentioned above, many hyperorchestral sounds emanate from the capacity to musicalize any sound by transforming it using digital music processes. In other words, following my hypothetical example before, the sound of wind could become a functioning musical instrument by using hybrid synthesis and other digital tools, resulting in a sound that is still connected to the source (the diegesis) while embracing a sonic mutation that enhances its expressive potential. Therefore, musical processes within the hyperorchestra would remain unnoticed without a sonic analysis of its music because they fall outside the paradigms that constitute traditional Western approaches to music theory and analysis.

Therefore, in calling this analytic approach sonic, I am emphasizing a standpoint that locates the sonic properties of music as the primary source material for musical analysis. Nevertheless, utilizing this approach does not disregard the traditional theoretical approaches for analyzing music, which, when appropriate, become similarly valuable for portraying a score's whole picture.

A sonic analysis highlights aspects beyond traditional musical characteristics of pitch, harmony, melody, and instrumentation. Thus, it incorporates the spectral properties (the characteristics of the frequency spectrum) of each of the sounds of the music. For example, a flute might be presented with different amounts of reverb, recorded with diverse amounts of air sound, or produced with an equalization process that removes part of its frequency range (filtering). These three cases are musical features that might become paramount in describing the musical characteristics of the music and its associated meaning. Moreover, any of these parameters might evolve over time, generating musical processes and effects comparable to changes in harmony, melody, or texture in a traditional sense.[3]

Hyperorchestral music adds another layer to the score analysis: an assessment of verisimilitude. Thus, assessing the degree of verisimilitude of an instrument or a sound involves a process of critically listening and comparing it to the cultural model that defines realism. For example, a sound perceived as unreal might generate specific meanings due to its unrealistic nature.

The analysis of hyperorchestral screen music must combine established screen music approaches that incorporate the analysis of the narration and narrative functions of the score in order to provide meaning and structure with a music analysis that is also capable of assessing its sonic features. This kind of analysis is supported by scoring practices detached from a linear process of conceiving the music first, then writing it, and finally recording it. Nonlinear processes to music making diminish the importance of the musical score and the Western music analytical frameworks that accompany it in favor of an approach that encompasses sound as the primer matter of music. The rest of the chapter is devoted to exploring the creative processes involving the hyperorchestra throughout the description of creative frameworks for the music creation process.

Music Creation Frameworks

Based on the previous discussion, music is an arbitrary, culturally defined subset of sound. Thus, to describe music requires a combination of aesthetics (and culture), technology, and pragmaticism. By technology, I mean what is technically possible at a given time (e.g., synthesizers require electricity to be invented), while by pragmaticism, I mean what is reasonably plausible within the culture (e.g., concert halls are designed with a musical model in mind that restricts the size of the ensemble and the location of the musicians by creating a stage). Writing music has almost always been limited by these constraints, which is why music composers have generally relied on frameworks for creating new pieces.

For instance, the score, the orchestral instruments, and an established set of performance practices have served as compositional frameworks for Western music creation. In conjunction with the score, each instrument provides an established sound output based on the information presented in the score and interpreted by the performer. As I described in Chap. 3, the orchestra is a model implicitly connected to how Western concert halls are designed. Equivalently, all musical traditions suggest a musical framework based on the boundaries and limitations of a sound that wishes to be considered music. Generally speaking, a new musical framework emanates when musical boundaries extend or change. To exemplify this process, I will explore the design of the ADSR model as a necessary framework that emanated with the development of synthesizers to ensure they remained within the musical borders. Thus, it is an example of a framework that pushed the boundaries of music by imposing some restrictions on synthesizers.

Example: Synthesizers and the ADSR Framework

The sonic possibilities of Western orchestral music expanded by adding new instruments and extending the techniques available to its instruments. However, the orchestra has barely evolved since the beginning of the twentieth century. At the same time, other musical styles that emanated from popular music have expanded the sonic possibilities of Western culture by using recording studios and electricity-driven devices. When a composer adds a new instrument to the orchestra, they add a new interface for music production. This interface becomes a new framework from which to generate new music. It might be that, as a result, the music produced with the added instrument extends the boundaries of what is considered music. With non-acoustic instruments, such as synthesizers, the process of expansion of the boundaries becomes much more noticeable. Acoustic instruments produce a limited and defined range of sounds, whereas the synthesizer can create a much wider variety of sounds that lack organicity.

Almost all synthesizers use the Attack, Decay, Sustain, and Release (ADSR) envelope model. These four states are the different stages a musical note conceptually goes through during its *lifecycle*. All physical sounds begin in a silent state. The physical body responsible for producing the sound needs some time to start vibrating in order to generate sound waves. Imagine playing a note on a piano: when the hammer hits the string, there is no sound. Once the string has been hit and the hammer no longer physically touches it, the string starts to vibrate, thus increasing its vibration amplitude, which is perceived as volume. This process is what is called the attack. After the attack stage, the musical note will recover from the attack and lower its amplitude (volume) until reaching a more stable state of vibration. During this stage, the vibration device recovers from the impact of the attacking device (the hammer in the piano). After this stage, there is a period of time when the note stays at a similar amplitude, the sustain stage. Finally, the note ends when the vibrating object returns to its non-vibrating stage, the release. This whole process is regularly modeled following a prototype similar to Fig. 5.2.

5 HYPERORCHESTRAL AESTHETIC FRAMEWORKS FOR THE SCREEN MUSIC... 197

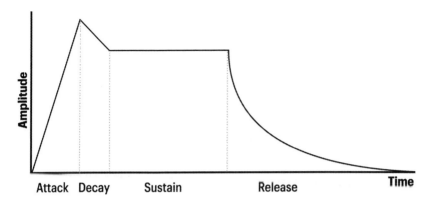

Fig. 5.2 Visual representation of the main principles of the Attack, Decay, Sustain, and Release (ADSR)

Fig. 5.3 Graphical representation of the sound wave of a timpani hit, with the ADSR labels superimposed

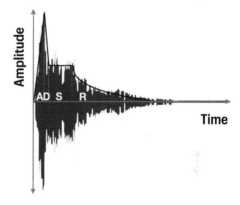

The release stage might be triggered by either the forced end of the note (the piano key is released and, therefore, the damper forces the string to stop vibrating) or because the vibrating source does not vibrate anymore (after a while, the piano string will stop vibrating). This template for the lifespan of a musical note roughly models how musical notes sound, especially for percussion instruments. In Fig. 5.3, the ADSR model is superimposed over a waveform of a timpani hit.

Synthesized instruments do not require an attack, decay, or release stage. As the sound is created using electric signals and without a physical vibrating medium, it can begin sounding at the desired amplitude and be cut without a release. However, modeling them through an ADSR envelope template brings them closer to how physical instruments react, thus stretching the boundaries of what is considered music less. In other words, a synthesized sound without ADSR might be considered a sound (a beep), whereas a synthesized sound with an ADSR envelope applied to it might become a musical note. However, modeling the sound of a note in terms of a generic ADSR opens the door to an expanded range of sound processes that go beyond what would be natural or achievable with physical instruments. Furthermore, it provides a framework for sound expansion that still preserves the connection with some physicality.

The example of ADSR envelopes reveals the necessity of creating frameworks that define music and how the flexibility of those structures is critical for expanding the boundaries of what is considered music in a given culture.[4] By establishing a virtual model inspired by physical processes but not restricted to them, utilizing the ADSR model allows for a curated expansion of the musical boundaries that feel culturally connected to the existing musical background. As I suggested above, parallel to the introduction of synthesizers, the boundaries of screen music have expanded with the addition of multiple sound sources, some of which are associated with diverse cultural backgrounds.

These processes, along with the new models they generated, have become the substrate for creating music in the hyperreal. In this chapter, I define the aesthetic frameworks for hyperreal music from these substrata. Next, I will provide a general model for music and hyperreality, which will interconnect with how recording music has affected the music creation process. After that, I will outline a model for the hyperinstruments and their creation. Finally, I will propose a framework for the hyperorchestra. I will exemplify these three frameworks through discussion and analysis of a few relevant audiovisual narratives.

Creating Music in the Digital Age: A Collaborative and Nonlinear Mode of Composition

Except for the music for the films in the silent era, screen music has always been a recorded medium. In Chap. 3, I suggested that recording music is inherently a hyperreal process because, during the recording, music transcends its pure physicality to become virtualized. Figure 5.4 provides a visual depiction of how music operates in hyperreality.

5 HYPERORCHESTRAL AESTHETIC FRAMEWORKS FOR THE SCREEN MUSIC...

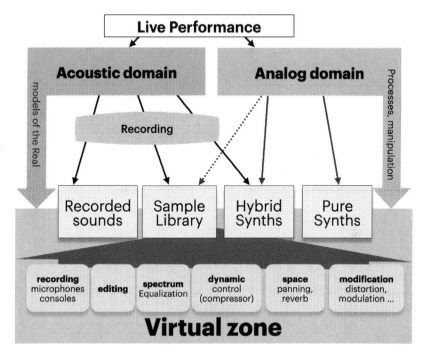

Fig. 5.4 Music in the hyperreal. This graphic shows how sound sources from the physical world are transported to the virtual area for processing. Once this happens, music becomes hyperrealistic

I differentiated the analog domain (music created with electricity) from the acoustic domain (organic instruments). Although electricity is part of humanity's physical world, its revolutionary nature goes beyond pure physicality. There is a crossover between the acoustic and the analog domains that I did not include for the sake of clarity, which involves electric instruments such as the electric guitar. They are acoustic instruments that require electrical amplification. The musical processes that go into the virtual zone involve recording.[5] Film music recording sessions brought acoustic music into the virtual. Then, it was edited, processed, and mixed. The final music mix is at the end of the process.

Similarly, creating sample libraries and hybrid synthesizers involves recording, processing, and mixing. Once the sounds are virtualized, they are used to generate virtual instruments that are autonomous from the physical reality.

In the virtual zone, music can be modified by editing, processing, and mixing. Editing involves selecting the takes or take fragments to generate a single linear music track. Editing already makes it possible to produce results that surpass the acoustic domain. For instance, it allows cutting the time required for a string performer to change from playing *pizzicato* to bowing. With mixing, it is possible to combine music that was never performed at the same time, rearrange the volumes of each of the instruments, and, in a similar manner as processing, modify the sound of the instruments by equalizing or compressing the dynamic range. The difference between mixing and processing is slight. However, by processing, I mean the modification of the sound creatively, beyond the intent of keeping the verisimilitude to a performance.

The Traditional Linear Scoring Process

The above model provides a general outlook on the interaction between music and hyperreality. It highlights recording as the conduit into the hyperreal. Figure 5.5 represents the traditional screen scoring process and its interaction with hyperreality.

The graphic outlines a linear process. It begins with the conceptual step of music creation. The conceptual stage draws from project-based materials (e.g., the temp track, the script, or production meetings), along with knowledge of film language and music theory. The composer would create the music at the conceptual stage using their understanding of the items above. From a Western perspective, the music would be written, orchestrated, and prepared. Once this process is completed, it is then performed and recorded. A performance involves the selection of specific instruments and performers for each of the instrumental parts, along with a place to record the music. Although the process of recording would ideally minimize any possible incidents, they might still happen. The recording virtualizes the performances, beginning with selecting and placing microphones and recording equipment. These devices are the link between the physical and the virtual. At the purely virtual level, music is assembled in a hyperreal process that involves, as aforementioned, editing, processing, and mixing.

The incorporation of sample libraries into the conceptual stage added a new element: the musical mockup. The composer would generate a digital

5 HYPERORCHESTRAL AESTHETIC FRAMEWORKS FOR THE SCREEN MUSIC...

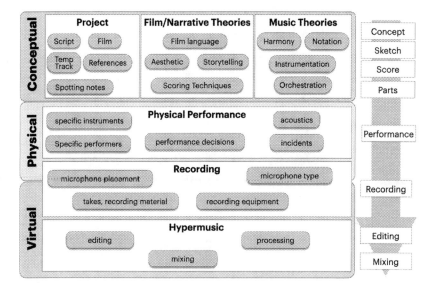

Fig. 5.5 Graphic visualization of the processes involved in a traditional movie scoring composition process

simulation of the score. As described in the previous chapter, the mockup became a very efficient communication for the conceptual stage. When that happens, the conceptual process merges with the virtual one, thus making the beginning and the end of the process part of the same realm, producing a sort of loop. Inevitably, the linear process collapsed after the introduction of the mockup, subsequently evolving into the following model.

The Contemporary Framework for Audiovisual Music Creation

As described in Chap. 4, sample libraries permeated into the final musical product. This transformed music creation and production, generating a nonlinear model. The music sequencer in the DAW is at the center of the music creation process. A DAW is a computer software that provides several functions. One of its functions is using MIDI's flexibility to generate hyperscores. In addition, the DAW integrates with varied virtual instruments that generate sound using MIDI information (Fig. 5.6).

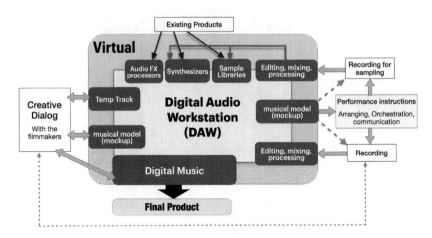

Fig. 5.6 Graphical visualization of a framework for contemporary music scoring. As it is a nonlinear process, there is no specific linear set of steps. Instead, the DAW becomes the core of the process

From the perspective of the DAW, synthesizers and sample libraries are equivalent devices: virtual instruments that input MIDI information in order to output sound. MIDI contains tempo information, and its messages are time-stamped, which means it is temporally equivalent to the Western score. This equivalency facilitates the process of music creation and any transcription process into a musical score that can be performed acoustically. MIDI tempo could potentially be ignored as well, opening the door to other means of musical expression. The DAW can also contain audio recordings that are placed on a timeline that aligns with the MIDI temporal information. The audio material within the DAW can be edited in a variety of ways. In addition, the DAW integrates with various sound processors, allowing the manipulation and modification of the sound that comes from either the audio samples or the virtual instruments. Finally, the DAW allows for the loading and synchronizing of a video track with its existing musical score.

A significant advantage of this framework is that a sonic rendering of the music is always available. It also allows for multiple versions and approaches to coexist simultaneously, increasing the capacity to communicate and collaborate even further. The music is sculpted and assembled virtually during the process. The right side of the graph shows two essential processes that involve recording. First, there can be recording sessions in order to create audio samples for the score. These audio samples might even become custom-made sample libraries specific to the movie. These samples integrate with the MIDI tracks by either being placed as audio files in the DAW or by being converted into a sample library, which will be operated through MIDI analogously to any other virtual instrument. The second process involves recording sessions that are closer (or equal) to the traditional scoring process. Thus, all or part of the instrumental material might be recorded. Each recording session might include an entire ensemble (e.g., the Western orchestra), just individual instruments, or instrumental sections, thereby increasing the mixing and editing possibilities. Once recorded, the music returns to the DAW (or stays if the same DAW is used for recording) while integrating with the rest of the digital musical elements.

Both procedures might require arrangement or orchestration for the physical instruments that will perform the music. Sometimes, the performer might create their part based on a provided mockup or idea. Sampling generally involves planning and design to generate the required sound material adequately. It is important to mention that recording is not limited to musical instruments. Anything that produces sound could be recorded and incorporated into a score. The final result might come entirely from the content garnered during the recording sessions, generating music akin to the traditional scoring model. Even in this case, the use of the DAW has made the process of music creation take place in the hyperreal.

This model prompts a nonlinear music creation process. The flexibility introduced by removing the need for linearity allows composers to adapt to the changes in the filmmaking process. For instance, digital movie editing allows continuous editing and adds a degree of nonlinearity to the process. A nonlinear music scoring process becomes necessary, so the score continuously adapts to the editing changes. Moreover, the music creation process can start generating musical demos long before there is any edited footage of the movie. Music inside the DAW can be conformed to new picture edits after being written.

Furthermore, digital files can easily be shared and duplicated, enabling multiple people to work on the music concurrently. Therefore, a team of music creators (in a broad sense) can quickly adapt existing musical material to synchronize with the latest cut of the movie. Thus, the process of movie scoring becomes scalable. Additionally, a digitized framework affords increased flexibility in the postproduction process. The music mix is habitually delivered in different blocks called stems. Thus, playing all stems at once results in precisely the music mix. In collaboration with the filmmakers, the dubbing mixer can reshape the music from the stems for better integration with the audiovisual narrative. Stems can also be used to create new music material without the need for the composer's intervention.

Below, I provide three diverse cases that illustrate the creative framework described above while highlighting its potential for storytelling and collaboration. Hans Zimmer's score for Christopher Nolan's *Inception* (2010) is an example of the expansion of orchestral sounds through a process of nonlinear recording and sound manipulation while creating a musical result that engages with the narrative. Ariel Marx' score for the limited series *A Small Light* (2023), created by Tony Phelan and Joan Rater, illustrates the power of contemporary scoring approaches in a score that is divided into three musical palettes following the show's narrative. Finally, I will describe how composer Bear McCreary has engaged his team of composers in his company Sparks and Shadows in a collaborative scoring process.

Example: Inception (2010), *Challenging Reality and the Impossible Orchestra*

Hans Zimmer's score for *Inception* (2010) exemplifies the expanded possibilities of creating meaning using music created in the framework described above. It is a movie in which a traditional scoring process would have fallen short of its narrative needs. Further, it exemplifies the necessity for a sonic analysis to tackle the different musical elements in the score.

Directed by Christopher Nolan, *Inception*'s narrative suggests that dreams may be equivalent to hyperreality. While dreams are not a representation of the physical world, they feel perceptually realistic when we are experiencing them. The plot revolves around a group of dream specialists who artificially create and share a dream with a person in order to steal information from them. The movie's narrative goes beyond questioning whether we might be living in a dream by asking if that question even matters, as it blurs the line between reality and dream from a perceptual or quasi-phenomenological point of view.

I will illustrate these points by using the architect training sequence (00:29:05). In the sequence, Ariadne, a new dream builder (an "architect"), learns how to design and transform a dream world in ways that transcend reality. The scene presents one of the most astonishing images of the movie, whereby Ariadne decides to fold the dream world. The music for the scene begins when Ariadne starts to manipulate the world in a manner that would not be physically possible; in Ariadne's words: "My question is, what happens when you start messing with the physics of the world?" [6] Ariadne is building a world from Cobb's, the main character and mentor, dreams.

The musical score for the sequence, as is the case for the rest of the movie, maintains coherence with the narrative and its philosophy. The orchestral part of the ensemble is comprised primarily of brass and strings. In addition, there is a formidable percussion complement (synthetic and recorded), electric guitar, and various synthesizers. The harmonic and melodic structure of the music at this moment contains only a repeated progression of four chords (g minor, F♯ Major, E♭ Major, B Major). The harmonic and melodic progression is a sort of wallpaper upon which the music is constructed. Orchestration, dynamics, and rhythm become the core musical elements. From these elements, I sample the three that are the most significant in relationship to both the framework outlined above and the hyperorchestra.

The Expanded Orchestra

The brass section sounds verisimilar even though the rendered sound could not be produced in a Western live orchestral context. The acoustic recordings took place in Air Studios. Brass was recorded separately in an ensemble of six bass trombones, six tenor trombones, four tubas, and four French horns. The horns were located at the gallery level above the stage (Zimmer and Nolan 2011). Zimmer argues that he assembled the biggest brass section ever in a studio. It also more than triples the amount of brass in the vast majority of Western orchestral pieces. It would most likely be impossible to have this amount of brass at a louder dynamic to balance with a string section in a concert hall while the strings played in a reasonably soft dynamic. Even if using hundreds of strings could make this possible (which is doubtful), the hall required to host all the musicians would be so large that it would add a significant amount of reverb, diluting the power of the music and the overall effect. The music sounds verisimilar to an orchestral sound while also sounding like a maximized version of reality. It exemplifies a nonlinear process of recording that allows the composer to mix orchestral sections in a hyperreal manner.

While the massive brass permeates the score in many ways and functions, one signature sound became so iconic to be given a name: the low brass-like sounds now generally referred to as "braams." They have permeated the scoring practices, and they have been present in a significant number of trailers since then. Zimmer explains how these sounds were created and that it all originated from an idea in the script:

> I made the sound, but that means nothing. Chris wrote the sound in his screenplay to Inception. It was his way of showing time slowing down. We booked a studio for the next day with 10 brass players, and we had a piano in the middle of the room with a brick on the sustained pedal. So the brass would play into this piano, and all the strings would be vibrating—and that's the sound of Inception. (Zimmer 2022)

Indeed, Nolan details these sounds in the shooting script as:

> INT. DILAPIDATED HOTEL ROOM—DAY
> In the distant background, strange MASSIVE low-end MUSICAL TONES start, sounding like DISTANT HORNS. (Nolan 2010, 14)

The creation of "braams" highlights the collaborative power that emanates from the contemporary scoring process. It allows for fluid communication between notes on the script, the ideas of the composer, the director, and the rest of the creative minds. It also hints at the vast possibilities for creating complex new meanings through music through hyperinstruments.

An Impossible Crescendo

The crescendo effects are also carefully measured to enhance the emotional reaction to the scene. They begin as a slow increase in the dynamic, become quite pronounced toward the last third of the effect, and then end abruptly. The masterfully crafted *crescendo* produces the psychoacoustic sensation that the music is louder than what is possible in reality. As discussed in Chap. 3, musical notation is vague when attempting to precisely notate the amount of dynamic change in a passage. Figure 5.7 depicts an attempt to notate the *crescendo* I just described as precisely as possible.

Figure 5.8 shows how a typical Piano Roll notation in the DAW would notate this *crescendo*, which reveals a much closer approach to the dynamic gesture.

5 HYPERORCHESTRAL AESTHETIC FRAMEWORKS FOR THE SCREEN MUSIC... 207

Fig. 5.7 A progressive crescendo written utilizing a traditional musical score notation

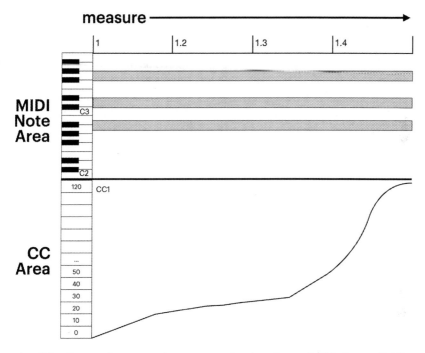

Fig. 5.8 Progressive crescendo representation based on a DAW piano roll. The top frame is used to write the note, whereas the bottom frame is used to write continuous data. In this figure, a 0 value in this lower area means the lowest possible dynamic and the highest value (127) means the highest possible value. The top numbers are the measure and beats

Carefully calculated crescendos are a fundamental tool to generate expressivity within an audiovisual sequence. The possibility of manipulating, with precision, the increase in the dynamics at any moment becomes a tool for synchronizing the music with the content of the scene.

Expanding the Sound Palette with Synthesizers
The remainder of the ensemble for the sequence consists primarily of a set of synthesizers. They can be divided into three approaches: synths that emulate brass-like sounds, lower-ranged thunder-like sounds, and airy synths. They fully integrate into the soundscape without being recognized as extraneous elements. The brass-like synthesizers may be perceived as an extension of the dominant brass sound of the expanding chords. Similarly, the airy sounds integrate into the whole soundscape, functioning as a sonic tail to the *decrescendos*. The lower-range synthesizers become especially apparent when Cobb's projections start to become hostile to Ariadne once they perceive that their world is being changed.

By using the musical tools described above, the composer produces musical meaning through innovative sound associations that would not be possible within a purely traditional orchestral scoring process. Thus, *Inception*'s score exemplifies how modern narratives rely on the innovations of the medium to produce sophisticated works, intellectually-provoking narratives, and nuanced meanings. For instance, the sequence described above depicts Ariadne's discovery process of the possibilities dream-world-building offers to surpass the physical world. Thus, discovering the capacity to fold a world is a crucial turning point for the character. The viewers, though, have already seen a few spectacular manipulations of the dream world before this sequence, which means the sequence is less surprising for the audiences than it is for Ariadne.

In this context, the music serves to convey Ariadne's emotional shock. Hans Zimmer's score conveys the emotional intensity of the moment while unveiling Ariadne's character development. Unreal crescendos and airy sounds create an otherworldly sensation that illustrates the hyperrealistic world Ariadne is creating. Similarly, the morphing of the orchestra into brass-like synth sounds becomes more evident when the characters walk through the manipulated dream world, making the music mimic the manipulation process. Additionally, low-register synthesized sounds are employed when Cobb's projections start to manifest. Sounds at these low frequencies would be challenging to produce acoustically, becoming a potent signifier of Cobb's subconscious that fuels these projections and their hostility. Later on, in my analysis of the music in *Annihilation* (2018), I will further explore the concept of organicity versus synthetic as a means of musical meaning.

Example: A Small Light (2023), Nonlinear Process and the Artisan Score

This example aims to illuminate how the nonlinear contemporary scoring process has allowed for increased stylistic diversity and experimentation in scores crafted from what we could define as an artisan score.[7] The limited series *A Small Light* (2023) explores the tragedy of Anne Frank and her family through the lens of the people who help them hide, especially Otto Frank's secretary, Miep Gies. The title is taken from a famous quote by Gies, "Even a regular secretary, a housewife or a teenager can turn on a small light in a dark room," and sets the overall narrative for the show. While the pillars of the story are the commonly known tragical historical facts (the Franks hiding for two years until they are discovered), the show's primary focus is on the lives of the resistance and the acts of courage they did to save lives and to fight the Nazi invasion. It combines moments of leisure and everyday activities to remind us that they were all still humans trying to live their lives with their actions under occupation. The show's composer, Ariel Marx, created three different sound palettes to differentiate the three realities the show was depicting sonically:

> The first is the score for pre-war Amsterdam, levity in the annex, the friendship between Miep and Otto etc. This palette has a lot of warmth—plucked strings, playful melodies, embellished clarinet lines etc.
>
> The second palette is a bit more serious and consequential and reflects the increasing pressure Miep and Jan are under. This palette is much more in the classical/neoclassical world with strings, keys, and electronics. While there is a strong sense of melody in these themes, there is also an urgency, and tension with an underbelly of darker acoustic and electronic elements.
>
> The third palette is all about tension, in all its little and large forms throughout the series. This was probably the most contemporary of approaches, and it uses a lot of electronics, percussion, and harsh, extended techniques on acoustic instruments. (Dreldon 2023)

Managing three simultaneous sound palettes (which would be the equivalent of ensembles in traditional scoring practices) is a clear example of the potential offered by the utilization of the DAW and nonlinear scoring practices. I have called the scoring for the show Artisan[8] because it uses an approach that is based on the individuality of the composer to conceive the musical soundscape for the show in a unique manner and in which the composer is working fundamentally alone. As a multi-instrumentalist,

Marx played many of the lines in the music while also collaborating with individual performers who provided additional performance recordings.

Conceiving three musical soundworlds that interact with how the story was told is a process greatly facilitated by nonlinear composing with the DAW at the center. In the traditional scoring model, having these three soundworlds would have meant keeping them in the composer's imagination until they were orchestrated and recorded at the end. While this is certainly possible, it prominently constricts the creative process in shaping the sound world, especially in creating new sounds that are not directly available. Thus, sound sculpting with the aim of developing sounds to fit diverse narrative and storytelling purposes becomes much easier and much expanded in this model. It puts the composer at the center of the process, allowing them access to and influence the whole sound creation process.

Further, the existence of digital versions of the music to be used in discussions with the rest of the creative team certainly allows for increased experimentation. The creative team of the show is able to listen to and approve the music or request changes without significantly interfering with the process. Thus, it seems reasonable to assume that through this method, the composer feels compelled to greater degrees of experimentation rather than aiming to play it safely so as not to disappoint the showrunners when they listen to the music at the very end of the process.

With this example, I wanted to emphasize that the nonlinear creative process I outlined provides a much-increased degree of experimentation and makes it possible for composers to become sound artisans. While the nonlinear process is also helpful for assembling and coordinating composer teams, as I will detail in the following example (making it a model that facilitates the industrialization of the artistic process), it is as essential for empowering and nurturing experimentation using an artisan approach to scoring.

Example: Bear McCreary, Sparks and Shadows, and the Composing Teams

In this example, I explore the collaborative potential a nonlinear process of scoring has to facilitate the creation of efficient and musically cohesive composing teams. To be clear, the process I describe here is not incompatible with the artisanship I just described, as they often complement each other. In this case, though, my focus is on how the nonlinear process allows for a division of labor akin to industrial processes while retaining quality and artistic value. Well-known infamous cases during the Golden Era have shown how challenging it is to create music for a film at a certain speed across several composers without making it feel disjointed and lowering the artistic quality.[9]

Composing assistant teams started to be widely assembled since digital technologies allowed the shift to the nonlinear composing framework I outlined. It has taken a few years, though, for this process to be solidified enough to become publicly acknowledged. The case I am describing revolves around composer Bear McCreary and his company Sparks and Shadows, who has started to receive official credit for the music they compose.[10] McCreary explains this change in a blog post devoted to the music for *Percy Jackson and the Olympians* (2023):

> This series' "Music by Sparks & Shadows" credit is relatively new. After carving my own path into the media scoring business and building a loyal team of additional music writers along the way, I am proud to nurture the next generation of successful screen composers. I have enthusiastically supported Sparks & Shadows, a collective formed of my most talented protégés, to branch out into their own projects. In addition to *Percy Jackson and the Olympians*, I am proud to see Sparks & Shadows awarded well-earned credits on many major projects, including *Halo*, Paramount+'s series adaptation of the iconic game series, Kevin Smith's *Masters of the Universe: Revolution*, as well as the second season of Apple+'s *Foundation*, the Blumhouse and Lionsgate feature film *Imaginary*, and Sony's beloved videogame experience *God of War Ragnarök: Valhalla*, among others. (McCreary 2024)

While this acknowledgment has effects on labor conditions and credit—and also on how audience members, producers, creators, and directors react to the fact that there is more than one composer—my focus here is on the process.[11] The music credits for *Percy Jackson and the Olympians* credit Bear McCreary for the themes, and Sparks & Shadows for the Music. In a first impression, this does not seem particularly revolutionary. In the traditional scoring process, a composer could write down some thematic material on staff paper and have another composer develop the score based on these themes, such as how John Barry's theme for James Bond has been used in all Bond films.

Let's explore the vast differences that modern nonlinear composing offers to the classical model I outlined above. First, the themes would reside in a DAW file (generally called a session). These themes would, at least, contain a finalized demo of how they sound, which would serve as a means of discussion with the show's creative team. The composers in Sparks & Shadows would receive these sessions that contain MIDI data, the information of which virtual instruments are assigned to which MIDI data, audio recordings, and audio processing information. Each composer has a computer that makes these files easily interchangeable. This means they all use the same virtual instruments, reverbs, and other tools. Therefore, they all share similar hardware and software, which is usually called a DAW template. Music can be easily co-written by several members of the team. They can also use part of the material from one cue and incorporate it into another by sharing their sessions beyond the thematic material. A revision might be done by the same composer or by someone else. Similar to software development practices, version numbers are routinely used to organize the collaborative effort. Further, composers might also be in charge of conforming tasks, which means the combination of material from several pre-existing cues to create (conform) a new musical cue. This process generally involves merging musical information from different sessions and writing additional musical elements to glue everything together.

Without delving too much into the technicalities of the process, the paragraph above exhibits the impact that a DAW-centric nonlinear composing process has on a collaborative approach to music creation. Somewhat simplifying, music is not shared at a conceptual stage (a mockup) but at a stage comparable in quality to how it will be at the end of the process. The collaboration is not a realization of a shared conceptual idea but a real collaborative music creation work at the production stage. Doing so lands results that are much more cohesive and renders a score that feels seamlessly composed by a single person. In sum, it brings the advantages of effective teamwork practices developed since the post-industrial era in the realm of scoring with the aid of necessary technology.

Hyperinstruments: A Timbral Revolution

A hyperinstrument is an instrument of the hyperorchestra and thus inhabits the hyperreal. As they pertain to screen music, hyperinstruments are conveyors of meaning, capable of a higher degree of specificity than their purely acoustic counterparts. Creating a hyperinstrument is not necessarily a matter of technological transformation but an attitude toward using sound specificity to provide curated meanings that contribute to the narrative, similar to how spectral music is commonly defined (Feinberg 2000a, 2).

As I described before, an instrument is an interface for music creation that generates a framework from which to produce music. One consequence is that instruments are intricately connected to culture and tradition. Thus, modifying instruments impacts the aesthetics of a given culture and might prevent the maintenance of a cultural tradition.

For instance, an instrument from a Western orchestra has an expected set of performance instructions that can be accomplished, which will generate an expected sound. Thus, a violinist will be able to play the pitches within the register of the instrument in a set of predefined techniques or performance modes to produce a result that will be generically attributed to the instrument. For the instruments of the Western orchestra, though, there are two additional features to consider. First, the instruments have barely evolved in over a century because they reached a state where any changes to improve anything would also probably have a tradeoff.[12] In other words, these instruments are the best they can be to fulfill the role they were designed for. Relatedly, performers and ensembles routinely perform pieces from the past, which would invalidate any changes to their instruments that would prevent them from either playing or maintaining the quality of their performance of older repertoire.

Thus, new music written for the Western orchestra needed to adapt to the instrumental restrictions and inability to evolve its instruments. For example, composers have envisioned means to produce new sounds without modifying the instruments, commonly referred to as extended techniques. They are techniques that extend the established practices of the given instrument within the Western cultural framework. From this viewpoint, an extended technique might be considered a predecessor of a hyperinstrument, as it generates a sound that is outside of the established cultural framework in an attempt to generate sonic specificity. Most extended techniques focus on expanding the sound possibilities of the instrument. For instance, the effect of a string performer playing *sul ponticello* (placing the bow closer to the bridge instead of its regular position) is mainly sonic. The intention of the composer, when asking for *sul ponticello*, is to generate a type of sound that is specific and intentional. For example, Michael Giacchino extensively used the *sul ponticello* technique in the score for *Lost* (2004–2010) to signify a sense of eeriness and potential danger.

Hence, the utilization of extended techniques denotes an attitude to music focused on the effect of timbre to modulate artistic expression, which can be applied to the creation of meaning. Electric instruments (e.g., the capacity to add effect pedals to the electric guitar) and synthesizers also expanded timbre similarly. The attitude toward creating hyperinstruments emerges from this background, taking it a step further aesthetically and technologically. Figure 5.9 models the definition of a hyperinstrument, which shares common ground with the previous frameworks.

The graphic aims to emphasize the two aspects that shape a hyperinstrument: sonic specificity via means of production and the association of narrative meaning to the sound of the instrument. I will revisit the concepts in the graphic in the following chapter to describe modes of

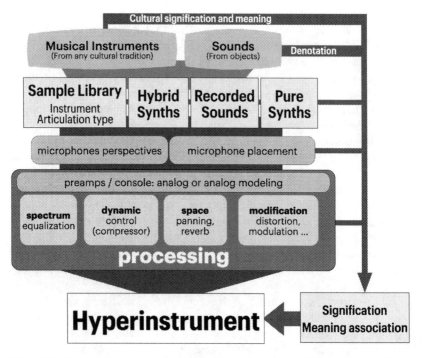

Fig. 5.9 Graphical representation of the hyperinstrument design framework

hyperinstrumental creation as a hyperorchestration tool. For now, I will focus on the aesthetic implications as they relate to the creative process.

Thus, writing for hyperinstruments requires a willingness for sonic specificity. For example, imagine a passage meant to be performed by a clarinet playing *staccato*. Traditional orchestral writing would write the passage in the clarinet part and mark *staccato*, accepting as appropriate the result that a sufficiently trained performer would provide. Hyperinstrumental design and writing would involve either (a) selecting from different staccato articulations in diverse clarinet sample libraries to find the precise sound that best fits the musical intention or (b) designing a clarinet recording in the same degree of specificity. Further, the performance will be specific to a performance tradition (not necessarily the Western orchestral clarinet performance). The sonic result would either become part of the final score or be recorded, edited, and mixed from this degree of specificity. Similarly, creating a hyperinstrument could also involve carefully selecting the desired microphone placement to achieve a desired idea or transforming the sound of the instrument by adding sound processing.

Therefore, the necessity for shaping a sound that signifies a specific meaning is present at all the stages of the design of the hyperinstrument. For instance, for Nolan's *Dark Knight* trilogy (2005–2012), Zimmer and his team created a sample library of Batman's cape swish sound that would be integrated into the score, functioning as a percussion instrument. This hyperinstrument directly denoted Batman by musicalizing the sound of one of his most iconic gadgets via sonic materialization. Another example is the reversed sounds used in *Gravity* (2013), which portrayed a somewhat terrifying depiction of outer space and the absence of sound.

One of the implications of creating instruments that are specifically customized for a specific purpose is that they lose the universality of the traditional orchestral instruments. They are frequently project-specific entities designed to provide narrative content in a manner that makes the sounds of the score unique and thoroughly tailored to the project. In sum, a hyperinstrumental attitude acknowledges the importance of crafting an explicit sound that is attached to a specific narrative meaning while contributing to creating a musical soundscape that makes the movie unique. The examples below will further clarify the concept by analyzing specific instances of hyperinstrumental design and their connection to the narrative needs of the audiovisual piece.

Example: Man of Steel *(2013)*, a Multicultural Drum Orchestra to Represent Humankind

One of the most prominent features in the music for *Man of Steel* (2013), composed by Hans Zimmer, is the utilization of sophisticated hyperinstruments. The drum ensemble became one of his most groundbreaking creations for the film. To form the hyperinstrument, the music team brought together twelve of the top drummers in Los Angeles (Zimmer 2013a). The drummers came from different musical traditions. During the recording session, the drummers began each take in unison, following a rhythmic pattern given by Zimmer. Then, they were asked to introduce rhythmic variations in accordance with their own personal drumming style. The initial intention was to apply the concept of a sectional sound to the drums. As Zimmer points out:

> I've used drums before in scores, but if you have one drummer, it sounds a bit cheesy. It is a little bit if you have one solo violin; it's always sort of right in your face, but if you have a string section, it sounds beautiful. I thought, what if we could get the twelve greatest drummers and melt them into one giant machine of energy? And we did that! (Zimmer 2013c, 1:04)

However, one element substantially differentiates this example from a string section. Whereas the string ensemble aims to create a homogenous sound, the "drum orchestra" purposely incorporates the individual cultural traditions of its performers. Furthermore, the drums were recorded using both individual close microphones for each drum set and microphones placed in the center of the stage. Thus, in addition to the individualities of each drummer's performance style, the sound of the drum orchestra is also the result of mixing a set of microphones capable of highlighting the individuality of each player. Therefore, Zimmer's hyperinstrumental design for the drum orchestra differs from the sound a generic drum ensemble might produce. In terms of meaning, the score for the film aimed to produce an earthly feeling that directed the attention of the narrative toward humankind instead of the depiction of a superhero. Zimmer states:

> My inspiration for the music came from trying to celebrate all that is good and kind in the people of America's heartland, without cleverness or cynicism. Just from the heart. I wanted the epic sound of the fields and farms stretching past the horizon, of the wind humming in the telephone wires.

5 HYPERORCHESTRAL AESTHETIC FRAMEWORKS FOR THE SCREEN MUSIC... 217

The music is less about the icon that Superman is, and more about the outsider with extraordinary powers and his struggle to become a part of humanity. (Rolling Stone 2013)

The "machine of energy" (the drum orchestra) was not meant to represent a superhuman but to portray the power of the epic that emanates from a diversity of voices that constitute humankind, who are also capable of sounding unified. It also provides the movie sound specificity with a sonic texture that has never been done before, highlighting a sort of organized chaos that symbolizes humanity's biggest strengths and vulnerabilities. The sonic result of the drum ensemble for most of the score is a subdued but highly energetic epic. The movie's sound effects are generally sharp and spectrally dense, a product of the sound design technologies that unfolded with digital sound editing and manipulation, which allows them to acquire the role that traditional orchestral percussion hits used to have.

While the sound of the drum ensemble modestly appears on Superman's planet, Krypton, most of its role relates to humanity. A pristine example is the three-part climax of the film. At that moment, Zod, the Kryptonian antagonist, aims to terraform Earth, destroy humanity, and repopulate it with genetically pure Kryptonians. Zod deployed two terraforming machines on opposite sides of the Earth. There are no drums when Superman destroys the first device (1:52:00-1:54:50). The music is focused on his decision to side with humanity instead of with his genetic legacy. The second device is destroyed in a coordinated effort by humans and significantly features the drum ensemble. It is a much more arduous task that unfolds a much more chaotic action sequence, in which the drum ensemble serves to reinforce the unity through the diversity idea that the narrative is portraying. Finally, the third part of the climax involves the final fight between Superman, who has now fully embraced Earth, and Zod. The score now *rewards* Superman with the humanity-linked drum ensemble after he fully commits to humanity.

On the opposite musical side, there is the Superman theme. The only similarity to Williams' iconic theme for the same character is in the opening 5th interval and a certain reliance on wide intervals. Whereas Williams' theme is outward, Zimmer's is inward. The theme appears first when Superman is born, and it is performed by French horns (which are generally warmer and more heartfelt than the trumpets of Williams' theme). However, the most memorable renditions of the theme happen in an even more intimate musical setting through an upright piano. Echoing his thoughts about making the score about the American people, such as Kansas farmers, who "never get celebrated," Zimmer aimed to represent them in the theme by cueing them "to on an old upright piano, and it was an old upright piano. I'm not a great keyboard player, I've played it, and it could have been better. Every time I got someone who was a real pianist and played it, it lost all its quirkiness and heart" (Weintraub 2013). Zimmer's thought process represents what I describe as the hyperinstrumental design process. In this case, the specificity of the sound to produce the intended meaning does not only involve selecting a precise sound source (a very singular upright piano that is slightly out of tune and maintenance) but also the performer (himself as a nonprofessional piano player).

Technically speaking, the drum orchestra was recorded and then sampled to create sonic material to construct the score nonlinearly, following the creative process outlined in the first framework. The sessions generated a set of recordings that would serve to design a sample library to create the score. They were integrated into the film's scoring process by becoming bespoke virtual instruments and audio loops. The score has other noteworthy elements that help to define how a messianic mythical hero struggles to integrate into American society as an outsider. For instance, similar to the drum orchestra, there is an ensemble of steel guitars.

The score for *Man of Steel* exemplifies many of the potentials related to hyperinstrumental design and conception, from the capacity to portray varied and specific meanings. The drum orchestra converted a staple of high-stakes action films, the percussion hits, into something much more profound and narratively significant without necessarily compromising its key role in the narration. Similarly, a hyperorchestral attitude is so liberating as to be able to conceive a main theme played using a non-pristine-sounding instrument and with the quirks of a non-pristine performance. These features become assets to implement a vision designed to produce powerful meanings that resonate with strong emotional connections. Finally, virtual instrument designers picked up the concept and started releasing libraries based on uncommon ensembles (e.g., a marimba ensemble). The company 8dio released a series called *Acoustic Ensembles*, and Spitfire Audio released what they called *Swarms*. After that, this instrumental technique became widespread and an affordable available option for a wide range of composers through the use of sample libraries.

Example: Chernobyl *(2019) and the Sound of Radiation*

Hildur Guðnadóttir's score for the limited series *Chernobyl* (2019) shows another angle from which to approach the creation of hyperinstruments.[13] The show retells the events of the nuclear tragedy at the Chornobyl nuclear power plant. One of the principal locations of the shooting was in a decommissioned nuclear power plant in Lithuania. Guðnadóttir, along with field recording engineer Chris Watson, traveled during shooting to record sounds and the ambiance of the power plant (Kraft and Holmes 2019, 27:55). While the example from *Man of Steel* focused on the creation of hyperinstruments that emanated from musical instruments, in this example I want to focus on the utilization of sound objects as the source for hyperinstruments. Due to radiation, Watson and Guðnadóttir were wearing protective equipment, which would have prevented any real interaction with the power plant (like singing). One of the main sources of sound material ended up being a door:

> Guðnadóttir put contact microphones on the door and recorded its incredibly high-pitched sounds. "We ended up pitching them down so they would be in an audible range, then orchestrating them into the score," she explains. "I used the sounds in the funeral music that highlights the hospital scenes with the radiation victims." (Burton 2019)

Compared to the process of designing the drum orchestra in *Man of Steel*, which followed a concept attached to a desire to provide specific meanings to the movie, the conception of the score in *Chernobyl* had a different route. It resembled a sound hunting process in an environment that was meaningful for the narrative, a nuclear power plant, and the show, as it was a primary shooting location. Thus, the location was significant, and the hope was that the sounds recorded in that location would also become meaningful for the score. At the same time, the process outlines a sort of self-reflexive process for the composer. Being there becomes an inspiration for the music, while the sound-hunting process is informed by the composer's ideas about the score. It does not only become a lived experience from which to draw a needed inspiration to craft music to represent something as complex as radiation, but also a self-guided search for meaningful sounds in that environment. The team also captured the necessary sonic data to create a simulation of the metallic reverberation of the environment—called an impulse response that creates convolution reverbs (Størvold and Richardson 2021, 32).

Finally, Guðnadóttir made a significant portion of the sounds in the score come from these recordings, self-limiting her sound sources for the show as a means for increased creativity. Regarding the reverb, it was extensively used to process the composer's voice heavily, "implying a ghostly agency that—from time to time—calls out from deep within the musical texture" (Størvold and Richardson 2021, 38).

From a hyperinstrumental viewpoint, the sound-capturing process in the power plant explores the denotative power of sound objects, how they provide meaning for the score, and how they induce an artistic state of mind to produce meaning-inducing sonic results. The recordings at the power plant were guided by a composer in search of specific and useful sound material to craft the score, and the recording journey in the location served to guide her sonic ideas to produce meaningful hyperinstruments for the show.

Example: World Building Through Hyperinstruments in Dune *(2021–2024)*

The score for *Dune* (2021–2024), directed by Denis Villeneuve and based on Frank Herbert's book of the same name, combines the two hyperinstrumental approaches defined for *Man of Steel* and *Chernobyl* while incorporating additional strategies related to world-building. Hans Zimmer visited the desert following a similar process I detailed above for *Chernobyl*:

> There was a moment when I disappeared into Monument Valley and the desert in Utah and Arizona to check the veracity of my ideas. How does the wind howl through the rocks? How does the sand grit in your teeth? It's just vastness and endlessness. (Burlingame 2021)

While Zimmer's trip to the desert—as a means to corroborate if his existing musical ideas represented wind and sand—is more intentional, the desert visit also seems to be an experience that enriches and inspires the composer based on the desert's materiality. Similarly but much more brutally than in *Man of Steel*, Zimmer assembled 30 bagpipe players to create a massive ensemble sound (and loud, arriving at 130dB) to represent the diegetic scene containing bagpipe players during the Atreides landing to Arrakis (King 2021). At the same time, the first solo bagpipe sound was actually an electric guitar performance heavily transformed and manipulated (Zimmer 2022).[14] These are all powerful examples of the creation of hyperinstruments for the movie. However, I will focus on the elements of the score that go even beyond the models already defined in its mission to represent a new world.

Dune's duology is, surprisingly, Zimmer's first time scoring a non-Earth science fiction or fantastic movie. Zimmer's focus is on world-building in a manner that distances it from scores of *Dune*-inspired universes such as *Star Wars*. Zimmer states that as a 13-year-old, he was confused with the scores for those kinds of films: "Why do all these science fiction movies have European orchestras, orchestral sounds, romantic period tonalities about them? We're supposed to be on a different planet, a different culture. We're supposed to be in the future" (2022, 0:55). Therefore, in addition to not using an orchestra, "Zimmer didn't want any of the culturally diverse instruments identifiable, so he disguised everything" (Desowitz 2021). According to Zimmer, the objective was to try "to do things that are humanly impossible by pushing the envelope of technology," and by asking "for more things to superimpose the sonic quality of one instrument onto another so you would [create] these impossible sounds" (Desowitz 2021).

The will to create instruments that generate impossible sounds immediately signals a hyperinstrumental approach. Before dissecting the approach in more detail, I'll explore a relevant concept from film language as it relates to the movie: the mise-en-scène. There are two main traditions for mise-en-scène design (world-building): theatrical or naturalistic. While a naturalistic approach is meant to conceive a film world that is as close as possible to our own (realistic or familiar), a theatrical approach presents worlds that are either exaggerated or unfamiliar to us (fantastic, unrealistic) (StudioBinder 2020, 3:50). These two approaches are not discrete, but continuous, which means each movie will have a degree of both approaches. John Williams described how George Lucas wanted the music for *Star Wars* to be "emotionally familiar" (Byrd 1997, 416), which highlights how Lucas wanted to use music to make a very fantastical world (theatrical) closer to our own experiences (naturalistic).

Zimmer's instinctive opposition to the scoring approach outlined above is certainly indicative of an aesthetic view that is detached from the Hollywood traditions represented in films such as *Star Wars*. It indicates an aesthetic vision in which the music integrates much more into the film fabric by blending with the rest of the elements that constitute the film language. It also serves to provide context on the reasons for the emergence of the hyperorchestra, with its power to transcend existing musical structures to provide meanings through sonic specificity in a manner that makes music much more relatable to the rest of the elements of film language.

Zimmer goes as far as to align the score's sonic palette to the movie's color palette. Talking about the *Dune* films, Zimmer recalls that his process starts "with creating a sound world. One of the things that I've always done is that I spend a long time looking at the colour palette and talking to the director of photography. What's this going to look like? What colours are you going to be using? What's the colour palette of this planet? And that seeps over into the colour palette of the music" (Inglis 2024, 125). From the myriad organological approaches to hyperinstrumental design in the score for *Dune*, I will focus on three areas.

The Voice

While *Dune* (the original book and, by extension, the movies) creates a unique and detailed world that encapsulates many planets and thousands of years of history, it is still relatable to us because it is mostly populated by humans. Thus, the naturalistic part of the mise-en-scène is humans that are relatable (sometimes, unfortunately, too much) to us. *Dune* exemplifies that science fiction is appealing because it lets us focus on the core elements of humankind by eliminating the realistic wrap that is the everyday world.

This is one of the reasons why the score also features the voice in order to create an emotional link with the audience in a manner that is faithful to the mise-en-scène. The main vocalist, Loire Cotler, crafted a vocal style intended to be unidentifiable from any culture on Earth through the process of merging influences:

> Stylistically, Cotler drew on everything from Jewish niggun (wordless song) to South Indian vocal percussion, Celtic lament to Tuvan overtone singing. Even the sound of John Coltrane's saxophone was an influence, she said. "When you start to hybridize these far-flung influences and techniques, interesting sounds start to happen," she said. "It's a vocal technique called 'Hans Zimmer.'" (King 2021)

Whereas the voice is the realistic link between *Dune*'s universe and ours, the cultural traditions attached to the musical use of the voice are much linked to Earth. At the same time, Frank Herbert's reference to the Middle East and its desert is rather evident. Villeneuve took it further by identifying *Lawrence of Arabia* (1962) as a predecessor for his version of *Dune* and its source material—T.E. Lawrence's autobiography *Seven Pillars of Wisdom* (1926)—as a significant influence for Herbert (Villeneuve 2021). Further, Villeneuve argues that "the idea that Lawrence will fall in love with another culture and try to help this culture in order to fight against colonialism and realize at the end that himself will be an instrument of this colonialism [...] has a strong link with Paul Atreides' journey in *Dune*" (2021, 1:10).

From a hyperinstrumental design perspective, the voice is a powerful source material in *Dune*'s score. As I delineated in the graphical representation of a hyperinstrument, musical instruments might provide meaning through cultural signification in addition to their sound properties. *Dune*'s hyperinstruments present a sophisticated version of the first in tandem with the second. For instance, in the iconic chant created by Cotler and that Zimmer refers to as the "cry of the banshee" (2022, 7:25), the sonic result does not represent any of the Earth's musical traditions but, at the same time, it seems like a blend of some of the ones mentioned above. The result is akin to an additive synthesis process (combining two sound sources together in a synthesizer) but for cultural musical traditions. Thus, the *additive cultural synthesis* process, to give it a name, serves to engage with the idea of worldbuilding that is vaguely inspired by the location and cultures of certain historical events without any clear reference. The roughness of the *cry of the banshee* also incorporates a search for a particular meaning-inducing kind of sound. Zimmer told Cotler to sound as if she was eating sand.[15] From this angle, meaning is created through a process of sound materialization in tandem with an artistic inspiration process similar to what I described in *Chernobyl*.

The present example illustrates the vast array of possibilities that the first part of the hyperinstrumental design (the sound source) offers to create the most complex meanings. Further, the initial vision for the instrument is polished through either recording techniques or sound processing and manipulation. The result is an extremely specific instrument in terms of sound and meaning.

Custom-Made Wind Instruments for Recording

Zimmer told Pedro Eustache, the score's core wind player, "Don't play it like a flute. Play it as if it was the wind whistling through the desert's dunes" (2022, 9:07). In addition to a creative process similar to what I just outlined for the voice (using a multitude of instruments from varied cultural traditions and crafting new performance techniques to try to align with the specific meaning of sounding like wind), there was also a process of physical creation of new recorded instruments. Zimmer emphasizes the amount of effort Eustache put into buying many PVC pipes to try to generate the sound they were aiming for. Eustache describes that he "actually made a sub-contrabass duduk by putting" a duduk (Armenian double reed instrument) embouchure "into a very long tube of PVC." Further, Eustache "cut the thing to get the different tones. So it is an instrument that doesn't exist anywhere" (Zimmer 2022, 10:22). This process adds a new perspective to the design of hyperinstruments. The PVC sub-contrabass duduk is an instrumental design conceived to produce sounds that will be recorded, not as a fully functional musical instrument. The design assumes proper microphone placement and processing to extract the part of the frequency information necessary to create a hyperinstrument that carries the intended meaning.

In addition, Zimmer and Eustache explain how another double-reed instrument, the Zerna, was used to create the sound of the bagpipe ensemble—blended with the bagpipe ensemble, electric guitar, sound processing, and many other sound sources. This process of hyperinstrumental design starts with a concept that spectral composers named "instrumental synthesis" (Fineberg 2000b, 85) as an acoustic process of timbral combination that mimics how synthesizers produce additive synthesis by merging sound sources.

Expanding the Synthesizer Capabilities

The second layer of hyperinstrumental design contains the samplers and the synthesizers. This is generally a layer in which composers implement or program their recordings or ideas in existing technology. Thus, I have not particularly emphasized its instrument-building capabilities further than that. As I mentioned in the previous chapter, Zimmer and his company have a long history of working with developers to create music software for their needs, including one of the first powerful software samplers in 1994 (Zimmer 2021). Similarly, there is a well-known relationship between Zimmer and synthesizer company U-he, which makes the Zebra synthesizer. Zebra was expanded for Hans Zimmer as a bespoke product due to his needs for the *Dark Knight*. The expanded *Zebra* was later released to the public as ZebraHZ. Similarly, Zimmer worked with Urs

Heckmann, U-he's boss, to expand Zebra even further for *Dune*. Zimmer recalls that "'Urs was asking, why do I really need five resonators?' Zimmer beams. 'I need five resonators because I have this vision of how things are supposed to sound!'" (Spice 2024).

In terms of hyperinstruments, Heckman and his team become virtual luthiers, which is a concept that also aligns with the vast possibilities of hyperinstruments and the hyperorchestra. While a luthier is a person who creates acoustic instruments (strings), the virtual version creates tools that allow the composer to create virtual instrument instances. For instance, a resonator (referred to above) is a synth model (conceptually akin to how ADSR is a model for a note) that aims to reproduce the vibration process that acoustic instruments have in their resonant chambers. Thus, conceptually speaking, one resonator is enough to model how the sound is amplified in an acoustic instrument. Zimmer asked to be able to incorporate five consecutive resonators (ZebraHZ allowed for 3) to develop sounding strategies that, even grounded in models of the real, completely surpass it even at the conceptual level. Speaking about resonators, Zimmer also collaborated with a company, Le Voix de Luthier, which creates acoustic resonators for synths. Their products are acoustic resonating wood structures (like a violin or a very small piano) in which the synth sounds are played and rerecorded to emulate an acoustic quality (Inglis 2024).

In this exploration of hyperinstruments in *Dune*, I focused on new concepts that complemented what I had discussed in *Man of Steel* and *Chernobyl*. In addition, I focused on how hyperinstruments have become a key element that facilitates the creation of the mise-en-scène in which the music can better merge with the rest of the audiovisual elements to fulfill a common world-building goal.

The Hyperorchestra and the Generation of Meaning

A framework for the hyperorchestra encompasses music creation for the purposes of the generation of meaning in the hyperreal by using processes of sound sculpting that generally include the creation of hyperinstruments. Analogous to hyperinstruments, writing for the hyperorchestra is an aesthetic attitude made possible by technological innovation in virtualization and sound processing. Given its virtual and fluid definition, the hyperorchestra is a less firm ensemble than the Western symphonic orchestra, which is deeply grounded in a cultural background. A piece written for the Western symphonic orchestra will sound reasonably balanced and coherent if the composer follows fundamental orchestrational principles. The main reason is that as an ensemble, the Western orchestra is pre-designed in all its elements, as I detailed in Chap. 3. The potential of the hyperorchestra is that it allows the composer to create any sound combination imaginable, going beyond the limits of physicality. The implication, though, is that the hyperorchestra does not have an established design comparable to the Western orchestra.

The statement above does not negate the sophistication in techniques and tools that involve traditional orchestration, nor should it indicate that orchestration has ever been static and lacking evolution. To that end, Dolan (2013) is a starting point for unfolding the historical evolution of orchestration since Haydn connected to a sensibility for timbre that is usually overlooked in analyses of eighteenth-century music. Further, McAdams et al. summarize recent research in orchestration by proposing *A Taxonomy of Orchestral Grouping Effects Derived from Principles of Auditory Perception* (2022). The article outlines sophisticated timbral combinations and summarizes previous scholarship on the matter, with a particular focus on the generation of new sounds through the skillful combination of two or more orchestral instruments—an acoustic process of sound sculpting.

Further, the intention of the instrumental combination might be to generate a timbre that resembles a known sound to create a signification process. For example, Debussy mixed the English horn with a trumpet in *Le Mer* to "replicate the foghorn of a ship at sea" (McAdams et al. 2022). Therefore, this example from *Le Mer* proposes a process of intentional sound sculpting to generate a denotative association that adds narrative content to the piece. While this conclusion could indicate that this is, in fact, a hyperorchestral process based on my definition above, this is not precisely the case. It is an example of the aesthetic foundations of the hyperorchestra, and it shows an aesthetic attitude relatable to the hyperorchestral process. However, it falls short of the specificity of the sound object and its intended meaning. For instance, combining a trumpet with an English horn to represent a foghorn is a cogent idea to conceive a hyperinstrument. However, the hyperinstrument would require specific sound sources, careful design of the microphone techniques, and so on in order to create a virtual instance that maximizes its meaning creation intent. Similarly, its meaning-creation purpose should determine its sonic placement in space and sonic evolution.

The hyperorchestra utilizes the power afforded by digital processes to virtualize music for rendering music that is intentional in its sonic design to portray meanings and a soundworld that shapes the audiovisual story world of the audiovisual piece. Figure 5.10 represents the framework for constructing the hyperorchestra.

Analogous to the model for the hyperinstruments, any sound sculpting process will be designed to carry meaning and integrate with the audiovisual storytelling process. For example, a virtual space that replicates the sound of an acoustic concert hall will be assessed by its degree of verisimilitude, thus carrying narrative meaning. Thus, in *Interstellar* (2014), the cathedral in which the organ was recorded contributed to its technological and religiosity—to put it in Nolan's terms—meaning associations.

Concurrently, established musical devices integrate with the hyperorchestra as well. While the hyperorchestra's most relevant addition is the introduction of a wide set of sound sculpting techniques to generate meaning, that does not exclude the utilization or incorporation of already established musical and scoring devices. More important for this discussion is the interaction between these devices and sound sculpting to

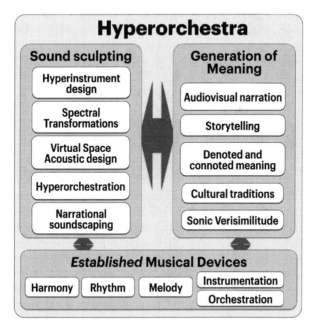

Fig. 5.10 Graphical representation of a conceptual framework for the hyperorchestra

expand the possibilities for meaning generation. For instance, harmony could be expanded through sound sculpting to incorporate spectral harmonic processes to generate meaning. Doing so might involve sound processing in tandem with orchestration. Therefore, writing music using a hyperorchestral model involves negotiating the generation of meaning.

At the same time, the different sounds are distributed around the spatial image and the sound spectrum to generate the desired soundscape. The spatial image might be stereophonic if the sound is stereo or if the surround speakers are only used for reverberation purposes. Further, the spatial image might involve the whole space if the composer and mixer utilize spatial audio technologies such as Dolby Atmos.

The sound canvas for the hyperorchestra is the humanly audible sound spectrum. Combining the different sounds in a hyperorchestra involves deciding which space each hyperinstrument will occupy in the soundscape. This process might interact with the definition of the hyperinstruments in a virtual ensemble. For instance, a filter might be required to restrict a hyperinstrument's spectral range. Hence, hyperorchestral scoring—as the overall contemporary scoring process—is similarly fluid and nonlinear. Hence, hyperorchestral decisions blend and permeate the definitions of the hyperinstruments.

In addition to meaning-related decisions, sound sculpting is also aesthetic. Generally, there are multiple ways to generate a specific musical meaning. As I will explore in the analysis below, director Alfonso Cuarón made an aesthetic decision not to include any percussion in *Gravity* (2013). Each aesthetic decision contributes to creating a unique soundscape for the audiovisual object in which they are embedded.

Closely related to the aesthetics is the design of the virtual space where the music will sound. A virtual space does not necessarily follow a purely three-dimensional design. In other words, the instruments do not necessarily need to be placed in a single imaginary three-dimensional hall. Designing a virtual space with this amount of variation and possibilities is challenging and essential, considering that the objective is to generate a cohesive, aesthetically appealing sound. In most instances, a very heterogeneous sound space might decrease the effectiveness of the result, diminishing the music's impact on the narrative.

In parallel with sound sculpting, meaning generation is a broad and multifaceted process. The sounds that generate hyperinstruments come from a wide range of sources. Some of these sources are attached to ordinary objects that are part of everyday life. The cape sound from *The Dark Knight* trilogy is a clear example. Similarly, some hyperinstruments in *Interstellar*'s track "Dust" are modeled to denote the sound of the dust-filled wind. Thus, in addition to the associations generated by cultural traditions attached to existing musical instruments, meaning can also be produced through sounds directly associated with human activities, experiences, or objects that hold narrative significance for the movie they will be part of.

Further, in this vast landscape of meaning generation through unrestrained use of sound, it is essential to assess the degree of verisimilitude of the resulting sound (sonic verisimilitude as it appears in the figure). Achieving sonic verisimilitude is not always a goal, but it is a noteworthy feature to take into consideration. For instance, the massive brass and impossible crescendos in *Inception* (2010) were reasonably verisimilar, although they attached a level of intensity that seemed to extend beyond the physical world. In doing so, the music invited the viewer to associate dreams with reality while exploring their capacity to surpass it. Therefore, the degree of verisimilitude of the score concerning the audience expectations is a critical feature that outlines diverse paths for the music in its capacity to generate meaningful content for the audiovisual narrative.

As mentioned above, meaning can be generated in the hyperorchestra through referential meaning in established musical devices. In the most possible simple example, a minor chord might be used to signify sadness. However, the possibility of generating meaning from a much more comprehensive range of perspectives and the chance to create vibrant and varied soundscapes could alter the effect of established ways to produce referential meaning. For example, the minor chord might easily be eclipsed by an overly positive soundscape or might have its meaning modified (e.g., to signify nostalgia) by finely sculpting its sound spectrum using spectral harmonic principles.

Throughout the framework for the hyperorchestra, I highlighted the vast possibilities of sound variability and meaning generation that it offers while identifying the possible risks that emanate from such a flexible device. The hyperorchestra should be considered a cultural entity with expansive expressive power at the expense of having solid and established foundations. In other words, creating music with the hyperorchestra offers an enlarged range of musical prospects at the price of losing the safety net that the Western symphonic orchestra model provides. The concepts I just outlined will be expanded in the next chapter as I describe hyperorchestration techniques.

All the examples presented in this chapter showcase the use of a hyperorchestra. The two additional examples I am presenting below from *Gravity* (2013) and *Annihilation* (2018) present decisions and processes at the ensemble level. From that viewpoint, they exemplify the hyperorchestral process of sound sculpting and sound selection to produce meaning that follows the ideas and aesthetics of the film. In doing so, the discussion in the two examples below also serves as an introduction to the final chapter devoted to the techniques for hyperorchestration.

Example: Gravity *(2013): Scoring the Soundlessness of Outer Space*

One of the most remarkable elements in *Gravity* (2013) is its treatment of sound, as the movie attempts to reproduce the impossibility of sound propagation in outer space. This does not mean that sound is not possible in space when using human technology. There is breathable air inside the space shuttle and the spacesuits, thus the possibility of sound propagation. Moreover, electromagnetic waves, such as radio frequencies, differ from mechanical waves, such as sound, in that they are carried in a vacuum. Therefore, it is possible to transmit sound between different air-filled spaces if radio transmission is used. Any impact these spaces receive will produce sound inside them, as the collision will generate mechanical waves in the air of those spaces.[16]

Making a movie that attempts to portray the absence of sound transmission in outer space is challenging in terms of sound design and sonic perspective. It also involves establishing a set of moviemaking decisions. An important decision revolves around determining the relationship between the visual and sound perspectives, which usually differ. If the camera were positioned in outer space, there would be no sound from this perspective. However, the sound in the movie typically mirrors the sound perceived by the characters, making the sonic narration from the characters' point of view while providing a visual shot structure that aims to portray a much more objective narration.

Chris Benstead, the music editor of the movie, explained that Cuarón wanted to avoid the perception of an orchestra behind the screen. Thus, there was "a great deal of digital manipulation of live recorded orchestral material" through sound design processing (Mera 2016, 103). Further, the orchestral recordings followed the nonlinear approach I described at the beginning of the chapter. As Mera (2016) points out, "Orchestral recordings are no longer aurally sacrosanct; they become source materials ready to be transformed" (103). For instance, they recorded a bass section separately in Abbey Road studios to create one of the recurrent motives in the movie by "digitally manipulating and cutting [them] off" (103). The score has numerous relevant elements and scoring techniques like the ones described above. I will focus on just two that are interconnected: the extensive utilization of reversed sounds and the compulsory absence of percussion instruments as prescribed by the director.

Reversing a sound is a standard studio processing technique that consists of reading the recording backward. Figure 5.11 portrays an original sound (a note performed with a strong attack) and its reversed version. The effect works best on sounds with a strong attack and initial decay along with a longer release.

When reversed, the sound has a slow-paced *crescendo* at the beginning, culminating with an extreme dynamic increase that is suddenly cut (if the attack is short). The end of the sound is unnatural and harsh. The result is highly vivid, employing material that, while it was recorded acoustically, cannot be reproduced in a physical reality. Reversed sounds that are generated from a sound with a fast and strong attack are dramatic, as they produce an almost impossible *crescendo* and a very sudden release. It is challenging to generate a *crescendo* that increases the amplitude of the sound as quickly as a reversed sound can produce. This is due to the natural properties of musical instruments and, more generally, to the properties of any material that is able to produce sounds. In both cases, the

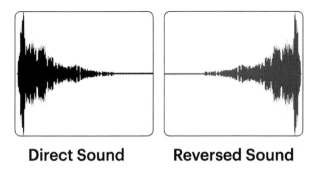

Fig. 5.11 Graphic representation of direct and reversed sound waveforms

physical material would need to change its vibratory state, which takes some time.

As shown in Fig. 5.12, an instrument needs to vibrate at a higher amplitude to sound louder. The vibrating materials, such as strings or the air in the case of wind instruments, need time to adapt. Thus, creating a fast crescendo is difficult for most instruments. Moreover, suddenly cutting the sound just after reaching the loudest point is not possible. This would involve physically stopping the instrument from continuing to vibrate and cutting any reverberation in the room.

The reversed sound is generally very effective when synchronized with a fade-to-black editing technique, especially after revealing something visually striking. In *Gravity*, the editing effect I just described appears reversed in the opening titles. First, the movie shows text on a black background. Then, the music generates an extremely wide crescendo that ends with a reversed sound of an ensemble. Finally, an image of Earth from outer space is shown in total silence, which serves as an establishing shot for the movie.

In addition to the dramatic effect created by a swelling crescendo after the text that states that "Life in space is impossible" (Cuarón 2013), the total silence that follows, in conjunction with a shot of Earth, reminds us that, in space, the physical laws of our planet do not apply. Therefore, the impossible sudden cut of the reversed sound, without any reverberation, emphasizes the necessary detachment from the everyday rules of life in

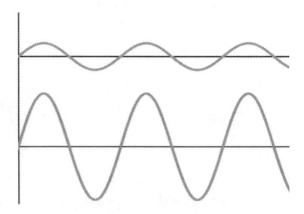

Fig. 5.12 Graphic representation of different amplitudes in sine waves

humanity's natural environment. The impossible nature of the reversed sound helps to generate the diegesis of outer space that wholly differs from the physical rules of the ground. The sound qualities of the reversed sound also physically connect with the space debris traveling around Earth at 20,000 miles per hour, which is also faster than anything in the physical reality, including bullets. The succession of reversed sounds in the score also provides an aural context to represent the high-speed debris, which, due to its extreme velocity, is difficult to represent visually accurately.

The reversed sound is also a tool that helps the composer, Stephen Price, overcome the absence of percussion, as requested by director Alfonso Cuarón: "You can't use percussion. It's a cliché; we can't do that" (Rosenbloom 2013). The sharp attack and exceptionally rapid decay of the reversed sound serve as a creative replacement for percussion. There are other techniques that Price employs to replace some of the effects of percussion:

> The sound will move all around you—sort of attack you almost. You feel as overwhelmed as she is, hopefully. With that are these feelings of heartbeats and breaths, and a lot of the immediate human side of things comes from these pulsations rather than rhythms in the score. It sometimes works as a heartbeat, other times it complements the sound design heartbeats that were there. Sometimes the pulses that are there are accompanying breaths. And always, we were very careful to get the tempo so that it felt appropriate to the state that she was in. (Rosenbloom 2013)

The concept of creating pulsations to replace the musical effect of percussion integrates well with the sonic nature of reversed sounds, which works in conjunction with the heartbeat-type sound design. The absence of both percussion and any actual sound caused by the objects hitting each other also detaches the diegesis of outer space from terrestrial life. As Ryan states, when she loses a screw from the Hubble telescope, "In my basement lab, things usually fall to the floor," and when things fall to the floor, they produce a percussive sound. Using these two devices, the score contributes to the movie's worldbuilding conception from the director, assisting in creating a carefully curated soundscape.

The use of a hyperorchestral model made it possible for the music to fulfill all its functions without the utilization of percussion. By implementing sound processing techniques such as the reversed sound I just described, the composer provided himself with a series of hyperinstruments that could carry functions generally attributed to percussive instruments. Moreover, a reversed sound becomes unnatural and slightly more threatening than any percussive organic sound. It also holds a sense of urgency and tension that augments what can be done percussively. It also detaches the score from seeming orchestral, aided by the sound mix that freely places instruments in the surround, breaking any similarities with the sonic placement that would result from the music coming from an orchestral pit in the theater.

Example: Annihilation *(2018) and the Organic Corruption*

The movie *Annihilation* (2018) is the second collaboration between director Alex Garland and composers Geoff Barrow and Ben Salisbury after their success in *Ex Machina* (2015). In *Annihilation*, there is an area in a fictional present-day Earth called *The Shimmer* in which strange things happen. Communications of any kind cannot go in or out of that area, and no human being who has entered The Shimmer has been able to come back. In addition, The Shimmer keeps expanding. The movie follows a team of four scientists/explorers in their quest to understand what is happening inside that area and propose possible solutions to reduce the effects. The scientists discover a disorienting world in which the laws of biology and physics seem to have been slightly twisted, generating a new world that is surprising, beautiful, and menacing simultaneously.

Garland briefly describes the movie's theme as "about the nature of self-destruction in a literal sense: cells have life cycles and stars have life cycles and plants and the universe and us. You, me, everyone. But also psychological forms of self-destruction" (Bishop 2018). Genre-wise, the movie follows an extended revisionist Western framework, as explored by David Bordwell in *Zip, Zero, Zeitgeist* (2014). This definition helps explain why the score features an acoustic steel guitar for one of the main musical themes. It connects the movie with the Western genre and the territory—reminding us that the Shimmer is still part of Earth. The composers explained their approach in an interview:

> Salisbury: Films that *Annihilation* vaguely references—like *Southern Comfort*—those searching-in-jungles-and-backwoods-of-America-type films, it just felt right to put acoustic guitar there. Not just right, but also a little bit odd in a sci-fi film.

Barrow: Most sci-fi films start now with huge orchestral armies of synth and sound design. And this was a bit of a human story, so it was really important to just give it a sense of reality rather than going into Marvel synthworlds. (Beta 2018)

The introduction displays the decision-making process of assembling an ensemble appropriate for meaning generation and outlining the possibilities available. From these possibilities, I will focus on how the composers chose to use the sonic transformation of physical sound material to provide meaning that connected the score with The Shimmer and how it contrasted with the highly synthetic music used to represent the alien at the end of the movie. The analysis will exemplify the hyperorchestral framework and introduce hyperorchestration before I approach it in the following chapter.

The sound sculpting processes in the score give additional clues to the viewers in their quest to understand the complexities of the diegetic world inside The Shimmer. A key theme for the film is its depiction of a biological interpretation of the concept of *corruption of form* that acts as a signifier for the self-destructive nature of beings. The main character is a cancer researcher who is shown describing how a cancer cell is nothing more than a cell that has lost its rhythm, thus implying that the rhythm of cell division is integral to defining life on Earth. In The Shimmer, there are subtle transformations in plants and animals that combine the DNA of several species simultaneously. The characters debate how to classify these transformations: biological mutations, corruptions, or illnesses. In all cases, the characters describe everything in The Shimmer as organic and not artificial, highlighting how the notion of artificiality, corruption, and evolution is anthropocentric.

To make these events comprehensible, the plot has to provide information to show how the world inside The Shimmer functions and explain the laws of physics and biology that make it possible. The music plays a role in aiding the narrative in transmitting these topics. While the acoustic guitar supports the idea of the characters in their quests of discovery of the unknown, the rest of the musical elements inside the Shimmer come from acoustic recordings. The composers reserved the use of synthesizers and sound processing that would be associated with artificial transformation to identify the Alien at the end. The end is "the only time in the score that synths and electronics make an overt appearance" (Martinelli 2018).

Thus, the music for The Shimmer aimed for organicity while, at the same time, had to connect with the eerie mutations and biological corruption. I will highlight three of the multiple sonic resources the composers used to achieve this: the use of the Waterphone instrument, the utilization of saturation as a subtle type of distortion, and the use of a flanger.

Waterphone
The Waterphone, an instrument invented in 1965 by Richard Waters, has been featured in several scores, especially in the 1980s and horror genre. It has been described as an acoustic synthesizer due to its dual nature of being an acoustic instrument that produces sounds that seem artificial. However, the Waterphone produces sounds that are distinct from those we would expect from analog synthesizers. At the same time, it differs from most acoustic instruments due to its incapacity to produce a distinct and organized pitch structure and overtones. This limitation becomes a feature to associate its sound with the concept of corruption of form. Further, its acoustic nature, in tandem with the apparent artificiality of the sounds it produces, is a powerful resource to engage with the movie's philosophical debate on what we define as organic versus synthetic.

Thus, the ambiguous and sonically fluctuating nature of the waterphone serves as a fitting sound bed for the Shimmer and as a starting point for the music. One of the guidelines for the musical score was to create a journey in which the music evolved following the discoveries in the narrative while accompanying the characters in their interpretation of what corruption of form and mutation meant in that environment.

Saturation as an Organic Mode of Distortion
Distortion is a sonic process that increases the amplitude of the overtones present in a sound. Soft saturation is a subtle distortion type called as such for its origins in analog audio equipment. A sound with modest saturation applied tends to be perceived as richer and warmer due to the subtle and harmonious reinforcement of its overtones. Thus, in the context of this movie, saturation is an organic mode of sound transformation that is also connected with the idea of corruption (a highly distorted sound is something we qualify as corrupted). Saturation is applied to many of the musical elements in the score during The Shimmer sequences.

The amount of saturation (as in distortion) can be increased or decreased, creating musical shapes that resemble musical dynamics. It is a technique present in the score, generating a transformed process of dynamic change that relates to the corruption of the form concept. When a performer plays their instrument at an increased dynamic, the resulting sound is richer in overtones and even in inharmonic material. However, the sound stays within the range of what we consider the sound of the instrument. The process is similar with distortion (including saturation), but each increase detaches the sound further from its original source. In other words, mild saturation is very similar to dynamic change (aka the beauty of slight processes of biological corruption shown in the movie). When saturation increases, the sound starts to break down into unidentifiable noise.

Phaser and Flanger
The phaser effect—while present throughout the score—is specially featured toward the end of the film. It becomes considerably noticeable after the team realizes that, inside The Shimmer, everything, including the DNA, is refracted. This means that areas of the DNA of each living element inside The Shimmer are being distributed and incorporated into other beings. The idea of refraction refers specifically to the division of the DNA into essential pieces. A phaser (also a flanger) is a sound effect that produces a sonic result in which a moving area of the frequency spectrum is reinforced. Consequently, a phaser emphasizes or deemphasizes the overtones of a sound. The effect is closer to the idea of refraction as the phaser emphasizes areas of the spectrum of the sound in a manner that seems to isolate and separate them from the rest of the sound.

Strictly speaking, a phaser is a synthetic effect due to the nature of how it is produced. However, while it is technically a synthetic alteration to the shape of the sound, its results still sound organic because it does not add artificial sounds that were not there originally. Metaphorically, this effect resembles something like observing the sound spectrum through a moving magnifying lens. Describing it in the context of *Annihilation*'s narrative, a phaser generates a corruption of the form of the sound it effects by producing a significant alteration of what the sound is in itself.

Using a waterphone, soft saturation, and flangers serve to sculpt sounds that remain intrinsically attached to their physicality but appear formally corrupted by sonic processes that mimic refraction. Thus, the division of light in its different colors through a prism (light refraction) is relatable to sonic processes focused on transforming the overtones of a sound or its natural divisions. In addition, synthetic sound generation and transformation were left to represent the alien at the climax of the movie, increasing the impact of the reveal but also creating a soundworld that became clearly distinct and artificial.

Synthetic and Artificial Processes for the Alien
At the end of the movie—when the Alien entity appears—part of the sound is distorted using a digital bit crusher distortion (which is artificial in its nature). At the same time, a motive played on an analog synthesizer dominates the sonic scape. It is a way to signify the artificiality of the being, separating it from the environment created by its influence. It is a means to signify the conceptual difference between The Shimmer and the entity that produces it. Both the music and the visuals help to create a clear division between the artificiality of the alien and the biological corruption we see in The Shimmer.

Annihilation*: Digital Music Process, Hyperinstruments, Hyperorchestra, and Hyperorchestration*
Annihilation serves as an example of all the frameworks described in this chapter. First, it took advantage of the collaborative possibilities that a nonlinear digital process of music production offers. The composers explained that, in an "Alex Garland film, everybody who's in the post-production […] at any point can make a point about each other's roles and whether they think something works or doesn't. And that's why we like working with Alex because you feel part of this gang that is making a film, rather than just making music *for* a film" (Britt 2018). For instance, the synthetic thematic material for the alien was initially devised to represent The Shimmer (Martinelli 2018). Through a collaborative process, the score was shaped in the way I analyzed above as the consequence of feedback and discussion from multiple people in the post-production process.

The movie also presents a wide range of hyperinstruments created through a combination of recorded sources and processing, some of which I described above. Parallel to the creation of the hyperinstruments, the hyperorchestra emanated in three music groupings: a mostly untreated acoustic guitar, an acoustically processed organic material, and a synthetic material. As I outlined above, each of these groups fulfilled particular narrative meanings and were sonically shaped for their meaning-generation purposes.

Finally, the exploration of *Annihilation* serves as an introduction to the next chapter in hyperorchestration. The utilization of sound transformations, such as distortion or the flanger, is not only a means for hyperinstrumental creation but also hyperorchestration techniques based on mixing principles. For instance, defining the dynamic balance and the music's overall dynamic shape through soft saturation—an equivalent to using instrumental dynamics—is an example of hyperorchestration. Next, I will detail hyperorchestration from a theoretical point of view and provide an essential introduction to the expanded toolkit of the composer when orchestrating in this virtual environment.

Notes

1. Corey (2017) defines technical ear training as the "technical attributes of audio: timbre or tone color (through equalization and filtering), dynamics processing (compression and expansion), level, reverberation, delay, distortion, noise, and mix balances" (x). Critical listening skills are developed through technical ear training. Corey suggests that "there is no easy way to gain critical listening skills. It takes regular effort over time through technical ear training to improve and maintain critical listening skills" (x).
2. Buhler structures his discussion in contemporary cinema starting from Bordwell's influential definition of "intensified continuity" (Bordwell 2002, 2006, 121–138).
3. A fully developed analytical approach to sonic analysis is outside this book's scope and already covered in the literature. This type of analysis became necessary to discuss studio records of popular songs and their production process. Moylan's (2014) *Understanding and Crafting the Mix*, initially published in 2002, is a reference book on this area. Its target audience is sound engineers, mixers, and producers to provide them with analytical and theoretical tools to discuss their craft. This book is the culmination of Moylan's (1983, 1985, 1986, 1987) lengthy doctoral and postdoctoral research to develop a methodology of aural analysis that incorporated timbre, spatial relationships, and the description of sound sources. Moylan (2020) refines and expands his methodology while describing how to use it in popular songs.

   Corey's (2017) *Audio Production and Critical Listening: Technical Ear Training* is a detailed approach to all the audio production processes and a methodology for ear training to develop critical listening skills necessary for providing a detailed sonic analysis of any piece of music. Corey complements Moylan in delivering the essential grammar for Moylan's methodology, which assumes a degree of proficiency in critical listening.
4. The ADSR envelope should be considered one of several frameworks that define the creation of synthesized instruments.

5. Analog synthesizers could also be physically recorded. However, for clarity, I did not specify it on the graphic.
6. The music for the scene corresponds to the music in the track "Radical Notion" from *Inception*'s original soundtrack album (Zimmer 2010).
7. Other examples could include, among others, Nathan Barr's scores for *True Blood* (2008–2014) or *The Americans* (2013–2018), Ludwig Göransson's score for *The Mandalorian* (2019–), or Hildur Guðnadóttir's score for *Chernobyl* (2019), which I will discuss later.
8. Coincidentally, the Hollywood Creative Alliance actually awarded Marx with the first-ever Artisan Spotlight Award in 2024 for *A Small Light*.
9. See Wierzbicki (2009, 145–154) for a historical account of some of the critiques studios received when crafting scores that had multiple composers.
10. As in the previous example, this is not the only case, though it is certainly at the forefront of a new dynamic regarding how to credit teams, proposing a rather unique approach. Similarly, Hans Zimmer's joint venture *Bleeding Fingers* had its composers credited in several shows but not as a collective.
11. Composer team members have been receiving proper attributing in cue sheets (which is what land royalties) for decades, which is separated from receiving screen credit (which has no financial consequence per se). However, this is not always the case. Similarly speaking, these team members have been credited as assistants or co-composers for many years.
12. The differences in sound between the piano and the harpsichord exemplify the tradeoff associated with any instrumental development. In general terms, the piano has increased sounding possibilities and musical resources, such as a broader range of dynamic variety. However, the technical development of the piano was achieved at the expense of losing the delicate metallic sound of the harpsichord.
13. Tore Størvold and John Richardson (2021) provide a comprehensive analysis of the score that includes a spectral analysis in *Radioactive Music: The Eerie Agency of Hildur Guðnadóttir's Music for the Television Series Chernobyl*. They outline how, through meaningful sound capturing and sound processing, the score attempted to signify radiation, which is the process I define as part of a hyperinstrument framework.
14. The Scottish guitar player Guthrie Govan provides some clues about the collaborative process with Hans Zimmer in (The_Phoenician 2022). For instance:

> And when you hear the bagpipes, when they land on the new planet—the first bit of bagpipes you hear is actually me. It even fooled me when I went to see the film. I'd kind of forgotten—I thought maybe it was buried in the background somewhere, but apparently [it's] at the first several bars where it's just the lone bagpipes. It's great. That's about 20

tracks of guitar that I sent to Hans. Stack them all up and run them through kind of monophonic synths and stuff like that you can get eerily close [to a bagpipe].
15. Hans Zimmer, Melena Ryzik, Loire Cotler, Tina Guo "In Conversation and Q&A with Award-winning film composer Hans Zimmer" (press conference, New York, NY, March 14, 2024).
16. Mera (2016) provides a detailed description of how 3-D audio was utilized in the movie's score and soundtrack.

References

Beta, Andy. 2018. "'Annihilation': Geoff Barrow and Ben Salisbury Talk Its Haunting Score." RollingStone. https://www.rollingstone.com/music/music-features/annihilation-geoff-barrow-and-ben-salisbury-talk-its-haunting-score-197947/.

Bishop, Bryan. 2018. "Annihilation and Ex Machina director Alex Garland on using sci-fi to explore self-destruction." The Verge. https://www.theverge.com/2018/2/21/17029500/annihilation-ex-machina-director-alex-garland-sci-fi.

Bordwell, David. 2002. "Intensified Continuity Visual Style in Contemporary American Film." *Film Quarterly* 55: 16–28.

Bordwell, David. 2006. *The way Hollywood tells it: story and style in modern movies*. Berkeley: University of California Press.

Bordwell, David. 2014. "Zip, zero, Zeitgeist." *Observations of film art* (blog). http://www.davidbordwell.net/blog/2014/08/24/zip-zero-zeitgeist/.

Britt, Thomas. 2018. "The sound of The Shimmer: Interview with *Annihilation*'s Ben Salisbury and Geoff Barrow." popMATTERS. https://www.popmatters.com/ben-salisbury-geoff-barrow-interview-2573141300.html.

Buhler, James. 2020. "The End(s) of Vococentrism." In *Voicing the Cinema: Film Music and the Integrated Soundtrack*, edited by James Buhler and Hannah Lewis, 278–296. University of Illinois Press.

Burlingame, John. 2021. "Hans Zimmer on 'Dune' Score's Electronic Textures and Made-Up Choral Language … and His Head Start on Part 2." Variety.

Burton, Byron. 2019. "How 'Chernobyl' Composer Found Inspiration in a Real (and Radioactive) Power Plant." The Hollywood Reporter. https://www.hollywoodreporter.com/news/general-news/how-chernobyl-composer-found-inspiration-a-radioactive-power-plant-1228682/.

Byrd, Craig L. 1997. "Interview with John Williams." In *Celluloid Symphonies: Texts and Contexts in Film Music History*, edited by Julie Hubbert, 414–423. Berkeley and Los Angeles, California: University of California Press.

Corey, Jason. 2017. *Audio production and critical listening: technical ear training*. Second ed. New York: Routledge.
Desowitz, Bill. 2021. "'Dune': How Composer Hans Zimmer Invented a Retro-Future Musical Sound for the Arrakis Desert Planet." IndieWire. https://www.indiewire.com/features/general/dune-hans-zimmer-score-1234673017/.
Dolan, Emily. 2013. *The Orchestral Revolution: Haydn and the Technologies of Timbre*. Cambridge, UK: Cambridge University Press.
Dreldon. 2023. "Ariel Marx hears a unique hiding place that holds 'A Small Light'." On the Score. https://onthescore.com/ariel-marx-hears-a-unique-hiding-place-that-holds-a-small-light/.
Fineberg, Joshua. 2000a. "Spectral Music." *Contemporary Music Review* 19 (2): 1–5.
Fineberg, Joshua. 2000b. "Guide to the Basic Concepts and Techniques of Spectral Music." *Contemporary Music Review* 19 (2): 81–113.
Inglis, Sam. 2024. "Hans Zimmer & Friends: Dune." *Sound on Sound* 39 (6): 124–133.
King, Darryn 2021. "How Hans Zimmer Conjured the Otherworldly Sounds of 'Dune'." New York Times. https://www.nytimes.com/2021/10/22/movies/hans-zimmer-dune.html.
Kraft, Robert, and Kenny Holmes, "Hildur Guðnadóttir needs an outlet for her darkness," 2019, in *Score: The Podcast*.
Kulezic-Wilson, Danijela. 2020. *Sound Design is the New Score: Theory, Aesthetics, and Erotics of the Integrated Soundtrack*. Oxford University Press.
Lawrence, T.E., and A. Calder. [1926] 1997. *Seven Pillars of Wisdom*. Wordsworth Editions Limited.
Martinelli, Marissa. 2018. "*Annihilation* Co-Composer Ben Salisbury Explains How That Weird Little Melody Wound Up in the Film's Trailer." Slate. https://slate.com/culture/2018/02/annihilation-co-composer-ben-salisbury-explains-the-musical-cue-from-the-alien.html.
McAdams, Stephen, Meghan Goodchild, and Kit Soden. 2022. "A Taxonomy of Orchestral Grouping Effects Derived from Principles of Auditory Perception." *Music Theory Online* 28 (3). https://doi.org/10.30535/mto.28.3.6.
McCreary, Bear. 2024. "Percy Jackson and the Olympians." *Bear's Blog* (blog). March 12, 2024. https://bearmccreary.com/percy-jackson-and-the-olympians/.
Mera, Miguel. 2016. "Towards 3-D Sound: Spatial Presence and the Space Vacuum."
Moylan, William. 1983. *An Analytical System for Electronic Music*. Doctoral dissertation. Ball State University.
Moylan, William. 1985. "Aural Analysis of the Characteristics of Timbre." 79th Convention of the Audio Engineering Society, New York, NY.

Moylan, William. 1986. "Aural Analysis of the Spatial Relationships of Sound Sources as Found in Two-Channel Common Practice." 81st Convention of the Audio Engineering Society, Los Angeles, CA.

Moylan, William. 1987. "A Systematic Method for the Aural Analysis of Sound Sources in Audio Reproduction/Reinforcement, Communications, and Musical Contexts." 83rd Convention of the Audio Engineering Society, New York, NY.

Moylan, William. 2014. *Understanding and Crafting the Mix: The Art of Recording* (3rd Edition). Independence, KY, USA: Focal Press.

Moylan, William. 2020. *Recording analysis: how the record shapes the song.* New York, NY: Routledge.

Nolan, Christopher. 2010. *Inception.* [Shooting Script].

Rosenbloom, Etan. 2013. "Film Music Friday: Steven Price on Gravity." http://www.ascap.com/playback/2013/10/wecreatemusic/fmf-steven-price-gravity.aspx.

Sadoff, Ron. 2013. "Scoring for Film and Video Games: Collaborative Practices and Digital Post-Production." In The Oxford Handbook of Sound and Image in Digital Media, edited by Carol Vernallis, Amy Herzog, and John Richardson. New York: Oxford University Press.

Spice, Anton. 2024. "How Hans Zimmer's sonic experiments shaped the world of Dune: Part Two." Composer - Spitfire Audio. https://composer.spitfireaudio.com/en/articles/how-hans-zimmers-sonic-experiments-shaped-the-world-of-dune-part-two.

Størvold, Tore, and John Richardson. 2021. "Radioactive Music: The Eerie Agency of Hildur Guðnadóttir's Music for the Television Series Chernobyl." *Music and the Moving Image* 14 (3): 30–45. https://doi.org/10.5406/musimoviimag.14.3.0030.

StudioBinder. 2020. "What is Mise en Scene—How Directors Like Kubrick Master the Elements of Visual Storytelling" https://www.youtube.com/watch?v=3euNFd7-TCg.

The_Phoenician. 2022. "Guthrie Govan Describes Surprising Guitar Effects He Had to Produce While Recording 'Dune' Soundtrack, Explains How Working With Hans Zimmer Impacted His Playing." Ultimate Guitar Com. https://www.ultimate-guitar.com/news/general_music_news/guthrie_govan_describes_surprising_guitar_effects_he_had_to_produce_while_recording_dune_soundtrack_explains_how_working_with_hans_zimmer_impacted_his_playing.html.

Villeneuve, Denis. 2021. "Denis Villeneuve on LAWRENCE OF ARABIA | TIFF 2021" In "TIFF Originals." https://www.youtube.com/watch?v=HxejohkhRuQ.

Weintraub, Steve. 2013. "Hans Zimmer Talks MAN OF STEEL, How He Crafted the Score, Dealing with the Pressure of Following John Williams, Nolan's INTERSTELLAR, RUSH, and More." Collider. https://collider.com/hans-zimmer-man-of-steel-interstellar-rush-interview/.

Wierzbicki, James E. 2009. *Film Music: A History*. Routledge.

Zimmer, Hans. 2010. "Radical Notion." Warner Bros. Entertainment Inc.

Zimmer, Hans. 2013a. "Digital Booklet. Man of Steel (Original Motion Picture Soundtrack) Deluxe Edition." WaterTower Music.

Zimmer, Hans. 2013c. "Man of Steel Official Soundtrack | Behind The Scenes Percussion Session w/Hans Zimmer" WaterTowerMusic. https://www.youtube.com/watch?v=QTOMIyynBPE.

Zimmer, Hans. 2021. "Hans Zimmer's use of computers and samples in orchestral music" In "Mix with the Masters." https://youtu.be/_LHyNYRtwR8?si=VUrPPKEv0N3HB0Ep.

Zimmer, Hans. 2022. "How 'Dune' Composer Hans Zimmer Created the Oscar-Winning Score" Vanity Fair. https://www.vanityfair.com/video/watch/vf-tricks-of-the-trade-hans-zimmer.

Zimmer, Hans, and Christopher Nolan. 2011. "Hans Zimmer - Making Of Inception Score" Hans Zimmer - Making Of Inception Score. https://www.youtube.com/watch?v=gL5en8Y10OU.

CHAPTER 6

Hyperorchestration: Sonic Strategies for the Creation of Meaning

In the preface to the third edition of *The Study of Orchestration*, Samuel Adler (2002) begins by admitting that he failed 20 years before when he attempted to predict the evolution of Western orchestral music:[1]

> In 1979, I stated that music of the last quarter of the twentieth century would be even more complex and even more experimental than in the decades since World War II. New methods of notation would be devised, new instruments would be invented, and possibly even new concert spaces would be created to accommodate the cataclysmic changes that I predicted would occur. (ix)

Adler observed that orchestral music became simpler during the last quarter of the twentieth century (ix). Further, he believed that orchestration had followed a similar path, and "a more traditional approach to the orchestra seems to have regained a foothold, despite all of the previous focus on experimentation" (ix). However, I argue that Adler was only incorrect in restricting musical evolution to the acoustic world. As I outlined, digital music and virtual instruments generated new methods of notation, new instruments, new spaces, and new complex modes of sound creation.

This chapter employs the Western orchestra concept of orchestration (and instrumentation by extension) to explore a set of equivalent techniques that apply when working with a hyperorchestra. I define these techniques as hyperorchestration. The models and examples in the previous chapter will serve as source material to exemplify the hyperorchestration techniques I will identify, which I will complement with additional ones. As usual, these techniques are an addition to the existing ones, and their utilization does not exclude the use of traditional orchestration approaches in combination with these new ones. I start by providing a quick overview of what Western orchestration means. I incorporate the innovations of the Spectral movement and define hyperorchestration within this framework. Then, I explore a set of hyperorchestration tools: the creation of hyperinstruments, the use of mixing techniques, spectral transformation, and the combination and expansion of orchestral-like ensembles.

On Orchestration: A Birdseye Overview

The principles that govern traditional Western orchestration serve to establish the grounds for unfolding hyperorchestration techniques. Film music emanated from a model based on the nineteenth-century Western orchestra. Hence, the links with a Western orchestral framework are relevant even when no single orchestral instrument exists in the score. Adler (2016) opens *The Study of Orchestration* by providing his philosophical views of the orchestra.

> The orchestra is certainly one of the noblest creations of Western Civilization. The study of its intricacies will illumine many important areas of music. After all, timbre and texture clarify the form as well as the content of a host of compositions. Further, specific orchestral colors and even the spacing of chords in the orchestral fabric give special 'personality' to the music of composers from the Classical period to our own time. (5)

Adler articulates the established status of the orchestra as a cultural institution for Western culture while highlighting the importance of timbre in all facets of music and reminding us that orchestration also shapes the musical style of a composer. Regarding orchestration, Adler (2016) reminds the readers that:

> Scoring for orchestra is thinking for orchestra. When dealing with a composite instrument like the orchestra you must be completely familiar with the character and quality of the orchestra's components: the range and

limitations of each instrument as well as how that instrument will sound alone and in combination with other instruments. The timbre, strength, and texture of every segment of the instrument's range become crucial when you are creating orchestral color combinations. (611)

These two excerpts stress the interconnection between instrumentation and orchestration. Orchestrating is to combine the sound of the instruments to create musical textures and timbres. In order to properly combine the sound of the instruments, it is necessary to know not only how to write for them but also which sound you can expect to hear. An acoustic instrument might be misleading. Its physical integrity might suggest that it generates a cohesive set of sounds. However, it is precisely because of its physical nature that its sounds defy homogeneity, as the physical elements that constitute the instrument react differently depending on performance factors, such as pitch and dynamics. For instance, the timbre of a clarinet will change with the pitch.

Similarly, increasing an instrument's dynamic will both increase its volume and modify its timbral characteristics. At a certain degree of the dynamic level, the sound will begin to be significantly distorted compared to our mental representation of the sound of the instrument. Further, most instruments can be played using various performance techniques, generating diverse spectral shapes.

From a conceptual standpoint, orchestrating involves acknowledging that each instrument can generate a variety of sounds. However, this is limited to a contained scope (e.g., the timbre of a clarinet when played in a loud dynamic level cannot be achieved when playing in a soft dynamic). Orchestrating a musical piece for a live performance by a Western orchestra requires the utilization of these varied sounds in a practical and possible manner. Although each instrument can generate multiple sounds, it is generally only possible to generate one (or a few) simultaneously. Therefore, orchestrating involves managing the orchestral forces to achieve the desired results in the best possible manner. Moreover, orchestrating also implies planning how to use the instrumental forces to create a musical structure for the piece.

Spectral Orchestration

Throughout the book, I have mentioned some concepts related to a spectral attitude toward musical thought. If screen music had been considered from its beginning at the same artistic level as music for the concert stage, we would consider many of the examples and composers I have analyzed so far to share the same thought process as spectral concert composers. Thus, the hyperorchestra is a model grounded in a spectral attitude toward sound while also requiring the outcome to induce meaning. From this point of view, the ideas that constituted the core of the spectral music thought are relevant and serve as a link between traditional orchestration and hyperorchestration.

In *Did You Say Spectral?*, composer and cofounder of the Spectral movement Gérard Grisey (2000) reviewed the emergence of the spectral movement, which "offered a formal organization and sonic material that came directly from the physics of sound, as discovered through science and microphonic access" (1). Grisey's colleague, Tristan Murail, indicates how their initial aesthetic goal was to focus on sound over structure.[2]

> I think that it is chiefly an attitude toward musical and sonic phenomena, although it also entails a few techniques, of course. We were trying to find a way out of the structuralist contradiction. […] Also, at that time, the information that we required was not as readily available as it is today. Gérard Grisey and I had read books on acoustics that were designed more for engineers than for musicians. There we found rare information on spectra, sonograms, and such that was very difficult to exploit. (Bruce and Murail 2000, 12)

There are three ideas I would like to highlight from these initial thoughts. First, the movement began as a reaction to formalist or structuralist forms of musical composition. Second, they made sound the central element of music construction, which required technical knowledge to study it. Moreover, a proper study of sound demanded the aid of technology, which served to reveal its physical properties. Last, spectralism should primarily be considered an attitude toward music composition rather than a school. A spectral attitude involves paying closer attention to the sound and its nature.

Therefore, the spectral movement became closely connected with the development of technologies to analyze sound. Murail states, "there had been a historic conjunction between an aesthetic movement, the spectral movement, and the techniques, research, and software developed at the IRCAM" (Bruce and Murail 2000, 13). Daubresse and Assayag (2000), in a review of the relationship between technology and Spectral music, suggest:

Their [spectral composers] compositional techniques were already sufficiently rich and sophisticated to make them at ease in front of both analyses and synthesizers; they went from an acoustical and musical multi-representation to the programming of processes for the generation of symbolic or sonic material. Manipulating timbre –but also traditional instruments– with ease, freed from repetitive calculation, they certainly gave synthesis some of its first proofs of musical respectability. (62)

One of the earliest spectral techniques designed to enrich traditional Western orchestration was the translation of acoustical findings to generate new textures. The most well-known of these techniques is referred to as instrumental synthesis:[3]

Perhaps the most important idea emerging from early spectral music (though it was presaged in other musics [sic]) was the idea of instrumental (or orchestral) synthesis. Taking the concept of additive synthesis, the building up of complex sounds from elementary ones, and using it metaphorically as a basis for creating instrumental sound colors (timbres), spectral composers opened up a new approach to composition, harmony and orchestration. The sound complexes built this way are fundamentally different from the models on which they are based, since each component is played by an instrument with its own complex spectrum. Thus the result is not the original model, but a new, much more complex structure inspired by that model. The sounds created in this way keep something of the coherence and quality that comes from the model while adding numerous dimensions of instrumental and timbral richness and variety. (Fineberg 2000, 85)

Fineberg describes how the spectral composers employed acoustic processes derived from the concept of the Fourier transform, which is, broadly, the mathematical process of dividing any sound into a series of sine waves of different frequencies. They used the Fourier transform to shape an orchestral sound that was the product of additively inserting the different frequencies that constituted the harmonic spectrum of a sound.[4] As Fineberg points out, the result generates a complex sound spectrum due to the physical nature of the orchestral instruments, which do not behave simply as sine generators. The sound produced through orchestral or instrumental synthesis is purely acoustic, although it could not have originated without the aid of electronic means of sound analysis. Therefore, these are not purely acoustic processes, aesthetically speaking, because they transform the sound's nature beyond the culturally expected soundscapes of the symphonic orchestra.

Grisey outlined seven consequences of the spectral attitude. I want to stress these three:

- More "ecological" approach to timbres, noises, and intervals.
- Integration of harmony and timbre within a single entity.
- Integration of all sounds (from white noise to sinusoidal sounds). (Grisey 2000, 1–2)

All three features are crucial to define hyperorchestration. In essence, along with Schaeffer's theory of the sound objects I described in Chap. 3, the concepts described by the spectral movement resonate with the sound-building foundational ideas of the hyperorchestra—which also involves a spectral attitude toward sound. However, a crucial difference exists in how the generation of meaning is approached. By using the hyperorchestra, screen composers acknowledge the cultural anchors of the sounds and processes they use, which are employed to create meaning for an audiovisual narrative. Creating sounds for the hyperorchestra involves much more than timbral investigation, as it requires constructing an expressive layer of meaning. While creating timbres to fulfill a hedonistic purpose only is undoubtedly an option, it is rather ineffective in most cases for screen music. Therefore, the hyperorchestral timbres acquire a level of signification beyond their sound qualities. Nevertheless, the musical paradigm that emanates from the spectral school informs some of the hyperorchestration grounds while connecting the hyperorchestra to a broader cultural and historical trend in Western culture in which timbre has become an increasingly important parameter.

Hyperorchestration

As I briefly described, Western orchestration builds upon the established symphonic orchestra model, stabilizing several sound parameters. Thus, it studies timbre and texture as tools for musical expression and structure by delimiting them to the orchestra's instruments and their combination within the restricted environment of the orchestral set-up. The virtual and multifaceted nature of the hyperorchestra and its hyperinstruments brings hyperorchestration to break with those constraints while embracing a spectral attitude toward sound—akin to many of the axioms proposed by

Grisey and Murail. At the same time, the importance of producing meaning in its integration with the film language for narrative, philosophical, or, generically speaking, storytelling purposes distances hyperorchestral practices to some concert music.

Western orchestration defines instrumental timbre as a template. For instance, there is a clear distinction in timbre between a flute and the first violin section, but not between different models of flutes (of the same orchestral flute type) or different players. This allows for any Western-type orchestra in the world to play any piece written for orchestra without any further instructions than the orchestral score.

Hyperorchestration involves evaluating the sonic qualities of all the elements in the hyperorchestra, which become individual and unique instances that draw from sound recordings, physical instruments, synthesizers, recording techniques, and sound processing. It makes the creation of hyperinstruments one of the most crucial processes of hyperorchestration. Moreover, the placement of the hyperinstruments is not limited to an assumed position as it is in any orchestral ensemble. The placement of the hyperinstruments takes further advantage of its virtuality by not being static, thus making virtual space placement and movement across the space part of hyperorchestration. Hyperorchestration also extends the denotative and connotative associations in the Western orchestra by acknowledging that meaning is, in fact, one of the pillars of constructing a desired sound. Sonic specificity to render meanings and customized sound worlds is prioritized over any sense of performance standardization that the traditional Western musical system facilitated.

In the rest of the chapter, I will explore hyperorchestration techniques beyond established orchestration or arranging practices. First, I will revisit the creation of hyperinstruments from a hyperorchestration lens. Then, embracing a spectral attitude, I will propose that mixing and orchestration are analogous processes and suggest how mixing techniques directly relate to orchestration procedures. Afterward, I will explore how spectral transformations are valuable tools for blending orchestration and harmony to create smooth and subtle variations in the musical discourse. Finally, I will explore how hyperorchestration can also be used as a mode of augmented traditional orchestration, along with all the value that this carries with it.

Hyperinstrumentation and Virtual Organology

In *Toward a New Organology: Instruments of Music and Science*, Tresch and Dolan (2013) acknowledge that musicology is overcoming "the artificial divide that was created in the early twentieth century between the study of music (musicology) and the study of instruments (organology)" (278). Perhaps inspired by this structuralist divide, both orchestration treaties and pedagogical approaches to orchestration have tried to present instrumentation and orchestration as two distinct fields of inquiry. In the entry in Oxford Bibliographies on the topic, Paul Mathews (2020) describes both instrumentation and orchestration as "the body of technical knowledge required to arrange musical content for instrumental forces as well as the creative act of applying that knowledge with compositional intent," while alerting that "the usage of the words *instrumentation* and *orchestration* has not been consistent over time or between the European languages." Relatedly, Adler's (2016) orchestration book is divided into two sections—instrumentation and orchestration—but the introduction to the former is devoted to orchestration.

Nevertheless, Mathews (2020) suggests that instrumentation "refers to the body of knowledge about instruments: the mechanics of sound production and the techniques of performers" and orchestration "to the use of technical knowledge to assign musical content to instruments in an ensemble to achieve a sonorous effect." If the divide between instrumentation and orchestration is already tenuous in the very narrow world of the Western orchestra, it becomes even more entangled in the hyperreal. Tresch and Dolan (2013) urged to incorporate the study of instruments with the studies they pertain to, stressing that it became indispensable since the popularization of computers. Discussing Logic Pro (a DAW), they argue:

> Logic Pro transforms its embedded objects. Within this world, a guitar is no longer a physical prosthesis for the performer, liberating forms of artistic expression while simultaneously circumscribing the performer's range through its technical specifications and limitations. In Logic Pro, the instrument becomes synonymous with its effects; it becomes, as it were, purely aesthetic—a particular texture, a timbre, as well as a cultural resonance that can be conjured up with a few clicks. (280)

Since so much of the instrumentation process deals with instruments being "physical prostheses" for their performers—in Tresch and Dolan's terms—the virtualization of musical instruments decreases the importance of instrumentation as a discipline. Further, the "purely aesthetic" nature of these virtual sounds, as they emanate from hyperinstruments, brings the process of hyperinstrumentation even closer to the orchestration domain. Concomitantly, the study of instrumentation does not include the creation of new instruments, whereas, for hyperinstruments, this is a fundamental aspect. In fact, the study of instrumentation relies on instruments having an expected set of sonic outcomes.

With that in mind, hyperinstrumentation adds a new perspective that emanates from the absence of physical instrument templates that could be summarized in the following four areas as they relate to hyperinstruments:

- **Specificity over a generic timbral palette.** Traditional composting for physical instruments involves using them as generic timbres (e.g., a flute timbre without distinction of the flute model or the performer's style). Hyperinstruments become specific in that aspect and use this specificity to produce meaning.
- **Sonic practicality over conceptual templates.** Similarly, hyperinstruments have the resulting sound at their core. Thus, hyperinstruments are all about the sound result instead of the conceptual idea of how something will sound once performed.
- **Delimited capabilities over a multipurpose physical object.** Physical instruments are capable of producing a diversity of sounds through multiple performance techniques. Hyperinstruments are delimited by design, with delimited parameters the composer can interact with.
- **Hyperinstrument creation is a core process.** Conceiving and creating hyperinstruments is a mode of hyperorchestration, inseparable from the whole creative process. Once they are created, using hyperinstruments is more trivial than the traditional instrumentation process.

One consequence of the limitless possibilities of creating different hyperinstruments is that a guide is not really an option. However, there are salient aspects of the creation process of hyperinstruments as they pertain to screen music. I detail three approaches regarding the selection of sound sources below. Then, I outline key aspects of the design process.

Sound Source: Materialization and Musicalization of Sound Objects

In Chap. 3, I discussed how Chion (1994) coined the concept of materializing sound indices to describe how sound could make us feel the material aspects of its physical source (114). I also detailed how Mera (2016) brought Chion's concept to twenty-first-century film music to define a new mode of scoring that opposed the mainstream recording aesthetic "where instrumental recordings strive for effortless clarity and perfect evenness" and where "microphones are carefully placed to avoid scratchy or breathy sounds, intonation is always precise" (157). I suggested that this aesthetic approach is reminiscent of Wagner's Bayreuth design and its inherent ideology. I also briefly mentioned how Blier-Carruthers (2020) examined a similar issue in Western classical music recordings in *The Problem of Perfection in Classical Recording: The Performer's Perspective.* Blier-Carruthers summarized their view by stating that "sonic and technical perfection is now the norm, but is arguably not the most musically rewarding aim" (218) while suggesting that listeners are ready for a change in this paradigm.

Sound clarity and technical perfection are an outcome of the process of virtualization of the music experience through recordings, which became asynchronous modes of listening. Understandably, the sonic model for these recordings is music that is flawless in both the technical side of the performance and in the sound production. After all, we expect a printed book to be without grammatical errors and with clearly printed typography. Thus, it is reasonable to model a musical recording with equivalent features: no mistakes regarding the text (the score) and sonically as clear as possible. Further, this recording aesthetic seems the most adequate from the perspective of classical Hollywood aesthetics. Bordwell's (1985, 162–6) broadly accepted definition of the Classical style suggests that it requires a clear delimitation of the story world (the diegesis). The musical score is generally outside of the diegesis; thus, film narration should ensure audiences do not confuse it with diegetic sounds. From this viewpoint, a musical score that is as dematerialized as possible from its physical sources becomes a narration technique to ensure audiences do not confuse it with an element from the diegesis. From this angle, I believe Claudia Gorbman's

(1987) controversial definition of classical film music as being inaudible is relevant.[5] More than literally inaudible, the musical score sounds as transparent as possible by its clear sound and lack of mistakes.

While contemporary films have retained the essential framework of classical Hollywood aesthetics, they have also incorporated several changes and a great degree of flexibility over the rigidity of some stylistic elements (Bordwell 2006). One element that I believe emanates from the comparative analysis of recent and classical films is increased trust in audiences to understand more complex modes of storytelling. Bordwell's concept of *intensified continuity* and its development for sound and music (Bordwell 2006, 121–38; Smith 2013; Buhler 2020) details a set of techniques in which the spectators are able to understand much more about the world of the movie by being presented with an editing that it is less self-explanatory. In the same line of thought, film and sound editor Walter Murch (2001, 17–20) explained how early sound film required an editing structure that always preserved and clarified three-dimensional continuity. However, Murch explains how three-dimensional continuity became the least essential parameter in his approach to editing, summarized by what he called the rule of six.[6] Similarly, early twenty-first-century discussions about music and film diegesis (Stilwell 2007; Neumeyer 2009; Smith 2009; Winters 2010; Cecchi 2010; Yacavone 2012; Buhler 2019, 151–186) proposed a much more nuanced approach and identified several instances in modern movies in which the diegetic space was not as clearly preserved as one would assume following Bordwell's classical framework. All these examples seem to elucidate that movies evolved stylistically in a manner in which they relied on audiences to be able to decode a more sophisticated and complex film form.

In this context, a process of re-materialization of film music that does not necessarily follow the aesthetic ideals of flawless and cleanliness seems reasonable. If audiences are able to get a sense of the story world when the 3D continuity is not spoon-fed, they will also be able to identify as score music that is much more materialized. Mera's (2016) description of the string techniques in *There Will Be Blood* (2007) is a rigorous example of this process. If a clear instrumental sound is characterized by the maximization of a smooth and balanced harmonic spectrum over inharmonic material (with an aim to eliminate as much of the latter as possible without affecting the timbre too much), extended performance techniques in Jonny Greenwood's music for *There Will Be Blood* aim for the opposite.

Further, this change in the contextual framework triggered new ways to use sounds as part of the musical score. Dario Marianelli's score for *Atonement* (2007) has become an exemplar of using a diegetic sound (the typewriter) as part of the nondiegetic score to signify the main character's internal world. This is also a case proving that audiences were not confused and could follow the story. A few years before, Michael Giacchino used airplane fragments in *Lost* (2004–2010) to become part of the percussive sounds for the score of the TV show (Wigler 2016). By using diegetic objects to produce sounds for the score, the aim is to create meanings that generate a unique soundworld for the story and are more relatable to the ideas and storytelling. In Chap. 5, I exemplified this process with the score for *Chernobyl*, which used sound material from the power plant that was used to shoot the show, and *Dune*, with the creation of sounds and instruments that aim to replicate the desert.

Mera (2016) also suggests that "musical noise in instrumental music is tied to material causality and announces its hapticity" (158). Thus, Mera analyzes the haptic power of instrumental music in film scores that emanate through noise. For my present discussion, I generally avoid using the term noise by instead focusing on describing the spectral properties of sound. Instrumental music might be qualified as closer to noise when there is a significant amount of inharmonic spectral material (e.g., breathing, air, or bow sounds) when the harmonic part of the spectrum is uneven by reinforcing certain higher overtones (e.g., saturation or distortion, but also loud brass instruments), or when many *harmonious* sounds are playing together generating dissonances that produce a spectrum in which the shape of its harmonic part becomes very close to an inharmonic spectrum (e.g., the string clusters Mera analyzes in *There Will Be Blood*). Further, if a movie uses air sounds to represent air in the diegesis, we generally do not call it noise but just sound. We are also less prone to call noise to sounds produced in non-orchestral performance traditions and instruments—e.g., an electric guitar with distortion or a traditional shakuhachi performance. Regardless, Mera's point regarding hapticity stands, which supports my previous statement on why dematerialized orchestral music was efficient in developing the classical Hollywood style. However, it seems clear that in many twenty-first-century scores, hapticity has become an asset for designing a musical score connected to the audiovisual narrative that can enrich its meanings by seamlessly integrating with the audiovisual narrative.

Many hyperinstruments are created using a sound source that is highly materialized and strongly connected to the film world. Through the technology present in samplers and hybrid synthesizers, the sound source can be easily shaped to conform to a pitch structure, which can then be pitch-shifted to produce sounds based on the source at different pitches. Further, any of the mixing processes I will describe in the next section can be used to further process and modify the source to either musicalize it or transform it for meaning or aesthetic purposes. This process enhances the haptic connection of the music with both the composer's team and the audience. As I described in the music for *Chernobyl*, the process of recording sounds from the power plant that became the core of the score for the show was also a source of inspiration for the composer. The lived experience of wearing a protective suit while searching for sounds in the same location where the show was shot was inspirational and a guide to creating the score. At the same time, these recorded and processed sounds aimed to retain a haptic connection with the place in a manner that was felt by the audience.

Sound Source: Musical Traditions and Globalized Culture

The hyperorchestra allows for hyperinstruments to be created not only from various sound sources but also from instruments outside the Western orchestra. This includes modern instruments from any country (synthesizers, guitars, etc.), instruments from any cultural tradition (from the Irish whistle to the Indian bansuri), and also the use of orchestral instruments in non-standard performance practices (e.g., playing a string instrument with overpressure). As a cultural institution, the Western orchestra has an established setup and expected set of instruments, which means that any instrumental additions become apparent and meaningful. Unless the additions are subtle, the decision to incorporate instruments is noticeable.

Of course, scores without an orchestra have been part of movies for several decades, but even then, they generally become noticeable. Further, it is also undoubtedly usual in twenty-first-century screen music to have non-orchestral ensembles and to transform orchestral sections and instruments by applying hyperinstrumental design. This is, for instance, the case in *Dune* or *Annihilation*.

Hyperinstruments that have their sources in these non-orchestral instruments might approach their design from two approaches:

decontextualizing the instruments or keeping their cultural context. Generally speaking, a decontextualized approach aims to add additional fresh sounds to the orchestral palette to accomplish meaning-creation purposes. More frequently than not, a decontextualized approach engages in a materialization process as described above. For instance, using a non-orchestral flute (e.g., the Japanese shakuhachi or the Indian bansuri) will land a sonic result that is much more materialized. These instruments have much more air sound, and their overtone and pitch structure are less clear than the orchestral flute.

In this approach, performers plying those instruments might choose to emphasize the sonic and spectral differences of these flutes instead of embracing the inherent musical performance traditions that are attached to them. Similarly, recording techniques might reinforce the same sonic intent. John Williams used the shakuhachi in the second half of the opening cue of *Jurassic Park* (1993) with this precise objective. In the music mix, it is difficult even to recognize the flute as a shakuhachi, but it is also clear that it is not an orchestral flute. The added amount of air and pitch instability helps the music to portray a more mysterious and threatening environment, connecting the music to the woods in the jungle. Both the performance and the recording emphasize the materializing aspects of the sound instead of focusing on portraying its musical tradition.

Instruments can also serve to incorporate a cultural context or specificity. This generally implies that some or all the performance traditions and musical styles associated with the instrument are preserved. For example, John Williams used the shakuhachi again in the score for *Memoirs of a Geisha* (2007) in a manner designed to signify Japan. Williams explained that he aimed to "create an oriental atmosphere by using traditional Japanese instruments that would be supported by a broad, Western harmonic vocabulary" (classicFM), which he described as providing a universal emotional framework. Williams' aesthetic framework is undoubtedly attached to classical Hollywood scoring traditions that have become at least partially outdated by the use of the hyperorchestra. However, it reinforces my point on the importance of the pristinely and clearly recorded Western orchestra as the neutral standard for screen scoring. Thus, the statement also aligns with my description above that non-orchestral sound additions have become, at least until now, meaningful and noticeable.

Using sound sources contextualized within their cultural traditions tends to generate a sort of cultural materialization. Wierzbicki (2009) noted how, in 1936, producers were already aware that using music resembling a culture was an effective world-building strategy that could save money on set design (148–9). While the examples from that period generally drew from cultural clichés at best to derogatory associations at worst, they still help indicate the effect these techniques have on filmmaking. For the cultural materialization effect to be effective, audiences must recognize the sounds and associate them with an area, tradition, or culture.

This is where technological progress has been instrumental in developing a hyperorchestra that draws from various sonic sources. Going back to McLuhan's ideas of implosion and the Global Village I described in Chap. 1, instant communication and access to a much broader type of music and music creators through technologies such as music streaming has had a crucial role in providing audiences with a more globalized approach to music. Further, in tandem with the capacity for distributed asynchronous recording worldwide, the nonlinear scoring process has made it easy for music creators (for the screen and everything else) to produce music using a wider variety of cultural influences. This fact does not make the average moviegoer an expert ethnomusicologist, but it does indicate an attitude toward musical listening that is much less restricted to narrow cultural traditions. Further, this is most effective when the intended meanings are nuanced and subtle (e.g., to shape the film world in addition to other elements). Filmic resources designed for an immediate association (e.g., showing the Eiffel Tower or using an accordion to signify Paris) might need to be sourced from more cliched approaches.

Finally, in my analysis of the hyperinstruments in *Dune*, I outlined how cultural traditions could be merged to produce a new musical style with influences from those cultures without being a direct referent. The process allowed for the creation of a sonic identity for an imaginary universe that had clear ties with existing human cultural traditions. This merging process was done through vocal techniques in voice elements and by creating new instruments using existing instrumental parts (the duduk mouthpiece in PVC tubes).

Sound Source: Expanding Instruments

The third area on sound sources has existing instruments as a starting point. While most of the discussion on this area will be described in the next section as it pertains to sound manipulation (mixing) as a mode of hyperorchestration, it is worth underlining some aspects from the point of view of the source. Instruments can be expanded by merging them with sounds from another instrument or source. For example, air sound could be added to a violin-based hyperinstrument to add a sense of dreaminess or transcendence. In *Interstellar* (2014), Nolan and Zimmer used a church organ as a core instrument, which was merged with a sine-wave-like synth sound around the 200Hz area. The process most likely involved sound sculpting processing in a way I will describe in the next section (e.g., the organ sound had the 200Hz frequency lowered to allow the synth to merge). In this case, this merging process created a hyperinstrument that extended the religious meaning associations of the organ into space by making the sound of the organ appear to float in the void.

The Design Process

So far, I have not distinguished between hyperinstruments built from recordings used to create custom-made sample libraries, existing sample libraries, synthesizers, or recordings imported and manipulated directly into the DAW. While these would be central distinctions from the point of view of the distribution of labor, economics, or even music production workflow optimization, they are much less relevant from the point of view of aesthetics. Sample libraries contain recordings (samples) of performances conceived by music creators (sample library designers). If time and budget were not an issue, we would expect that a composer would choose to either use an existing sample library or decide to create their own just based on what best fits the aesthetic requirements of their idea.

Nevertheless, the nonlinear music creation process imposes similar flexibilities and limitations to all these approaches. I have already described many of the flexibilities allowed. The constraints emanate from the fact that once a recording has been made, it becomes the musical material from which to create the score. Once recorded, all instruments become virtualized instances. In other words, the traditional scoring process would allow the composer to conceive musical techniques for the performers until its last step: the recording sessions. In the nonlinear model, recording is part of the process and not a final step. Tresch and Dolan (2013) called virtual instruments "purely aesthetic" (280) for that very reason, as they become detached from the physical instrument, with its capabilities and limitations. Thus, once the hyperinstrument has been designed and created, they generally are much more constrained in what they can do due to their degree of specificity. Hence, this is why I emphasized that creating and designing hyperinstruments became an essential part of the composition process and, thus, an essential aspect of hyperorchestration. In the following section, I describe mixing techniques as a mode of hyperorchestration that can be used to create, design, and combine hyperinstruments.

Mixing as a Mode of Hyperorchestration

One central element of the hyperorchestration process is successfully negotiating the soundscape once the music is liberated from the restrictions of the standardized model of the symphonic orchestra. One consequence is that it brings mixing and orchestration even closer, becoming the same process. Simplifying, orchestration can be defined as the art and craft of combining musical instruments, while music mixing could be described as the art and craft of combining recorded musical sounds. Thus, they are essentially the same process in a virtualized music creation framework.

In this section, I explore mixing as a hyperorchestration modality. However, it is not an exhaustive and practical exploration of mixing. It is a theoretical approach to how mixing tools align with orchestration procedures. Thus, I focus on the mixing techniques that aid in the creation of meaning. For context, I start by analyzing the beginning of Mahler's First Symphony—an attempt to transcend the limitations of the orchestral setup by applying the acoustic equivalent of a mixing process.

Acoustic Mixing in Mahler's First Symphony

At the beginning of Mahler's *First Symphony*, the composer asks the trumpet players to perform as if they were far away. In concert performances of the piece, trumpet players are temporally placed offstage. Besides the effect that such spatial placement of the trumpets might have in terms of musical signification (an awakening call from far away), this unconventional placement engenders a new sonority that generates a new array of orchestral interactions. In terms of orchestration, this unorthodox placement implies that the conventional principles of orchestral trumpet scoring do not apply. In the score, Mahler notated the trumpet part with a *ppp* dynamic, which is softer than the *pp* written for the woodwinds playing just before the trumpets' entrance (Fig. 6.1).

Examining the most common performance practices for this beginning, one realizes that the *ppp* dynamic refers to the resulting loudness of the trumpets at the concert stage. In other words, the trumpet players are not performing a *ppp* dynamic but in a much louder dynamic (*mf* or *f*) to compensate for the attenuation of their sound due to their placement.

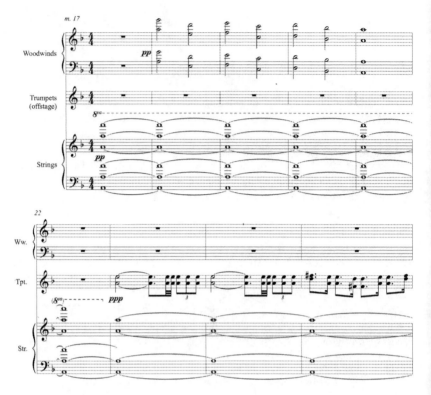

Fig. 6.1 Score reduction for Mahler's *First Symphony* (m. 17–25)

When the offstage trumpets interact with the clarinet, it sounds significantly louder than the trumpets while performing at a softer dynamic level.

Loudness is not the only sound property altered when the trumpets play offstage. The distance and walls between their location and the stage also alter the timbre of the trumpets. Thus, even though the performers could play onstage more quietly than the offstage sound, the result would be significantly different. Consequently, performing the opening of the trumpet part onstage in a quieter dynamic would substantially alter the sound that the composer envisioned for the beginning of the symphony and invalidate the effect.

This is an extraordinary example of using acoustic devices such as walls and distance to develop an acoustic mixing process. It is also intentional in terms of meaning (Mahler did that to portray an idea) by molding the sound spectrum of the trumpets (the walls attenuate the loudness of the higher frequencies the most while leaving most of the mid frequencies that we associate with bright brass). Further, it exemplifies the relevancy of instrumental distance, based on musical models (from the orchestra to a rock band), in which we expect the instruments to be close to each other. Concomitantly, it shows the evocative power of subtle variations of the instrument spectrum. With the hyperorchestra, ideas such as this become exponentially easier to achieve with a limitless set of sound transformation possibilities.

The Parameters of Sound (and Music)

In the practical book *The Art of Mixing*, David Gibson (2005) briefly describes the fundamental roots of sound:

> Sound has three components: volume (or amplitude), frequency, and time. That's it. Therefore, every sound manipulator used in the studio can be categorized as to whether it controls volume, frequency, or time. (75)

Following this, Gibson classifies the different processors into six main groups based on how the effects interrelate with the physical characteristics of sound. These groups originate in combining these three features: Volume, Frequency, Time, Volume over Frequency, Frequency over Time, and Volume over Time. In addition, the location of the sound is an additional parameter. While the distance from the sound source could be described using the three parameters indicated by Gibson, a sound at an equal distance from ours will be perceived differently because of the shape and position of our ears. Gibson incorporates this concept in his book, but he keeps it separate from the other parameters to differentiate between monophonic, stereophonic, and surround music.

The simplicity of this model—with only three variables plus space—is paramount to understanding that all sound processing relates to one or a combination of these areas. Thus, all sound or musical processes can be explained using these terms only. However, its simplicity does not facilitate the creation of theoretical approaches. Music adds a sense of organized formal structure to sound that can be formalized and described on top of this framework, grounded on the natural phenomenon of the harmonic series.

Fineberg (2000) summarized the most relevant concepts regarding structure in his *Guide to the Basic Concepts and Techniques of Spectral Music*. As I have mentioned before, the foundations of spectral music are closely related to the sonic principles of the hyperorchestra, which are in line with music mixing principles and studio production. While many sources discuss musical acoustics and the harmonic series, I use Fineberg's (2000) guide as the starting point because of its focus on aesthetics in relation to spectral attitudes to music.

The Harmonic Series
The harmonic series (85–6) is a mathematical phenomenon that appears in nature and is at the core of music structure. A frequency (the fundamental) triggers a set of other frequencies (overtones or harmonics) that are integer multipliers. For instance, a 200Hz fundamental frequency will have overtones at 400Hz, 600Hz, 800Hz, and so on. The distances between the first frequencies in the series determine perfect intervals (octave, fifth, and fourth) in our music system, followed by a major and minor third. The first notes of the series generate a major triad chord, which is complemented with the acoustic equivalent to a dominant 7th chord (the 7th is lower than it generally is in our temperate system).

Harmonic Spectra as a Mode of Natural Additive Synthesis
Additive synthesis is a technique for "building complex sounds through the combination of a large number of elementary ones" (84). The most elementary sound is produced by a sine wave, which represents only one frequency. The harmonic spectra (86) product of the harmonic series might be considered a natural version of additive synthesis in which each added frequency over the fundamental is one of the overtones in the series. Each of the overtones has a determined amplitude (volume) that generally decreases with higher overtones. However, there are infinite possible combinations of amplitudes of the overtones for the same organization, which we call pitch when it follows the harmonic spectrum.

Instrumental Spectra
Western orchestral musical instruments (as well as the rest of the instruments at varied degrees) developed to "have spectra which are very close to the pure harmonic spectra, so as to emphasize clarity of sound and pitch" (86). This idea aligns with the pursuit of clarity for recordings described before. Nevertheless, each instrument (and each register within

the instrument and dynamic level) has a distinct distribution of amplitudes within the harmonic spectrum. While the overall shape is for overtones to get sequentially quieter, each instrument, register, or dynamic level has a distinct distribution of amplitudes. Further, the resonant elements of an instrument emphasize certain areas of the frequency range (called formants), modifying the power of certain overtones (87–9). For example, Fineberg mentions the most evident examples: the "flute's weak fundamental tone in its low register," the clarinet spectrum that "tends to emphasize only odd numbered partials," or the brass instruments in a loud dynamic that "tend to have dissonant upper partials as the loudest components of their spectrum" (87).

While the design goal for many instruments is to maximize the harmonic spectrum and make it seem stable, this is not entirely possible. The following three concepts are part of an instrument's sound in combination with its harmonic spectrum.

Inharmonic Spectra
Some musical instruments (mainly grouped under the term unpitched percussion) do not have a harmonic spectrum but an inharmonic one, meaning their frequency content is not organized around the overtone series (91). It is important to emphasize that these instruments do have a spectral shape, though, which allows us to identify them sonically (a suspended cymbal sounds different from a bass drum).

In addition, all acoustic instruments designed to produce primarily harmonic spectral sound have inharmonic material due to their physicality. For instance, the air flowing through the flute, the performer's breathing sound, or the sound of the bow in contact with the strings in a violin produce inharmonic spectral content. Performance technologies (the design of the stage and the concert hall), performance techniques, and the classical recording process were designed to reduce the inharmonic sounds even more. For instance, the selection and placement of microphones are instrumental in minimizing the amount of air, breathing, or bow sound they capture.

Attack Transients
To make an instrument start to produce sound, physical action must be taken to alter the state of the materials. It requires additional physical strength, which generally generates additional sound. Fineberg calls these "mechanical parasites," such as "the scrapping of the bow before the pitch

has stabilized in a string instrument" or "the impact of the hammer in a piano" (90). The sound of the attack is generally in the form of inharmonic material and short in time. Performance techniques and instrumental design technologies usually try to minimize some of these sounds (e.g., all the felt around piano mallets). However, they are still an integral part of the musical discourse.

The Spectral Envelope
The spectral envelope "determines the appearance, disappearance, and changing relative amplitudes of various partials" (90). In other words, what we associate with the timbre of an instrument is not a static distribution of frequencies but a dynamic process that is currently very difficult to analyze or fully understand. This is in addition to the fact that each note produced by the instrument will have a different frequency distribution because:

1. each note has a different starting fundamental,
2. each register generates a different overtone structure due to the physical properties of the materials instruments are made,
3. the resonant frequencies tend to stay stable, which means they emphasize different relative frequency areas in relationship with the fundamental of the note, and
4. there are multiple variations in the harmonic and inharmonic sounds depending on dynamic changes in the performance (e.g., the amount of pressure applied to the bow or its location).

With all of that in mind, it is understandable that learning to orchestrate or to mix is daunting, especially because crafting universal methods is difficult, if not impossible. One faces a similar problem when trying to study or describe it. Still, learning orchestration and instrumentation has the advantages of a very discrete set of instances. This means that orchestrating is possible without knowledge of the spectral properties of the sound. With hyperorchestration (along with mixing), spectral understanding becomes indispensable. Breaking the discretization of sound objects and allowing limitless possibilities links the creative process back to the foundations of the acoustics of sound and the acoustic structures of music.

Notes, Pitch, Noise, and Timbre

With the above in mind, common terminology such as note, pitch, timbre, or noise becomes more vague. Dolan and Rehding (2021), in their introduction as editors to *The Oxford Handbook of Timbre*, emphasized that "to talk about timbre means to constantly define and redefine it" while acknowledging how all the authors in their edited book offer "a particular way of framing what timbre is, or could be" (2021, Introduction). Similarly, while the concept of pitch seems clearer as to the fundamental frequency of a frequency structure that is primarily harmonic, it is not without a degree of fuzziness. For example, the perception of pitch will be lower in sounds that follow the overtone structure less strictly (e.g., the flute's lower register). Relatedly, while both a bass drum sound and a suspended cymbal hit do not have a pitch because they possess an inharmonic frequency content, we generally associate the suspended cymbal as sounding higher (due to its frequency range) and thus somehow connect this to the concept of pitch.

Relatedly, what constitutes a note is also more ambiguous than one might think. Everybody would agree that a violin section playing together at the same pitch counts as one note. However, if we add to this sound a single flute in a manner that becomes unnoticeable on its own as it only contributes to adding additional higher-frequency content, would that constitute one or two notes?

Finally, the concept of noise within music could be associated with either unexpected sounds within a framework (e.g., excessive bow sound in a violin performance) or, from a spectral point of view, the inharmonic frequency content of sounds. Hainge (2013) would call the latter an approach from a physicist's viewpoint (3). However, the suspended cymbal or bass drum sound would become noises, which does not generally align with our perception.

From a traditional orchestration viewpoint, all these concepts become fairly straightforward by restricting the possibilities and possible sound outcomes. The study of timbre becomes a combination of examining instrumental and ensemble timbres. Instrumental timbre is the assumed frequency structure of a musical instrument within a given circumstance (pitch, dynamic, articulation). Once this is established, ensemble timbres become the real orchestration challenge: the resulting sound product of combining different instruments in varied circumstances. The timbral outcome of these combinations is a product of acoustic interactions between the bodies of the instruments (e.g., the sound of the violins resonates in the celli, thus modifying its resonant points), phase cancellations, and interactions within the orchestra (frequencies reinforce or cancel each other), and our psychoacoustic capacity to discern content within a certain frequency area.

Hyperorchestration (and mixing) has the advantage of utilizing sound analytical tools that help discern and identify sound properties while adding exponential complexity and opportunities for sonic combinations. To give one example, let's consider the previous scenario in which violins and a flute are playing in unison in a manner that the flute is only contributing to the higher frequency part of the resulting sound (the lower part of the frequency range in the flute is masked by the violins). If we decide to filter out the lower part of the flute, we might produce an ensemble timbre that is perceived as the same without the filter but leaving additional mixing room for other elements. However, if we were to listen to the flute alone, the timbral differences would be massive. In that case, has the hyperorchestrator/mixer changed the music's timbre or preserved it?

These questions highlight the ambiguities of the terms, which become even more major in hyperorchestration. At the same time, they also underline the importance of these terms to retain a connection and discuss the sound sources. Thus, concepts such as instrumental timbre or pitch are handy if used with the more objective concepts I just outlined. Considering the complexity of dealing with all these concepts and properties, I will add another theoretical source of knowledge that has been fundamental in developing hyperorchestral models: the process of creating synthetic sounds from scratch using synthesizers.

Synthetic Sound Design Principles

It is not a coincidence that many of the relevant figures who reshaped screen music at the end of the twentieth century to move toward the hyperorchestra were well-versed in working with synthesizers. Synths are not only the foundations for understanding samplers and all the realistic representations of acoustic instruments and performances but also a way to model and better understand the parameters I outlined in the previous section. Sound synthesis creates sounds out of processes instead of recordings. These sounds aim to at least relate to acoustic experiences, which means that synthesizer design needs to incorporate ways of modeling the acoustic world. Sound design with synthesizers (along with the design of the synths themselves) started by understanding and modeling music.

Thus, in addition to the basic concept of pitch and frequency, there was a focus on understanding how to model timbre and the life of a musical sound.

The Fourier theorem is indispensable for implementing synthesizers and many tools used to process audio. From the point of view of music, the theorem states that any sound can be expressed as a combination of single-frequency sounds at varying amplitudes. In other words, any sound can be recreated artificially by combining a set of single-frequency sounds.[7] A sound that produces a single frequency is generally regarded as a sine wave. This is because its graphical representation [amplitude(y) over time(x)] follows the graphical representation of a sinusoidal function [y=sin(x)]. Sine waves are smooth and periodic, which is why they correlate with a single frequency. The quicker their period, the higher the frequency. This means that they are easy to recreate artificially.

Synthesizers (at least in their essential form) generate sound through an electric device—voltage-controlled oscillators—that can generate alternate periodic electrical signals in the form of a sine wave or another shape. They generate sound by either combining multiple sine waves in a harmonic structure that resembles an acoustic instrument or by achieving a similar result by starting with a harmonically dense sound (created by a similarly periodic shape, such as a square, that contains infinite overtones) and then reducing its overtone content (Pejrolo and Metcalfe 2017, 53–59). The sound produced by the combination of these oscillators is generally controlled using the ADSR model (described in the previous chapter). The model, which aims to mimic the acoustic process of a note, is also instrumental in the pursuit of a tool that engages in models of the real. In addition, sound (such as white noise) might be added at the moment of the attack of the note to mimic the inharmonic content of the sound or during the note to model air or bow friction.

Therefore, while, theoretically, creating a synthesizer sound does not require any knowledge of acoustic instruments, the reality is that, in practice, it does. Synths created to become musical instruments are designed to extend music and, thus, interact with our interpretation of what music is based on the previous section. It also requires an analytical perspective by creating and applying synthetic models that resemble acoustic realities (e.g., ADSR). Further, designing a synth sound to become an instrument implies applying mixing to combine a group of sine waves or filter some of the frequencies of a square wave (or any other signals). For instance, making a synthesizer sound similar to a clarinet or a trumpet might involve changing some of the frequency content of the original sounds that came from the oscillators.

Designing synthesizer sounds also created broad categories that correlate with instrumental function within an orchestra or a band. A key type of synthesizer in screen scoring is the pad, which is generally smooth and somewhat static, resembling the sound of a sustained string section. Its overtone harmonic shape is similar to the string section while offering immense opportunities for sound variation, from a simplified number of overtones to a more complex upper register harmonic structure.

Therefore, conceiving mixing as a mode of hyperorchestration emanates from the practice of sound sculpting through synthesis, which, thanks to the evolution of digital technologies and DAWs, is combined with the utilization of acoustic instruments and recordings. In explaining these processes, I suggest equivalents with traditional Western orchestration whenever possible. I aim to demonstrate how close each mixing process is to similar acoustic techniques. However, using mixing tools in that way requires a mode of thinking (a spectral attitude) that was much more developed by composers or music creators well-versed in synthesizers than the ones whose main field of expression were orchestral ensembles. With all these concepts in mind, let's start by defining what mixing was before and is now from this paradigm.

Defining Mixing

At its core, music mixing emanated from recording. In its original meaning, mixing was the process of joining together the different recorded elements of a song to create a sound image that was as close as possible to the live sound that preceded the recording (Moylan 2014, 418). In *Understanding and Crafting the Mix*, Moylan (2014) outlined the importance of focusing, during the mixing process, on the creator's intended meaning for the music. This is achieved by adapting the different pieces captured during the recording (or created by the synthesizers) while putting them together. Moylan even suggests that mixing is effectively composing music:

> The process of planning and shaping the mix is very similar to composing. Sounds are put together in particular ways to best suit the music. The mix is crafted through shaping the sound stage, through combining sound sources

at certain dynamic levels, through structuring pitch density, and much more. (416)

Moylan's definition aligns with my approach of defining mixing as a mode of hyperorchestration. However, in Moylan's framework, mixing is contained within a few processes and strategies. Moreover, Moylan's approach is broadly linear, placing the mixing process at a very specific stage of the production of a song. The nonlinear model I outlined suggests a process in which the techniques associated with mixing become an integral and intertwined part of the creative process. In this environment, mixing evolves to include a much broader approach to sound modification.

Therefore, mixing comprises processes dedicated to placing a specific sound or virtual instrument within the virtual soundscape while shaping its sound spectrum. In other words, mixing is sculpting the sound and placing it on the virtual canvas presented to us. It also contributes to creating hyperinstruments and their associated meaning, thus acting similarly to how traditional orchestration operates when creating textures and timbres.

In the following sections, I describe a selection of mixing processes that I consider primary when used as a hyperorchestration tool: the creation of a sound perspective for a hyperinstrument, the utilization of sound processing tools, and the design of a virtual space in which to place the music. These processes do not exclude hyperorchestral music from being mixed in its original definition. While it is all reasonably interconnected, my focus is still on how mixing becomes hyperorchestration.

Combining Microphones: Sound Perspectives

In the hyperinstrument framework I proposed in the previous chapter, I included a stage that involves deciding the microphone placement and the final sound perspective of the hyperinstrument. This might be a decision based on an existing sample library that provides multiple sound perspectives or from a set of microphones placed during the recording process. The latter implies that the composer needs to have a good notion of how they want to record a sound or instrument to produce the desired hyperinstrument. The effects of this process on the creation of meaning are significant. Therefore, the process of generating a perspective is relevant because it has been instrumental in the recordings of many scores since the early 2000s, and they are also a general feature of a significant number of virtual instruments.[8] Thus, crafting a sound perspective based on an existing subset of options has become one of the creative processes when writing music using virtual instruments, which is not dissimilar from scoring decisions while using nonlinear customized recordings.

In the analysis of the hyperdrums in *Man of Steel* (2013), I described how using microphones placed close to each of the drums was essential to produce a sound mix that combined the cultural individuality of each performer while generating a cohesive drum ensemble sound. Recording nonlinearly and in isolated groups encourages the utilization of multiple and specific microphones to shape a detailed perspective in an approach that is aesthetically similar to deciding the sound perspective in a virtual instrument.

In *Joker* (2019), Hildur Guðnadóttir recorded her cello (or its variant, Hallodrophone) with fairly closely placed microphones, which emphasized the bow friction over the string sound and the uneven overtones at the attack. Played with more pressure than a traditional classical performance, the microphone placement helped to capture the extra friction of the instrument, creating a sound to identify Arthur's damaged and tortured personality before becoming the Joker. Relatedly, Ludwig Göransson recorded his wife playing the violin in *Oppenheimer* (2023) at his studio in a manner that made the solo violin appear almost like a home recording coming from a single microphone placed in a smaller-than-usual room. The solo violin, as it appeared when Oppenheimer met his future wife Kitty ("Meeting Kitty"), helped create a humane and common-man side of a character portrayed as the modern Prometheus throughout most of the film. Hence, the solo violin recording strategy facilitated us to connect with him at a human level.

One instrument that has radically transformed its expressive meaning through this process is the piano. In the widely influential score for *The Shawshank Redemption* (1994), Thomas Newman wrote a stylistically revolutionary piece of music with solo piano in *Brooks Was Here*. At that moment, the oldest inmate in the group of characters is released from prison. He is unable to adapt to the changes in society, writes a letter to his friends, and commits suicide. The music contains a subtle and spare solo piano theme that was recorded very close to the mallets (with additional equalization as I will detail in the next section). Thus, the microphones helped to materialize the mechanics of the piano, making the theme more intimate—as if the audience was listening with the ear inside the piano—and the sound more unsettling. Another subtle strategy of using the piano to evoke nostalgia appears in the score for *Blade Runner 2049* (2017). Wallfisch and Zimmer use the piano recorded fairly closely but pass it through a massive reverberation, creating a sensation of loss and remembrance. In the score, the piano is accompanied by bell sounds that reinforce the nostalgia due to its connection to childhood tropes. The piano melody for the main theme in *The Social Network* (2010)—"Hand Covers Bruise"—provides an even more suggestive example of the possibilities of employing the sound perspective as a musical tool to create evolving meaning.[9] The theme appears three times during the movie to signify the main character's (the portrayal of Mark Zuckerberg) detachment from reality. To do so, the piano is recorded further and further, almost becoming a distant childhood memory in the third and last version.

These examples show how the composer or the mixer gains access to several microphone recordings (or already mixed perspectives) from which to generate a specific sonic placement for the instrument at any moment in the score. Fig. 6.2, which is reminiscent of Moylan's templates for stereo analysis (2014), represents the three different mixes of the piano as they appear in *The Social Network* (2010).

With only these three recordings, it is possible to craft multiple customized perspectives by mixing the different microphone recordings. For example, one mix could be mainly created using perspective 1, adding

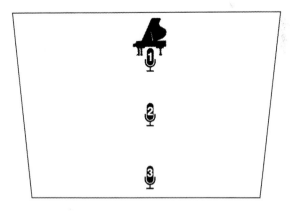

Fig. 6.2 Visual representation of the piano mixes in *The Social Network* (2010). The composers utilized three different microphone positions at varying distances from the source

some signal from perspective 3. Generating a sound perspective could be even more sophisticated if one eases the necessity to retain a realistic connection with the source. To provide just one example, these three recordings could create a piano sound that could not be generated acoustically by individually altering the position in the stereo field (panning) for some of the perspectives and mixing them together afterward (Fig. 6.3).

Altering the positioning of the microphones captured in the stereo field produces a significant result: it is impossible to establish a physical placement for the piano in a two-dimensional stereo image. The position of the piano becomes multidimensional and thus from the hyperreal, in which each additional perspective generates a new dimension.

To summarize, creating a sound perspective has the potential to tailor the meaning of the instrument and the music. One of the main reasons is that the process subverts the sound we expect based on the standard placement of microphones. Recording closer to the instrument increases its materialization by capturing much more of its mechanics (mallets, bow, air…). Similarly, recording the instrument further also affects our perception, as it deviates from the recording standard. In this case, we lose frequency content and detail while gaining the sound of the recording space, thus unveiling a materializing effect of the space. If standard microphone placement makes the recording space reasonably transparent to the listeners, placing the microphones further materializes the room in a similar way in which Mahler made us aware that the trumpets at the beginning of his first symphony were placed outside the stage.

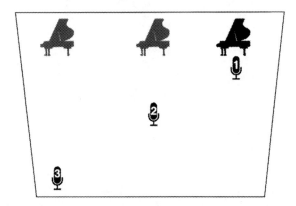

Fig. 6.3 Mixing perspectives with different panning

Spectral Shaping Through Equalization

The term equalization (EQ) is linked to the original purpose of these processors: to restore the *original* sound of the instrument that was transformed due to the recording process. As microphones do not capture sound evenly across frequency ranges, equalizers were meant to serve as a restoration tool following the recording process. Gibson (2005) provides a broad definition of equalizers and the complexity attached to their utilization during the mixing process:

> EQ is a change in the volume of a particular frequency of a sound, similar to the bass and treble tone controls on a stereo. It is one of the least understood aspects of recording and mixing probably because there is such a large number of frequencies—from 20 to 20,000Hz. The real difficulty comes from the fact that boosting or cutting the volume of any one of these frequencies depends on the structure of the sound itself: Each one is different. (p. 89)

Broadly understood, an equalizer can alter the volume of the restricted frequency range of the incoming sound signal (volume over frequency category).[10] Gibson (2005) also describes how the process of equalization has evolved along with what we consider a natural sound:

> These days natural is defined by what is currently on CDs and the radio. We have become addicted to crisper, brighter, and cleaner, as well as fatter, fuller, and bigger. [...] What we hear on the radio and on CDs these days is much brighter, crisper, and bassier than the real thing. If it isn't bright enough and doesn't have enough low-end, it won't be considered right. (195)

Still, Gibson's approach to equalization is traditional, mainly focused on generating the accepted cultural standard for a natural sound—even when the standard has become hyperrealistic. In another practical book on mixing, *The Mixing Engineer's Handbook*, Owsinski (2013a) provides an aesthetically expanded approach, when compared to Gibson's, to equalization:

> There are three primary goals when equalizing:
> 1. To make an instrument sound clearer and more defined
> 2. To make the instrument or mix bigger and larger than life

3. To make all the elements of a mix fit together better by juggling frequencies so that each instrument has its own predominant frequency range (25)

Owsinski offers some aesthetic insights that can be generalized to a broader range of hyperorchestration tools. Hence, Owsinski's triad of primary goals serves as a template for the main categories in which equalization might be used hyperorchestrationally. First, equalization might be used to modify the sound properties of a hyperinstrument or a sound combination and alter it within the confines of what is considered its natural sound (part of the hyperinstrumental design process). In traditional orchestration, the possibility of modifying the sound of an instrument is constrained. For instance, a solo violin might be asked to perform a passage instead of a violin section. Similarly, the section could play using a mute or *sul tasto*. These orchestrational decisions will alter the string sound to a certain degree: a solo violin will sound sharper and more intense than a whole section at the expense of becoming the sound of just one violin.

In addition to these resources, hyperorchestration allows the mixer to fine-tune the sounds by equalizing some of their frequencies, thus producing, for example, either a clearer or more diffused sound. Diverse equalization techniques could be applied to produce those effects. For instance, reducing the 3KHz area in the violins produces an effect roughly equivalent to using a mute, with the advantage that the composer can vary the amount of reduction, creating unlimited types of virtual mutes that do not exist in reality.

The second area in which equalization could be employed as a hyperorchestration mechanism is to stretch an instrument's perception of verisimilitude—expanding its sound possibilities—which would generally alter its associated meanings. By employing equalization to surpass its verisimilitude—as a representation of a physical instrument—it is possible to tailor the instrument's sound further to satisfy particular expressive needs. For instance, a region from the high-frequency area could be filtered (the signal is wholly muted in that area) to produce a mellow and partially obscure sound. Intense equalization might transform the original sound into something that barely resembles the source.

Finally, equalization is valuable in assigning certain frequency areas to each instrument to enhance and better shape the final sound. This is the approach that most resembles an extended mode of orchestration. For each instrument, the hyperorchestrator might prioritize which frequency ranges the instrument is allotted. The fewer the instruments in a frequency range, the clearer and more present they become. In this process, it is essential to consider how the overtones interact and their role in shaping the instrument's sound. If some of the frequencies of an instrument are cut and, therefore, some of its overtones are missing, the instrument's timbre might significantly change. At the same time, sounds in the same frequency range mask each other, thus diluting their contribution to the creation of the timbral content of the instrument. In acoustic orchestration, the composer might decide not to use brass in a passage where the flute plays a line to prevent the brass overtones from masking the flute sound. With hyperorchestration, it is possible to filter the frequencies of the brass section that collided with the flute line to preserve both instruments at the cost of modifying the timbre of the brass.

Revisiting "Brooks Was Here" from *The Shawshank Redemption*, the piano was not only recorded close but also had its higher frequencies attenuated. In doing so, Thomas Newman can evoke closeness and intimacy through the microphone placement while also suggesting a sense of nostalgia and distance—a product of the loss of high frequencies. Recording the piano from far away would have had a similar effect but at the expense of losing the intimacy produced by hearing the mallet sound. The solution—close microphones and equalization—preserved the feelings of intimacy and nostalgia without compromise.

The theme for the TV show *Daredevil* (2015–2018), composed by John Paesano, also provides a pristine example of the power of using EQ for evocative purposes. The strings in the theme represent the main character, Daredevil, a vigilante with complicated morals who acts at night only. Thus, strings provide an appropriate hero-like timbre for the character but would miss his ethically compromised side. The solution was to equalize them in a manner that resembles asking for the strings to play in a *sul ponticello* technique that is greatly exaggerated and obscured. Figure 6.4 is an approximation of the EQ used for the strings. Therefore, equalization served as a hyperorchestration technique to modulate the traditional meaning of the spiccato string sound—to signify the heroic nature—into the nuanced morals of Daredevil's character.

Frequency: Harmonic Density

A common problem in sound recording that was exacerbated with digital technologies is the failure to properly capture the nuances and details of

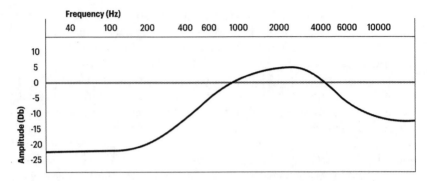

Fig. 6.4 String EQ Processing in the Strings of Daredevil. Transcribed by the author

the higher part of the harmonic spectra of the sound. While this happens for multiple reasons, I would like to focus on one common solution. When a sound is louder than what analog equipment can handle (e.g., the tape recorder), it loses its shape in its moments of maximum amplitude. In the simplest case—a sine wave—the wave becomes slightly squared. The consequence is that the wave no longer generates one single frequency as multiple overtones are added, generating a harmonic spectrum.

This process is called distortion. At subtle amounts and through the modeling of analog equipment, the process is called soft saturation. A consequence of saturation is that the resulting sound contains a denser harmonic spectrum produced by the addition of harmonic content. While this added harmonic material is artificial, it also balances the loss of higher-frequency harmonic content due to the recording and digitalization process. Further, the instability of the analog circuits in this situation makes the added harmonic content somewhat unstable and changing, thus approximately replicating the subtle variations of harmonic content at the higher frequencies when playing music acoustically that are lost when recording it (Fig. 6.5).

This remarkable coincidence has been revolutionary in preserving the recordings' sense of warmth and intensity, and it is a crucial element in the twenty-first century's effort to re-humanize digital music. For example, sample libraries suffer even more from the lack of higher-frequency content. They are short recordings that do not have enough time to accumulate higher frequency content and, even if they did, would sound unnatural

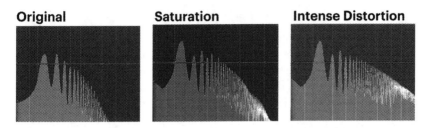

Fig. 6.5 Frequency representation of adding different levels of distortion to a sound

when looping the sound. This is why it is not uncommon to reduce the higher frequencies to create smoother samples at the expense of losing some of the higher frequencies. Thus, it is almost indispensable to use a certain amount of soft saturation in virtual instruments to restore some harmonic density and higher frequency content.

For the hyperorchestrator, it adds another dimension: the capacity to manage and interact with the harmonic density of the sounds. This is similar to asking a string player to increase bow pressure or the way dynamics work in brass instruments (*forte* sounds in brass are essentially equivalent to distortion in terms of harmonic density). Thus, it is possible to replicate these processes in any instrument through the careful use of distortion, uncovering the effect that harmonic density has in creating balance and differentiating instrumental layers (harmonically denser instruments tend to become foregrounded).

Even further, it unfolds the power of distortion for expressive and signification means. For instance, Alex Garland's *Ex Machina* (2015) contains a child-like theme representing the AI robot Ava, composed by Geoff Barrow and Ben Salisbury. The theme uses a children-like glockenspiel instrument to feature the melody. As Ava progresses and becomes more and more self-aware (and scary), the melody gets increased amounts of distortion to signify Ava's transformation. In the end, an 8-bit distortion style is used to transform the theme, making it impossible to recognize the original sound source. Each note sounds dissonant yet preserves a sense of innocence by not sounding too threatening. These nuanced meanings are possible thanks to the subtle way of operating timbre that these techniques afford composers.

Volume and Dynamic Control

In mixing terms, dynamic controls refer to changes in volume (amplitude) of either singular hyperinstruments or the whole mix over time. For instance, it is possible to decrease the volume of something recorded loudly to make it quieter than a softer sound. For example, this allows for the handmade PVC duduk in *Dune* to sound louder than instruments that would overpower it if they were playing together in the same room. While changes in volume can be easily programmed (drawn) in DAWs manually, there are sound processors devoted to automating it. Thus, they are dedicated to dynamic control by reducing or expanding the dynamic range—the difference between the loudest and the quietest sound—of a soundtrack. For example, the compressor—the most common of these effect processors—reduces the dynamic range by decreasing the volume of only the loudest sounds, which is attenuated beyond an established threshold. Then, the compressor can increase the amplitude (volume) of the sound. For example, it can increase the resulting sound proportionally to the amount of gain reduction, keeping the sound within the limits of the maximum amplitude level (Fig. 6.6).

The result is a sound with a decreased amount of dynamic variation. Applying compression in a percussion sound—a timpani hit—allows the hit to last longer as it delays the decay stage. A more constant sound in terms of its dynamic becomes perceptually more present. Another effect of compression is generating a thicker sound due to its sustained constant dynamic. The utilization of dynamic control processors allows for the extension of dynamic-focused orchestration principles, thus generating compelling new sounds that can emanate from the individuality of a single

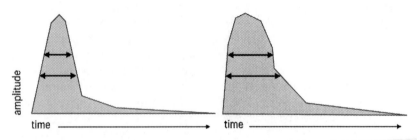

Fig. 6.6 Sketch of the effects of a compressor

instrument sound alone. A single instrument might become thicker than the whole ensemble by compressing its sound.

Compressed sounds can also become iconic and identifiable as a singular aesthetic. This is the case for the pop/rock piano sound, which is quite intensely compressed. While this type of piano treatment is common in pop songs, it is less common in screen music, which tends to treat the piano closer to the classical tradition. However, this is not the case in Dan Romer and Benh Zeitlin's score for *Beasts of the Southern Wild* (2012). In the climactic part of the movie (1:19:56), the music ("The Confrontation") contains a string chamber ensemble along with a compressed *pop* piano and drumkit. The piano sound is uncommon as a score with a chamber string ensemble, making the music sound closer to a vocal-less (aka instrumental) song. It makes the piano sound bold, somewhat trespassing the diegetic space to provide strength to the young but fearless main character of the sequence.

Virtual Space Design

Creating a virtual space for the hyperorchestra involves, at the technical level, utilizing microphone perspectives, various sound processors, reverberation processors, and spatial positioning tools. The nature of the virtual space is commonly two-dimensional. The stereo and the surround speaker design generate an aural image with no height. With increased precision, the surround speaker system reproduces the reflections produced by reverberations from the back of the hall. In screen music, creating a three-dimensional music mix requires using a technology such as Dolby Atmos (Dolby). However, even in Dolby Atmos, the music mix tends to be restricted to maintain the differentiation between the movie world and the nondiegetic material. Music mixer Alan Meyerson advises against Atmos mixes that have musical elements moving around the three-dimensional space: "If you are doing a movie, the one thing you don't want to do is have someone turn their head, right? You don't want them doing that when they're watching a movie. So, if I have a sound zipping around that's not connected to something on the screen, it's going to be very disconcerting. It's going to be very distracting" (Meyerson 2023, 27:40). Even with these constraints, Atmos allows the height of the space to be unfolded for sounds that emanate symbolically from the screen plane. Meyerson (2023) explains that he crafts a musical mix in four height layers: the first layer is equivalent to a surround mix and becomes the foundation. The

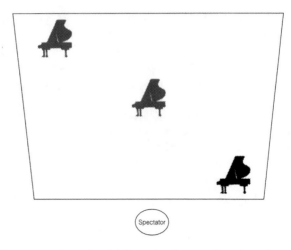

Fig. 6.7 Representation of multidimensional spaces based on the example from *The Social Network*

other three layers are on top of the foundation for some sound objects whenever necessary. In addition, Meyerson states that it is now expected to use Atmos-dedicated microphones during orchestral recordings (at about 16 feet of height).

Regardless of the limitations in the interaction between the music score and the diegesis, the music has an unlimited virtual space to place the music that would start at the screen wall in which the movie is screened (or the equivalent for TV). Moreover, employing a virtual space allows us to bypass the restrictions of the physical world and create acoustically impossible spaces. For example, the hypothetical example extracted from the piano theme in *The Social Network* generated a virtual space where a sound object was in different locations at the same time. From the audience's point of view, the model would generate the following instrument placement (Fig. 6.7).

This particular sound distribution might generate the impression that the piano is on the far right of a long rectangular area (Fig. 6.8).

Back to the basics, the traditional model of orchestral set-up, along with the principles of orchestration, is grounded in a mostly physically stable ensemble positioning. The principles that regulate the balance between instruments, the difference in their power, or how they mask other instruments all assume a fixed physical disposition. Thus,

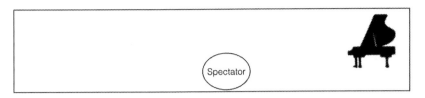

Fig. 6.8 Two-dimensional possible mental representation of the previous figure

stereophonic orchestral sound is, in practice, in terms of music composition, a one-dimensional model. From an aesthetic viewpoint, unlocking the space dimension is highly appealing. Mahler's example outlines the immense possibilities offered when expanding the sound dimensions while highlighting the associated challenges regarding the necessity to redefine the orchestration principles. Therefore, aside from examples similar to Mahler's, which are exceptional in the most common symphonic repertoire, there is no orchestrational equivalent to virtually expanding the space.

Mahler's example also hints that creating customized virtual spaces has great potential to generate meaning, especially when it can underline parallels between the visuals and the diegetic world (e.g., using a massive virtual space for the music when the diegesis is in outer space). Thus, it is a very enticing area for the hyperorchestrator. There are two areas in which the virtual space design becomes especially relevant in terms of the generation of meaning: the utilization of reverberation effects and the cohesiveness and verisimilitude implications of designing an evolved and sophisticated virtual space.

Reverberation Processors
There are two design approaches for reverberation effects. These effects allow the placement of a sound as if it were performed inside a space. The first approach is a synthetically designed digital process that emulates reverberation (commonly called algorithmic for its synthetic origin). The processors generate sound delays that replicate those created by a hall. The reverberation processors from the other group are commonly known as convolution reverbs. The reverbs in this second group are generated from a sound sample captured in a physical space (impulse response), which captures the natural reverberation generated inside a hall from the particular perspective of the microphone's location. It is similar to the HDR process of capturing the lighting of a hall, which I described in Chap. 2

(Prince, 2012, 192–193). Thus, using convolution reverbs has the potential to carry the meaning from their original spaces into the hyperreal, where it will evolve and interact with other meanings present in the diverse musical objects of the hyperorchestra. In the analysis of *Chernobyl*, I described how they captured an impulse response at the nuclear power plant, which was used to significantly transform the composer's voice.

The potential of algorithmic reverbs is that they do not replicate reality. First, they are capable of creating a reverberation that is more perfect than reality—analogously to Eco's statement about the perfect fake nature in Disneyland—which also helps separate the music from the diegesis whenever necessary. In other words, these processors might aid in partially dematerializing the musical score. For instance, a hyperorchestra containing strongly materialized hyperinstruments might benefit from this process to modulate the materialization effect over time to merge with the narrative adequately. In addition, this reverb approach facilitates the creation of impossible spaces that might enhance the creation of meaning. For instance, a quasi-infinite reverberation could be used to signify infinity either literally, in a movie in outer space, or metaphorically, in a narrative about transcendence.

The use of reverberation for meaning purposes is widespread in screen music. To give one example, the opening of *Oppenheimer* (2023) depicts a complex structure, foreshadowing the ideas and the film itself ("Fission"). In the middle of the complex sonic texture, the harp provides the first notes of the melody. It is recorded close—similarly to the piano in *Shawshank*—but with a reverb that represents an almost endless space. It makes the harp seem to float around the audience, who is then metaphorically floating around with the harp due to the closeness of the recorded sound. After that, an intensely processed solo violin takes the spot in a similar virtual space design. The main change, though, is that the solo violin does not have the aural fidelity and definition of a close recording. It is processed using distortion that makes it lose part of its spectral shape. All of these hyperorchestration decisions are evocative and foreshadow the themes of the movie, which combines the individual and ethical struggles of Oppenheimer—with a sense of historical consequentiality—with a portrayal of a field of physics—quantum mechanics—that escapes common human understanding.

Cohesiveness and Spatial Verisimilitude
Another important aspect to consider when designing a virtual space is evaluating the resulting cohesiveness. While virtually placing a symphonic

orchestra inside a bathroom could generate an intriguing sound, it would break the space's verisimilitude. Similarly, the coexistence of multiple two-dimensional virtual spaces will diminish the cohesiveness of the resulting soundscape.

Much akin to most of the features of the aesthetics of the hyperorchestra, a sound result that is more or less cohesive has advantages and disadvantages, depending on the meaning and functionality intended for the music. Generally, a non-cohesive sound would make the music more apparent and noticeable due to its peculiarities. It will also tend to be associated with some degree of unrealism, enhancing the theatrical nature of the audiovisual narrative, which might be related to the diegesis or the aesthetics of the whole film world. Therefore, from a hyperorchestral perspective, the cohesiveness of the virtual sound stage becomes another variable to evaluate in the process of sound and meaning creation.

As an example, the motive for The Shire in *The Lord of the Rings Trilogy* (2001–2003) contains a Western orchestra in tandem with some Irish instruments: mainly a Bodhrán, a dulcimer, and a fiddle (Adams 2010, 386–7). While the fiddle (a violin, after all) is traditionally mixed with the orchestra, the Bodhrán is mixed extremely to the left, and the dulcimer extremely to the right. In addition, they appear at the very front and without any reverberation, taking them out of the overall orchestral mix. This unusual mixing decision is surprising and diminishes the sense of cohesion and verisimilitude of the music mix. At the same time, it helps foreground these instruments, which are associated with the Hobbits and The Shire. If they were mixed with the *pizzicato* and other instruments in the orchestra, we would have had difficulty hearing them, thus losing their meaning generation capabilities.

Primarily Creative Processors

This last group of sound processing tools is broad in scope yet specific in its objectives. The effects used by this group aim to manipulate the sound by purposefully transforming it beyond its original shape. The clearest example is the utilization of processing pedals on electric guitars. Generally, processed electric guitars barely resemble the sound produced by the actual instrument. In fact, a processed electric guitar sound has become a recognizable singular instrument, distinguished from a guitar sound. The diverse processors involved in producing the processed electric guitar sound have served as the basis for developing a full range of sound processors applicable to any sound. While there are myriad creative effect processors, I will describe just two that are particularly relevant, which fall under a variety of categories according to Gibson's (2005) classification:

- Frequency over Time: Vibrato generators, Flangers
- Volume over Time: Tremolo generators (75)

Vibrato and tremolo generators are relevant examples because they can produce contained and controlled sound variation over time, making the sound of a hyperinstrument dynamic and generating a rhythmic pulse that could interact with the rest of the audiovisual material. In addition, these effects are modeled from acoustic instrumental techniques. Vibrato is a common technique for strings and some wind instruments, and it is essential for producing their most common sound. A string vibrato is the slight alteration of the frequency over time at a particular rate—for example, eight times per second—by moving the finger that is pressing the string to either side. In a vibrato sound processor, this is modeled by using a low-frequency sinusoid wave called low-frequency oscillator (LFO). They are physically equivalent to a sound wave, although they are not necessarily perceptible by the human ear. This allows them to efficiently modulate the sound by altering its frequency.

The tremolo effect diverges further from its physical counterpart. Tremolos are equivalent to vibratos applied over the amplitude (volume) instead of the frequency. They generate volume undulations, which might resemble the undulations produced by the bow change on a string tremolo, by similarly using an LFO over a volume controller.

The nature of these effects highlights how they extend traditional and orchestrational principles beyond their physical possibilities and how they apply to a broad range of sounds. The possibility of a fixed sound undulation over time also generates a rhythmic and metric effect that would not be possible to achieve with a long sound, thus making note attacks nonessential for generating meter and rhythmic patterns. In the analysis of the score for *Annihilation* (2018), I mentioned how the composers used flangers as a sonic representation of refraction.

Sound Processing and Aural Fidelity

Bordwell et al. (2020) define aural fidelity as "the extent to which the sound is faithful to the source as we conceive it" (284).[11] The word "conceive" is fundamental to comprehend that the concept does not necessarily link a recorded sound source with a sound from the physical world. As they state, "we do not know what laser guns sound like, but we accept the whang they make in *Return of the Jedi* as plausible" (284). Therefore, assessing a sound's aural fidelity involves analyzing its verisimilitude. Many of the tools described in this section were initially intended to restore the aural fidelity of recorded sounds. From this angle, equalization served to restore the original frequency spectrum before the recording. Further, using a reverb would place the instruments inside a hall. Similarly, mixing was originally conceived as the resulting process of joining all the elements to recreate a live experience.

In the aesthetics of the hyperorchestra, these possibilities expand beyond the objective of accurately representing a physical event. Similar to the concept of cohesiveness, aural fidelity becomes another dimension from which to generate meaning. Assessing the degree of fidelity of a hyperinstrument or a sound becomes an aesthetic decision linked to the functions the sound is expected to fulfill.

Moreover, in music, the concept of aural fidelity interacts non-obviously with the notion of materialization described before. In terms of fidelity, hearing the sound of the piano mallets (thus materializing the piano sound) means a socially uncommon closeness to the piano during a performance. Therefore, that piano sound is genuinely faithful to the source but not to how we are used to listening to the source. I believe that in this incongruency resides the evocative power of the closely recorded piano sound, with its capacity to evoke intimacy while preserving a sense of standard orchestral sound. Similarly, I mentioned that Zimmer purposedly used a slightly detuned piano sound to perform the theme of *Man of Steel* himself, to provide an imperfect performance. Chion (1994, 116) mentions a detuned piano as a materializing force to make it seem diegetic, which is clearly not the case in this situation.

Nevertheless, both a detuned piano and an imperfect performance materialize the sound. Analogously, while the performance maintains the aural fidelity of what it represents, it detaches from the fidelity of an expected piano performance (flawless in the sound and execution). Thus, the tension between sounds that have a high degree of aural fidelity (one could say even higher than the stylized flawless recordings) but that defy our expectations based on conventions becomes mostly efficient for producing meaning.

Spectral Transformations: Timbre, Harmony, and Dynamic Hyperorchestration

Spectral transformations—variations in the spectrum of a sound—are a dynamic mixing process. For instance, using a filter to add or subtract frequencies from a hyperinstrument varyingly falls inside this category. This process has been instrumental in modeling an approximation to the timbral fluctuations associated with dynamic change in synthesizers. In other words, using the volume on a synthesizer to reproduce instrumental dynamics sounds much more artificial than reducing the sound's overall amplitude (volume) by filtering some of the higher frequencies. The latter process is closer to how acoustic instruments work: when the dynamic increases, it generally triggers an increase in the higher overtone content. While an in-depth discussion of the effects of this process falls outside the scope of this book, as it would need to discuss the link between pitch-based harmonic approaches and spectral harmony, I present some relevant highlights as they pertain to the current discussion.

The overtone series is intimately connected with many harmonic approaches, as a note's first and most audible overtones generate a major triad chord. As I described before, Grisey (2000) considered the "integration of harmony and timbre within a single entity" (1–2) as one of the pillars of a spectral attitude. Similarly, the additive synthesis process of crafting the sound of a synthesizer by combining a group of sine waves following an overtone structure blends the concept of timbre and harmony.[12]

Further, in discussing the harmonic density of a sound, I stated that a process such as soft saturation (or distortion) increases the amount of higher overtone content in a sound. A significant increase in harmonic density generates dissonance within a single note entity, suggesting that consonance and dissonance are much more continuous than a set of discrete states. This was already a fact in traditional Western orchestration: a dissonance on a piano sounds less dissonant when played on the strings and, frequently, even less dissonant if different sections of the orchestra play the two dissonant notes. However, an instrumental design of orchestral instruments based on achieving a balanced and fairly homogenous harmonic spectral shape for each instrument minimized the harmonic variability of playing a note in different timbres. In hyperorchestration, harmonic density is one of the parameters used to craft and combine hyperinstruments, which forces a more acoustically accurate approach to the concept of dissonance and consonance.

In a very general sense, musical discourse can be understood as processes of tension and release, which also includes the process of increasing and decreasing tension. This aligns with David Huron's (2006) cognitive theory of expectation (ITPRA), which I mentioned in Chap. 2. While dynamics and other musical devices also play a significant role in these processes, functional harmony, as well as managing dissonances and their resolutions, are central. Thus, in musical styles modeled into what we call the Western common practice, the authentic cadential process is the epitome of a tension/release process: the dominant portrays the moment of maximum tension that resolves into the tonic, the release. Processes of tension/release are also modulated by the use of common notes between chord progressions, which not only maintain a cohesive musical discourse but also generate a state of less tension due to a decrease in the perceived harmonic change. The degree of reliance on common notes in chord progressions is generally regarded as the level of voice-leading parsimony in the harmony of the piece of music.

In music for the screen, the processes of tension/release are generally associated with the events in the visual narrative, which means they cannot rely on structural elements of the musical discourse. Voice-leading parsimony tends to aid in the creation of musical flow that is less reliant on predesigned musical structures and more prone to be able to adapt to the actions of an audiovisual narrative. To that end, Frank Lehman (2018), in *Hollywood Harmony: Musical Wonder and the Sound of Cinema*, describes how many Hollywood scores have chord progressions that possess significant voice-leading parsimony (143). This is one reason why screen music benefits from Neo-Riemannian theory, a harmonic analysis method that privileges parsimonious chord progressions (88).

Using spectral transformations, it is possible to change the harmonic content of a sound (or a group of sounds) from being very tense to much more relaxed (or even from being extremely dissonant to being consonant). This can be achieved by manipulating the harmonic density of the sound. In its simplest form, the result is two distinct sounds that emanate from the same origin and have very different spectral harmonic content. From this viewpoint, they could be treated as two distinct spectral harmonies, following Grisey's suggestion that timbre and harmony cannot be separated. While pitch-based harmony relies on discrete entities (pitches) to create harmonic change, changes in the spectrum (harmonic spectral transformations) can be continuous. From this angle, spectral transformations add a new tool for the screen composer: the capacity to create subtle changes in the (spectral) harmony of the passage that would be impossible using pitch-based harmony. Thus, this process allows for slight changes in tension. They highlight the intrinsic relationship that already existed between orchestration and harmony.

One of the clearest examples of this process is especially evident in the first season of *Mr. Robot* (2015–2019), created by Sam Esmail and scored by Mac Quayle. The score is entirely built with synths in the first season and uses spectral transformations as a core technique to shape the musical discourse. The show follows Elliot—a hacker—battling corporate forces in a dystopic capitalist society like ours. Due to the show's topic, there are many hacking sequences of Elliot programming a computer. From the point of view of storytelling, a hacking sequence is challenging as it portrays a high-stakes action that could potentially have severe consequences (such as changing the world order). Still, at the same time, it is visually static and unexciting.

In one of the first hacking scenes (S1E1, 0:30:25), Elliot fixes a hacking attack but has second thoughts and leaves part of the hacking device in place for him to access later. During the scene, a filter is used extensively to generate the equivalent of a smooth alternating harmony between two harmonic areas: one with very few overtones and another that is richer and sounds more dissonant. The changes between harmonic areas do not necessarily reflect narrative changes but just the necessity to fluctuate between harmonic regions to provide a sense of progress. Toward the end of the scene, the higher parts of the spectrum are saturated in a musical gesture that resembles a cadential process. This is achieved by opening the filter to unveil the fully spectrally saturated sound (dissonant to the average ear) and adding a few additional sounding elements. The possibilities of spectral transformations are vast as they span throughout harmony, orchestration, and musical flow, making them an increasingly employed device in contemporary screen music scores that use hyperorchestral models.

Expanding Western Orchestration Principles with the Hyperorchestra

In this final section, I explore two aesthetic principles that guide the combination of hyperinstruments beyond the utilization of mixing techniques. The following principles expand traditional orchestration techniques with the possibilities offered by the hyperorchestra: augmenting and expanding instrumental sections and combining extended sections and instruments.

Augmenting and Expanding the Orchestral Sections

In the analysis of *Inception* (2010), I argued that the score contained a massive brass section, which became iconic as an archetype of expanding sections from the traditional orchestra. Taking a different approach, the score in *The Man of Steel* (2013) served as an example of new orchestral sections from ensembles of single-instrument instances. The drum ensemble became a section within the percussion section of the hyperorchestral ensemble for the score.

Augmented or expanded sections attain increased independence. While they integrate within the hyperorchestra, they preserve a distinctive presence. The traditional Western orchestral placement was designed to create an already *mixed* and balanced disposition. For instance, the brass section is in the background, supporting the strings. Hyperorchestration negated the requirement for a fixed instrumental mix. Therefore, the sections in the hyperorchestra are autonomous sound entities, and the composer has the freedom to make them evolve and generate new sonic environments. The definition of a section within an orchestra dissolves, which allows for a more flexible approach to their construction.

In this context, the possibility of augmenting, extending, and creating new sections appears. The expansion process is grounded in the principle that defines a section: a structured group of instruments that produces a cohesive output through the amalgamation of diverse sound sources. The drum ensemble generated its ensemble sound by joining a set of recordings utilizing close microphones in addition to general room microphones. The sound retained the intensity and clarity of an individual drum and added power to the ensemble. Similarly, the traditional orchestral string sections in the same score were mixed with an emphasis on the close microphones, thus generating a distinct orchestral string sound: a blend of sectional power and soloistic intensity.

The individual treatment of each section allows for the expansion of the number of performers without significant compromises. In live performances or recordings with the full orchestra in the same room, there is a necessary correlation between the number of performers and the minimum reverberation due to the hall's dimensions. Placing a single player in a small room is possible, but this becomes impossible with larger ensembles. Recording techniques (e.g., using close microphones) minimize the amount of reverberation captured. Further, using sample libraries (exclusively or as an addition) increases the means for expanding the ensemble's dimensions.

Consequently, the acoustic correlation between ensemble size, reverberation, and individualistic sound dissolves in the hyperorchestra. A colossal brass ensemble could be placed in a virtual space that could only hold a few players. Further, the ensemble might still preserve the intensity of a single instrument recorded closely. Moreover, the virtualization of the sections produced by sample libraries and nonlinear recording allows for overdubbing (having the section more than once). For instance, Lorne Balfe's opening theme ("Alethiometer") for the show *His Dark Materials* (2019) contains three distinct string sections. One string section (the B section) plays sustained chords for the whole theme. The other section (A) plays the melodic elements, including legato accompanying lines. The third string section (and overdub of the A section) plays short (*spiccato*) accompaniment notes. The three string sections play all at the same time.[13]

The examples from *The Man of Steel* revealed the possibility of creating new sections that did not exist in the traditional orchestral ensemble. Aesthetically, they derive from deconstructing the concept of an instrumental section. These new ensembles utilize some of the properties associated with an instrumental section by implementing them in new sound paradigms. The hyperdrums would not be possible if all the music for the score was recorded at once. Moreover, recording them using only sectional microphones would not have generated the particular sound intensity and power that the drums in *Man of Steel* aimed for.

Expanding the orchestral sections also comes from the performance side. With computer-aided technology, it is possible to generate impossible crescendos, such as those described in the analysis of *Inception*'s (2010) score. Thus, the performance element of the ensemble sound has also extended virtually to allow for acoustically impossible gestures generated by the modification of the recorded sounds or by the utilization of carefully programmed sample libraries.

Sonic Combination

Sonic combination refers to the process of merging different sections and instruments. Balancing and combining instruments and sections is one of the focuses of traditional orchestration. Adler's proposal to divide musical elements into three main categories is a well-accepted paradigm for organizing orchestration:

1. *Foreground*: the most important voice, usually the melody, which the composer wants to be heard most prominently;
2. *Middleground*: countermelodies or important contrapuntal material;
3. *Background*: accompaniment, either chordal or using polyphonic or melodic figures.(Adler, 2016, 126)

Once the composer decides which musical items pertain to each category, the role of orchestration is to create the balances and combinations that best achieve the desired results, making the foreground voice prominent, the middleground ideas distinctly heard but in a secondary position, and the background ideas non prominent but filling the soundscape. With the hyperorchestra, the process of combining instruments and sections becomes much more flexible, akin to the rest of the elements discussed in this chapter.

Volume control is a standard hyperorchestration device that achieves balance while expanding the traditional orchestra. For instance, volume mixing can balance the sound of a brass section playing *fortissimo* with a string section playing in a moderately soft dynamic. This process might create a collateral effect: the string section might seem bigger as its volume is increased—even if the sound is still softer—compared to the brass section.

The sonic placement of the instruments and sections also affects their combination and unity as a section. For instance, if a string section plays a sustained chord and spiccato accompaniment simultaneously—such as in *His Dark Materials*—both sounds will generally emanate from the same virtual location. Thus, it will sound like an acoustically impossible expanded section. Frequently, the reverberation of the short and long notes differs, adding another layer of virtual space complexity while producing verisimilar results.

In parallel, the success of introducing new hyperinstruments depends on how its role is negotiated in terms of its combination with the other instruments. If the new instrument needs to have a soloistic role, the process of instrumental combination must consider this fact. Otherwise, not only might the singular sound of the instrument be lost, but the associated meaning might also not permeate properly.

As a final matter, composers must assess how their utilization affects the perception of verisimilitude in their music when applying hyperinstrumental combinations. This is comparable to the evaluation of aural fidelity when employing mixing tools for hyperorchestration. The assessment of how hyperorchestral techniques reshape the perception of verisimilitude focuses on the resulting sound as experienced by the audience. Moreover, the evaluation process needs to consider the desired level of verisimilitude to fulfill the narrative needs in terms of added meaning. This assessment will allow for the permanent awareness of the implications of particular hyperorchestrational procedures. Hyperorchestrating is a means of sound expansion and development, which, like any similar process, involves balancing what is gained against what is lost.

Notes

1. This text on the preface was removed in the fourth edition (Adler 2016).
2. Serialism and its related techniques were the dominating compositional approaches in the 1960s when Murail and Grisey started to develop a spectral attitude. These compositional approaches are what Murail identifies as structuralist, as they aimed to create a pre-established musical discourse through the serialization of all the elements in a musical piece.
3. In the previous chapter, I discussed the music in *Dune* and referenced the bagpipe ensemble sound as an evolution of this technique.
4. For instance, Grisey's *Partiels* is modeled after the sound spectrum of a low E performed by a trombone.
5. See Jeff Smith (1996), *Unheard Melodies? A Critique of Psychoanalytic Theories of Film Music*, for a comprehensive critique of Gorbman's approach that follows a theoretical framework akin to Bordwell's models.
6. Murch (2001) identified six weighted parameters for an ideal film edit: emotion (51%), story (23%), rhythm (10%), eye-trace (7%), two-dimensional plane of the screen (5%), and three-dimensional space of action (4%).
7. The Fourier theorem is explained plainly in the majority of introductory books to music technology or synthesizer design (e.g., Pejrolo and Metcalfe 2017, 36; Hosken 2011, 38–40). Similarly, it is also often mentioned that the Fast Fourier Transform (FFT) is an algorithm that can compute a close

approximation of a division of a sound into single frequencies very efficiently in terms of computing (Pejrolo and Metcalfe 2017, 176).
8. They are also called microphone positions, although the term might be misleading. Each position does not necessarily reflect the sound captured by a single microphone; it might result from the sounds captured by several microphones already mixed to create a perspective.
9. I discussed this theme from *The Social Network* in more detail in (Casanelles 2016).
10. See Gibson (2005, 89–120) for a more detailed description of equalizations and equalizers.
11. Jeff Smith (2009) also discusses the concept of aural fidelity in relation to the creation of the diegesis.
12. In *Timbre as Harmony–Harmony as Timbre*, Robert Hasegawa (2021) provides an overview of these approaches that go beyond spectral composers.
13. While the score is not published, Lorne Balfe shared some of the scores publicly during the 2020 pandemic.

References

Adams, Douglas. 2010. *The Music of The Lord of the Rings Films: A Comprehensive Account of Howard Shore's Scores* (Book and Rarities CD).
Adler, Samuel. 2002. *Study of Orchestration*. Third ed.
Adler, Samuel. 2016. *Study of Orchestration*. Fourth ed.: W. W. Norton & Company.
Blier-Carruthers, Amy. 2020. "The Problem of Perfection in Classical Recording: The Performer's Perspective." *The Musical Quarterly* 103 (1–2): 184–236.
Bordwell, David. 1985. *Narration in the fiction film*. Madison, Wis.: University of Wisconsin Press.
Bordwell, David. 2006. *The way Hollywood tells it: story and style in modern movies*. Berkeley: University of California Press.
Bordwell, David, Kristin Thompson, and Jeff Smith. 2020. *Film Art: An Introduction*. 12th ed.: McGraw-Hill Education.
Bruce, R., and T. Murail. 2000. "An Interview with Tristan Murail." *Computer Music Journal* 24 (1): 11–19. http://www.jstor.org/stable/3681847.
Buhler, James. 2019. *Theories of the Soundtrack*. New York: Oxford University Press.
Buhler, James. 2020. "The End(s) of Vococentrism." In *Voicing the Cinema: Film Music and the Integrated Soundtrack*, edited by James Buhler and Hannah Lewis, 278–296. University of Illinois Press.
Casanelles, Sergi. 2016. "Mixing as a Hyperorchestration Tool." In *The Palgrave Handbook of Sound Design and Music in Screen Media Integrated Soundtracks*,

edited by Greene Liz and Kulezic-Wilson Danijela, 57–72. London, England: Palgrave Macmillan.

Cecchi, A. 2010. *Diegetic versus nondiegetic: a reconsideration of the conceptual opposition as a contribution to the theory of audiovision*. Worlds of Audiovision.

Chion, Michel. 1994. *Audio-vision: sound on screen*. New York: Columbia University Press.

Daubresse, Eric, and Gérard Assayag. 2000. "Technology and Creation- The Creative Evolution." *Contemporary Music Review* 19 (2): 61–80.

Dolan, Emily, and Alexander Rehding. 2021. "Timbre: Alternative Histories and Possible Futures for the Study of Music." In *The Oxford Handbook of Timbre*, edited by Emily Dolan and Alexander Rehding. Oxford Handbooks Online: Oxford University Press.

Fineberg, Joshua. 2000. "Guide to the Basic Concepts and Techniques of Spectral Music." *Contemporary Music Review* 19 (2): 81–113.

Gibson, D. 2005. *The Art of Mixing: A Visual Guide to Recording, Engineering, and Production*. Artistpro.

Gorbman, Claudia 1987. *Unheard melodies: narrative film music*. London Bloomington: BFI Pub. Indiana University Press.

Grisey, G. 2000. "Did You Say Spectral?" *Contemporary Music Review* 19 (3): 1–3.

Hainge, Greg. 2013. *Noise Matters: Towards an Ontology of Noise*. New York: Bloomsbury Publishing Plc.

Hasegawa, Robert. 2021. "Timbre as Harmony—Harmony as Timbre." In *The Oxford Handbook of Timbre*, edited by Emily Dolan and Alexander Rehding. Oxford Handbooks Online: Oxford University Press.

Hosken, Dan. 2011. *An Introduction to Music Technology*. NY: Routledge.

Huron, David. 2006. *Sweet anticipation: music and the psychology of expectation*. Cambridge MA: MIT Press.

Lehman, Frank. 2018. *Hollywood Harmony: Musical Wonder and the Sound of Cinema*. Oxford University Press.

Mathews, Paul 2020. Instrumentation and Orchestration. Oxford Bibliographies.

Mera, Miguel. 2016. "Materializing Film Music." In *The Cambridge Companion to Film Music*, edited by Cooke Mervyn and Ford Fiona, 157–172. Cambridge: Cambridge University Press.

Meyerson, Alan. 2023. "Alan Meyerson: Mixing The Movies Part 1 - Immersive Audio" In "*Sound on Sound Magazine*." https://youtu.be/7NQJmAyM65I?s i=wLCtM0gL5Ifwsh2M.

Moylan, William. 2014. *Understanding and Crafting the Mix: The Art of Recording* (3rd Edition). Independence, KY, USA: Focal Press.

Murch, Walter. 2001. *In the blink of an eye: a perspective on film editing*. 2nd edition. Los Angeles, California: Silman-James Press.

Neumeyer, David. 2009. "Diegetic/Nondiegetic: A Theoretical Model." *Music and the Moving Image* 2 (1): 26–39. http://www.jstor.org/stable/10.5406/musimoviimag.2.1.0026.

Owsinski, Bobby. 2013a. *The Mixing Engineer's Handbook*, 3rd Edition. Cengage Learning PTR.

Pejrolo, Andrea, and Scott B. Metcalfe. 2017. *Creating Sounds from Scratch: A Practical Guide to Music Synthesis for Producers and Composers*. New York, NY: Oxford University Press.

Prince, Stephen. 2012. *Digital Visual Effects in Cinema: The Seduction of Reality*. Rutgers University Press.

Smith, Jeff. 1996. "Unheard Melodies? A Critique of Psychoanalytic Theories of Film Music." *Post-theory: Reconstructing Film Studies*: 230–47.

Smith, Jeff. 2009. "Bridging the Gap: Reconsidering the Border between Diegetic and Nondiegetic Music." *Music and the Moving Image* 2 (1). http://www.jstor.org/stable/10.5406/musimoviimag.2.1.0001.

Smith, Jeff. 2013. "The Sound of Intensified Continuity." In *The Oxford Handbook of New Audiovisual Aesthetics*, edited by John Richardson, Claudia Gorbman and Carol Vernallis. Oxford University Press.

Stilwell, Robin J. 2007. "The Gap between diegetic and nondiegetic." *Beyond the Soundtrack: Representing Music in Cinema* 1st: University of California Press.

Tresch, John, and Emily Dolan. 2013. "Toward a New Organology: Instruments of Music and Science." *Osiris* 28: 278–298. https://doi.org/10.1086/671381.

Wierzbicki, James E. 2009. *Film Music: A History*. Routledge.

Winters, Ben. 2010. "The non-diegetic fallacy: Film, music, and narrative space." *Music and Letters* 91(2): 224–244. https://doi.org/10.1093/ml/gcq019.

Wigler, Josh. 2016. "Carlton Cuse and Michael Giacchino Reflect on 'Lost' at Hollywood Reunion Concert." *The Hollywood Reporter*. https://www.hollywoodreporter.com/tv/tvnews/carlton-cuse-michael-giacchino-reflect-932318/.

Yacavone, Daniel. 2012. "Spaces, Gaps, and Levels." *Music, Sound, and the Moving Image* 6(1): 21–37. 10.

CHAPTER 7

Conclusion

This book aimed to contribute to the analytical tools for understanding the functions of music within film language from the perspective of a spectral approach to timbre that encompassed its varied capacity to provide meaning through interactions with the physical and the hyperreal. Therefore, it adds new tools to toolkit of the existing scholarship of analytical approaches in orchestration, harmony, melody and motives, rhythm, tonality/atonality, and others. For instance, a melodic analysis of Loire Cotler's "cry of the banshee" for the *Dune* score will certainly shed some light on its expressive meanings. Similarly, Thomas Newman's open harmonies in "Brooks Was Here" reinforce the meaning of intimate nostalgia I outlined with the recording and processing of the piano. My analyses were constrained by the scope of this book, which allowed them to be more specific and become clear examples of what I was describing.

With this book, I also aimed to emphasize the pivotal role of digital tools in the creation of screen music and, by extension, the importance of this knowledge in facilitating more detailed score analysis and interpretation. While this book is not a history of scoring technology, I provided some historical snapshots of these virtual tools to underline their importance in the history of screen scoring. Due to their ephemeral nature, I believe there is a historical-musicological urgency to describe and catalog them. While a violin has remained the same piece of technology for centuries and has a physical presence—even if screen music would not use

© The Author(s), under exclusive license to Springer Nature Switzerland AG 2024
S. Casanelles, *The Hyperorchestra*,
https://doi.org/10.1007/978-3-031-75193-6_7

violins anymore—most of the first virtual instruments, sequencers, and processors do not work anymore with modern computers, are being erased from the internet when companies release newer versions, and their virtual trace risks getting lost.

I began this book by advocating that film composers should be considered filmmakers who use music, akin to cinematographers, editors, or screenwriters. I did so by proposing that cinema—and the rest of audiovisual narratives that followed—is a medium that unfolded its full potential with digital tools. Film editing, which is at the core of the art due to its medium-specific quality, seemed to be born to be digital. I suggested the same for music with the hyperorchestra: digital tools allowed for music to fully become filmmaking and not be a complement or addition to film. This statement is not about how to analyze film—for decades, screen music scholarship has demonstrated the importance of the music score as an integral part of the narrative. Instead, it is about how digital tools expanded musical functions to dissolve within an integrated approach to film language. Therefore, I see digital tools as a way to culminate the idea of total artwork (*Gesamtkunstwerk*) by not only combining different arts but also merging them into one.

This mode of thinking was thoroughly developed by Danijela Kulezic-Wilson (2008, 2015, 2020) in her approach to an integrated soundtrack in which all the elements (not only the music) were approached musically. Similarly, Walter Murch's (2001) editing philosophy—who also was the first person to receive a sound design credit—suggests a more fluid and unified approach to film language, which leaped forward with the introduction of digital editing.

I have also emphasized that collaboration and fluid dialog are paramount for music to become integrated into the film fabric. This is one of the reasons why I started by introducing McLuhan's media theory. By describing the Global Village, McLuhan made us aware that with the capacity for instantaneous communication triggered by electricity, everything changed: human evolution became not only expansive but also a process of implosion. In doing so, there was a potential to manage globalized village-like human interactions and relationships.

Through the nonlinear model of screen scoring, I presented a roadmap for how extensive collaboration and dialogue can be in any screen project. This model allows, when necessary, to shift from a score designed for interchangeable performers (studio musicians) to develop much more meaningful and personal collaborations with them. We are generally unable to recall the names of the performers who worked with Korngold,

Steiner, or Herrmann, all of whom were impressive studio musicians. In contrast, most people could name at least a few of Hans Zimmer's collaborators—even if only Lady Gaga, Billie Eilish, or Tina Guo. With the hyperorchestra, I proposed a model of music creation that prioritizes sonic specificity and the creation of meaning, which is much more easily achieved through collaboration with individuals instead of writing music for generic instrumentalists to perform it. Composers can inspire these performers to become passionate, engaged, and more emotional collaborators, accentuating the power of human relationships in creating art. Many of these performers become true collaborators with the composer(s) by also contributing to the creation of music through this process. Hence, they contribute to the musical score in many more ways, which enriches the final result. Technology has significantly facilitated this process on many levels, including the ability to collaborate remotely from anywhere in the world (or during a lockdown due to a global pandemic).

Similarly, the twenty-first century has seen the emergence of composer collaborators (to name a few: Reznor and Ross, Barrow and Salisbury, Son Lux, and Zimmer with many others) and composer teams (e.g., Bear McCreary and Sparks & Shadows, or Bleeding Fingers). Throughout the book, I have also described similar interactions between directors and composers. Further, collaboration is also much more fluid with other members of the filmmaking team, especially music editors, whose functions are frequently divided between themselves and members of the composing team, while music editors' functions also merge with what scoring used to be.

In an age of uncertainty due to the exponential progress of technological development—exacerbated by the introduction of generative Artificial Intelligence models—, meaningful human-to-human interactions that share an artistic vision through passion, emotion, and common ideology are more important than ever. These are, at least for now, humanity's medium specificity.

References

Kulezic-Wilson, Danijela. 2008. "Sound Design is the New Score." *Music, Sound, and the Moving Image* 2 (2): 127–131. https://doi.org/10.3828/msmi.2.2.5.

Kulezic-Wilson, Danijela. 2020. *Sound Design is the New Score: Theory, Aesthetics, and Erotics of the Integrated Soundtrack.* Oxford University Press.

Kulezic-Wilson, Danijela. 2015. The Musicality of Narrative Film. London: Palgrave Macmillan.

Murch, Walter. 2001. *In the blink of an eye: a perspective on film editing.* 2nd edition. Los Angeles, California: Silman-James Press.

References

Bibliography

Abramovitch, Seth. 2015. "'Braaams' for Beginners: How a Horn Sound Ate Hollywood." The Hollywood Reporter. https://www.hollywoodreporter.com/movies/movie-news/braaams-beginners-how-a-horn-793220/.

Adams, Douglas. 2010. *The Music of The Lord of the Rings Films: A Comprehensive Account of Howard Shore's Scores* (Book and Rarities CD).

Adler, Samuel. 2002. *Study of Orchestration*. Third ed.

Adler, Samuel. 2016. *Study of Orchestration*. Fourth ed.: W. W. Norton & Company.

Air Studios. n.d. "History." https://www.airstudios.com/history/.

Arturia. 2024. "True Analog Emulation." Accessed January 2024. https://www.arturia.com/products/technology/tae%C2%AE.

Atkin, Albert. 2013. "Peirce's Theory of Signs." http://plato.stanford.edu/archives/sum2013/entries/peirce-semiotics/.

Auslander, Philip. 2008. *Liveness: Performance in a Mediatized Culture*, Second Edition. New York: Routledge.

Barthes, Roland. 1977. *Image-Music-Text*. Hill and Wang.

Baudrillard, Jean. 1993. *Symbolic Exchange and Death*. Sage Publications.

Baudrillard, Jean. 1994. *Simulacra and Simulation*. Ann Arbor: University of Michigan Press.

Baudrillard, Jean. 2000. *The Vital Illusion*. New York: Columbia University Press.

Baudrillard, Jean. 2005. *The Intelligence of Evil or tile Lucidity Pact*. New York: Berg.

© The Author(s), under exclusive license to Springer Nature Switzerland AG 2024
S. Casanelles, *The Hyperorchestra*,
https://doi.org/10.1007/978-3-031-75193-6

Beta, Andy. 2018. "'Annihilation': Geoff Barrow and Ben Salisbury Talk Its Haunting Score." RollingStone. https://www.rollingstone.com/music/music-features/annihilation-geoff-barrow-and-ben-salisbury-talk-its-haunting-score-197947/.

Bishop, Bryan. 2018. "Annihilation and Ex Machina director Alex Garland on using sci-fi to explore self-destruction." The Verge. https://www.theverge.com/2018/2/21/17029500/annihilation-ex-machina-director-alex-garland-sci-fi.

Blier-Carruthers, Amy. 2020. "The Problem of Perfection in Classical Recording: The Performer's Perspective." *The Musical Quarterly* 103 (1–2): 184–236.

Bordwell, David. 1985. *Narration in the fiction film*. Madison, Wis.: University of Wisconsin Press.

Bordwell, David. 2002. "Intensified Continuity Visual Style in Contemporary American Film." *Film Quarterly* 55: 16–28.

Bordwell, David. 2006. *The way Hollywood tells it: story and style in modern movies*. Berkeley: University of California Press.

Bordwell, David. 2012. *Pandora's Digital Box: Films, Files, and the Future of Movies*. The Irvington Way Institute Press.

Bordwell, David. 2014. "Zip, zero, Zeitgeist." *Observations of film art* (blog). http://www.davidbordwell.net/blog/2014/08/24/zip-zero-zeitgeist/.

Bordwell, David, and Kristin Thompson. 2012. *Film art: an introduction*. New York: McGraw-Hill.

Bordwell, David, Kristin Thompson, and Jeff Smith. 2020. *Film Art: An Introduction*. 12th ed.: McGraw-Hill Education.

Borges, J. L. 1999. Collected Fictions. Penguin Books.

Bregman, Albert S. 1990. *Auditory Scene Analysis: The Perceptual Organization of Sound*. Cambridge, MA: MIT Press.

Britt, Thomas. 2018. "The sound of The Shimmer: Interview with *Annihilation*'s Ben Salisbury and Geoff Barrow." popMATTERS. https://www.popmatters.com/ben-salisbury-geoff-barrow-interview-2573141300.html.

Bruce, R., and T. Murail. 2000. "An Interview with Tristan Murail." *Computer Music Journal* 24 (1): 11–19. http://www.jstor.org/stable/3681847.

Buhler, James. 2019. *Theories of the Soundtrack*. New York: Oxford University Press.

Buhler, James. 2020. "The End(s) of Vococentrism." In *Voicing the Cinema: Film Music and the Integrated Soundtrack*, edited by James Buhler and Hannah Lewis, 278–296. University of Illinois Press.

Buhler, James. 2021a. "Blank Music: Marketing Virtual Instruments." In The Oxford Handbook of Music and Advertising, edited by James Deaville, Siu-Lan Tan and Ron Rodman, 93–118. Oxford University Press.

Buhler, James. 2021b. *Music, Digital Audio, Labor: Notes on Audio and Music Production for Contemporary Action Film. Music in Action Film: Sounds like Action!* New York: Routledge.

Buhler, James. 2024. "Composing for the Films in the Age of Digital Media." In *The Mediations of Music: Critical Approaches after Adorno*, edited by Gianmarco Borio, 144–162. London: Routledge.

Buhler, James, and David Neumeyer. 2016. *Hearing the movies: music and sound in film history.* Second edition. New York, New York: Oxford University Press.

Burlingame, John. 2021. "Hans Zimmer on 'Dune' Score's Electronic Textures and Made-Up Choral Language … and His Head Start on Part 2." Variety.

Burton, Byron. 2019. "How 'Chernobyl' Composer Found Inspiration in a Real (and Radioactive) Power Plant." The Hollywood Reporter. https://www.hollywoodreporter.com/news/general-news/how-chernobyl-composer-found-inspiration-a-radioactive-power-plant-1228682/.

Byrd, Craig L. 1997. "Interview with John Williams." In *Celluloid Symphonies: Texts and Contexts in Film Music History*, edited by Julie Hubbert, 414–423. Berkeley and Los Angeles, California: University of California Press.

Campbell, Joseph. 2008. *The hero with a thousand faces.* Third ed. Novato, California: New World Library.

Casanelles, Sergi. 2013. "Hyperorchestra hyperreality and Inception." Music and the Moving Image, New York.

Casanelles, Sergi. 2015. "The Hyperorchestra: A Study of a Virtual Ensemble in Film Music That Transcends Reality." New York University. https://www.proquest.com/docview/1777237483.

Casanelles, Sergi. 2016. "Mixing as a Hyperorchestration Tool." In *The Palgrave Handbook of Sound Design and Music in Screen Media Integrated Soundtracks*, edited by Greene Liz and Kulezic-Wilson Danijela, 57–72. London, England: Palgrave Macmillan.

Casanelles, Sergi. Forthcoming 2024. "Atmospheres, Synths, and Spectral Transformations in Scores for TV." In *The Oxford Handbook of Music in Television*, edited by James Deaville, Jessica Getman, Ronald Rodman and Brooke McClorke. Oxford: Oxford University Press.

Cecchi, A. 2010. *Diegetic versus nondiegetic: a reconsideration of the conceptual opposition as a contribution to the theory of audiovision.* Worlds of Audiovision.

Chan, Melanie. 2008. "Virtually Real and Really Virtual: Baudrillard's Procession of Simulacrum and The Matrix." *International Journal of Baudrillard Studies* 5 (2).

Chion, Michel. 1994. *Audio-vision: sound on screen.* New York: Columbia University Press.

Chion, Michel. 2009. *Film, a Sound Art.* New York, NY: Columbia University Press.

Chion, Michel. 2011a. "Dissolution of the Notion of Timbre." *Differences* 22 (2–3): 235–239. https://doi.org/10.1215/10407391-1428906

Chion, Michel. 2011b. "Let's Have Done with the Notion of 'Noise'." *Differences* 22 (2–3): 240–248. https://doi.org/10.1215/10407391-1428906a.

Cook, Nicholas. 2013a. "Bridging the Unbridgeable? Empirical Musicology and Interdisciplinary Performance Studies." In *Taking It to the Bridge: Music as Performance*, edited by Cook Nicholas and Pettengill Richard, 70–85. University of Michigan Press.

Cook, Nicholas. 2013b. "Beyond Music: Mashup, Multimedia Mentality, and Intellectual Property." In *The Oxford Handbook of New Audiovisual Aesthetics*, edited by Richardson John, Gorbman Claudia and Vernallis Carol, 53–76. Oxford University Press, USA.

Corey, Jason. 2017. *Audio production and critical listening: technical ear training*. Second ed. New York: Routledge.

d'Escriván, Julio. 2012. *Music Technology*. Cambridge, UK: Cambridge University Press.

Daubresse, Eric, and Gérard Assayag. 2000. "Technology and Creation- The Creative Evolution." *Contemporary Music Review* 19 (2): 61–80.

De Souza, Jonathan. 2017. *Music at Hand: Instruments, Bodies, and Cognition*. New York, NY: Oxford University Press.

De Souza, Jonathan. 2018. "Orchestra Machines, Old and New." *Organised Sound* 23 (2): 156–166.

De Souza, Jonathan. 2021. "Timbral Thievery: Synthesizers and Sonic Materiality." In *The Oxford Handbook of Timbre*, edited by I. Dolan Emily and Rehding Alexander, 346–379. New York: Oxford University Press.

Desowitz, Bill. 2021. "'Dune': How Composer Hans Zimmer Invented a Retro-Future Musical Sound for the Arrakis Desert Planet." IndieWire. https://www.indiewire.com/features/general/dune-hans-zimmer-score-1234673017/.

Dolan, Emily. 2012. "Toward a Musicology of Interfaces." *Keyboard Perspectives* 5: 1–13.

Dolan, Emily. 2013. *The Orchestral Revolution: Haydn and the Technologies of Timbre*. Cambridge, UK: Cambridge University Press.

Dolan, Emily, and Thomas Patteson. 2021. "Ethereal Timbres." In *The Oxford Handbook of Timbre*, edited by Emily Dolan and Alexander Rehding. Oxford University Press.

Dolan, Emily, and Alexander Rehding, eds. 2021a. *The Oxford Handbook of Timbre*. Oxford Handbooks Online: Oxford University Press.

Dolan, Emily, and Alexander Rehding. 2021b. "Timbre: Alternative Histories and Possible Futures for the Study of Music." In *The Oxford Handbook of Timbre*, edited by Emily Dolan and Alexander Rehding. Oxford Handbooks Online: Oxford University Press.

Dreldon. 2023. "Ariel Marx hears a unique hiding place that holds 'A Small Light'." On the Score. https://onthescore.com/ariel-marx-hears-a-unique-hiding-place-that-holds-a-small-light/.

Eco, Umberto. 1990. *Travels in Hyperreality (Harvest Book)*. Mariner Books.

Emmerentze Jervell, Ellen. 2019. "Icelandic Artist Drew Sounds from Power Plant to Compose 'Chernobyl' Soundtrack." Billboard magazine. https://www.billboard.com/music/music-news/hildur-guonadottir-icelandic-artist-chernobyl-soundtrack-interview-8527454/.

Federman, Mark. 2004. "What is the Meaning of the Medium is the Message?". http://individual.utoronto.ca/markfederman/MeaningTheMediumisthe Message.pdf.

Fineberg, Joshua. 2000a. "Spectral Music." *Contemporary Music Review* 19 (2): 1–5.

Fineberg, Joshua. 2000b. "Guide to the Basic Concepts and Techniques of Spectral Music." *Contemporary Music Review* 19 (2): 81–113.

Gibson, D. 2005. *The Art of Mixing: A Visual Guide to Recording, Engineering, and Production*. Artistpro.

Göransson, Ludwig 2024. "How 'Oppenheimer' Composer Ludwig Göransson Created 'Can You Hear The Music?' | Behind the Song" Variety. https://youtu.be/fWvX4M1dXss?si=cGwGIqIegDSHWAX7.

Gorbman, Claudia 1987. *Unheard melodies: narrative film music*. London Bloomington: BFI Pub. Indiana University Press.

Grisey, G. 2000. "Did You Say Spectral?" *Contemporary Music Review* 19 (3): 1–3.

Hainge, Greg. 2013. *Noise Matters: Towards an Ontology of Noise*. New York: Bloomsbury Publishing Plc.

Hasegawa, Robert. 2021. "Timbre as Harmony—Harmony as Timbre." In *The Oxford Handbook of Timbre*, edited by Emily Dolan and Alexander Rehding. Oxford Handbooks Online: Oxford University Press.

Henson, Christian. 2015. "Spitfire Walkthrough - Evo Grid #1: Strings" Spitfire Audio. https://www.youtube.com/watch?v=xwxM14oSZnY.

Heyde, Herbert. 1975. *Grundlagen des natürlichen Systems der Musikinstrumente*. Leipzig: VEB Deutscher Verlag für Musik.

Hornbostel, Erich M. von, and Curt Sachs. 1961. "Classification of Musical Instruments." *The Galpin Society Journal* 14: 3–29. https://doi.org/10.2307/842168.

Hosken, Dan. 2011. *An Introduction to Music Technology*. NY: Routledge.

Huron, David. 2006. *Sweet anticipation: music and the psychology of expectation*. Cambridge MA: MIT Press.

Hurwitz, M. 2011. "Sound for Picture: Hans Zimmer's Scoring Collective - Composer Collaboration at Remote Control Productions." In The Routledge Film Music Sourcebook, edited by James Wierzbicki, Platte Nathan and Colin Roust, 254–257. Routledge.

Inglis, Sam. 2024. "Hans Zimmer & Friends: Dune." *Sound on Sound* 39 (6): 124–133.

Jessica AS. February 13, 2015. "!!SPITFIRE - Evo Grid 1 - Strings - RELEASED... If you liked our Scary Strings you'll love this!!!" KVR audio forum. https://www.kvraudio.com/forum/viewtopic.php?t=432062.

Jung, Hwa Yol. 1984. "Misreading the Ideogram: From Fenollosa to Derrida and McLuhan." *Paideuma: Modern and Contemporary Poetry and Poetics* 13 (2): 211–227.

Karlin, Fred, and Raybund Wright. 2004. *On the Track: A Guide to Contemporary Film Scoring*. Routledge.

Kellner, Douglas. 2020. "Jean Baudrillard." The Stanford Encyclopedia of Philosophy, Winter 2020 Edition.

King, Darryn 2021. "How Hans Zimmer Conjured the Otherworldly Sounds of 'Dune'." New York Times. https://www.nytimes.com/2021/10/22/movies/hans-zimmer-dune.html.

Kirn, Peter. 2005. "East West Stormdrum Sample Library: In-Depth Review." https://cdm.link/2005/07/east-west-stormdrum-sample-library-in-depth-review/.

Kittler, Friedrich 1999. *Gramophone, Film, Typewriter (Writing Science)*. Stanford University Press.

Kmet, Nicholas. 2018. "Orchestration Transformation: Examining Differences in the Instrumental & Thematic Color Palettes of the *Star Wars* Trilogies." In *John Williams: Music for Films, Television and the Concert Stage*, edited by Emilio Audissino. Brepols.

Knakkergaard, Martin. 2015. "The Music That's Not There." In *The Oxford Handbook of Virtuality*. New York, NY: Oxford University Press Inc

Kraft, Robert, and Kenny Holmes, "Hildur Guðnadóttir needs an outlet for her darkness," 2019, in *Score: The Podcast*.

Kulezic-Wilson, Danijela. 2008. "Sound Design is the New Score." *Music, Sound, and the Moving Image* 2 (2): 127–131. https://doi.org/10.3828/msmi.2.2.5.

Kulezic-Wilson, Danijela. 2020. *Sound Design is the New Score: Theory, Aesthetics, and Erotics of the Integrated Soundtrack*. Oxford University Press.

Kulezic-Wilson, Danijela. 2015. The Musicality of Narrative Film. London: Palgrave Macmillan.

Kurzweil, Ray 1990. *The Age of Intelligent Machines*. Kurzweil Foundation.

Kurzweil, Ray. 2005. *The singularity is near: when humans transcend biology*. New York: Viking New York.

Lancelin, Aude (interviewer), Gary Genosko, and Adam Bryx (translators). 2004. "The Matrix Decoded: Le Nouvel Observateur Interview with Jean Baudrillard." *International Journal of Baudrillard Studies* 1 (2).

Lawrence, T.E., and A. Calder. [1926] 1997. *Seven Pillars of Wisdom*. Wordsworth Editions Limited.

Lehman, Frank. 2018. *Hollywood Harmony: Musical Wonder and the Sound of Cinema*. Oxford University Press.

Libin, Laurence. 2001. Organology. Oxford University Press.

Linoff, Marci. 2022. "How to Become a Motion Capture Actor." https://www.backstage.com/magazine/article/how-to-become-a-motion-capture-actor-73824/.

Lowder, J. Bryan. 2014. "How Interstellar's Stunning Score Was Made." http://www.slate.com/blogs/browbeat/2014/11/18/making_interstellar_s_score_hans_zimmer_s_soundtrack_explored_in_exclusive.html.

Martinelli, Marissa. 2018. "*Annihilation* Co-Composer Ben Salisbury Explains How That Weird Little Melody Wound Up in the Film's Trailer." Slate. https://slate.com/culture/2018/02/annihilation-co-composer-ben-salisbury-explains-the-musical-cue-from-the-alien.html.

Mathews, Paul 2020. Instrumentation and Orchestration. Oxford Bibliographies.

Mayfield, Matt. 2012. "AF002 Audio Domains and Waves." https://www.youtube.com/watch?v=I__cjo82SQY.

Mayfield, Matt. 2016. "The Acoustic, Analog, and Digital Domains - Digital Audio Foundations Video Tutorial: Linkedin Learning, Formerly Lynda.com." https://www.linkedin.com/learning/digital-audio-foundations/the-acoustic-analog.

McAdams, Stephen, Meghan Goodchild, and Kit Soden. 2022. "A Taxonomy of Orchestral Grouping Effects Derived from Principles of Auditory Perception." *Music Theory Online* 28 (3). https://doi.org/10.30535/mto.28.3.6.

McCreary, Bear. 2024. "Percy Jackson and the Olympians." *Bear's Blog* (blog). March 12, 2024. https://bearmccreary.com/percy-jackson-and-the-olympians/.

McLuhan, Marshall. [1964] 1994. *Understanding Media: The Extensions of Man*. Cambridge, Mass.: MIT Press.

McLuhan, Marshall. 1969. *Counterblast*. London: UK: Rapp &Whiting Limited.

Mera, Miguel. 2013. "Inglo(u)rious Basterdization? Tarantino and the War Movie Mashup." In *The Oxford Handbook of Sound and Image in Digital Media*, edited by Carol Vernallis, Amy Herzog, and John Richardson. Oxford University Press.

Mera, Miguel. 2016a. "Materializing Film Music." In *The Cambridge Companion to Film Music*, edited by Cooke Mervyn and Ford Fiona, 157–172. Cambridge: Cambridge University Press.

Mera, Miguel. 2016b. "Towards 3-D Sound: Spatial Presence and the Space Vacuum."

Meyerson, Alan. 2023. "Alan Meyerson: Mixing The Movies Part 1 - Immersive Audio" In "Sound on Sound Magazine." https://youtu.be/7NQJmAyM65I?si=wLCtM0gL5Ifwsh2M.

Moylan, William. 1983. *An Analytical System for Electronic Music*. Doctoral dissertation. Ball State University.

Moylan, William. 1985. "Aural Analysis of the Characteristics of Timbre." 79th Convention of the Audio Engineering Society, New York, NY.

Moylan, William. 1986. "Aural Analysis of the Spatial Relationships of Sound Sources as Found in Two-Channel Common Practice." 81st Convention of the Audio Engineering Society, Los Angeles, CA.

Moylan, William. 1987. "A Systematic Method for the Aural Analysis of Sound Sources in Audio Reproduction/Reinforcement, Communications, and Musical Contexts." 83rd Convention of the Audio Engineering Society, New York, NY.

Moylan, William. 2014. *Understanding and Crafting the Mix: The Art of Recording* (3rd Edition). Independence, KY, USA: Focal Press.

Moylan, William. 2020. *Recording analysis: how the record shapes the song.* New York, NY: Routledge.

Moylan, William, Lori Burns, and Mike Alleyne. 2022. *Analyzing Recorded Music Collected Perspectives on Popular Music Tracks.* Milton: Taylor & Francis Group.

Murch, Walter. 2001. *In the blink of an eye: a perspective on film editing.* 2nd edition. Los Angeles, California: Silman-James Press.

Neumeyer, David. 2009. "Diegetic/Nondiegetic: A Theoretical Model." *Music and the Moving Image* 2 (1): 26–39. http://www.jstor.org/stable/10.5406/musimoviimag.2.1.0026.

Nolan, Christopher. 2010. *Inception.* [Shooting Script].

Obumneke, S. Anyanwu, Emaeyak P. Sylvanus. 2022. "Music Production Technology in New Nollywood Soundtracks: Context, Application, and the Effect of Globalization." *Music and the Moving Image* 15 (1): 22–37.

Owsinski, Bobby. 2013a. *The Mixing Engineer's Handbook,* 3rd Edition. Cengage Learning PTR.

Owsinski, Bobby. 2013b. *The Recording Engineer's Handbook,* 3rd Edition. Cengage Learning PTR.

Pawlett, William. 2007. *Jean Baudrillard: Against Banality (Key Sociologists).* Routledge.

Pejrolo, A. 2005. *Creative Sequencing Techniques for Music Production: A Practical Guide to Pro Tools, Logic, Digital Performer and Cubase.* Routledge.

Pejrolo, A., and R. DeRosa. 2007. *Acoustic and MIDI Orchestration for the Contemporary Composer: A Practical Guide to Writing and Sequencing for the Studio Orchestra.* Kidlington, GBR: Focal Press.

Pejrolo, Andrea, and Scott B. Metcalfe. 2017. *Creating Sounds from Scratch: A Practical Guide to Music Synthesis for Producers and Composers.* New York, NY: Oxford University Press.

Persing, Eric. 2009. "Psychoacoustic Sampling" Spectrasonics. https://vimeo.com/5748896.

Phoenix, Nick, Austin Tony, and Pacemaker. 2011. "Quantum Leap RA Virtual Instrument User's Manual." http://www.soundsonline-forums.com/docs/QL_RA_Manual.pdf.

Prasad, Anil. 2004. "Miroslav Vitous: Freeing the Muse." Innerviews: music without borders. https://www.innerviews.org/inner/vitous-1.

Prince, Stephen. 1996. "True lies: perceptual realism, digital images, and film theory." *Film Quarterly* 49 (2): 27–37. https://doi.org/10.2307/1213468.

Prince, Stephen. 2010. "Through the Looking Glass: Philosophical Toys and Digital Visual Effects." *Projections* 4 (2): 19–40. https://doi.org/10.3167/proj.2010.040203.

Prince, Stephen. 2012. *Digital Visual Effects in Cinema: The Seduction of Reality.* Rutgers University Press.

Rogers, D., Phoenix N., Bergersen T., and Murphy, S. 2009. *EastWest/Quantum Leap Hollywood Strings Virtual Instrument User's Manual.*

Rosenbloom, Etan. 2013. "Film Music Friday: Steven Price on Gravity." http://www.ascap.com/playback/2013/10/wecreatemusic/fmf-steven-price-gravity.aspx.

Sadoff, Ron. 2013. "Scoring for Film and Video Games: Collaborative Practices and Digital Post-Production." In The Oxford Handbook of Sound and Image in Digital Media, edited by Carol Vernallis, Amy Herzog, and John Richardson. New York: Oxford University Press.

Saussure, Ferdinand. 1998. *Nature of the Linguistic Sign.* Boston: Bedford/St. Martin's Press.

Sample Modeling. 2024. "Technology: a brief overview of our proprietary technology." Accessed 2024. https://www.samplemodeling.com/technology/.

Schaeffer, Pierre. 2017. *Treatise on Musical Objects: Essays across Disciplines.* Translated by Christine North and John Dack. Oakland, CA: University of California Press.

Sharf, Zack. 2020. "Christopher Nolan Says Fellow Directors Have Called to Complain About His 'Inaudible' Sound." IndieWire. https://www.indiewire.com/features/general/christopher-nolan-directors-complain-sound-mix-1234598386/.

Smalley, Denis. 1994. "Defining timbre - Refining timbre." *Contemporary Music Review* 10 (2): 35–48. https://doi.org/10.1080/07494469400640281.

Smith, Jeff. 1996. "Unheard Melodies? A Critique of Psychoanalytic Theories of Film Music." *Post-theory: Reconstructing Film Studies*: 230–47.

Smith, Jeff. 2009. "Bridging the Gap: Reconsidering the Border between Diegetic and Nondiegetic Music." *Music and the Moving Image* 2 (1). http://www.jstor.org/stable/10.5406/musimoviimag.2.1.0001.

Smith, Jeff. 2013. "The Sound of Intensified Continuity." In *The Oxford Handbook of New Audiovisual Aesthetics*, edited by John Richardson, Claudia Gorbman and Carol Vernallis. Oxford University Press.

Spice, Anton. 2024. "How Hans Zimmer's sonic experiments shaped the world of Dune: Part Two." Composer - Spitfire Audio. https://composer.spitfireaudio.com/en/articles/how-hans-zimmers-sonic-experiments-shaped-the-world-of-dune-part-two.

Spitfire Audio, 2015, "EVO GRID 1 - If you liked our 'SCARY STRINGS' you'll love this!!."

Staier, Andreas. 1997. Schubert, F. – The Late Piano Sonatas D 958 - 960. Teldec - Das Alte Werk.

Steward, Dave. 1994. "Organising Your Sample Library." Sound on Sound. https://www.soundonsound.com/techniques/organising-your-sample-library.

Stewart, Dave. 2010. "EWQL Hollywood Strings." Sound on Sound. https://www.soundonsound.com/reviews/ewql-hollywood-strings.

Stewart, Dave, and Mark Wherry. 2003. "Vienna Symphonic Library: Orchestral Cube & Performance Set First Editions." Sound on Sound. https://www.soundonsound.com/reviews/vsl-orchestral-cube-performance-set.

Stilwell, Robin J. 2007. "The Gap between diegetic and nondiegetic." *Beyond the Soundtrack: Representing Music in Cinema* 1st: University of California Press.

Størvold, Tore, and John Richardson. 2021. "Radioactive Music: The Eerie Agency of Hildur Guðnadóttir's Music for the Television Series Chernobyl." *Music and the Moving Image* 14 (3): 30–45. https://doi.org/10.5406/musimoviimag.14.3.0030.

StudioBinder. 2020. "What is Mise en Scene—How Directors Like Kubrick Master the Elements of Visual Storytelling" https://www.youtube.com/watch?v=3euNFd7-TCg.

Tan, Sui Lan, Cohen Annabel J., Lipscomb Scott D., and Roger A. Kendall, eds. 2013. *The Psychology of Music in Multimedia*. Oxford University Press.

Tapp, Tom. 2024. "Denis Villeneuve: "Frankly, I Hate Dialogue. Dialogue Is For Theatre And Television"." Deadline. https://deadline.com/2024/02/denis-villeneuve-movies-corrupted-by-tv-1235838780/.

The_Phoenician. 2022. "Guthrie Govan Describes Surprising Guitar Effects He Had to Produce While Recording 'Dune' Soundtrack, Explains How Working With Hans Zimmer Impacted His Playing." Ultimate Guitar Com. https://www.ultimate-guitar.com/news/general_music_news/guthrie_govan_describes_surprising_guitar_effects_he_had_to_produce_while_recording_dune_soundtrack_explains_how_working_with_hans_zimmer_impacted_his_playing.html.

Tommasini, Anthony. 2013. "Wearing a Wire at the Opera, Secretly, of Course." https://www.nytimes.com/2013/06/30/arts/music/wearing-a-wire-at-the-opera-secretly-of-course.html.

Tresch, John, and Emily Dolan. 2013. "Toward a New Organology: Instruments of Music and Science." *Osiris* 28: 278–298. https://doi.org/10.1086/671381.

Turgeon, Sebastien. 2019. "The Problematic Case of Sound Amplification at the Royal Swedish Opera." Opera Wire. https://operawire.com/the-problematic-case-of-sound-amplification-at-the-royal-swedish-opera/.

Vary, A. 2013. "Inside The Mind (And Studio) Of Hollywood's Music Maestro." http://www.buzzfeed.com/adambvary/hans-zimmer-film-composer-inside-his-studio.

Vienna Symphonic Library. "Capturing Timeless Classics." Accessed 2024a. https://www.vsl.co.at/en/AboutUs/Silent_Stage.

Vienna Symphonic Library. "About Us: From Dream to Reality." Accessed 2024b. https://www.vsl.co.at/en/AboutUs/History.

Villeneuve, Denis. 2021. "Denis Villeneuve on LAWRENCE OF ARABIA | TIFF 2021" In "TIFF Originals." https://www.youtube.com/watch?v=HxejohkhRuQ.

Vitous, Miroslav. "Symphonic Orchestra Samples." Accessed 2024. https://www.miroslavvitous.com/symphonic-orchestra-samples/.

Vogler, Christopher. 1992. *The Writer's Journey: Mythic Structures for Storytellers and Screenwriters.* M. Wiese Productions.

Wartenberg, Thomas E. 2003. "Philosophy Screened: Experiencing The Matrix." *Midwest Studies In Philosophy* 27 (1): 139–152. https://doi.org/10.1111/1475-4975.00076. https://onlinelibrary.wiley.com/doi/abs/10.1111/1475-4975.00076.

Weintraub, Steve. 2013. "Hans Zimmer Talks MAN OF STEEL, How He Crafted the Score, Dealing with the Pressure of Following John Williams, Nolan's INTERSTELLAR, RUSH, and More." Collider. https://collider.com/hans-zimmer-man-of-steel-interstellar-rush-interview/.

Wherry, Mark. 2002. "Media Adventures: Hans Zimmer and Jay Rifkin." Sound on Sound. https://www.soundonsound.com/people/media-adventures.

Wierzbicki, James E. 2009. *Film Music: A History.* Routledge.

Winters, Ben. 2010. "The non-diegetic fallacy: Film, music, and narrative space." *Music and Letters* 91(2): 224–244. https://doi.org/10.1093/ml/gcq019.

Wigler, Josh. 2016. "Carlton Cuse and Michael Giacchino Reflect on 'Lost' at Hollywood Reunion Concert." The Hollywood Reporter. https://www.hollywoodreporter.com/tv/tv-news/carlton-cuse-michael-giacchino-reflect-932318/.

Yacavone, Daniel. 2012. "Spaces, Gaps, and Levels." *Music, Sound, and the Moving Image* 6(1): 21–37. 10.

Zimmer, Hans. 2001. The Gladiator Waltz. Universal Classics Group.

Zimmer, Hans. 2010. "Radical Notion." Warner Bros. Entertainment Inc.

Zimmer, Hans (Rctec). 2012. "Hans Zimmer Sound?" VI Control. https://vi-control.net/community/threads/hans-zimmer-sound.24544/page-2#post-3614029.

Zimmer, Hans. 2013a. "Digital Booklet. Man of Steel (Original Motion Picture Soundtrack) Deluxe Edition." WaterTower Music.

Zimmer, Hans. 2013b. "Oil Rig. Man of Steel (Original Motion Picture Soundtrack) Deluxe Edition." WaterTower Music.

Zimmer, Hans. 2013c. "Man of Steel Official Soundtrack | Behind The Scenes Percussion Session w/ Hans Zimmer" WaterTowerMusic. https://www.youtube.com/watch?v=QTOMIyynBPE.

Zimmer, Hans. 2014a. "Digital Booklet. Interstellar (Original Motion Picture Soundtrack)." WaterTower Music.

Zimmer, Hans. 2014b. "Dust. Interstellar (Original Motion Picture Soundtrack)." WaterTower Music.

Zimmer, Hans. 2014c. "S.T.A.Y. Interstellar (Original Motion Picture Soundtrack)." WaterTower Music.

Zimmer, Hans. 2021a. The Dune Sketchbook (Music From the Soundtrack). WaterTower.

Zimmer, Hans. 2021b. "Hans Zimmer's use of computers and samples in orchestral music" In "Mix with the Masters." https://youtu.be/_LHyNYRtwR8?si=VUrPPKEv0N3HB0Ep.

Zimmer, Hans (Rctec). 2021c. "Hans Zimmer's Dune soundtrack -- only using U-he Dark Zebra." VI Control. https://vi-control.net/community/threads/hans-zimmers-dune-soundtrack-only-using-u-he-dark-zebra.114041/post-4974255.

Zimmer, Hans (Rctec). 2022a. "Abbey Road vs Air Studios." https://vi-control.net/community/threads/abbey-road-vs-air-studios.100100/post-5176469.

Zimmer, Hans. 2022b. "How 'Dune' Composer Hans Zimmer Created the Oscar-Winning Score" Vanity Fair. https://www.vanityfair.com/video/watch/vf-tricks-of-the-trade-hans-zimmer.

Zimmer, Hans, and Christopher Nolan. 2011. "Hans Zimmer - Making Of Inception Score" Hans Zimmer - Making Of Inception Score. https://www.youtube.com/watch?v=gL5en8Y10OU.

Zone, R. 2012. *3-D Revolution: The History of Modern Stereoscopic Cinema* (1st ed.). The University Press of Kentucky.

AUDIOVISUAL NARRATIVES

Abrams, J.J. (creator), and Michael Giacchino (composer). *Lost*. ABC, 204-10.

Anderson, Paul Thomas (creator), and Jonny Greenwood (composers). *There Will Be Blood*. Paramount, 2007.

Bertolucci, Bernardo (director), Ryuichi Sakamoto, David Byrne, and Cong Su (composers). *The Last Emperor*. Columbia Pictures, 1987.

Cuarón, Alfonso (director), and Steven Price (composer). *Gravity*. Warner Bros. Pictures, 2013.

Darabont, Frank (director), and Thomas Newman (composer). *The Shawshank Redemption*. Columbia Pictures, 1994.

Esmail, Sam (creator), and Mac Quayle (composer). *Mr Robot*. USA Network, 2015–2019.

Favreau, Jon (creator), and Ludwig Göransson (composer). *The Mandalorian*. Disney+, 2019–2023.

Fincher, David (director), Trent Reznor, and Atticus Ross (composers). *The Social Network*. Columbia Pictures, 2010.

REFERENCES 315

Garland, Alex (director), Geoff Barrow, and Ben Salisbury (composers). *Ex Machina*. A24, 2014.

Garland, Alex (director), Geoff Barrow, and Ben Salisbury (composers). *Annihilation*. Paramount, 2018.

Goddard, Drew (creator), and John Paesano (composer). *Marvel's Daredevil*. Netflix/Disney+, 2015–2018

Goyer, David S., Josh Friedman (creators), and Bear McCreary (composer). *Foundation*. Apple TV+, 2021–.

Hudson, Hugh (director), and Vangelis (composer). *Chariots of Fire*. 20th Century-Fox, 1981.

Jackson, Peter (director), and Howard Shore (composer). *Lord of The Rings: The Fellowship of the Ring*. New Line Cinema, 2001.

Jackson, Peter (director), and Howard Shore (composer). *Lord of The Rings: The Two Towers*. New Line Cinema, 2002.

Jackson, Peter (director), and Howard Shore (composer). *Lord of The Rings: The Return of the King*. New Line Cinema, 2003.

Kubrick, Stanley (director), and Wendy Carlos (composer). *A Clockwork Orange*. Warner Bros., 1971.

Lean, David (director), and Maurice Jarre (composer). *Lawrence of Arabia*. Columbia Pictures, 1962.

Lynch, David (director), and Angelo Badalamenti (composer). *Mulholland Drive*. Universal Pictures, 2001.

Nolan, Christopher, and Hans Zimmer (composer). *Inception*. Warner Bros., 2010.

Nolan, Christopher, and Hans Zimmer (composer). *The Dark Knight Rises*. Warner Bros., 2012.

Nolan, Christopher, and Hans Zimmer (composer). *Interstellar*. Paramount Pictures, 2014.

Nolan, Christopher (director), and Ludwig Göransson (composer). *Oppenheimer*. Universal Pictures, 2023.

Nolan, Christopher (director), James Netwon Howard, and Hans Zimmer (composers). *Batman Begins*. Warner Bros., 2005.

Nolan, Christopher (director), James Newton Howard, and Hans Zimmer (composers). *The Dark Knight*. Warner Bros., 2008.

Philips, Todd (director), and (composer) Hildur Guðnadóttir. *Joker*. Warner Bros. Pictures, 2019.

Rater, Joan, Tony Phelan (creators), and Ariel Marx (composer). *A Small Light*. National Geographic, 2023.

Riordan, Rick, Jonathan E. Steinberg (creators), Bear McCreary, and Sparks and Shadows (composers). *Percy Jackson and the Olympians*. Disney+, 2023.

Scott, Ridley (director), and Vangelis (composer). *Blade Runner*. Warner Bros., 1982.

Scott, Ridley (director), and Hans Zimmer (composer). *Gladiator*. DreamWorks Pictures, 2000.

Snyder, Zack (director), and Hans Zimmer (composer). *Man of Steel*. Warner Bros., 2013.

Spielberg, Steven (director), and John Williams (composer). *Jurassic Park*. Universal Pictures, 1993.

Spielberg, Steven (director), and John Williams (composer). *Minority Report*. 20th Century Fox, 2002.

Spielberg, Steven (director), and John Williams (composer). *Memoirs of a Geisha*. Columbia Pictures, 2005.

The Wachowskis (directors), and Don Davis (composer). *The Matrix*. Warner Bros., 1999.

Thorne, Jack (creator), and Lorne Balfe (composer). *His Dark Materials*. HBO, 2019–2022.

Villeneuve, Denis (director), and Hans Zimmer (composer). *Dune: Part One*. Warner Bros. Pictures, 2021.

Villeneuve, Denis (director), and Hans Zimmer (composer). *Dune: Part Two*. Warner Bros. Pictures, 2024.

Weisberg, Joe (creator), and Nathan Barr (composer). *The Americans*. FX, 2013–2018.

Wright, Joe (director), and Dario Marianelli (composer). *Atonement*. Universal Studios, 2007.

Wyatt, Rupert (director), and Patrick Doyle (composer). *Rise of the Planet of the Apes*. Twentieth Century Fox, 2011.

Zeitlin, Benh (director & co-composer), and Dan Romer (co-composer). *Beasts of the Southern Wild*. Fox Searchlight Pictures, 2012.

Zemeckis, Robert (director), and Alan Silvestri (composer). *Forrest Gump*. Paramount Pictures, 1994.

Index[1]

A
Abbey Road, 147, 231
Accordion, 259
Acousmatic, 72–82, 96, 97
Acoustically, 202, 208, 231, 238, 274, 278, 282, 289, 292, 293
Acoustic Ensembles, 218
Acoustic instrument, 2, 4, 7, 14, 16, 21, 95, 102n35, 121, 123, 128, 129, 136, 142, 155, 158, 159, 177, 196, 199, 209, 225, 236, 247, 265, 268–270, 288
Acoustic means, 20, 71, 86, 92
Acoustic recordings, 20, 124, 132, 205, 235
Acoustic waves, 192
Additive synthesis, 102n31, 223, 224, 249, 264, 288
Adler, Samuel, 102n32, 245, 246, 252, 293, 294n1
Aesthetics, 2, 6–9, 11–13, 20, 29, 31, 34, 47, 51–55, 57n2, 63, 65, 67–73, 75, 77–81, 87, 88, 90, 93–97, 99n14, 101n26, 120, 122, 124–126, 132, 133, 149, 151, 152, 156, 162, 165, 168, 172–175, 178–181, 189–239, 248, 252–255, 257, 258, 260, 264, 276, 281, 283, 285, 287, 291
Air Studios, AIR, 158, 169, 205
Albion, 166, 169
Amplitude, 14–18, 20, 21, 136, 192, 196, 197, 231, 232, 236, 263–266, 269, 278, 280, 286, 288
Analog
 emulation, 176–177
 synthesizer, 7, 85, 102n35, 167, 176–177, 236, 238, 240n5
Annihilation, 208, 230, 234–239, 257, 286
Arnalds, Olafur, 180
Articulations, 111, 116, 123, 124, 136, 140, 146, 154, 159, 160, 172, 182n8, 215, 267

---

[1] Note: Page numbers followed by 'n' refer to notes.

© The Author(s), under exclusive license to Springer Nature Switzerland AG 2024
S. Casanelles, *The Hyperorchestra*,
https://doi.org/10.1007/978-3-031-75193-6

Artificial intelligence, 103n35, 170
Artisan score, 209–210
Arturia, 85, 102n35, 176
Atmosphere, 178, 183n25
Atonement, 256
Attack, Decay, Sustain, and Release (ADSR), 150, 195–198, 225, 239n4, 269
Attack transients, 265–266
Audiovisual narrative, 2–6, 10, 12, 13, 20, 26, 27, 32, 34, 43, 91, 94–97, 175, 180, 189, 191, 198, 204, 229, 250, 256, 285, 289, 300
Aural fidelity, 284, 286–287, 294, 295n11
Auslander, Philip, 42, 49, 61, 68, 88
Authorship, 13, 46, 49–52, 62, 88, 155

B
Bagpipe, 220, 224, 240–241n14, 294n3
Balfe, Lorne, 292, 295n13
Bansuri, 257, 258
Barrow, Geoff, 234, 235, 279, 301
Bass drum, 174, 265, 267
Baudrillard, Jean, 9, 17, 25–35, 37–41, 47, 54, 95–97, 100n18, 132
Beasts of the Southern Wild, 281
Beethoven, Ludwig Van, 190
Bespoke, 165, 166, 224
  virtual instruments, 162, 164, 218
Blade Runner, 86, 176
Blade Runner 2049, 273
Bleeding Fingers, 240n10, 301
Bodhrán, 285
Bordwell, David, 42–44, 234, 239n2, 254, 255, 286, 294n5
Braams, 8, 15, 206

Brass, 8, 15, 64, 86, 97, 138, 165, 205, 206, 208, 229, 256, 263, 265, 277, 279, 291–293
Buhler, James, 57n2, 92, 132, 140, 144, 145, 152, 180, 183n16, 193, 194, 239n2, 255

C
Camera, 6, 46–49, 54, 55, 69, 70, 100n16, 230
Campbell, Joseph, 57n7
Cello, 17, 89, 128, 135, 143, 153, 272
Chamber Strings, 169
Chernobyl, 20, 162, 219–220, 223, 225, 240n7, 256, 257, 284
Chion, Michel, 3, 75–77, 79, 174, 193, 254, 287
Cinesamples, 158
Clarinet, 158, 169, 209, 215, 247, 262, 265, 270
Classical Hollywood, 43, 159, 254–256, 258
Communication protocol, 89, 108, 111, 112, 182n11
Compression, 15, 239n1, 280
Computer
  computer graphic imagery (CGI), 5, 48–56, 88–92, 95, 103n40
  languages, 40
Concert hall, 64, 68–71, 75, 100n16, 147, 157, 158, 168, 195, 205, 227, 265
Consciousness, 36–38, 45
Consonance, 288, 289
Cook, Nicholas, 62, 63
Corruption of form, 235, 236
Creative processors, 285–286
Crossfade, 144
Cry of the banshee, 223, 299
Cuarón, Alfonso, 228, 230, 232, 233
Cultural connotations, 87, 111

D

Damage Library, 165
Daredevil, 277
Dark Knight, The, 7, 177, 215, 224, 229
De Souza, Jonathan, 81, 83, 86, 99n14, 102n32
Deep sampling, 137, 150
Dematerialized, 80, 96, 254, 256
Desert of the real, 26
Diegesis/diegetic, 44, 53, 76, 79, 194, 220, 233, 235, 254–256, 281 285, 287, 295n11
Digital
   cinema, 16, 25–56, 193, 194
   means, 3, 16, 18
   music, 2, 5, 15, 18, 107–181, 191, 192, 194, 238–239, 245, 278
   synthesizers, 108, 167, 176–178
   tools, 2, 5, 12, 97, 107–181, 194, 299, 300
Digital Audio Workstation (DAW), 16, 80, 94, 95, 97, 101n28, 107, 117–119, 176, 182n5, 201–203, 206, 207, 209–212, 252, 260, 270, 280
Disneyland, 28–30, 34, 41, 93–95, 123, 142, 154, 284
Dissonance, 256, 288, 289
Distorted Reality, 178
Distortion, 15, 236–238, 239n1, 256, 278, 279, 284, 288
Diva, 177
Dolan, Emily, 10, 64, 65, 83–85, 103n37, 177, 178, 226, 252, 253, 260, 267
Dolby Atmos, 228, 281
Drum, 7, 8, 89, 115, 164, 167, 171, 173–175, 183n24, 216–219, 272, 291, 292
Drum ensemble, 216, 217, 272, 291
Duduk, 171, 224, 259, 280

Dulcimer, 285
Dune, 8, 125, 220–225, 256, 257, 259, 280, 294n3, 299
Dynamic crossfading, 137–139, 151
Dynamic levels, 67, 71, 82, 115, 129–131, 137–139, 247, 262, 265, 271

E

Early music, 78, 79
EastWest, 158, 163
Eco, Umberto, 27–29, 93, 94, 142, 154, 284
Editing, 1–3, 5, 6, 19, 50, 68, 77, 95, 97, 117, 200, 203, 217, 232, 255, 300
Effect processors, 107, 280, 286
8-bit distortion, 279
8dio, 144, 145, 183n19, 218
Electric guitar, 14, 172, 199, 205, 214, 221, 224, 256, 285
Electronic means, 7, 249
Epic percussion, 167, 173–175, 177
Equalization (EQ), 15, 150, 194, 239n1, 272, 275–278, 287, 295n10
Esmail, Sam, 290
Ethereal timbres, 103n37, 167, 177–178
Evo Grid 001 Strings, 179
Evolve, 165
Ex Machina, 234, 279

F

Fiddle, 285
Filmmaker, 2–6, 8, 13, 50, 57n2, 132, 166, 204, 300
Filter, 47, 50, 228, 268, 269, 277, 288, 290
Final mix, 18, 68, 98n9, 121

Flanger, 236–238, 286
Flute, 19, 64, 89, 91, 101n27, 158, 169, 171, 191, 194, 223, 251, 253, 258, 265, 267, 268, 277
Fourier theorem, 102n35, 269, 294n7
Fourier transform, 249
French horn, 121, 137, 205, 217
Frequency
  area, 15, 266, 268, 276
  range, 99n12, 192, 194, 265, 267, 268, 275–277
Functional toolkit, 161, 168, 175
Fundamental, 19, 44–46, 92, 98n1, 115, 117, 127, 132, 135, 137, 139, 173, 177, 207, 226, 253, 263–268, 287

G
Galloway, Alexander, 109, 110
Garland, Alex, 234, 238, 279
Generation of meaning, 3, 9, 11, 171, 225–239, 250, 283
Giacchino, Michael, 213, 256
Gladiator, 7, 125, 126, 173, 174
Global Village, 36, 37, 41, 172, 259, 300
Glockenspiel, 279
Golden Era, 211
Gollum, 49–53, 88, 89
Göransson, Ludwig, 240n7, 272
Gravity, 215, 228, 230–234
Greenwood, Jonny, 79, 255
Grisey, Gérard, 95, 248, 250, 251, 288, 289, 294n2, 294n4
Guðnadóttir, Hildur, 162, 219, 220, 240n7, 272
Guitar, 14, 74–76, 171, 172, 199, 205, 214, 218, 221, 224, 234, 235, 238, 240–241n14, 252, 256, 257, 285

H
Harmonic
  content, 15–17, 278, 289
  density, 277–279, 288, 289
  series, 263, 264
  spectra, 264, 278
  spectrum, 19, 249, 255, 264, 265, 278
  harmonically dense sound, 269
Heavyocity, 161, 165, 178
Henson, Christian, 163, 178, 179
High Definition Range (HDR), 48, 283
His Dark Materials, 292, 293
Hollywood Strings, 158, 168
Hollywood Studio Orchestra, 168
Huron, David, 44, 45, 289
Hybrid, 99n14, 152, 153, 159, 167, 175, 177–180, 194
Hybrid synthesizers, 19–21, 87, 88, 167, 177–178, 180, 191, 199, 257
Hyperinstrument/hyperinstrumental, 9–12, 17, 94, 101n24, 103n42, 189, 190, 198, 206, 212–229, 234, 238–239, 240n13, 246, 250, 251, 253, 257, 259–261, 271, 276, 280, 284, 286–289, 291, 293, 294
Hyperinstrumentation, 252–261
Hyperorchestra/hyperorchestral, 2, 3, 5–7, 9, 11–13, 17, 27, 28, 31, 32, 34, 42, 46, 56, 61–97, 103n42, 107–181, 189–239, 245, 248, 250, 251, 257–259, 263, 264, 268, 271, 281, 284, 285, 287, 290–294, 300, 301
Hyperorchestration/hyperorchestrational, 9, 10, 12, 17, 99n15, 103n42, 215, 230, 235, 238–239, 245–294

Hyperorchestrator, 268, 276, 279, 283
Hyperreal, 26–56, 63, 76, 87, 92–94, 96, 103n42, 128–151, 189, 198–200, 203, 205, 212, 225, 252, 274, 284, 299
Hyperrealistic, 29, 72, 76, 94, 148, 199, 208
Hyperreality, 9, 11, 17, 25–56, 62, 92, 93, 96, 175, 198, 200, 204
Hypertext, 38, 40–42, 57n3

I
Imagination, 5, 32, 37, 44–46, 74, 122, 155, 210
Implosion, 35–38, 40–42, 259, 300
Impulse response, 220, 283, 284
Inception, 8, 9, 165, 204–208, 229, 240n6, 291, 292
Indexicality, 46–49, 55, 56
Industrial Revolution, 33, 40, 65
Inharmonic
  frequency content, 267
  material, 237, 255, 265, 266
  spectra, 265
  spectral material, 256
  spectrum, 256
Instrument
  instrumental combination, 161, 226, 294
  instrumental spectra, 264–265
  instrumental synthesis, 224, 249
Instrumentation, 194, 245, 247, 252, 253, 266
Intensified continuity, 239n2, 255
Interface, 62, 81, 83, 84, 88, 90, 107, 109–120, 126, 131, 164, 182n5, 182n11, 183n15, 196, 213
  effect, 109–120, 164
Interstellar, 8, 227, 229, 260
ITPRA, 44, 289

J
Joker, 272
Jurassic Park, 53, 54, 258

K
Keyboard, 83, 84, 89, 107, 109–115, 118, 148, 182n6, 218
Kubrick, Stanley, 190
Kulezic-Wilson, Danijela, 193, 194, 300
Kurzweil, Ray, 1, 39

L
Last Emperor, The, 7
Lawrence of Arabia, 223
Layering, 134–139, 148
Le Voix de Luthier, 225
Legato, 129, 131–133, 139–145, 149, 154, 160, 182n8, 292
Live
  experience, 61, 69–71, 287
  liveness, 42, 49, 61, 69, 142
  recording, 61, 68, 69, 100n16, 165
Loop/looping/loops, 17, 19, 133–135, 137, 149, 150, 164, 167, 173–175, 179, 183n24, 201, 218, 279
Lord of the Rings, The, 6, 49, 51, 89, 174
Lost, 213, 256
Low frequency oscillators (LFO), 286

M
Mahler, Gustav, 183n22, 261–263, 274, 283
Man of Steel, 8, 125, 126, 216–220, 225, 272, 287, 291, 292
Marianelli, Dario, 256
Marx, Ariel, 204, 209, 210, 240n8

Materialization, 77, 79, 161, 223, 254–259, 274, 284, 287
Materialize/materialized/ materializing, 78, 79, 97, 255, 257, 258, 272, 274, 284, 287
Materializing sound indices, 76, 77, 254
Matrix, The, 25–27, 30, 31
McCreary, Bear, 204, 210–212, 301
McLuhan, Marshall, 11, 27, 28, 35–42, 45, 55, 64, 65, 67, 72, 73, 81, 82, 102n32, 103n38, 109, 140, 172, 259, 300
Meaning, 2–4, 9, 11, 13, 14, 17, 18, 26, 34, 36, 37, 41, 49, 55, 56, 63, 79, 87, 94, 95, 110, 125, 145, 149, 157, 162, 165, 166, 171, 173, 177, 178, 181n2, 189–191, 194, 195, 204, 206, 208, 212, 214–216, 218–220, 222–239, 245–294, 299, 301
Mechanical waves, 192, 230
Media theory, 38, 81, 300
Mediation, 40, 61, 68, 83, 110, 117
Medium is the message, the, 35
Medium-specific, 48, 57n8, 300
Memoirs of a Geisha, 258
Mera, Miguel, 77–80, 97, 165, 230, 231, 241n16, 254–256
Meyerson, Alan, 281, 282
Microphone perspectives, 148, 281
Microphone positions, 148, 183n17, 273, 295n8
Microphones, 15, 68–73, 77, 98n9, 99n10, 99n11, 99n12, 100n16, 146–148, 162, 192, 200, 215, 216, 219, 224, 226, 254, 265, 271–275, 277, 282, 283, 291, 292, 295n8
Mise-en-scène, 95, 221, 222, 225
Mixing
  mixed, 61, 68, 69, 71, 152, 156–158, 168, 199, 215, 226, 271, 273, 285, 291, 295n8

  music mix, 199, 203, 204, 258, 281, 285
  techniques, 72, 246, 251, 260, 261, 291
  tools, 261, 270, 294
Mockup, 3–5, 12, 14, 16, 18, 120–128, 132, 156, 157, 160, 163, 164, 172, 200, 201, 203, 212
Models of the real, 53, 56, 225, 269
Moog, 14, 84–86
Moylan, William, 239n3, 270, 271, 273
Mr. Robot, 290
Murail, Tristan, 248, 251, 294n2
Murch, Walter, 1, 255, 294n6, 300
Music
  creation process, 92, 107, 127, 189, 195, 198, 201, 203, 260
  musical instruments, 4, 10, 14, 16, 19–21, 62, 72, 81–86, 88, 91, 101n27, 102n32, 113, 191, 194, 203, 219, 223, 224, 229, 231, 253, 261, 264, 265, 267, 269
  musical note, 19, 21, 85, 88, 113, 114, 196–198
  musical score, 3, 17, 19, 21, 27, 44, 46, 62, 64, 65, 67, 68, 73, 89, 98n5, 108, 111, 112, 117, 118, 146, 155, 157, 160, 193, 195, 202, 205, 207, 236, 254–256, 284
  music-creation process, 93
  production, 1, 19, 92, 97, 109, 110, 196, 238, 260
Music Instruments Digital Interface (MIDI)
  Continuous Controllers (CCs), 113–116, 131, 182n4, 182n8, 182n9
  Note Off, 113, 114
  Note On, 113, 114
Musique concrète, 73, 75

N

Narration, 195, 218, 230, 254
Narrative, 2–7, 9, 10, 12–14, 17, 20, 26, 27, 32, 34, 43–46, 57n2, 72, 79, 91, 94–97, 165, 166, 175, 180, 189–191, 193, 195, 198, 204, 205, 208–210, 213–217, 219, 226–229, 235–238, 250, 251, 256, 284, 285, 289, 290, 294, 300
Native Instruments, 175
Newman, Thomas, 272, 277, 299
Noise, 31, 32, 77–79, 90, 96, 146, 154, 157, 193, 237, 239n1, 250, 256, 267–269
Nolan, Christopher, 8, 177, 204–206, 215, 227, 260
Nondiegetic, 193, 256, 281
Nonlinear, 1–3, 12, 16, 18, 19, 67, 95, 119, 141, 145, 175, 189, 190, 195, 198–212, 228, 230, 238, 259, 260, 271, 272, 292, 300
  processes, 12, 19, 189, 195, 202, 205, 209–210
Non-orchestral ensembles, 257
Non-Western instruments, 148, 149, 163, 171, 172
Note transition, 139–145, 154

O

Omnisphere, 161, 162, 166, 178
Ontology, 42, 46–52, 56, 57n8, 68, 69, 86, 88
Oppenheimer, 272, 284
Orchestral ensemble, 68, 96, 167, 169, 251, 270, 292
Orchestral score, 12, 123, 128, 159, 251
Orchestration, 10, 12, 17, 64, 65, 91, 99n15, 102n32, 123, 124, 128, 136, 156, 157, 161, 164, 167, 170, 179, 203, 205, 226, 228, 245, 246, 250–253, 261, 266, 267, 270, 271, 276, 277, 280, 282, 283, 288, 290–294, 299
Orchestrator, 122, 124, 159, 161
Orders of simulacra, 28, 29, 32–35, 37, 38, 40, 95, 96
Organ, 111, 227, 260
Organology, 9–11, 19, 82, 83, 102n32, 252–261
Original source, 79, 81, 82, 237
Oscillator, 20, 87, 102n31, 150, 269, 270
Outer space, 54, 215, 230–234, 283, 284
Overpressure, 78, 101n25, 257
Overtone, 17, 19, 128, 222, 236, 237, 256, 258, 264–267, 269, 270, 272, 277, 278, 288, 290

P

Panning, 7, 15, 76, 274
Peirce, Charles, 46
Perceptual realism, 11, 42, 52–54, 92
Percussion, 82, 167, 173–175, 177, 197, 205, 209, 215, 217, 218, 222, 228, 231, 233, 265, 280, 291
Percy Jackson and the Olympians, 211
Performance, 4, 8, 19, 21, 46, 49–52, 62–64, 67, 68, 70–74, 76–80, 84, 86, 88–91, 93, 94, 96, 98n4, 98n5, 98n6, 98n8, 100n16, 101n23, 103n40, 108, 112, 114, 116, 118, 120, 122–124, 126, 129, 132–137, 139–143, 145, 147–149, 154, 155, 157–162, 164, 165, 167–169, 171, 172, 176, 180, 183n20, 195, 200, 210, 213, 215, 216, 218, 221, 224, 247, 251, 253–258, 261, 265–268, 272, 287, 292

Persing, Eric, 161, 162
Perspective image, 38, 39
Phase, 3, 36, 137, 148, 150, 268
Phaser, 237–238
Philosophy, 11, 14, 26–28, 30, 35, 56–57n1, 122, 205, 300
　philosophical, 11, 26–42, 56, 76, 92–97, 166, 236, 246, 251
　philosophical inquiry, 26, 30
Phonetic alphabet, 37, 38
Photograph, 2, 42, 46–48, 53
Physical means, 88, 91, 126, 180
Piano, 3, 16, 19, 64, 70–72, 77, 78, 83, 93, 99n14, 99n15, 101n26, 102n35, 107, 109, 111, 113, 115, 117–120, 132, 142, 148, 156, 162, 183n20, 196, 197, 206, 207, 218, 225, 240n12, 266, 272–274, 277, 281, 282, 284, 287, 288, 299
Piano concerto, 70–72, 93, 99n14
Piano Roll, 117–120, 206, 207
Pitch, 9, 19–21, 65, 82, 98n2, 108, 113, 115, 118, 128, 131, 132, 134, 139–141, 143–145, 147, 150, 160, 163, 172, 182n7, 194, 213, 236, 247, 257, 258, 264, 265, 267–269, 271, 289
Pitch structure, 172, 236, 257, 258
Pizzicato, 89, 116, 133, 136, 155, 182n8, 182n13, 200, 285
Placement, 64, 68, 69, 148, 160, 215, 224, 226, 234, 251, 261, 265, 271–274, 277, 282, 283, 291, 293
Planet of the Apes, The, 89
Plot, 43, 44, 204, 235
Predesigned musical phrases, 172
Prince, Stephen, 11, 42, 47, 48, 50–55, 58n10, 58n13, 92, 284
Process of virtualization, 39–42, 56, 72, 86, 254

ProjectSAM, 158, 170
Psychoacoustic sampling, 161

Q
Quantum Leap Symphonic Orchestra, 147
Quayle, Mac, 290

R
Radical illusion, 31, 39, 47
Realism, 5, 11, 42, 52–54, 63, 92, 123, 132, 150, 152, 155, 157–161, 178, 194
Reality, 4–6, 9, 17, 25–27, 29, 31–34, 37–56, 58n10, 62, 63, 69, 72, 73, 76, 86, 87, 92, 93, 96, 101n22, 109, 124, 126, 128, 129, 132, 133, 136, 137, 141, 146, 150–155, 159–163, 168, 170, 175, 177, 193, 200, 204–209, 229, 231, 233, 235, 269, 273, 276, 284
Recorded music, 10, 62, 63, 68–73, 93
Recording, 2–4, 7, 8, 10, 11, 16, 18–21, 46, 47, 51, 53, 58n10, 61, 63, 68–81, 85–87, 92–94, 96, 97, 99n15, 100n16, 100n19, 101n23, 101n26, 101n30, 102n31, 107, 117, 121–124, 127, 128, 131–135, 137, 138, 141, 143, 144, 146–152, 154–165, 168–170, 175–180, 182n14, 183n19, 195, 196, 199, 200, 202–205, 210, 212, 215, 216, 218–220, 224, 230, 231, 235, 251, 254, 257–260, 264, 265, 268, 270–275, 277, 278, 282, 284, 287, 291, 292, 299
　music, 68, 93, 198

techniques, 78, 168, 223, 251, 258, 292
technology, 11, 61, 64, 96
Replicate reality, 132, 146, 160, 161, 168, 284
Replication, 4, 120, 123, 132, 134, 153, 155, 158, 168, 175
Resonant, 225, 265, 268
Resonators, 225
Reverb/reverberation, 15, 73, 117, 146, 147, 183n17, 194, 205, 212, 219, 220, 228, 232, 239n1, 273, 281, 283–285, 287, 292, 293
Reversed sounds, 215, 231–234
Rise & Hit, 175
Risers, 175
Romer, Dan, 281
Round robin, 19, 139, 141, 154

S
Sable Strings, 169
Sadoff, Ron, 149, 168, 190
Salisbury, Ben, 234, 279, 301
Sample
    library, 19, 20, 21n2, 87–94, 101n29, 107, 108, 117, 121, 124–128, 130, 133, 134, 138, 140, 142–144, 146–150, 153–160, 162–164, 167–170, 172, 177, 179–181, 183n21, 183n23, 199–203, 215, 218, 260, 271, 278, 292
    sample-based, 85, 86, 93, 102n34, 107, 124, 125, 127, 152, 153, 163
    sample-based virtual instruments, 63, 85–93, 107, 109, 121, 124, 127, 152
    sampler, 19–21, 85, 86, 89, 108, 124, 129–131, 133, 134, 138,
139, 143, 144, 150, 154, 157, 183n19, 183n21, 224, 257, 268
    sampling, 102n31, 125–151, 153, 154, 158, 161, 162, 165, 169, 172, 176, 179, 182n14, 203
Saturated, 290
Saturation, 236–237, 239, 256, 278, 279, 288
Saussure, Ferdinand de, 32, 38
Scary Strings, 163, 179
Schaeffer, Pierre, 73–77, 80, 96, 101n22, 250
Schubert, Franz, 78, 79
Shakuhachi, 171, 172, 256, 258
Shawshank Redemption, The, 272, 277
Silent Studio, 146, 147
Simulacra, 28, 29, 32–35, 37–41, 95, 96, 120–127, 132
Simulacra and Simulation, 25, 28
Simulation, 6, 9, 17, 26, 29–36, 39, 120–123, 132, 150, 155, 201, 219
Sine wave, 82, 102n35, 135, 232, 249, 260, 264, 269, 278, 288
Slate + Ash, 180
A Small Light, 204, 209–210, 240n8
Smith, Jeff, 295n11
Social Network, The, 27, 273, 282, 295n9
Sonic
    analysis, 190–195, 204, 239n3
    combination, 268, 293–294
    material, 6, 63, 218, 248, 249
    model, 127, 254
    possibilities, 68, 73, 191, 196
    rendering, 202
    verisimilitude, 229
Sony scoring stage, 158
Sound
    design, 5, 20, 134, 166, 180, 193, 217, 230, 233, 235, 268–270, 300

Sound (*cont.*)
  object/objects, 63, 72–81, 94, 117, 143, 148, 153, 160, 162, 163, 171, 219, 220, 226, 250, 254–257, 266, 282
  palettes, 8, 84, 208, 209
  perspective, 70, 146–148, 230, 271–274
  processing, 134, 153, 163, 167, 175–177, 215, 223–225, 228, 233, 235, 240n13, 251, 263, 271, 285–287
  processors, 102n35, 117, 147, 155, 202, 280, 281, 285–286
  properties, 65, 115, 223, 262, 268, 276
  qualities, 134, 233, 250
  recording, 19, 86, 93, 156, 175–178, 251, 277
  source, 62–63, 69, 71, 73, 76, 87, 96, 101n22, 102n31, 150, 152–153, 159, 163, 176, 178, 191, 198, 199, 218, 220, 223, 224, 226, 239n3, 254–260, 263, 268, 270, 279, 287, 291
  synthesis, 150, 177, 268
Soundscape, 93, 149, 178, 208, 209, 215, 228, 229, 233, 250, 261, 271, 285, 293
Soundworld, 79, 210, 227, 238, 256
Sparks & Shadows/Sparks and Shadows, 204, 210–212, 301
Specificity, 48, 95, 124, 136, 171, 190, 212–215, 217, 218, 222, 226, 251, 253, 258, 260, 301
Spectral
  envelope, 266
  movement, 95, 246, 248, 250
  spectralism, 248
  spectrum, 10, 16, 19, 20, 58n10, 94, 95, 135, 138, 146, 163, 192, 194, 228, 229, 237, 249, 255, 256, 263–265, 271, 278, 287–290, 294n4
  transformation, 246, 251, 288–290
Spectrasonics, 161, 162, 166, 178, 183n25
Spitfire/Spitfire Audio, 158, 159, 162, 163, 166, 169, 178–180, 218
Star Wars, 91, 221
Stereo, 15, 68, 228, 273–275, 281
Stereo image, 274
Stereophonic, 228, 263, 283
StormDrum, 161, 173, 174
Story
  storytelling, 3–8, 11, 14, 27, 32, 43–45, 94–96, 124, 132, 142, 204, 210, 227, 251, 255, 256, 290
  world, 227, 254, 255
Strings, 4, 10, 17, 64, 78, 79, 81–83, 91, 96, 97, 101n22, 101n25, 101n26, 102n35, 111, 114, 116, 123, 124, 129, 133, 136, 138–140, 142, 144, 149, 150, 158–162, 164, 169, 179, 196, 197, 200, 205, 206, 209, 213, 216, 225, 232, 255–257, 265, 266, 270, 272, 276–279, 281, 286, 288, 291–293
  ensemble, 79, 98n1, 136, 216, 281
Structuralist, 248, 252, 294n2
Studio, 10, 44, 49, 63, 69, 72–81, 86, 94, 96, 100n20, 101n30, 117, 121, 146, 147, 158, 159, 174, 183n17, 196, 205, 206, 231, 239n3, 240n9, 263, 264, 300, 301
Sul ponticello, 101n25, 133, 213, 277
Surround, 29, 234, 263, 281
  speakers, 228, 281
Suspended cymbal, 265, 267
Swarms, 218
Symphobia, 158, 170

Synhtestrator, 90
Synthesis, 86, 87, 102n31, 102n34, 150–152, 161, 167, 168, 177, 194, 223, 224, 249, 264, 268, 270, 288
 synthesis-based, 152
 synthesized, 62, 81, 82, 153, 198, 208
 synthesized instruments, 85, 87, 197, 239n4
 synthesizers, 7, 8, 14, 19–21, 63, 81–87, 89, 92, 93, 96, 101n29, 102n31, 102n34, 102n35, 103n36, 107, 113, 114, 122, 125, 129, 135, 150–153, 175–177, 195–198, 202, 205, 208, 214, 223–225, 235, 236, 249, 251, 257, 260, 268–270, 288, 294n7
 synths, 102n34, 159, 176–178, 208, 225, 235, 241n14, 268, 269, 290
Synthetic, 91, 150–151, 167, 205, 208, 235–238, 268–270, 283

T
Taiko drum, 174, 175
Technology, 1–3, 5, 6, 9–13, 17, 27, 29, 31, 34–38, 43, 48, 50, 54, 57n2, 58n13, 61, 64, 75, 82, 83, 85, 88, 92, 96, 108, 111, 117, 120–122, 124, 125, 128, 129, 132, 134, 137, 154, 156, 157, 160, 170, 179, 180, 189, 192, 195, 211, 212, 217, 221, 224, 228, 230, 248, 257, 259, 265, 266, 270, 277, 281, 292, 294n7, 299, 301
 technological evolution, 27, 121
There Will Be Blood, 79, 80, 255, 256

Timbral, 64, 65, 71, 88, 92, 97, 99n15, 137, 138, 171, 180, 190, 212–226, 247, 249, 250, 253, 267, 268, 277, 288
Timbres, 9–11, 16, 21, 62, 65, 73, 79, 81, 82, 84, 85, 93, 99n14, 99n15, 100n20, 101n26, 101n27, 114, 122, 137, 138, 149, 166, 173, 177–178, 214, 226, 239n1, 239n3, 246, 247, 249–253, 255, 262, 266–269, 271, 277, 279, 288–290, 299
Time stretching, 21, 133–134
Timpani, 64, 174, 197, 280
Tremolo, 116, 123, 124, 133, 136, 182n8, 286
Trombones, 98n3, 205, 294n4
True Digital Emulation, 176
Trumpet, 96, 217, 226, 261–263, 270, 274
Tubas, 205
Typewriter, 109, 110, 256

U
U-he, 177, 224, 225

V
Vangelis, 86, 176
Verisimilar, 4, 5, 48, 49, 71, 124, 128, 132, 142, 153, 159, 205, 229, 293
Verisimilitude, 49, 72, 88, 123, 135, 194, 200, 227, 229, 276, 283–285, 287, 294
Vibrato, 89, 90, 116, 124, 129, 131, 132, 137, 138, 143, 144, 150, 151, 160, 181n2, 286
Vienna Symphonic Library (VSL), 143, 144, 146, 147, 153–155, 157, 158, 168

Villeneuve, Denis, 8, 220, 223
Violins, 4, 7, 10, 14, 16, 82, 83, 89,
    94, 101n27, 108–111, 114–116,
    123, 124, 129, 132, 133, 140,
    142, 143, 153, 155, 160,
    182n10, 182n13, 216, 225, 251,
    265, 267, 268, 272, 276, 284,
    285, 299, 300
Virtual, 2, 26, 61, 107–181,
    250, 299
  instrument, 4, 21, 31, 63, 107–181,
    198, 200, 245, 260, 271, 272,
    279, 300
  organology, 11, 252–261
  reality, 17, 27, 34, 39, 42–56, 72,
    128, 133
  space, 21, 227, 228, 251, 271,
    281–287, 292, 293
Virtualization, 11, 27, 44, 56, 62–94,
    177, 225, 253, 292
  process, 39–42, 56, 63, 81, 97, 123,
    165, 254
  virtualized, 94, 176, 198, 199,
    260, 261
Voice-leading parsimony, 289
Voltage-controlled oscillators, 269
Volume, 14, 16, 21, 99n15, 114, 131,
    137–139, 146, 150, 166,
    183n15, 196, 200, 247, 263,
    264, 275, 280–281, 286,
    288, 293

W
Wagner, Richard, 75, 77, 254
Waterphone, 171, 236, 237
Western civilization, 26, 39, 41,
    52, 55, 246
Western culture, 37, 52, 82, 168, 171,
    196, 246, 250

Western music
  Western musical notation, 62, 63
  Western musical practice, 109,
    111, 140
  Western musical score, 62, 64, 111,
    117, 157
  Western music theory, 62, 74, 155
  Western orchestra, 8, 10, 74, 96,
    108, 122, 167–171, 203, 213,
    226, 245–247, 251, 252, 257,
    258, 285
  Western orchestral music, 95, 140,
    167, 196, 245
Western society, 26, 31, 36, 37, 39, 49
Wikipedia, 41
Williams, John, 168, 169, 217,
    221, 258
Woodwind, 64, 101n22, 136,
    169, 261
World-building, 8, 43–46, 220–225,
    233, 258
Written language, 37, 38, 40, 103n38

Y
Yamaha CS-80, 86, 176
Yamaha DX-7, 85
Yoda, 91

Z
Zebra, 7, 8, 177, 224, 225
Zebra2, 177
ZebraHZ, 177, 224, 225
Zimmer, Hans, 5–9, 21n1, 21n2, 120,
    125, 126, 134, 147, 156–158,
    165, 166, 169, 177, 204–206,
    208, 215–218, 220–225, 240n6,
    240n10, 240n14, 260, 273,
    287, 301

Printed in the United States
by Baker & Taylor Publisher Services